A MACROECONOMICS MODEL AND STABILISATION POLICIES FOR THE *OPEC* COUNTRIES

For my parents
and
for my wife and my daughters

A Macroeconomics Model and Stabilisation Policies for the *OPEC* Countries

With special reference to the Iraqi economy

A. KHALIK SALMAN
Mid Sweden University
Östersund, Sweden

Routledge
Taylor & Francis Group

LONDON AND NEW YORK

First published 1999 by Ashgate Publishing

Reissued 2018 by Routledge
2 Park Square, Milton Park, Abingdon, Oxon, OX14 4RN
711 Third Avenue, New York, NY I 0017, USA

Routledge is an imprint of the Taylor & Francis Group, an informa business

Publisher's Note
The publisher has gone to great lengths to ensure the quality of this reprint but points out that some imperfections in the original copies may be apparent.

Disclaimer
The publisher has made every effort to trace copyright holders and welcomes correspondence from those they have been unable to contact.

A Library of Congress record exists under LC control number: 97074448

ISBN 13: 978-1-138-61364-5 (hbk)
ISBN 13: 978-1-138-61368-3 (pbk)
ISBN 13: 978-0-429-46435-5 (ebk)

Contents

Figures and diagrams

Tables

ix

Acknowledgments

I am especially grateful to Professor Glyn Davies, Professor Gary Akehurst, and Professor C. J. Green for getting me started on this analytical journey, and for their unending encouragement through the years it has taken me to complete it. Also thanks to the editorial staff at Ashgate, in particular Anne Keirby, Sarah Markham, Pauline Beavers, and Amanda Richardson. Finally, thanks to my family who have helped me persevere in the challenges of scholarly research.

Preface

The intention of this book is to make it possible for those wishing to learn about macroeconometric models to acquire the skills needed to understand and evaluate models. It is aimed at postgraduates and professional economists, in either the public or private sector. The book can be used as part of a course in applied macroeconometrics. It assumes some understanding of standard macroeconomics theory, and although an econometrics background is useful, it is not necessary. The treatment is not particularly mathematical for, although a familiarity with matrix algebra is assumed, alternative ways of describing modelling methods are given. The book can also be used as a guide in interpreting models and their results for those who use the products of model-based exercises. Too often users of models are unsure whether the results that they are presented with reflect a particular view of how the economy functions, or are the result of specific (often very technical) assumptions by the modeller. After reading this book the model user should be able to understand why different models or different approaches result in different conclusions.

The motivation for publishing this book has come from lecturing to students and professional economists, both in the developing countries (*OPEC* countries) and in some European countries, about macroeconometric models and their properties. There is no one source that gives a description of both technical matters and empirical features of macroeconometric models in the *OPEC* countries and in Iraq. Furthermore, the international references suffer from shortage of these kinds of references. This book is more international in nature, for it gives the reader a sight into models of different economies, as well as multicountry models. My debt to many colleagues in the macroeconomics modelling profession is immense, and many of the ideas in this book come as a result of joint work and many conversations. Thanks to Prof. Glyn Davies and Prof. Gary Akehurst for getting me started on this subject. Christopher J. Green has been an enormous influence on me, as has his tremendous ability to understand technical problems. I am deeply grateful to him for his guidance and encouragement throughout the writing of this work. The list of others to whom I am indebted is extensive, but I should like to mention particularly J. Harbour and Ms. Joan Wright at the University of Wales-Cardiff Business School. I would like to thank Prof. Kirkpatrick for his encouragement to publish this work. I would like to acknowledge the encouragement given to me by Prof. Peter Apell and Arne Fagerström at the University College of Borås in Sweden, and Prof. Ronny Norén, Dennis Lans and Ann-Charlotte Staverfelt at the Mid Sweden University, Östersund. Needless to say, I am responsible for any errors and omissions in this book. Thanks are also due to my daughter Noor Salman, Mr. A.H. Al-Masri at the University of Göteborg for tolerant and efficient help with preparation of the manuscript and for the forbearance of my family while this book was in preparation.

1 An introduction to macroeconomic modelling

This book is concerned with macroeconomic models. These have been used regularly for the last 30 years or so. They have been used by the private sector, in academic institutions and in government and official agencies to analyse the economy and to evaluate macroeconomic policies, and to make predictions about the likely future behaviour of the economy (forecasts). Macroeconomic model has become widely accepted as the standard approach to forecasting and policy evaluation in the industrial economies of Europe, North America and Japan, because of the growing awareness of the importance of work of this kind, the last three decades, in particular, have witnessed an accelerated growth in the construction and estimation of macroeconometric models for both industrial and less developed countries (LDCs). As economic links between nations have increased, so there have been attempts to incorporate the joint dependence of economics, either through linked models or by construction of global (world) models. Despite the fact that macroeconometric modelling is now an established activity, it has not been without its critics. This book is an attempt to describe how macro models have developed, to give a picture of their current level of development, and to examine some of the issues, both economic and technical, that arise in their construction and use. Particular emphasis is placed upon the policy implications arising from different macro models. The book is about the construction of models through econometric estimation methods. Macroeconomic models in general use have tended to follow a rather aggregate time-series approach, and the book therefore rather inevitably centres on this, but at the same time it critically compares the usefulness of the 'standard' modelling approach with models based on other methods, such as vector autoregressive methods (VARs), computable general equilibrium (CGE) models and representative agent models.

The material in this book is part of my PhD thesis, which was in the University of Wales-Cardiff Business School in the UK and it reflects my experience as a researcher in the field of macroeconomic models. This analysis involved model construction, policy analysis, forecasting and comparative model analysis with a variety of models of differing economies and global economy. Some of the material has been published in other places, especially in international conferences and by Journal, so that the intention of this book is not originality, but rather to assemble a reasonably comprehensive account of modelling methods and findings.

1

Research in this area for the OPEC countries' economies and Iraqi economy, however, is still in its infancy. To date, there have been only two main models for this economy. These models could be described as incomplete to the extent that they neglected the prices, wages, and supply labour force and also neglected the export sector and influences on the economy. Unfortunately the early model builder sought to transplant the structure of the proto-type Keynesian model that had been developed mainly for industrialised economies to the construction of the Iraqi model. It was not surprising that these models performed poorly and were incapable of dealing with the major issues relevant to the Iraqi economy. Another serious problem that the early model builders were confronted with was the lack of consistent data series and the appropriate computer software. Consequently, these existing econometric models were never fully implemented and they appeared only in print. In fact, most of the estimated models were neither complete nor were they fully tested for their validity. The properties of these earlier models therefore, remain unknown.

This book has been aroused by the need to construct a model that incorporates interactions among the production block; the aggregated demand block, the employment block; the price block; the government block; the financial block and the foreign sector block. We have been also motivated by the need to take account of the changing structure of the economy brought about by the increasing share of the oil sector in GDP and its dominance of the foreign sector as against the deteriorating performance of the agricultural sector.

In recent years, there has been a pressing need to develop such a model. This need is particularly strong in those agencies that are charged with responsibility for policy formulation. One such official agency is the government. Since the early 1970s, there has been a fundamental change in the development strategy in Iraq. In particular, unlike the earlier period when the public sector played only a passive role, in the post-1970 era the Ministry of Planning and the Government have been much more active in the pursuit of discretionary economic policies. As a result, official agencies and the Central Bank have been engaging more frequently in the use of monetary and fiscal policies with twin objectives of stabilising economic fluctuations caused by the large swing in export prices and promoting economic growth and development.

The book has been divided into nine chapters. Chapter 1 introduces the subject matter. It discusses the motivation, the objectives of research exercise, the methodology adopted and the layout of the study.

Chapter 2 provides a general survey of the performance and problems of the Iraqi economy. It discusses the main characteristics of the economy, and its growth performance during the period 1968-1980, structural changes in Iraqi economic sectors and lastly discusses the major macroeconomics development problems such as inflation and work-force.

Chapter 3 is concerned with the indirect impact of the oil sector revenues on the planning machinery and economic growth during the period 1950-1980. This chapter will firstly focus on the literature on the role of the public sector in the development process, and the role of oil in providing a suitable basis for economic development plans and diversification, as well as the relative importance of oil export revenues for the ordinary budget for the period 1968-1980. Our concern with oil export revenue is crucial because this revenue represents about 90 per cent of the total Iraqi revenue.

Chapter 4 examines the interaction of the oil export sector and the indigenous sectors of the Iraqi economy. The direct impact may be discussed in terms of the flow of resources between the oil sector and non-oil sectors. Here, we will examine the demand-induced influences, including the 'Backward Linkages' that initial the flow of resources from the indigenous sectors to the oil sector. Then, we will look at the supply-induced influences, the 'Forward Linkages' that amount to a reverse flow of resources from the oil sector to the rest of the economy. The demand-induced influences or 'Backward Linkages' refer to these forces that are directly associated with growth of demand in the oil export sector resulting from the expansion of operations in that sector; in the case of the supply-induced influences or 'Forward Linkages' on the other hand, we try simply to explain the linkage of non-oil export sectors on the economy.

Chapter 5 focuses on a review of the relevant existing work in relation to the Iraqi economy. In particular, it reviews work on production function, impact demand functions and the two existing macroeconometric models of the economy. At the same time, this chapter deals with the specification and estimation of the macro model.

Chapters 6 and 7 examine the properties of the models. In particular, Chapter 6 represents the within sample tracking results of the Iraqi model, while Chapter 7 shows the sensitivity of the model to various exogenous shocks.

In Chapter 8, we present some illustrations on the application of the model to econometric analysis. In particular, we examine the effects of export fluctuations on the economy.

The last chapter gives a summary of the main findings of research work, the conclusions and the limitations of the model.

1.1 A brief objective of the book

Detailed macroeconomic models are often the output of the combined efforts of a team of researchers usually made up of professional economists, econometricians and special agencies. More often than not the size, the structure, the details and the level of sophistication and consequently the objectives of macroeconometric models are determined by the personnel constraint, the limited time, financial resources and data availability. These factors have been very much in evidence in the course of our own study. As a result, the objectives of the study are limited to the following:

a.	The first major task is the construction of a macroeconomics model of Iraq. Beside using the model to analyse the export sector, it can be applied to study the effects of other macroeconometric policies on the economy;

b.	Estimation of the model using annual data mostly from 1963 to 1986; and

c.	Simulation of the model in order to observe its tracking ability and its response to certain exogenous shocks.

In doing so, the research is based largely on the Keynesian short-run macro theory. However, sufficient emphasis was given to the short-run determination of sectoral output. Substantial modifications in the standard specification are sometimes necessary in order to incorporate the characteristics of developing economy. Within each block farther disaggregation is made in order to examine the structure of the component parts in some detail.

Another important development in this area relates to the export sector. In this study we wish to take into account the linkages between exports and other sectors of the economy. Moreover, we also had to recognise the degree of fluctuations and the severity of their impact on the economy in relation to the other sectors of the economy (Adams and Behrman, 1981). Following these suggestions, an econometric analysis with the use of an integrated macroeconometric model is being used here to examine the effects of export fluctuations on the economy. This point is of particular importance because none of the previous studies either investigated the measurement of fluctuations in export prices and its effects on the sectors of the economy, or used an econometric analysis with the use of an integrated macroeconometric model to examine the effects of the fluctuation on the economy.

Furthermore, in the formation of the model, we wish to take into account of the growing importance of the oil sector in the economy. This factor distinguishes the Iraqi economy from the majority of the other developing economies and a model purporting to describe the behaviour of such an economy must pay adequate attention to that sector.

1.2 Data resources of estimation models

One of the problems of macroeconomics model building in developing countries such as Iraq, as observed by UNCTAD staff "is the lack of reliable and adequate data over a length of time" (R.J. Ball, 1966). For this reason certain econometric problems such as those posed by the limited degree of freedom and errors in variables are inescapable.

The data used in this study was compiled from a variety of official sources, one of these is an Iraqi official source. Ministry of Planning agreed to give the available data and available input-output table to the researcher for the years 1968,

4

1976 and 1980. The Iraq-Iran war has made the data during the 1980s highly secretive.

The estimation periods for the equations are not uniform. They differ considerably depending on the length of the data period available and variables that determine a particular endogenous variable. Hence, whilst some equations were estimated over the period 1960 to 1986 (26 observations), most were estimated over the period 1963 to 1986 (23 observations) and one (the service equation) was estimated over the period 1968 to 1986 (18 observations).

The data used for estimation were obtained from numerous sources. The major sources, however, are the following:

1. The Ministry of Planning of Iraq;
    a. Annual Abstract of Statistics (annual series)
    b. Industrial Survey of Iraq (various issues)
    c. Iraqi Trade Summary (annual series)
    d. Digest of Statistics (various issues)
    e. Central Statistics Office (C.S.O.) publication of all national development plans.
2. Central Bank of Iraq;
    a. Annual reports and statement of accounts
    b. Economic and fiscal review.
3. United Nations, year book of international trade statistics (various issues) and other United Nations publications.
4. Various issues of both the IECD economic outlook and OECD main economic indicators.

1.3 The methodology of the current macroeconomic modelling

In existence are two widely used techniques that can be adopted in specification of a macro-economic model of an economy. These are the econometric and input-output techniques. An input-output model describes the structural interdependence in terms of demand and supply relationships of an economy in equilibrium. This technique has many and obvious uses for both policy makers as well as analysts. Since it indicates final demand for goods and services and inter-industry transactions required to satisfy that demand, the technique can serve as a planning and forecasting device. Also an up-to-date input-output table can be used by policy makers to project full employment levels of over-all demand.

However, data on the input-output tables flows of the main sector of the economy and that for many individual years are inadequate in Iraq. Also, the technique depicts a situation of an economy in equilibrium. In this study we are concerned with an analysis of an economy in the short-run. This means we allow for situations of disequilibrium and indicate some of the mechanisms that will be

5

brought into play when there is such a disequilibrium. We have therefore opted for an econometric model.

An econometric model based on national income accounts involves specification and estimation of a system of structural equations that attempt to describe the functioning of the economy. Such a technique can be used, among other things, to assess the probable policy implications of policy variables as well as to assess the influence of other exogenous variables on the key variables of the economy.

In this work the specification of equations explaining each endogenous variables is, as might be expected, influenced by previous related work in both advanced and developing countries. Accordingly, an attempt is made to specify equations which have a theoretical basis but which also pick up some salient features of the Iraqi economy.

We, therefore, favour the adoption of the ordinary least squares (OLS) method and Two-stage least squares (2TSL) method to avoid the problems of 'simultaneous equations bias' and the problem of an insufficient degree of freedom. These methods are used in estimating equations in the model employing annual data mostly from 1963 to 1980.

When the disturbance term is serially correlated, an appropriate transformation will be made according to an autoregressive scheme so as to ensure, as far possible, efficient estimates.

The selection of estimated equations to be used for simulation will be based on relevant economic theory with regard to the signs and sizes of the parameters as well as on the basis of standard statistical criteria. These criteria include R (the adjusted coefficient of determination) t-value as well as Durbin-Watson or H statistic. Equations that are economically unreasonable in terms of signs and/or sizes of parameters, even if they satisfy the conventional statistical tests, are rejected. Equally, those that are economically sensible but do not meet requirements of the standard statistical tests are also dropped. All satisfactory equations are then subjected to simulation within the sample period so as to assess the validity of the model in terms of its response to certain exogenous shocks. The assessment of the model with respect to its tracking ability is carried out employing simple graphical techniques and summary performance statistics such as mean absolute percentage error (MAPE), root mean square error (RMSE), and root mean squares percentage error (RMPSE), Theil's inequality statistics (U1 and U2) and so on. Other simulation exercises will be approached adopting standard counterfactual techniques.

Further reading:

Bodkin (1991), Smith (1990), Smith (1993).

2 The macro economy: performance, structure and problems

Iraq now stands at the crossroads of economic development. 1980 witnessed the completion of the second five-year period of development planning and the implementation of the third Development Plan (1976-1980). In marked contrast to most other developing nation, and as a result of the oil price rise from 1970 onwards, there has been no shortage of finance to promote economic activity; but finance alone cannot guarantee progress and problems have been encountered in converting financial into productive, physical resources particularly problems associated with inflation and manpower shortages. The two development plans to date have shared common objectives. In seeking a higher rate of growth in Gross Domestic Product (GDP) emphasis has been placed upon the development of human resources through better standards of education, training and health. Diversification of the economy has been strongly encouraged, recognising the need to conserve deplorable oil reserves and to maximise, over the long term, the earnings from oil. However, such objectives are not immediately achievable: the perquisite for the creation of an industrialised economy is the establishment of a physical infrastructure in the form of transport and communication facilities, telecommunication and electricity and water-supply networks. This has been the focus of attention over the last ten-year period and has been accorded a strong emphasis in the development policy. This in turn has affected the nature of, and extent to which, economic progress has taken place, and has helped maintain and strengthen the country's defence and internal security. Economic achievement can be measured not only by the growth of output and productivity but also by the changing structure of the economy and in the light of the above objective, growth performance, by any standards has been impressive. The Iraqi economy grew dramatically over the period of study 1968-1980. GDP in current prices rose from I. D 1076 million in 1968 to I. D 13503.0 million in 1980, at the average growth of about 25.22 per cent per annum. While GDP in constant 1969 prices rose from I. D 1033.4 million in 1968 to I. D 1499.2 million in 1974, and GDP in constant 1975 prices rose from I. D 3974.3 million in 1975 to 6571.8 million in 1980, with a higher average growth rate in the period 1975-1980, approximately 36.6 per cent per annum. This compares favourably with an average growth rate in the period 1968-1974 of 6.4 per cent per annum and indeed exceeds the targets laid down in the period covering the second development plan. Actual growth performance of

GDP during the period 1970-1980 grew by an average of 28.6 per cent per annum. By 1970-1980 GDP at current prices was I. D 56922.5 millions and non-oil GDP had reached ID 25227.2 millions.[1]

Although international comparisons in this context are somewhat debatable, and must be viewed with caution, growth rates in the developed world were clearly no match for the Iraqi experience. For instance, taking the period 1974-1980, real GDP grew by only 2.9 per cent per annum in the USA and by 2.7 per cent per annum in West Germany. The average annual growth rate of real GDP for the OECD countries was only 3.5 per cent per annum between 1969 and 1979. The explanation for the discrepancy is largely to be found in differences in growth potential, with the Iraqi economy benefiting from the transfer of labour from agriculture to more productive employment as well as from the surplus of both financial and energy resources. These factors alone do not make growth inevitable, as most other oil-rich developing economies have not equalled the Iraqi performance. Real GDP in Venezuela, for instance, grew at only 4.9 per cent per annum on average from 1974 to 1979. As Diagram 2.1 indicates, both productivity growth and increase in GDP per head of population in Iraq were also exceptional GDP per head of population rose by 20.60 per cent from 1968-1980, and non-oil GDP per head by 13.45, GDP per employee in the same period grew by 16.535 for the total economy and by 9.7 I. D in the non-oil sector. This illustrates the tremendous advances made in the average standard of living in Iraq in recent years. Real GDP per head of population by 1980 was over I.D 1022.9 and real output per employee in the non-oil sector had reached over I.D 1738.36 per annum.[2] Economic development means more than simply increasing the volume of output of goods and services; it implies a maturing of the institutional and organisational framework of the economy and a change in the composition of output towards industrial output, at the same time maintaining adequate resources in agriculture.

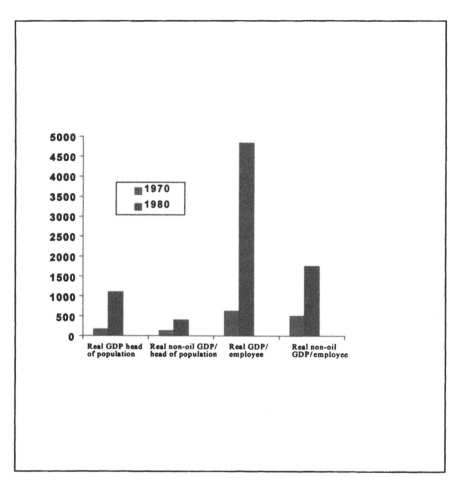

Diagram 2.1 Indicators of productivity and the standard of living 1970-1980

This increased maturity is recognisable in the country in a number of areas - later chapters will represent this institutional development more fully, but there are several major examples; the Ministry of Industry has taken more responsibility for achievement of a steady and industrialisation process; it is now working effectively for the protection and encouragement of the domestic industry and for sound regional development This is being accomplished through various departments covering foreign capital investment, industrial protection, industrial cities and industrial licensing. A wide variety of government financial institutions have also been introduced and have established themselves very quickly; these offer financial assistance for most developing sectors of the economy. This chapter provides an outline of the economic flow in Iraq, Gross Domestic Products and its compositions; consumption (private and public), investment. The next section details the structural changes in the Iraqi economy. The final section discusses the major macroeconomics development problems such as inflation and manpower.

2.1 Economic flow in Iraq

All market-oriented economies can be depicted, more or less accurately, with a diagram such as Figure 2.2. This schematic representation shows business firms and households facing each other in two types of markets. In the goods markets, firms sell their products to households. In the resources markets, they purchase the services of resources from the households. The incomes provided to the households in return for the services provided are just sufficient to purchase the goods and services produced by the firms. Such a representation provides a useful first approximation as to how market-oriented economies work in general, but this must be modified to aid our comprehension of any particular economy. This is especially true if the government plays a large role in the economy and if the foreign sector of the economy is relatively large, both of which are true of Iraq. Figure 2.3 presents an expanded depiction of the Iraq economy, with the relative size of the various flows represented by the width of the arrows. This representation is still only a rough first approximation of the structure of the economy. It does not, for example, demonstrate savings by the private sector, nor does it break down government expenditures into the oil and non-oil sector. Still, it does provide a striking impression of the degree to which Iraq's economy differs from those on which textbook models are based.

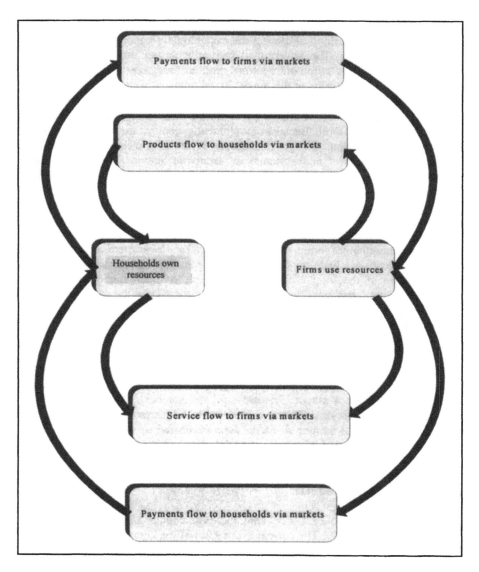

Figure 2.2   Schematic diagram of a market–oriented economy

11

Figure 2.3 reveals at least three features which set the Iraqi economy apart.

Perhaps the most striking of these is the exceptionally important role played by the government sector. The government naturally derives most of its immense income from the sale of crude oil. Personal and business taxes are negligible, and are likely to remain the same in the future. In the financial year 1979, for instance, total government revenues represented about 88.8 per cent of the national Gross Domestic Production GDP of this revenue, almost more than 90 per cent derived from the sale of crude oil. Because government revenues are so large, and are independent of taxation, the government is in an almost unique position to influence both the level and structure of economic activity. The expenditures through which the government exercise its influence are quite varied. They include direct expenditure on consumption and on large-scale investments as well as the provision of loans and other financial assistance to other economic agents in the economy. While the government's expenditures on consumption (education, defence, etc.) are quite large,[3] a large part of its economic activity is directed towards encouraging economic growth, either by direct investment or by providing funds for enterprises which are judged likely to contribute to economic growth. A second feature of the Iraqi economy is its degree of interdependence with the world. This interdependence has increased dramatically as the national income from oil export rose, and simply reflects the increased standard of living which that income has made possible. In the financial year 1979, export accounted for 58 per cent of GDP. For the same period, imports represent 22 per cent of GDP. The percentage of total consumption and investment goods which were imported was, of course, much greater. A final feature of the economy is the relatively large fraction of the GDP which is paid for the use of foreign owned resources. Chief among these features is labour. Presently, a large number of Iraq's labour force consists of foreign workers. This is considered to be a transitory situation Long-term plans call for the training of native labour with the requisite skills to reduce the dependence on foreign labour.

2.2 Gross domestic products

As we can see from Table 2.1 and Table 2.2, these contain a summary of the GDP for the period 1968-1980. The current I. D values of the components are indicated in Table 2.1. Table 2.2 adjusts the data for price changes, using the GDP price deflator with 1975 as the base year. It also indicates the percentage of total GDP which derives from each sector for the period 1970-1980.

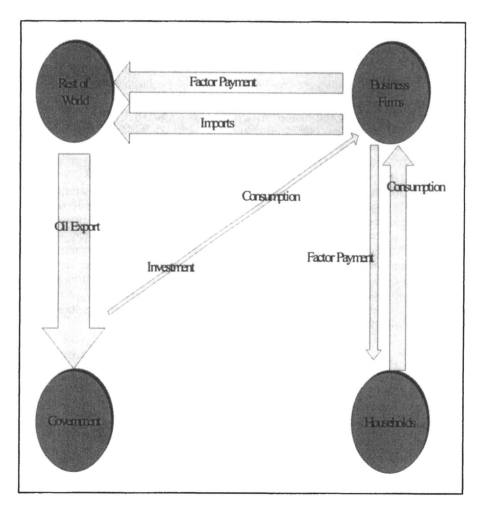

Figure 2.3 Schematic diagram of the Iraqi economy

Note: Payments for goods and services are indicated. Relative size of flows are indicated by the width of the arrows. These are estimated by the authors from various official sources. The estimation is not precise. The width of the arrows should be interpreted as showing orders of magnitude only.

It is no surprise that the oil sector is the largest single contributor to the GDP. Its relative importance, always great, fluctuates with the rate of crude oil production and its price. The relative importance of this sector fell after 1974 but then rose again in 1979 and 1980. Since then, it has fallen again. In stark contrast, the non-oil sector is much less volatile. Among the non-oil sectors, the largest is construction. This is followed by transportation and government services, and trade and finance.[4]

Iraq is unusual for the relative importance of one sector, oil production. It is also unusual for the relative unimportance of another sector, agriculture. Even allowing for some understatement of agricultural output due to subsistence farming and herding, agriculture accounts for a small share of the total amount output when we compare Iraq to developed as well as less developed countries. The growth rate of the economy has been staggering regardless of whether real or monetary measures are used. A good deal of the growth in nominal GDP during the 1970s represented price changes, but an inspection of Table 2.1 leads to the conclusion that, even after taking inflation into account, the real out-put has increased at a very rapid rate by comparison with almost any economy at almost any time in history. This growth has not been shared at all evenly among the sectors of the economy. The most striking gains have been in the construction and trade sectors of the economy. This gain. especially in construction, may be temporary, reflecting the period of transition in which Iraq currently finds itself. The sectors which have been growing (relatively) most slowly are agriculture and government services agriculture has declined, in relative terms, for instance, from 19.1 per cent in 1968 to 5.7 per cent in 1980. This is because of the rapid growth of the other sectors of the economy. The agricultural sector is examined in much more detail in another section. That government services have fallen in relative importance is a striking testimonial to the rapidity of overall growth, for government services have been rising quite rapidly by almost any standards.

Table 2.1 Gross domestic product according to economic sector for the period 1968-1980 (at current prices)

Economic sectors	1968	1969	1970	1971	1972	1973	1974	1975	1976	1977	1978	1979	1980
Agriculture	205.8	201.4	194.6	215.8	260.1	210.6	278.4	311.6	429.0	498.4	550.5	612.0	722.0
Mining and quarrying:	348.0	343.2	370.5	512.9	407.3	574.3	2036	2062	2826	2115	3730	6750.0	8679
a. Crude oil	341.6	335.9	362.6	507.8	400.0	563.4	2023	2043	280	3090	3702	6713.0	8638
b. Other	6.4	7.3	7.9	5.1	7.3	10.9	13.6	18.7	21.9	25.3	27.8	36.9	40.0
Manufacturing	94.6	103.0	116.0	118.5	140.0	157.6	187.8	270.6	379.8	418.8	506.2	629.0	631.0
Construction	36.8	38.5	40.6	43.6	45.2	57.6	155.5	356.1	483.2	415.9	559.3	994.0	915.0
Electricity, water	14.9	16.8	12.7	11.9	13.7	16.0	13.7	17.2	22.5	27.4	42.9	37.8	59.0
Total commodity	693.1	702.0	734.4	902.7	866.3	1016	2672	3017	4140	4475	5389	9022.0	1105
Transport & storage	65.8	69.1	71.2	79.7	85.9	88.5	124.1	184.7	249.1	294.8	375.5	557.0	50.0
Wholesale & retail	86.9	90.1	98.6	94.4	102.6	115.2	168.9	208.7	245.3	294.8	428.4	655.0	565.0
Banking & insurance	13.1	15.5	19.6	22.1	21.8	26.2	48.0	89.1	96.5	100.6	103.2	189.0	169.0
Distribution sectors	165.8	174.7	189.4	196.2	210.3	229.9	341.0	483.4	590.9	690.2	902.1	1400.0	1236
Total services	217.9	242.5	275.3	297.7	233.3	352.6	509.9	605.7	650.7	773.1	934.8	124.0	1209
GDP of factor cost	1080	112.0	1199	1398	1399	1599	3523	4105	5382	5939	7225	11653	1350
GDP excluding oil	742.2	784.2	836.5	888.8	998.9	1035	1500	2062	2578	2849	3523	4940.0	4864
Population	8.9	9.1	9.4	9.8	10.1	10.4	10.8	11.1	11.5	12.0	12.4	12.8	13.0
Per capita income	121.1	123.1	127.6	142.5	138.5	153.7	326.2	369.8	469.9	494.9	685.7	911.0	1022

Source: Calculated from Ministry of Planning, Iraq, Economic Development, Economic Indicators for Iraqi Development, 1964-1969, and for the period 1970-1980, Volumes 1978, 1981 and 1982.

Table 2.2   Distribution of gross domestic product according to the main economic sectors for the period 1970-1980 (at constant prices 1975=100)

Economic sectors	1970	1971	1972	1973	1974	1975	1976	1977	1978	1979	1980
Agriculture-forest/fishery	319.1	331.5	401.4	306.1	362.1	311.6	384.2	373.9	378.4	377.5	391.0
Crude oil	1481	1606	1383	1916	1841	2043	2620	2641	3164	3951	3400
Other mining & quarrying	15.0	9.6	13.4	18.3	17.7	18.7	19.2	21.6	27.0	27.7	27.0
Manufacturing sectors	155.9	181.6	196.7	212.7	227.8	270.6	333.9	372.9	210.2	481.7	513.0
Construction	77.6	89.5	85.8	116.0	216.7	356.1	406.1	339.2	449.2	719.7	611.0
Electricity & water	9.2	10.8	9.5	12.7	15.2	17.2	20.6	25.0	29.8	40.0	38.0
Commodity sectors	2058	2229	2090	2582	2681	317	3785	3773	4459	5516	4983
Transport & storage	87.7	95.9	98.9	98.7	130.6	184.6	222.8	248.0	307.5	418.8	341.0
Wholesale & retail trade	131.1	117.9	133.4	143.1	186.6	208.7	220.2	243.4	333.6	492.3	389.0
Banking & insurance	21.5	23.9	23.4	24.5	48.9	89.1	95.4	98.5	100.5	141.7	106.0
Distribution sectors	240	238	256	269	366	482	548	590	742	1053	837.0
Service sectors	358.4	375.3	390.1	410.0	552.4	605.7	598.6	667.1	776.5	952.0	851.0
Total GDP	2657	2842	2736	2361	3599	4105	3932	5030	5977	7520	6671
Total national income	2139	2246	2315	2910	3103	3693	4665	4748	5822	7145	6558

Source: Calculated from Ministry of Planning, Iraq, Economic Development, Economic Indicators for Iraqi Development, 1964-1969, and for the period 1970-1980, Volumes 1978, 1981 and 1982.

This rapid economic growth has not been without accompany difficulties. A major problem has been acquiring labour in sufficient quantities to produce the expanding flow of goods and services. The difficulties encountered in this respect will be discussed in more detail in another section of this Chapter. Also, Iraq suffered severe inflation in the years immediately following the first major increase oil prices This inflation in large part reflected Table 2.1 bottlenecks which were acute in the early transitional years but which have become much less *so* as the requisite infrastructure has been put in place. In what follows, we shall briefly review the components of the GDP.

2.2.1 Expenditure on the gross domestic product

We have briefly examined the composition of the GDP and of the income that is generated in the process of producing the output. The demand for a nation's output can be broken down into three major components; consumption (private and government), investment and net exports. In what follows, we examine the structure of the expenditures in relatively broad terms. Then we focus on investment expenditure and consumption in more detail. It is instructive to compare expenditure on GDP in a few countries (refer to Table 2.3). The data in this table reveals some remarkable differences between the patterns of the three Arab oil countries, Iraq, Saudi Arabia and Kuwait and the other nations. Probably the most obvious difference is the disproportionately low level of private consumption expenditures in the Arab oil countries, compared with either developed or less-developed countries. This difference mainly reflects the unusually large difference between income and wealth: the Arab oil nations' incomes have risen dramatically during the past decade, but adjustments of consumption to such a dramatic change can be expected to occur with a lag.[5] Also notables are the high levels of imports and exports relative to GDP and the relative size of the balance of trade. The large positive balance of trade, of course, is offset by capital flow which provides Iraq with productive assets other than crude oil and its domestic capital stock.

Table 2.3 Expenditures on GDP, by type selected countries

Economic sectors	Iraq	Kuwait	Saudi Arabia	Austria	USA	Bolivia	Egypt	Pakistan
Private consumption	24	26	18	55	65	69	72	83
Government consumption	23	11	23	18	21	10	12	10
Gross fixed capital formation	18	11	25	25	16	17	21	12
Change in stocks	-	-	1	3	-	2	1	1
Exports	58	84	68	39	10	17	21	12
Imports	-22	-31	-35	-41	-11	-16	-24	-23
GDP	100	100	100	100	100	100	100	100
Export less Import / GDP	36	52	33	-2	-1	1	-2	-11

Notes: Data are for 1980. All entries percentages. Percentages might not add up to 100 due to rounding. They should total to 100 due to the accounting identity, Y=C+I+G(X-M)+ST. In the table above, C= private consumption, I= gross fixed capital formation, G= Government expenditures, X= exports, M= imports, and ST= additions to stocks.

Sources: 1. All the data for all countries (excluding Iraq), estimated and computed from International Monetary Fund, - Washington, DC. 2. Foreign Trade, 1970-1980, Foreign Trade Section, Ministry of Planning, Iraq, April 1982. 3. Economic Indicators, 1970-1980, Ministry of Planning, Baghdad, August, 1982.

2.2.2 *Private and government consumption*

To some extent, the low fraction of income spent on private consumption reflects the large amount of consumption expenditures by the government. Still, including governmental consumption expenditures, total consumption expenditures remain a relatively small fraction of total income. Because it can limit its consumption to a small fraction of total income, Iraq was in the fortunate position of being able to save and so to escape what is often perceived as a vicious cycle of underdevelopment.[6]

From the period 1968-1980, private consumption in Iraq has grown at an annual rate of 19.5 per cent. this contrasts with 24.8 per cent annual rate of GDP growth. Private consumption has fluctuated much less than GDP, so its share of GDP has ranged from a low of 21.1 per cent to a high of 52.6 per cent during the period of study. The lowest figure was for 1973, just after the jump in revenues due to the rise in crude oil prices. Before that private consumption's share of GDP was much larger. Also, it appears to be going back to its pre-1974 level. In 1978, before the second large price increase and the increase in Iraqi production, the share had reached to 38.8 per cent (see Table 2.3), but in 1980 the share had again declined because of the war between Iraq and Iran.

While private consumption has not risen as rapidly as GDP, government consumption expenditures have risen slightly faster than GDP (as noted above, these contain a large non-consumption component). The average annual rate of growth is 26 per cent. These expenditures are of two types. Considerable in-kind transfer payments are made to private citizens. In addition, the government has expanded very large amounts to upgrade its administrative infrastructure, which was inadequate to deal with the rapid increase in economic activity that the nation has experienced in the past two decades.

2.2.3 *Investment (gross fixed formation)*

The central importance of physical capital accumulation to economic development is generally recognised. Indeed, in some models, notably the Harrod-Domar model, this is the sine qua non of development. Such a mechanistic view of development has given way to emphasis on development of other resources, but capital accumulation remains of central importance.[7] Given this fact or economic life, the few nations which do not experience constraints on the amount that they can invest in physical capital are indeed fortunate.

Iraq has been in this enviable position for the past decade. Its oil revenues are sufficient to allow it to invest to the extent of its absorptive capacity. As a result, Iraq has an almost unique opportunity to determine the rate and type of economic development which are consistent with its overall social and political goals. The immensity of the available funds does not, of course, mean that no choices have to be made. Rather it means that no investment which is deemed to be worthy need be foregone due to insufficient funding.

19

Perhaps the most fundamental question facing most less developed nations is how to invest more. For Iraq, this question is replaced with two closely related questions. What is the optimum rate of investment in domestic capital formation? And probably more important is what types of investment are optimal? Capital accumulation is not an abstraction, rather it consists of roads, machines, buildings, other physical assets and human capital. For a nation whose entire capital stock is being built almost from the ground up, within a generation, reference to the aggregate in which the composition is ignored will not do.

Regarding the question of how fast a nation can accumulate capital (its 'absorptive capacity') much has been written. The definition of 'absorptive capacity' remains unclear, but the motivation behind the concept is quite clear: a country which has a poorly developed physical and social infrastructure can absorb only a limited amount of investment without encountering severe bottlenecks and probably experiencing an unacceptably high inflation rate.[8] Calculations of just what a nation's absorptive capacity is at any particular time must be tentative. In the period immediately following the oil price increase of the 1970s Iraq did experience some of the bottlenecks to be expected as a nation approaches its absorptive capacity. Many of these centred around inadequate port facilities, telecommunications, and cement and electricity production. By 1980 these bottleneck had been largely eliminated and Iraq was experiencing rapid investment with only moderate inflation.

Most of the total investment has been made by the government. The government's share has been rising, from 53.0 per cent in 1968 to 80.3 per cent in 1980. Private investment has fallen in relative terms. Though it has expanded in absolute terms. Except for rather larger investment in 1969, the oil sector investment has been relatively small, and has declined throughout the last half of the decade in relative terms.[9] These trends are quite apparent in Figure 2.4.

Table 2.6 presents a summary of the relative importance of each sector investment providing average values for the period considered.

The percentage of GFCF in the GDP increased from about 12 per cent in 1968, at 1975 constant prices, to 32.9 per cent in 1980. The level of investment during the 1968-1980 period was lower than in the period 1973-1980. The average annual rate of growth for the first period was about 12.5 per cent while the average annual rate of growth for the second period was about 25.3 per cent,[10] this was mainly due to the increases in oil revenues and the resulting balance of trade surplus which Iraq enjoyed over this period.

The rate of capital formation, and its distribution between construction, transport equipment and machinery, is a big factor in the determination of output growth in the country I. D values terms gross fixed capital formation rose from I. D 270.2 million in 1968 to I. D 2198.2 million in 1980 (at constant 1975 prices); With the increase in the ratio of capital formation of the GDP from 11.5 per cent in 1968 to 32.9 per cent in 1980 (at constant 1975 prices).[11]

There is a much discernible change in the type of investment being undertaken among 1968 and 1980. By 1980 construction accounted for 52.9 per cent of gross capital formation, or I. D 1165.5 million (at constant 1975 prices), compared to only I. D 270.2 in the 1968 percentage of capital formation; construction tends to be the least productive of capital expenditure, particularly residential construction: but there has been a noticeable shift away from residential construction from 1980 onwards.

The data presented above provide a clear picture of an economy achieving rapid industrial development, with the lead being taken by the government sector. However, although this picture obviously needs to be expanded further it is a depiction of the nature and effects of the data above and the information presented here.

A major shortcoming of any measure of physical capital accumulation is that it does not provide information on the extent to which the economy's 'human capital' is being developed.[12] Investments in human capital show up in the accounts as government consumption on items such as education and health care, and even defence, as we have pointed out earlier.

Table 2.4 Expenditure on private and Government consumption level 33 and its percentages for the period 1968-1980

Year	Private consumption 1	% 1/3	Government consumption 2	% 2/3	GDP 3
1968	543.3	52.5	220.4	21.3	1034.5
1969	565.1	52.6	242.5	22.6	1074.2
1970	609.9	52.3	268.4	23.1	1167.0
1971	664.5	49.4	308.9	22.9	1345.2
1972	657.4	48.5	332.8	24.5	1356.5
1973	556.7	35.8	410.4	26.4	1555.5
1974	727.5	21.1	796.2	23.1	3453.2
1975	1584.0	39.3	918.0	22.8	4034.8
1976	1820.0	34.7	1241.0	32.6	5252.5
1977	2230.0	38.7	1270.0	22.0	5761.2
1978	2734.0	38.8	1728.0	24.5	7040.6
1979	2939.0	27.6	1677.0	16.1	10632.8
1980	3330.0	24.7	3224.0	24.1	13503.0

Source: Ministry of Planning, C.O.S., Iraq, for the period 1968-1980.

Table 2.5 Investment by sectors (private and public), for the period 1968-1980

Years	GI	1/3 %	PI	2/3 %	GCF
1968	75.8	53.0	67.2	46.9	143.0
1969	78.5	49.9	78.8	50.1	157.3
1970	101.1	45.6	84.0	45.4	185.1
1971	105.0	53.9	89.7	46.1	194.7
1972	114.7	52.8	102.4	47.2	217.1
1973	218.9	75.8	69.7	24.2	288.6
1974	542.7	86.3	85.9	13.7	628.6
1975	913.3	85.9	149.1	14.1	1062.4
1976	1112.4	83.2	224.1	16.8	1336.5
1977	1230.9	83.4	245.8	16.6	1476.7
1978	1646.4	82.6	346.6	17.9	1993.0
1979	2264.4	83.4	449.8	16.6	2714.3
1980	2562.8	80.3	630.0	19.7	3192.8

Note: GI= Government's investments. PI= Private investment. GCF= Gross domestic fixed capital formation.

Source: Economic Indicators of Economic Development in Iraq, Economic Department, Ministry of Planning, Baghdad, 1976, 1980.

Table 2.6 Gross domestic fixed capital formation and relative importance of economic sectors (at constant prices,'75=100)

Economic sectors	1968	1969	1970	1971	1972	1973	1974	1975	1976	1977	1978	1979	1980	RG
Agriculture	32.6	43.2	42.9	58.3	56.7	60.0	62.4	76.0	116.5	150.5	169.9	232.4	263.3	11
%	12.1	14.6	13	15.3	14.9	12.0	7.7	7.2	9.8	11.8	10.7	11.7	12	
Mining	2.3	2.1	13.9	19.0	23.3	54.2	103.5	87.1	136.8	159.3	152.8	179.5	22.6	7
%	0.9	0.7	4.2	5.5	6.1	10.9	12.9	8.2	11.5	12.5	10	9.0	1.0	
Manufacturing	70.5	76.8	78.8	79.2	89.8	121.0	162.6	242.0	223.7	256.4	252.6	371.3	233.8	21
%	26.1	26	23.7	22.8	23.6	24.3	20.2	22.7	18.8	20.2	16	18.6	14.7	
Construction	3.1	7.5	7.1	9.0	8.7	12.4	27.5	35.9	46.4	26.5	29.4	47.4	129.6	2
%	1.1	2.5	2.1	2.6	2.3	2.5	3.4	3.4	3.9	2.1	1.9	2.4	5.9	
Electricity & water	16.8	16.3	22.4	20.3	19.3	17.3	42.0	70.1	96.7	127.3	235.1	160.2	330.5	7
%	6.2	5.5	6.7	5.8	5.1	3.5	5.2	6.6	5.9	10.0	14.5	8.0	15.0	
Commodity sectors	125.3	145.9	165.1	180.8	197.8	264.9	398.0	511.1	593.1	720.0	834.3	990.8	1070	50
%	46.4	49.3	49.7	52.0	52.1	53.1	49.4	48.1	49.9	56.7	52.7	49.7	48.7	
Transport & storage	34.6	31.8	42.0	44.4	48.5	53.3	194.5	320.7	351.6	221.5	219.2	330.8	254.7	16
%	12.8	10.7	12.6	12.8	12.8	10.7	24.1	30.2	29.6	17.4	13.8	16.6	11.6	
Wholesale & retail	13.8	9.9	12.5	10.1	11.4	36.7	30.0	33.7	50.2	51.7	97.7	72.1	115.6	4
%	5.1	3.3	3.8	2.9	3.0	7.4	3.7	3.2	4.2	4.1	6.2	3.6	5.3	
Banking & insurance	2.1	2.4	2.8	4.6	2.3	10.7	1.7	4.6	2.2	1.9	2.8	3.1	4.0	0
%	0.8	0.8	0.8	1.3	0.6	2.1	0.2	0.4	0.2	0.2	0.2	0.2	0.2	
Distribution sectors	50.5	44.1	57.3	59.1	62.2	100.7	226.2	359.0	404.0	275.1	319.7	406.0	374.3	21
%	18.7	14.9	17.3	17.0	16.4	20.2	28.1	33.8	34.0	21.7	20.2	20.7	17.0	
Services sectors	94.4	105.9	109.4	107.6	119.8	133.1	182.3	192.3	191.8	278.8	428.3	595.6	754.3	27
%	34.9	35.8	32.9	30.9	31.6	26.7	22.6	18.1	16.1	21.6	27.1	29.9	34.3	
G.D.F.C.F.,GDF/GDP	270.2	295.9	332.2	347.5	379.8	498.7	806.5	1062	1189	1270	1582	1993	2198	18
%	11.5	12.1	12.5	12.2	13.9	15.3	26.0	25.9	24.1	25.3	26.5	26.5	32.9	

Note: RG = Rate of growth.

Source: Economic Indicators, Economic Development in Iraq, Economic Department, Ministry of Planning, October 1981, August 1982.

Table 2.7 Gross domestic fixed capital formation by sectors for the period 1968-1980 (at current prices)

Economic sectors	1968	1969	1970	1971	1972	1973	1974	1975	1976	1977	1978	1979	1980
Agriculture	16.8	22.5	23.0	29.0	31.3	33.9	47.8	76.0	131.2	175.6	213.4	315.9	3829
Mining & quarrying	1.2	1.1	7.6	10.4	13.2	30.7	79.6	87.1	156.8	185.7	193.2	245.7	33.3
Manufacturing	36.4	40.1	42.5	43.4	50.3	69.1	123.7	242.0	248.4	298.9	317.0	502.9	471.0
Construction	1.7	4.0	3.9	5.1	5.0	7.8	21.3	35.9	77.7	148.6	36.0	63.2	178.0
Electricity & water	8.7	8.5	12.1	11.0	10.7	9.8	32.1	70.1	49.7	30.4	288.8	218.5	482.0
Commodity sector	64.8	76.2	82.1	98.9	110.5	151.3	304.5	511.1	633.8	839.2	1048.4	1246	1346
Transport & storage	20.6	81.2	26.8	27.7	31.0	32.5	156.6	230.7	397.8	254.2	278.0	450.0	361.0
Wholesale & retail	7.4	5.4	7.9	6.3	7.0	22.6	25.0	33.7	54.8	59.4	122.8	97.8	168.0
Banking & insurance	1.1	1.3	1.5	2.5	1.3	6.1	1.4	4.6	2.5	2.2	3.6	4.2	5.9
Distribution sectors	29.1	24.9	36.2	36.5	39.3	61.2	183.0	359.0	455.1	315.8	404.4	552.0	534.0
Ownership-welling	26.0	23.3	32.8	34.4	39.2	45.1	45.3	78.3	101.2	162.3	252.6	318.0	353.0
Public Administration	4.6	4.0	5.2	5.4	5.9	12.3	41.1	52.0	56.2	85.3	135.0	239.2	381.0
Services	18.5	19.8	21.8	19.5	22.1	18.7	34.7	62.0	60.2	84.1	156.4	258.9	397.0
Total services	49.1	56.1	59.8	59.3	67.2	76.1	141.1	192.3	217.6	321.7	543.4	816.1	112.0
G.D.F.C.F.	143.0	137.2	185.1	194.7	217.0	288.6	628.0	1062	1337	1477	1996.2	2714	3193
G.D.F.C.F./GDP	13.4	14.2	15.4	14.2	15.6	18.2	18.8	25.9	29.2	25.9	28.5	26.6	23.8

Source: Economic Indicators, Economic Development in Iraq, Economic Department, Ministry of Planning, October 1981 and August 1982.

A second limitation of the data presented here is that only gross investment is described. This prevents a reliable estimation of the accumulated capital stock. Any estimation of depreciation rates must be a risky undertaking when there has been so much investment in such a short time period, and in a region which has physical characteristics so different from those of countries for which reliable depreciation data are available.

2.3 Structural changes

Sectoral development does reflect the objectives laid down in the development plans. As Tables 2.1 and 2.2 demonstrate, no major sector has shown a decline in real output; nevertheless there are marked differences in expansions of sectors. As is to be expected the agriculture sector was one of the slowest growing sectors within the period of study.

In this part of this chapter, we will briefly focus on the agriculture and manufacturing sectors, and let the reader judge the growth from the above tables.

2.3.1 Agricultural sector

The period of study has witnessed monumental changes in the size and nature of Iraq's agricultural sector. In 1968 this sector employed 50.0 per cent of the country's population, primarily in the style of farming that had been practised for generations. By 1980 the fraction of the labour force employed in agriculture had fallen to one-third. That third of all markets accounted for only 15.9 per cent of non oil GDP and only 5.5 per cent of GDP. This decline was caused by the high contribution of the oil sector to GDP, especially after 1973 which increased from 29.5 per cent in 1972 to about 64 per cent in 1980. Therefore as a result of the vast size of increase in the oil sector, the contribution of non-oil sectors has been declining proportionately despite the absolute amount of development which had taken place in these economic sectors.

Before the discovery of oil, agriculture played a much more significant role in the Iraqi economy, as Iraq was primarily an agricultural country. Some of the products of this agricultural economy, notably dates, wheat, barley, cotton, vegetables were quite famous.

The growth of cities and industry have upset the equilibrium that had been established over generations.[13] Local products became less competitive and local techniques, however efficient under previous conditions, became almost irrelevant. The most striking cases in point are the reform land, soil salinity and the labour force.

Along with the increased competition from abroad and new technology, three other factors have dramatically affected Iraqi agriculture. Consumption patterns have changed, partly because more consumers are expatriates and partly because of the huge jump in Iraqi citizens incomes. This has resulted in significant changes in

25

consumption patterns. The second factor is that the cities attract many workers from farming. This attraction largely stems from the relatively high-paying jobs that are available in the urban areas, but also from the availability of superior services, such as education and health care, in the cities. Finally, the cities themselves are encroaching on agricultural lands. The relative decline of agriculture is not unusual in growing economies. Still, the rate at which the relative importance of this sector of Iraqi's economy has been declining is unusually rapid.

However, the agricultural sector has a special role in the Iraqi economy as it has in most of the developing countries being the main source for meeting some of the domestic demand for food and being, the main source of raw materials for the domestic industries like tobacco, dairy products, beverages, etc. At the same time, agriculture in Iraq has good prospects, for further growth, given the availability of fertile land, water resources and means of finance.[14]

A. *An overview of Iraqi agriculture* before turning to specifics that apply to individual regions of Iraq, and to the crops that are of most importance, a few general comments are in order In almost all of Iraq the climatic conditions are quite unstable and dictate to a great extent as to whether commercial agriculture is feasible, and, if so, how it is be practised. Soil salinity over a large part of the country rules out any but the most irrigated rural area. Iraq's agricultural resources consist of about 12 million hectares of potentially cultivable land, equivalent to about one-fourth of the total area of the country. Less than two thirds of cultivable land is cultivated of which one-half is irrigated. Owing to the widespread practice of the follow system, however only about 50 per cent of the land is cultivated in any one year.

B. *Agricultural products* the most important agricultural winter crops are cereals, especially in the north part of Iraq, where the rainfall is sufficient to grow important crops such as wheat and barley. The data available indicates quite clearly that production levels were declining during the period of study, for instance, on 000'ton the volume of wheat production declined from 135.692 (x000')ton in 1969 to 1.300 (x000')ton in 1980. Whilst corresponding figures for barley show a decline from 992-419 (x000')ton in 1968 to 600 (x000')ton in 1980.[15] In addition, summer crops such as rice and cotton are grown in areas in central and southern Iraq which are irrigated from the twin rivers, Tigris and Ephratery. Dates are another important summer product. Thus, for instance, during the period 1968-1980, the average date production accounted annually for 8.85 per cent to the total value of agriculture production.

As can be seen from Table 2.8 the ratio of the value of foodstuff production to the total value of agricultural output, was higher than that of animal production. During the period 1968-1976, the value of foodstuff average accounted for 63.71

Table 2.8 Value of agriculture products in Iraq for the period 1968-1976

Items	1968	1969	1970	1971	1972	1973	1974	1975	1976
Food stuff	1,26984	1,12557	1,27874	1,38945	1,90561	1,31994	1,92826	2476	2,85771
Field crops	75319	58259	71497	81137	118893	66356	96043	80262	1,15912
Vegetables	16303	17119	16697	22704	17308	21088	32534	72322	63221
Fruits and Dates	14213	18545	16371	16448	18723	22388	35383	52396	60877
Others	21149	18634	23309	18656	34637	22162	28866	42692	45761
Animal products	62943	70553	76691	75761	8,6923	1,01939	1,10921	1,35122	1,56656
Dairy products	10118	10647	11271	10650	12492	13803	18675	20720	27597
Meat	25806	29949	32307	42566	36518	41814	48945	63318	72291
Hide, Skin and Eggs	7766	8954	10420	11827	15335	17335	23058	25913	36463
Others	1185	11900	12688	10718	12928	13928	16109	19198	15707
Grand total	1,89927	1,83110	2,04565	2,14706	2,77484	2,33933	3,03747	3,82794	4,42427
Ratio 1/3%	66.8	61.47	62.51	64.71	68.67	56.42	63.48	64.70	64.59
Ratio 2/3%	33.14	38.53	37.49	35.29	31.33	43.58	36.52	35.30	35.41

Note: Unavailable data for the years 1977, 1978, 1980.

Source: E.F. Penrose, International Relations and National Development, Iraq, London, 1978, p. 456.

per cent, whilst the corresponding figure for animal products was 36.78 per cent for the same time.

C. *Agricultural productivity* the income level among the agricultural population remains relatively low. In part, this reflects continued use of primitive techniques (low-yield seeds, inefficient irrigation and limited mechanisation) by a large but declining number of farmers. Another contributing factor is the size of agricultural holdings, for instance, during 1970-1975, the average holding size of irrigated land was from between 10 hectares and 15 hectares depending on the type of irrigation crops and type of land, and non-irrigation land to 250-500 hectares, depending on the average rainfall of the region. Some of the small holdings were profitable orchards and greenhouses, but many more were subsistence farms. An estimated large number of the small farms produced for their owners' consumption and not for sale.[16]

While a large number of traditional farms are quite small, there is rapid growth in the number and importance of large mechanised farms. The creation of these farms is facilitated by the availability of large tracks of virgin land and by the low cost of capital funds. These farms have become important in wheat production.

Some most remarkable large-scale enterprises have been managed by the government during the period under study. For example. Before 1968, the government owned 17 large scale farms and local co-operatives. This number increased from 473 in 1968 to 1935 in 1978, and 1893 in 1980. The collective farms settlement in 1972, increased from 6 in 1972 to 79 in 1978, while it declined to 33 in 1980.[17]

D. *Government agricultural policy* at the same time that the government is pursuing policies designed to further industrial development, it is implementing measures to encourage a vital agricultural sector according to the agricultural development plans, 1970-1975 and 1976-1980.

The need for a sound agricultural sector has long been recognised and supported by the government. The need for a sufficient level of production strategic food and the opportunities for good levels of agricultural incomes underlie the agricultural policies and plans of the government.

The implementation of this policy involves various government agencies. The Iraqi Agricultural Bank provides a wider range of financial services to the agricultural sector. In spite of agricultural credit, it still makes a small contribution to production and or farming activities, but, in recent years, a change has come about in providing loans. For instance, the amount of total loans spent on improved supplies of inputs increased from 14 per cent in 1970 to 41.9 per cent in 1980. At the same time, the total loans provided by the agricultural co-operative Bank to farmers increased from I. D 1027 million in 1970 to I. D 24072.0 million in 1980 (see Table 2.7).

Along with action directly encouraging production, the general move towards developing an infrastructure on which industries can rely has not ignored agriculture. Extensive efforts have been made to survey, develop and distribute to unused arable lands and to build a system of dams that will provide a more reliable water supply for agriculture in many regions. A network of main, secondary and agricultural roads is being constructed in order to link production centre with marketing centre. The next section deals with these policies.

E. *Subsidies and supports*   the support for agriculture begins at the level of research and development. At the other end of the production process, the government purchases many farm products at prices which are well above the market price. The government's programme of incentives consists of three parts; subsidiaries purchase of machinery and equipment; provision of inputs such as electricity, fertiliser and seeds at below cost price! and direct output subsidiaries, typically in the form of price floors.

The agricultural banks' subsidies for provision of machines during the 1970-1980 period accounted for over 9.0 per cent of total subsidies, with subsidies for animal feed purchases accounting for another 19.6 per cent, and agricultural improved inputs supplies accounting for another 41.9 per cent. Subsidies for other purposes accounted for over 24.0 per cent (Table 2.9).

By far the most important price support programme involved the production of wheat. The ministry of agriculture purchases wheat from local farmers and international markets. As the price paid to farmers has been high, the response has been a marked increase is total production.

Summary

Agricultural production has not grown as fast as the economy as a whole over the period of study, but perhaps more importantly, its nature has changed dramatically during this period. Traditional herding and agriculture have given way to highly capital intensive techniques of animal husbandry and farming. Iraq has approached self-sufficiency in many types of agricultural products and produces a substantial quality of other products.

Table 2.9 Some indications of Iraqi agricultural sector during the period 1968-1980

Year	Improved input supplies	%	Agriculture machines	%	Market	%	Development of live stock	%	Other Purpose	%	Total
1970	139.0	14.0	151.0	15.0	354.0	35.0	222.0	22.0	161.0	14.0	1027
1971	968.0	54.0	278.0	16.0	344.0	19.0	52.0	3.0	156.0	8.0	1798
1972	833.0	38.0	517.0	24.0	349.0	16.0	300.0	14.0	201.0	8.0	2200
1973	1056.0	38.0	616.0	22.0	319.0	11.0	4920	18.0	303.0	11.0	2784
1974	1142.0	38.0	336.0	12.0	119.0	4.0	718.0	25.0	590.0	20.0	2905
1975	1586.4	26.8	3076.3	52.1	136.1	4.0	921.7	16.0	199.9	3.4	5920
1976	2004.8	22.8	3446.7	39.2	354.0	4.0	2513.7	28.6	477.1	5.4	8796
1977	3758.5	40.4	2345.1	25.2	398.8	4.3	2094.1	22.5	698.2	7.5	9295
1978	5859.4	42.6	1369.7	90.1	817.7	6.0	2248.3	16.3	3470.4	25.2	13766
1979	9293.3	43.8	1901.1	9.1	888.5	4.2	4800.2	22.6	4341.4	20.5	21214
1980	10077.5	41.9	2146.2	9.0	121.5	5.0	4728.8	19.6	5909.9	24.6	24072

Sources: Ministry of Planning, Iraq, C.S.O., Annual Abstract of Statistics, Volumes 1976, 1978 and 1980.

To a great extent the increased output can be traced to government policies which encourage a viable domestic agriculture. The government has provided numerous implicit subsidies to farmers and in some cases has guaranteed a price which is above the world market price of the product.

2.3.2 The manufacturing sector

The manufacturing sector is currently a small part of Iraq's economy, accounting for well under 10 per cent of the GDP. This contrasts with 35 per cent in a highly developed country like the United States and 25 per cent in a developing nation such as India, which places a great emphasis on manufacturing. In terms of employment, the picture is much the same: in 1980, manufacturing. Employed just over 350,000 workers or about 12.7 per cent of the total civilian workers. Over the past decade, the rate of growth of employment in the manufacturing industry has been just 9 per cent, compared to an overall employment growth rate of just 8.9 per cent for the same period (see Tables 2.12 and 2.13).

The value added in the manufacturing industries grew from I. D 94.6 million in 1968 to I. D 709 million in 1980 at a rate of about 11 per cent during the 1968-1974 period and about 27 per cent during 1975-1980 period. The most important single manufacturing band is the production of consumer goods for direct consumption, such as food, beverage, tobacco, textiles, which accounts for about 34.7 per cent of manufacturing production. Consumer durable goods began to be produced in Iraq only during the early seventies, and then only in assembly plants.

Other products worth mentioning is refined petroleum which has a share of about 22 per cent, while the chemical industries account for 5.2 per cent of manufactures. Intermediate construction goods (non-metallic industries) account for about 15 per cent of manufacturing production and the miscellaneous sectors account for about 8 per cent. The production of capital goods has been negligible, its weight in total manufacturing output being insignificant as we clearly saw in Table 2.10.

The relative growth of this sector, particularly during the seventies, has been due to a number of factors. First, a substantial increase in the total resources of Iraq that has provided unique opportunity for the rapid development of the country. Secondly, the government has emphasised the importance of industrialisation in its development programmes and plans. Consequently. The allocation of finance to the industrial sector has rapidly increased. During the 1970-1980 period, the industrial sector received I. D 5329 million but the figure for the previous plan was only I. D 3307.6. The implementation efficiency rate was on average about 62 per cent during the same period.

Table 2.10 Index number of quantity of production in manufacturing industries for the period 1968-1980**

	F	T	C	P	CH	M	MS	GIN
Weights	34.7*	7.5*	7.9*	22.0*	5.2*	14.8*	7.9*	100*
1968	112.7	118.1	161.0	147.1	169.7	137.5	99.9	130.1
1969	120.8	137.5	168.4	159.9	188.8	139.4	127.6	141.3
1970	123.6	161.0	205.9	163.3	106.9	140.6	163.1	151.6
1971	135.8	194.5	284.2	182.4	241.9	165.4	194.5	176.5
1972	132.5	215.4	181.8	195.4	269.5	185.0	221.1	191.5
1973	167.1	275.5	281.8	196.5	259.6	194.0	272.3	207.0
1974	175.9	268.0	303.5	215.0	310.3	182.4	330.3	221.7
1975	216.0	255.4	313.6	315.7	342.7	196.5	353.7	263.2
1976	288.1	286.1	350.4	403.3	371.9	240.2	407.1	324.9
1977	369.2	204.1	388.9	456.1	391.4	412.6	452.9	399.1
1978	421.2	311.8	407.0	587.4	405.7	480.9	579.5	468.8
1979	428.0	208.3	379.5	643.6	413.9	560.9	657.3	499.3
1980	406.9	382.6	371.8	533.9	412.0	477.4	607.1	451.8
1981	485.7	434.0	428.2	564.6	520.1	750.9	566.7	539.3

Note: F= Food, Beaver and Tobacco T= Textile C= Clothes and Shoes CH= Chemical products M= Non-Metallic MS= Miscellaneous GIN= General Index No. P= Petroleum refinery.
* The weights used in table as indicative of the relative importance of the various commodity groups during the period of study. ** At constant prices 1962= 100.

Sources: C.S.O., Annual Abstract of Statistics, 1974, 1976, 1983, Ministry of Planning, Baghdad, Iraq.

Diagram 2.3 shows the industrialisation process in Iraq and the importance of government policy, as well as the role of oil revenues in industrial development.

There are several factors which have contributed to delays of industrial development. The low rates of implementation were not the only reason underlying slow industrial development. Industry in Iraq has suffered from other serious problems, many of which are of the kind typically experienced by developing countries. The small size of the Iraqi market has been a constraining factor, limiting many establishments to a level of production well below their economic capacity. This has forced per units cost of production up, thus making local products less competitive with imported substitutes.[18]

Shortages of qualified managers and skilled labour is believed to be the most serious bottleneck in the industrial sector, and the k import-substitution industrialisation itself has contributed to the T retardation of growth of industry. It has created a new set of t demands for a variety of imports such as machinery, spare parts, raw materials and semi-finished goods.

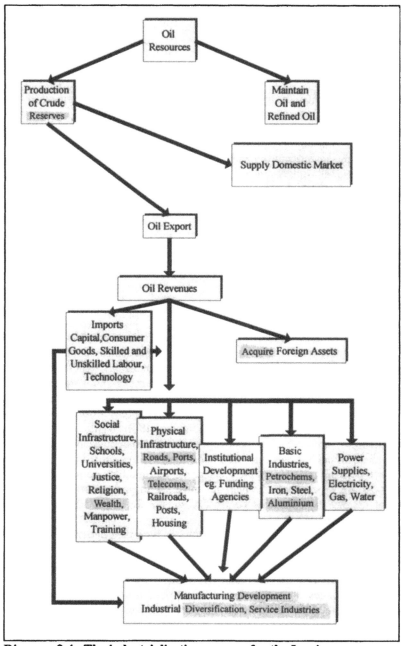

Diagram 2.4   The industrialisation process for the Iraqi economy

Not only does the policy of import substitution create demand for imported inputs and equipment, but the rise in per capita income is likely to raise the developing countries propensity to import, all the more so, because distribution of income in favour of the urban sector and higher income groups, whose expenditures pattern typically has the highest component of imports (Little et al 1970, p.63).[19]

Furthermore, Iraqi industry has also suffered from lack of enthusiasm on the part of the private sector. Iraqi entrepreneurs are accustomed to employing their capital in trade, rather than industry, and in investment in small and quick-yielding projects.

However, the manufacturing industry has performed relatively well especially after the national development plan of 1976-1980 accorded priority to petrochemicals and metallurgy. This was a new economic policy which changed the structure of production in favour of intermediate and capital goods.

Finally, the development of the industrial sector during the seventies was facilitated by the lack of foreign exchange constraints, as the rising level of oil revenues provided all the foreign exchange necessary for the importation of capital equipment and spare parts.

2.4 External trade and the balance of payments

Imports most of Iraqi industrial development has been dependent on the replacement of imported consumer goods by domestically produced substitutes However, much of the relative development has taken place inefficiently behind the protective wall of high tariffs and other trade restrictions, and has often been assembly plants requiring large scale imports of intermediate and capital goods. Because of the limited capacity of the domestic economy to produce the capital and intermediate goods required by an expanding industrial sector, a rate of growth has resulted in relatively high import dependence. As can be seen from Table 2.11, that the share of capital goods to the total imports increased from 26.4 per cent in 1968 to 48 per cent in 1980. While the share of intermediate goods imports in total import was 32.3 per cent on average, most of these gods being used in the industrial sector. The consumer goods, on average for about 30 per cent of total imports during the 1968-1980 period.

More importantly there was no trend towards increased dependence on imports as a whole. However, the share of imports in GDP increased dramatically after the fourfold increase in crude oil prices in 1973. Such that in 1980, imports constituted more than 16.5 per cent of gross domestic product. A continuation of this state of affairs clearly hinges on the performance of the oil sector. Because, the Iraq's capacity to imports depends on the foreign exchange which it received from the oil export.

34

Table 2.11 Import of consumer, capital and intermediate goods for the period 1968-1980

Years	(A)	(B)	(C)	(D)	A/D %	B/D %	C/D %
1968	56.6	58.1	49.3	144.2	39.2	26.4	34.2
1969	59.4	44.7	52.4	156.5	38.0	28.6	33.5
1970	59.8	48.9	71.7	181.7	92.9	26.9	39.5
1971	100.2	60.1	86.3	247.9	40.4	24.3	34.8
1972	68.4	73.8	90.0	234.7	29.2	31.4	38.4
1973	84.5	87.9	95.9	270.2	31.6	32.5	35.5
1974	271.9	200.6	297.8	773.4	35.2	25.9	38.5
1975	336.4	610.4	473.5	1426.9	23.6	42.8	33.2
1976	254.9	555.3	331.9	1150.9	22.1	48.2	28.8
1977	315.7	708.7	290.5	1323.2	23.9	53.6	21.9
1978	340.3	754.8	361.3	1473.6	23.1	51.2	24.5
1979	397.2	782.4	533.5	1738.9	22.8	44.9	30.7
1980	548.2	1050.8	580.7	2208.1	24.8	47.6	26.3

Note: A= Consumer goods. B= Capital goods. C= Intermediate goods. D= Total Import.
Source: Ministry of Planning, Foreign Trade Section, Iraq, April 1982.

Exports total exports grew, during the period, at an average compound rate of about 33 per cent per annum. We can say that the rate of growth of total exports was dominated by the rate of growth of oil exports. The percentage of oil exports to total exports was 94 per cent in 1968.

So that the share of non-oil exports in total export was about 6 per cent, the proportion declining to the lowest point of 1.3 per cent in 1979. The latter decrease in non-oil exports was due to the big increase in crude oil exports, which increased from about I. D 422 million in 1972 to I.D 6314 million in 1979. This sharp increase was due to oil nationalisation in June 1972, and to the rapid increase in oil prices during the seventies.

Finally, one must remember that although the export revenues from crude oil play such important roles in promoting the balance of trade, this may contain vital risks to the economy, as these revenues encourage the slowing Down of the growth of economic activities outside the oil sector. Furthermore, when these revenues are hit by any crisis which could cause a noticeable decline in their value, it would be inevitably reflected in the balance of payments, resulting even in deficit position, as it was in 1967, 1972, when oil revenues declined substantially.

According to foreign trade statistics, the balance of trade during the period of study was in deficit, but when oil is included in total exports, the results are positive, showing an increasing surplus during the whole period, because the revenues from oil exports grew at an annual rate of growth of 34 per cent during the 1968-1980 period, thus accounting for about 97 per cent of the total exports. The aggregate surplus continued at a relatively high level throughout the period.

The overall balance of trade surplus increased from I. D 221.5 million in 1968 to I. D 4659 million in 1979, as a result of the impact of higher crude oil exports after the increasing of oil prices in 1973. Therefore the Iraqi economy relied mostly one commodity in its exports, that is crude oil, the Iraqi economy was wide open to changes in the external, political, and economic events in the world. These events affected its capacity of imports and the stability of its economic development.

However, it is important to note that if we exclude oil from total exports the picture changes immediately in the opposite direction, the balance of trade suffered a serious deficit during the period as a whole. See Table 2.12.

Table 2.12   Trade balance of Iraqi economy 1968-1980

| Years | Total imports | Total exports of | | Total exports | Balance of Trade | |
		Non-oil exports	Oil exports		Inc. oil exports	Exc. oil exports
1968	144.1	21.5	344.5	356.7	221.5	-122.7
1969	156.5	22.0	346.2	368.2	211.7	-134.5
1970	181.7	22.5	368.1	390.6	208.9	-159.2
1971	247.9	22.8	526.2	549.0	301.9	-225.1
1972	234.7	28.5	421.5	450.1	215.4	-206.1
1973	270.2	32.4	677.4	709.8	439.6	-237.8
1974	773.4	38.0	2325.7	2323.7	1580.3	-745.4
1975	1426.9	35.4	2584.4	2619.8	1192.9	-1391.5
1976	1150.9	46.4	2875.6	2922.0	1771.1	-1104.5
1977	1323.2	42.4	2979.0	3021.4	1698.2	-1280.8
1978	1473.6	62.9	3781.0	3843.9	2370.3	-1410.7
1979	1738.9	83.5	6314.0	6397.5	4658.6	-1655.4
1980	2208.1	121.8	3510.7	3632.5	1424.4	-2086.3

Source: Ministry of Planning, Foreign Trade Section, Iraq, April 1982 and Table 2.11.

The balance of payments despite the rapid growth in the value of imports, oil exports have always been sufficient to maintain the balance of payments in healthy surplus. As Table 2.13 shows, the size of this surplus has increased from I.D 25.3 million in 1967 to I. D 1005 million in 1978. The cumulative payments surplus reflected in a dramatic change in official capital and monetary gold this period of ID 715.7 million, and oil exports has achieved contribution in increasing Iraqi cumulative payment surplus. For instance, the oil exports contribution increased from I. D 272 million in 1967 to I. D 3262.2 million in 1978. This indication had reflected the healthy financial state of the Iraqi economy.

36

Table 2.13 Iraqi balance of payments summary 1967-1978

Years	CB	C	PC	CM	CG
1967	25	272	-27	0.6	-1.9
1968	55	345	-38	-2.9	-18
1969	54	347	-48	0.1	9
1970	35	378	-37	0.2	-2.1
1971	68	526	-72	-0.8	-36
1972	75	421	-78	0.5	-52
1973	253	625	155	-2.7	175
1974	690	1943	-103	-67	715
1975	840	1820	-144	24	9
1976	736	2273	-296	-19	-861
1977	882	3151	-209	-5	-731
1978	1005	3262	-134	-37	-931

Note: CB= Current account balance; Including official transfer payments and goods and services C= Oil sector capital transaction PC= Other private capital; Including inward direct investment, short-term and long-term private capital and error and omissions CM= Commercial banks CG= Capital Gold; Including non-monetary gold, allocation of SDR and monetary sector.

Source: Iraqi Central Bank, *"Bulletin"*, January-December 1978, Statistical Department.

2.5 Major macroeconomic development problems

2.5.1 Inflation

The major problem encountered in Iraq was in the middle year of the last decade, the occurrence of an unacceptably high rate of inflation. This seriously threatened to jeopardise the development programme creating shortages of raw materials and consumer goods and affecting the viability of investment projects in both the public and private sectors; it led to an uncertain and hence risk business environment and undermined the standard of living enjoyed by certain sectors of the community, particularly those at the lower end of the income sale.

Two main indicators of the rate of inflation are available in Iraq. The cost of living index is now based upon surveys for middle income families in the country, spending an average of I.D 200.500 per month. As such, it is not a totally accurate indicator of inflation. Particularly, it rends to underestimate the actual rate of inflation since it does not cover all prices and, because it reflects primarily movements in consumer goods prices, it is affected by the large subsidisation programme introduced by the government in the mid-1970s. Nevertheless it is influenced by changes in imported consumer goods prices, which is not the case for the second indicator, the non-oil GDP deflator. This indicator does vary more with changes in capital goods and non-retail prices. Whichever indicator is chosen, the conclusions which emerge (see Table 2.14) are the same. During 1974 and 1976 the average annual inflation rate stood at approximately 10 per cent per annum; from 1977 onwards the inflation rate has declined to a level which compares very favourably with Western economies.

The cause of inflation during this period was not difficult to ascertain. The government had always been aware that accelerating its own expenditures too much could lead to inflation. In the interest of economic development in the mid-1970s it had been prepared to walk a tight rope between pushing economic growth to its limits and maintaining price stability. In this it went too far, the economy was unable to absorb the massive expenditure programmes of 1975 and consequently prices rose. To some extent inflation was imported but as Table 2.11 shows, import price rises could not be blamed entirely for its occurrence in Iraq.

The government was not slow to react. It immediately froze its part of expenditure at its 1976-1977 level. Some large public expenditure projects were postponed. At the same time, the government introduced price controls on some commodities and upon rents, as well as alleviating the hardships of low income groups through a policy of high subsidisation of basic foodstuffs. One area where prices had escalated was in relation to government contracts. Excessive inflationary expectations were being built into contract prices, particularly for wage and raw materials costs. The government responded by imposing lighter controls on contract prices.

Table 2.14 Inflation rates in Iraq

Years	CL	CLT	GDP*	RG	MP	RMP
1968	66.9	1.5	104.4	-	-	-
1969	70.1	4.8	105.5	1.1	-	-
1970	73.8	5.3	108.8	3.1	100.0	-
1971	76.4	3.5	122.8	12.9	106.0	6.0
1972	80.4	5.2	120.2	-2.1	115.0	8.5
1973	84.7	5.3	124.8	3.8	145.0	26.1
1974	91.3	7.7	235.8	88.9	182.0	25.5
1975	100.0	9.5	239.9	1.7	195.0	7.1
1976	118.0	18.0	279.8	16.6	196.0	0.5
1977	124.1	5.2	270.8	-3.2	216.0	10.2
1978	144.3	16.2	300.4	10.9	241.0	11.5
1979	163.4	13.2	350.6	16.7	269.0	11.6
1980	163.0	-0.24	390.9	-	288.1	7.1

Note: CL= Cost of living index. CLT= Rate of growth of CLT; for middle income Iraqi families. GDP *= Non-oil GDP deflator. RG= Rate of growth of GDP deflator. MP= Import price index. RMP= Rate of growth of import price index.

Source: This table estimated and computed variously from National Account Department, C.S.O., Ministry of Planning, Iraq.

The gap between spending and supply was also narrowed by encouraging the growth of domestic production capacity and by allowing imports to fill this deficiency in domestic production. However, it was not simply a question of allowing imports, more one of creating the ability to import. Inflation had arisen partly because ports in Iraq were unable to accommodate the vast import levels stimulated by development expenditures. By the beginning of the 1970s ports were congested; excessive delays were occurring in the import of raw materials and consumer goods and congestion surcharges were adding to import costs. The newly formed Ports Authority was charged with the task of remedying this situation as we shall see later.

This is one other feature of past inflation in Iraq which is not obvious from general price indicators. This is its structural character. Inflation has changed relative prices in the country as same sectors have incurred higher inflation rates than others. This is especially true of the housing sector, where the growth of the urban population put pressure on accommodation in 1970-1980 and raised rents by over 40.6 per cent in 1980 alone. During the same year the cost of food, drink and tobacco rose by approximately 14.8 per cent, whilst fabric and clothing costs fell. Recognising these differentials the government-controlled rents accelerated the house-building programme and extended the government financial assistance available for residential construction.[20]

It is interesting to note the role of monetary forces alongside fiscal measures. In Iraq the rate of growth of the money supply is mainly dependent upon three factors; the amount of domestic government expenditure, the growth of credit to the private sector and the net private balance of payment deficit; the first of these factors has proved the most influential. The money supply continued to grow throughout the last decade, the rate of growth responding to changing growth rates in government spending. At the same time, in the late 1970s, there was an increase in the private sector's balance of payment deficit as the value of imports rapidly expanded. This has also contributed to the lower growth rate of the money supply.

The causal direction appears to have been from government spending to the money supply and, in turn, to prices. It would have, consequently, been impossible to restrict the growth of the money supply, as an anti-inflationary device, without also putting limits on government spending. The inflation experience of 1973/74 meant that the velocity of the circulation of money was not stable during these years; the ratio of national product to money supply was at its highest ratio in 1974/1975 falling again in 1976.[21]

2.5.2 Work-force

Typical developing economies have a labour surplus. In the case of Iraq, the abundance of oil revenues and the ability created to buy capital goods has transformed it into the position of a labour-deficient economy, resulting in a number of manpower problems. Not only is the volume of domestic labour inadequate to support economic development at a rapid rate, it is also lacking in the skills required in the expanding sectors.[22] Iraqi labour productivity was relatively low by international standards when the oil boom came; as Table 2.12 shows, the majority of labour in the producing sectors was employed in the low productivity agricultural sector. By 1980 around one-quarter of the total work force was still to be found in agricultural employment.

The deficiency in volume and quality of Iraq manpower has been counteracted by government policies which are both short and long-term in nature. The immediate solution to the labour shortage was to import skilled, and unskilled labour on a large scale. This in itself has given rise to further manpower problems. The government does not wish to remain so dependent upon expatriate labour. Consequently it proposed, in the second development plan 1976-1980, to restrict the growth of the non-Iraqi labour force. At the same time it recommended a substitution of skilled for unskilled expatriate labour particularly as the construction sector has reduced its unskilled manpower requirements.

The long-term solution is clearly to encourage the growth of the Iraqi labour force and to raise the average productivity level of Iraqi workers. Productivity levels have been improved by extending the quantity and quality of education facilities for technical, commercial, agricultural and general vocational training. Particular emphasis has been placed upon educational courses which meet the needs of both the public and private sector. This will be shown in more detail in later chapters.

Table 2.15 demonstrates the major changes that have taken place in sectoral employment since 1970. There was a strong movement of labour away from the agriculture sector, for instance, the ratio of workers in the agriculture sector declined from 52.47 per cent of the total employment of the Iraqi economy in 1970 to the 33.62 per cent in 1980. This was mainly due to the attraction of higher wages in the Construction sector and in industrial employment. Output levels were improved therefore in agriculture by increased productivity, but this sector still remains one of the lowest in labour productivity in the country.[23] Moreover, it is highly probable that labour will continue to move out of agriculture despite the government's resolve to promote self-sufficiency in foodstuffs. Indeed the government anticipates a further allocation to agricultural employment, this would be consistent with its declared policy to deploy manpower to those sectors, with the greatest potential for growth and highest productivity levels.

There are nevertheless several unwelcome features among these sectoral employment trends. There has been a high ratio of the labour force employed in the services sector. From 1970 to 1980, the labour force movement in this sector was approximately 226,000 workers, or 6.2 per cent of the labour force increasing in the service sector from 1970 to 1980 (see Table 2.16). Many of the service industries were of relatively low labour productivity and therefore some switching of labour was helpful to output growth. The government sector absorbed further employees in this period, and in particular a higher proportion of the more productive Iraqi labour available to the more productive sector of the economy.

Table 2.15 Total employment in Iraq, and its distribution by economic sectors, 1968-1980*

Years	A	MQ	M	E	B	T	TM	S	EM
1968	1253.6	15.0	173.8	12.8	66.0	140.0	116.6	281.2	2159.0
1969	1306.4	15.0	176.4	12.9	67.0	145.0	119.1	392.9	2234.7
1970	1385.7	16.0	179.0	13.0	67.0	150.0	125.0	402.6	2338.3
1971	1434.7	16.5	184.9	13.7	69.0	160.0	128.3	414.3	2426.1
1972	1469.1	17.5	206.7	16.5	70.5	168.7	132.6	420.5	2502.1
1973	1398.4	10.5	209.3	16.3	92.7	175.7	135.0	523.6	2569.5
1974	1325.6	19.2	216.5	17.0	105.0	182.5	137.2	644.9	2643.8
1975	1215.4	20.0	227.8	18.3	185.9	190.7	141.6	809.1	2808.8
1976	1041.2	32.9	233.2	20.3	289.4	210.3	166.5	955.1	2949.3
1977	941.1	36.7	282.7	23.1	318.3	222.6	176.5	100.1	3001.1
1978	941.1	35.5	302.8	26.1	350.2	235.8	187.1	1047.5	3126.1
1979	941.1	39.3	324.3	28.7	385.2	249.7	190.3	1035.4	3202.0
1980	941.1	43.7	356.2	31.5	423.7	264.4	210.0	1010.6	3308.1

Note: A= Agriculture MQ= Mining and Quarrying M= Manufacturing E= Electricity and Water B= Building and Construction T= Trade and finance TM= Transport and Communication. *All figures in thousands.

Sources: 1. This table was calculated and estimated from Ministry of Planning, C.O.S., various years, Iraq.
2. Ministry of Planning, Iraq, The Manpower Planning Commission: The Realities of Population, Manpower Wages during the period 1976-1980 and 1984.

Table 2.16 Numbers of employment in the economic sectors, 1970-1980

Economic sectors	A	B	C	D %
Agriculture & Fishery	914.0	941.0	27.0	0.3
Mining & Quarry	16.0	43.7	27.7	10.3
Manufacturing	150.0	356.0	205.0	9.0
Construction	67.0	423.7	356.7	20.2
Electricity & Water	13.0	31.5	18.5	9.2
Commodity Sectors	116.0	1796.2	1680.2	4.4
Transport & Storage	154.0	210.2	56.2	3.4
Wholesale & Retail	150.0	264.4	114.4	5.8
Banking & Insurance	6.9	26.7	19.8	14.5
Distribution sectors	306.9	501.3	194.4	5.0
Services sectors	275.0	501.0	226.0	6.2
Total	1741.9	2798.5	1056.6	-

Note: A= Employment ('000) 1970 B= Employment ('000) 1980 C= Change in Employment 1970-1980 ('000) D= Growth of employment as a percentage.

Sources: 1. C.S.O., Annual Abstract of Statistics, 1978. 2. The Economic Planning Commission: Iraqi economy realities during 1970-1978, Ministry of Planning, Baghdad, Iraq. 3. The Manpower Planning Commission: The Realities of Population, Manpower Wages during 1976-1980, Ministry of Planning, Iraq.

Notes and references

1. Economic indicators of Economic Development in Iraq, Economic Department, Ministry of Planning, Baghdad, reports for 1960-1976 and 1970-1980 periods, published in 1976-1980.
2. Calculated from Table 2.1 and Table 2.2.
3. We follow the accounting procedure of referring to these expenditures as consumption items. In fact, expenditures on education and health are probably better thought of as an investment, because they increase the productivity of the work-force. Also, a substantial share of military expenditures are for the building of hospitals and for training, and should be considered as investment as well.
4. Even the figures reported in Table 2.1 and Table 2.2 do not fully reveal the importance of petroleum in the economy. Most of the other sectors would decline dramatically (though becoming relatively more important) if oil revenues were to diminish for a prolonged period. This is even true of agriculture, that receives substantial subsidies derived from oil revenues, see the exchange between T.H. Stanffer, *Measuring oil addition: growth versus expansion in a renter economy*, Middle East Economic Survey, Vol. XXIV, No.5, 16 November, 1981.
5. The increased income of the 1970s probably contained a large amount of income which would be considered as transitory in Friedman's sense of the term, Milton Friedman's, *A theory of the consumption function*, National Bureau of Economic Research, Princeton, NJ, 1957.

6. For a discussion of the dilemma facing many less-developed countries, refer to E. E. Hagen, *The Economics of Development*, Irwin, Homewood, 1975.

7. For a more useful discussion of the issues surrounding capital accumulation and economic development, increasingly, economists are stressing the importance in the development process of human capital, in the form of investment in education and training, health and migration, rather than physical capital, see C.P. Kindleberger, *Economic Development*, Wiley, New York, 1965, p.84.

8. Johany discusses this issue in *The Myth of the OPEC Cartel*, Wiley, Chichester, 1984, pp.60-65.

9. Calculated from Table 2.3.

10. Calculated from Table 2.4.

11. Ibid.

12. The concept of human capital traces primarily to G. S. Becker and T.W. Schultze. See B.F. Kiker (ed.), *Human Capital*, Columbia University Press, New York,1971.

13. The data available reveal the vast expansion of the cities in relation to the total and urban population, it shows that urban population, as a percentage of total population, increased from 54.4 per cent in 1970 to 65.70 per cent in 1965. See the World Bank, World Department Report Social indicator data sheet, August 1979.

14. The Quarterly Economic Review of Iraq, *Annual Supplement*, London, 1981. See also for more details:
    a. Frederick W. Axelgard (ed.), Iraq in Transition: *A Political, Economic, and Strategic Perspective*, published in Britain by Mansell Publishing Limited, London Inc., 1986.
    b. Lloyds Bank Group, *Iraq Economic Report*, 1985.

15. Beside the influence of the rainfall on the fluctuation agricultural output, the civil war in Northern Iraq until 1975 played a role in low agricultural production. See Quarterly Economic Review of Iraq, op.cit., p. 11 and European Publication, London, 1983/1984, p.361.

16. N. Akhan, *Pattern of Agricultural Development in Arab Countries*, the Arab Planning Institute, Kuwait, 1979, pp.167-71. This comments on FAO Census Bulletin No.17, May 1977 and see also published by Ernest Benn Limited, London, 1978.

17. Ministry of Planning, C.O.S., *Table 32/3, 1978 and 1980*.

18. Al-Eyd, A. K., *Oil Revenues and Accelerated Growth*, Praeger, publisher, USA, 1979, and see also, Lloyd G. Reynolds, *Economic Growth in the Third World, 1950-1980*, Yale University, 1985, p.339.

19. Little, I., Scitovsky, T. and Scott, M., *Industry and Trade in some developing countries*, New York Oxford University Press, 1970.

20. Central Statistical Organisation, *Annual Abstract of Statistics*, Ministry of Planning, Iraq, 1978, 1980.

21. Central Bank of Iraq Bulletin, *Statistical Department, January-December, 1978*.

22. Ibrahim (ed.), *Arab resources, the transformation of a society*, Centre for Contemporary Arab Studies, Washington, DC, Croom Helm, London, 1983, and see Shaw, R. P., *Manpower and education shortages in the Arab World, An Interim Strategy*, New York, Praeger, 1981, and also see World Bank, *Research Project on International Labour Migration and Manpower in the Middle East and North Africa*, USA, September, 1980.

23. Thelbald, R. and Jawad, S., *Problems of Rural Development in Oil rich economy, Iraq, 1958-1975 the Contemporary state*, edited by Niblock, T., University of Exeter, 1983.

3 The indirect impact of the oil export sector revenues on the planning machinery and economic growth during the period 1950-1980

The significance of the oil export sector, as noted earlier, extends far beyond its financial contribution. In addition to revenue, the oil sector's direct contribution is to foreign exchange earnings, the balance of payments, employment, GNP, not to mention energy supply and use as domestic inputs. However, more important from a long-term perspective, is the indirect contribution of the sector to the economy's development and structural change, i.e. *"the indirect impact deriving from expenditures of oil revenues by control government to cover the foreign exchange components of ordinary budget, development programmes and defence allocation"* (Keith Mclachlam, 1981).

Taking all the direct and indirect effects of the oil exports revenue into account, it can be argued that *"for nations with enormous oil deposits such as Venezuela, parts of Middle East and North Africa, oil is the economic life"* (Michael Tanzer, 1969). It is also true that oil is *"necessary for economic development"* (ibid.). Yet, it is difficult to agree with the view that *"these countries represent prime candidates for testing the validity of the theory of economic development through unbalanced growth...."* (ibid.). An unbalanced growth pattern may be feasible, and it has certainly been historically practical, but what is economically or technically possible may not always be socially desirable. Rapid capital accumulation, especially in a single sector which is not fully integrated with the rest of the economy, may lead to socio-economic chaos and to an under-utilisation of resource which may prove socially wasteful.

Therefore, when a single commodity such as oil plays a vital role in the economy and when that product is a exhaustible resource, it is crucial that not only the asset itself be handled by a sound and rational production utilisation programming policy, but also that the actual and potential proceeds from it be utilised in a way that contributes most effectively to achieving a stage of self-sustaining economic growth.

Efforts, have been made with growing frequency by the Iraqi government to strengthen the linkages between the oil sector and the rest of the economy. In Iraq, in addition to the increase in the price of oil and nationalisation of oil industries, the establishment of a number of projects such as petrochemical industries and other concerns during the last decade have enhanced linkages between the oil and other sectors. Yet, it is widely recognised that in all the major petroleum exporting developing countries, the oil sector is essentially isolated from the rest of the economy. The relationship between the oil and non-oil sectors at this point in time is essentially financial, with the former providing funding for the extensive development of the latter. This has often caused in a developing country a dualistic type of development in which a modern sector exists side by side with a traditional sector. Moreover, by its nature, the oil industry is capital intensive rather than labour intensive, employing only a relatively small portion of the labour force in light of its undeniable predominance in the economy as a whole. A major part of Iraqi has no direct bond with the overriding source of their nation's wealth.

The degree of isolation and/or dualism varies, of course, from country to country. This phenomenon may be due in part to the technological, political and economic structures of the oil industry and of the nation in question. It can also be traceable in part to the inability of the existing domestic industries and markets to supply the quantity and quality of required materials and services.

This aspect of the oil sector that is being weakly integrated with the rest of the economy-once again necessitate the diversification of the economy by rational and effective utilisation of the oil proceeds.

This chapter will review the literature on the role of the public sector in the development process and the role of oil in providing a suitable basis for economic development plans and diversification, as well as the relative importance of oil export revenues for the ordinary budget for the period 1968-1980. We are concerned with the oil export revenue, because this revenue represents more than 90 per cent of the total Iraqi revenues during the period under study.

3.1 Public expenditure, development and welfare maximisation

As already stated, the goal of public expenditure in LDCS is the development of the economy. The importance of this stems from the fact that with development, welfare can be increased in proportion with the level of output of the economy. According to Kishnawamy, 1965, p.81:

For all countries, the indictable elements in a development policy can be grouped under two main requirements: 1. an enlargement of the supply of those factors of production whose relative scarcity is inhibiting growth and 2. attainment of a pattern of factor - use which secures the maximum social net product.

Given these requirements, that aspect of fiscal policy concerned with the role of public expenditure in developing countries (LDCS) has increasingly become allocated. It is concerned with allocating more resources for investment and restricting consumption (Raja J. Chellaih, 1969).

With regard to investment, the public sectors function is to decide which forms of investment to undertake so as to ensure that the rate of growth of the economy is accelerated. This requires public expenditure activities of the widest variety. Such a strategy ensures that the available capital in a given economy is channelled into maximising output capacity which, in turn, leads to improved welfare (P. N. Rodan, 1964, p.8; W.T. Newlyn, 1961).

The attempts to enhance growth and development through development plans have led the public sector in LDCS to engage in a series of marginal choices between the use of single factors or the combination of various factors of production. However, the growth of output per head depends on the one hand, on the available natural resources, and on the other hand, on human behaviour. If growth is to take place, three conditions must hold true:

i. There must exist some genuine effort to economise, either by reducing the cost of any given product or by increasing the yield from any given input of effort, or of other resources;
ii. Increase of knowledge and its application especially in the rapid accumulation and application of knowledge in production, and
iii. Increasing the amount of capital or other resources per head (Arthur Smithies, Vol. 71, 1961, pp.255-272).

Two broad approaches for enhancing development have been adopted to meet the above conditions. The first is through capital formation, as exemplified by national development plans in LDCS. The second, is through increased input of effort and skill by personnel. According to Arthur Smithies, the type of growth primarily dependent on capital accumulation can be called the Ricardian growth model, while the type primarily dependent on more skilled effort can be called the Malthusian growth model.

The Ricardian model requires a much more rigorous limitation of consumption than does the Malthusian growth, model. For LDCS, the process of development involves striking a balance between the above two approaches. This is corroborated by Bangs who states that:

It would appear that many of the LDS in their development planning, at least, hold an implicit Ricardian concept of growth since they place such a heavy emphasis on investment especially in the public sector. This does not mean, however, that they wholeheartedly accept that other Ricardian prescription, e.g. about limiting consumption (Robert, B. Bang, 1968, p.20).

The implication of the above statement is quite clear: while investment is being enhanced, consumption is also permitted to increase, in order to maximise the welfare of the people, but the influence of the *Ricardian* view on economic development has led to the enlargement of public sector investment expenditures.

However, if investment is to generate welfare maximisation, an effective method of categorising public expenditure must be established. This is absolutely imperative because development expenditure must take in all growth including expenditure. A functional allocation of public expenditure is the most effective way of selecting investment that maximises productivity and thus welfare in economy.

This is because such a process *"greatly improves the distribution of government resources between consumption and development purpose, and among the various sectors of the economy"*, Rascheed O. Khalid, 1969, p.65.

Investment projects must be chosen in terms of productive efficiency and improvement of economic organisation. These issues are essential because they affect the capacity to increase output in a given economy and thus the ability to maximise welfare (Johne H. Alder, 1969, p.415).

Increasing development through public expenditure also requires the Government to ensure the growth in productive capacity. For an increase in public expenditure is justified only as long as the stimulating effects of additional expenditure on productive effort including capital formation lead to increased total economic production. This is the best way for material welfare to be improved upon (Al. Sayigh, Yusif, 1982, pp.77-79).

As the functional budgetary process implies, the allocative efficiency between consumption and investment in the budget must be the principle if accelerated growth rate is to be achieved (Raja, T. Chelliah op. cit., pp.38-40). If welfare is to be maximised, governments in LDCS must direct revenues to effect maximum long-run increases in output (Jesse Burhead, 1956, p.466).

In seeking to increase output, it is pertinent to remember that government investment, especially in social overhead capital, creates external economies for both the public and private sector. For example, improved roads, and rail transport lower the costs of shipping goods and open up private investment opportunities. Electric power projects will attract additional private investment and make farther Government investment cheaper. Because of the importance of external economies, major emphasis should not be placed on the income-producing aspect of direct investment by government.

This view has also been echoed by Walter Heller who states that balanced economic development depends on assigning priorities to projects according to their chances of being self-liquidating (Walter Heller, 1975, p.9). The central issue, therefore, is the capacity of government investment to maximise overall output in the economy rather than whether or not a project is paying its way. However, investment that maximises overall output of the economy can also be economically feasible.

To sum up, we can say that, if public expenditure is to enhance development and thus maximise the welfare of the people in a given society, the public sector must be concerned with the level and structure of its expenditure. Effort must be directed to those areas that ensure an overall increase in output of the economy so as to meet both current and future needs.

3.2 The effect of oil export revenues on the economic development programmes, and plans for the period 1950-1980

The devising of development plans has been the most popular activity of the governments of underdeveloped countries since World War II (Arthur W. Lewis 1969, p.37). When one considers that there has been very little success in development planning in most of these countries, one is apt to ask oneself what such a country does, if anything, having laboriously come up with a scheme?

A development plan must promote growth if it is to be a worthwhile enterprise. Meanwhile, more importantly, development which is broadly based on a plan's guidelines must generate a higher rate of growth than one based only on government budgetary allocation which is undertaken without the overall guidance of a comprehensive plan. The nub, therefore, is what function does a development plan perform, which cannot be performed by the annual budgetary policies of an ordinary government? This is an important question which a country contemplating the initiation of an economic development plan will have to ask itself when considering the poor correlation between development planning in a developing country and the ensuring economic growth (ibid.).

A realistic comprehensive plan must create a better environment for growth by providing a "sense of direction and consistency" (W. F. Stolpher, 1964). The purpose of annual budgets then is to convert the overall objectives of plans into annual projects with concomitant expenditures. A plan need not replace a government budget nor similar fiscal concerns; what it does is to provide an overall framework within which government expenditures and policies might be geared towards the long-term development of the country concerned? We can then say, that the plan would lend a sense of direction to governments and other public organisations on the one hand, and to the private sector on the other, so that consistency is achieved between government policies and the reactions of the private sector to them.

If a development plan is to inject a consistency into the public sector and in the economy as a whole, a feasible and rational assessment of priorities must be ensured. The plan must provide the framework within which the government, through its policies, together with the private sector's response, would act in order to achieve a reasonable rate of growth. If the rate is higher than that which could be realised in a situation where a plan does not exist, then one can infer some improvement resulting from the implementation of a plan.

Therefore, it would appear that development plans have not been performing successfully in most developing countries and several reasons have been given for this failure. They are:

1. Financial constraints.
2. Physical bottle necks.
3. Bias towards:
   a. Macro-plans,
   b. Urban development at the expense of rural development,
   c. Plan formulation vice versa plan implementation,
   d. Excessive industrialisation to the detriment of agriculture,
   e. Unrealistic targets often based on political expediency,
   f. Inadequate data bases or profitless basic survey,
   g. Inadequate specification of major targets and programmes designed to achieve them,
   h. A shortage of qualified work-force and administrative capacity all these are regarded as the causes for failures of development planning in developing countries (G. M. Meier, 1976, Chapter 13).

While careful planning is essential for poor countries trying to expand and maximise the range of their limited resources, it is also vital for countries with an available but narrow base of sources, particularly those with extractive and wasteful assets such as oil, which are attempting to diversify their economic base and to preserve and utilise their temporary wealth. There are other reasons why Iraq may benefit from a comprehensive development plan. One of the principle barriers to the successful implementation of a plan is financial or capital constraints. This having been eliminated in Iraq, it therefore stands a better chance than most developing countries of carrying out the projects which are put forward in a plan. Secondly, although financial and capital constraints may not exist in Iraq's case, other constraints do: human, administrative and physical ones. Nevertheless, the chief purpose of the plan is to ensure the "efficient use of a country's resources in accordance with certain rationally determined priorities for the attainment of nationally cherished goals" (ibid.). Moreover, as will be discerned from the discussion in this section, the history of planning in Iraq shows that greater efforts at development planning were made when Iraq found itself with surplus funds in the 1970s, but history also relates that the need for a development plan goaded that country into action in the 1980s.

In a country like Iraq, in which most of the state revenue comes from oil, the need exists for rationale allocation by the government. Allocation through physical and social infrastructure expenditure is not enough.[1] It must be stressed once again that more rational allocation mechanism is necessary in terms of the efficient utilisation of limited physical and administrative capacity, which is just as important as the utilisation of financial capital. The government of Iraq thus hopes that a comprehensive development plan, as the one for 1980-1985 will provide the necessary control direction for development in order to reduce waste, diversify the economy and ensure some internal consistency in government finances and in the overall development process of the Iraqi economy.[2]

3.2.1 The planning machinery during the period 1950-1969

Before discussing the history of the role of oil export revenue in economic development plans, it is necessary to give a brief background of the Iraq economy. The recent economic history of Iraq shows the agricultural sector was the backbone of the economy before oil. The quantity of agricultural exports continued to rise unimpeded, despite the relative fall in their prices these include cotton, wheat, barley, in addition to pastoral products like wood (Hasan, M. S. 1982, pp.348-358). The most important agricultural exports are dates and cotton. The foreign exchange earned from these provided the funds for capital imports for the development process of the country. These funds were not sufficient because agricultural revenue did not total the requirement of current expenditure of the government. For example, total government revenue rose moderately from an average of slightly over $12 million a year in the period 1946-1950 (Edith and Penrose, 1978, p.150). Until the 1950s, state revenue was too small to finance integrated large scale development programmes. For this reason, agricultural techniques remained backward leading to low output and productivity.[3] Socio-political factors were also to blame. In these circumstances there were virtually no industries of any substance and there was serious unemployment in the rural areas. For instance, the growth of rural population was higher than that of production, by a factor of 2. This resulted in a fall in the output per head of the rural and agricultural population. Thus the annual output of grain fell from 1,000 kilos per head of rural population in the 1980s to 560 kilos during 1930 and further to 505 kilos in 1950 (Hussan, M. S. op. cit., p.352). Development efforts concentrated on providing rudimentary services such as river control and water storage. Because of the central role of agriculture, all development efforts were geared to increase its export. Thus, the land and water resources formed the backbone of the economy before the advent of oil (Fahim, I. Qubain, 1958, 17-36, and IBRD, 1952, p.1).

Oil was discovered in Iraq in the 1920s. Thus at independence, oil had already been discovered in the north but there was little exploration in other parts of the country. In the initial stages, Iraq oil was developed principally by British and French companies under the auspices of the Turkish petroleum company (*Tpc*). The appropriation of ownership was as follows: Britain 70 per cent, France 20 per cent, and the Iraqi government 10 per cent (Michael Fanzer, 1969, Chapter 23). After independence, the Iraqi petroleum company (*Ipc*) a consortium of companies from Britain, France and the USA, was formed. It became the principle company in the Iraq oil business. Continuous conflict between the company and the government over lease holdings and royalty payments coupled with the development of alternative sources of petroleum kept both production of and revenues from oil at a pitifully low level.

The argument for planning in Iraq dates back to the 1950s when it was found necessary to inject some rationality into the economy after the government established a development board to serve as a vehicle for the utilisation of the rising oil revenue. The need for some sort of economic plan, particularly in government financial matters, was expedited by the desire to establish stability in the Iraqi economy (Lord Salter, 1955, p.97).

In the 1950s the Iraqi government established a Development Board to handle the task of developing Iraq. The main functions of the development board were; the presentation of a general economic and financial plan for the development of resources of Iraq and the raising of the standard of living of her people. This plan defined the general programmes to be undertaken by the board and included in its scope, but was not limited to projects in water conserving, flood control, irrigation, drainage, industry and mining or communication by river, land and air (Law No.23, 1950, p.126).

The Development Board prepared its first development programme as shown in Table 3.1 and called for a planned expenditure amounting to I. D 65.7 million to be financed from oil revenue. The planner's estimate of oil revenue during the programme period was I.D 29.4 million, and it accounted for 86.7 per cent of the total fund protected by the Development Board.

The first development programme was replaced in 1952 by the second development programme for the fiscal years 1951/1952-1955/1956 (The Middle East and North Africa, 1966/1967, p.280). The main underlying factor of the second development programme was that in the same year, an agreement was reached between the Iraqi government and the oil companies which led to an increase of 50 per cent in the government's share of the profits derived from crude oil export in 1955. However, only 70 per cent of oil revenue was donated to the development plan. The remaining oil revenue (30%) was channelled into financing ordinary government expenditure. The first development programme called for total planned expenditure amounting to I. D 65.7 million, while the second development programme (1951/1952-1956/1957) called for a planned expenditure of I.D 155.4 million against estimated revenues of I. D 168.7 million of which 97.6 per cent was oil revenue (see Table 3.1). Thus as a main source of financing the development programmes, oil revenues continued to play an important role in their realisation. In the first development programme oil revenue was projected as 86.7 per cent of the total funds allocated for the programme. While in the second programme oil revenue accounted for 97.6 per cent of the total allocated for the programme (see Table 3.1).

In February 1955 a new third five-year development programme for the period 1955/1956-59/60 replaced the second development programme. The new programme for the period 1955/56-59/60 called for total expenditure of I. D 304.3 million against estimated total revenue of I. D 215.7 million, while oil revenue accounted for 99.7 per cent of total planned (see Table 3.1).

It can be seen from Table 3.1 that the Iraqi planners gave priority to the agricultural sector in the allocation of the planned expenditures. An illustration of this policy is given in the IBRD mission recommendations, which point out in a report on the Iraqi economy in 1951: *"any development programme for Iraq must obviously put primary emphasis on agriculture, especially, concerned with development of food control, irrigation and drainage*" (International Bank for Reconstruction and Development, 1955, PXI).

The above mentioned programme did not survive its projected period and was replaced in 1956 by a new development programme for the years 1955/56-1960/61. This new programme depended upon the recommendations of the Economist Lord Salter. However, the estimated total expenditure was I.D 500.1 million. The planned oil revenues accounted for 98.7 per cent of total planned revenues (see Table 3.1).

The development programme of the 1955/56-1960/61 period continued to the end of 1959. This was due to the Revolution of 1958 when the new regime adopted a fresh approach towards developing the Iraqi economy and in 1959 the Development Board was replaced by a Planning Board and the Ministry of Planning (Penrose, 11, pp.252-253). The New Economic Plan for the period 1959/60-1962/63 made provision for expenditure estimated to I. D 392.2 million (Table 3.1). So, although the new regime was concerned with the role of the oil export revenue in financing development expenditure, the percentage of oil revenue towards the development programme was reduced by 50 per cent, the remaining 50 per cent being allocated to the ordinary budget (Edith. W. Penrose, op. cit., p.253). The deficiency was to be financed from internal and external sources.

The provisional economic plan for the period 1959/60-1962/63 did not run its full course, being replaced by another five year plan that was more balanced in that it increased the allocations to agriculture whilst reducing those to building and housing (ibid.). In this plan, the planned total expenditure was of 556.3 million and total revenues of I. D 556.8 million. It was estimated that oil revenues would account for 69.5 per cent of total planned revenue (Table 3.1).

Finally in 1965 a new five year economic plan (1965/1966-1969/1970) came into being and this ran its full course. The total expenditure during the five years of this plan was set at I. D 561.2 and the total revenues were expected to balance with the total expenditure. It was expected that oil revenue would account for 69.5 per cent of total planned revenues (Table 3.1). Furthermore, during this period, actual expenditure, at a percentage of both planned and actual revenues, was relatively less than in the preceding two periods. Moreover, the sectoral pattern shifted in favour of the building and housing sector, mainly at the expense of agriculture. It can be seen that actual expenditures in the industrial sector more than doubled in their plan as compared with the previous one (Table 3.1). Also, actual oil revenues in this period accounted for 91.5 per cent of actual total revenues as compared with 82.2 per cent in the previous plan.

From what has been said so far, a significant difference appears between planned and actual expenditure and revenue for the programmes and economic development plans reviewed above. For instance, during the period 1951-1969 actual expenditure fell short of planned expenditure in agriculture. industry, transport and communication by 41.6, 50.2, 53.7 per cent respectively (Table 3.4). Furthermore, as can be inferred from the above, the expenditure in the plan after the 1960s shifted its emphasis from agriculture to industry, as compared with the 1950s, reflecting the shift from agriculture to industry that the regimes after 1960s adopted. For example, in the 1951-1960 period, actual investment in agriculture and industry accounted for 29.3 per cent and 12.9 per cent respectively of total actual expenditures. The corresponding percentages of the 1961-1969 period were 13.5 and 24.7 (see Tables 3.3 and 3.4).

Moreover, it is worth mentioning that the nature of development programmes for the period prior to 1958 was forever changing in the expenditures, content and emphasis. This may be explained by the fact that Iraqi revenue was characterised by instability as Iraqi planners at the time lacked both experience and the necessary data. Indeed, the plans for the Iraqi economy of that period kept changing and did not run their full course until 1965, political instability being the main explanation.

Another important point to be noted about the economic programmes and plans for the period 1950-1969 was the particular significance of the foreign trade sector in Iraq as a determinant of growth of income, investment and import capital. The non-oil exports part of this sector however, were neglected by Iraq's economic planners during their period; as was mentioned earlier, this sector (non-oil export) played a vital role in the Iraqi economy before the 1950s (Hussan, M. S., op. cit.). Furthermore, the industrial policy which was adopted during this time, was that the small contribution of the non-oil export sector should cover the development expenditure.

To round off the review, one should mention that oil export revenues constituted the main source for the finance of development expenditure for the period 1950-1969. Having shown that diversity of revenues does not exist in a tangible form so as to play an appropriate role in the Iraqi economy during the above period, oil export revenues can be said to have constituted the main source of foreign exchange receipts. Iraqi planners seemed to have failed to minimise dependence of the Development effort and the entire economy at large on the oil export revenues, and had not managed to create an important role for the non-oil sector such as agriculture. Thus efforts should now be concentrated on using revenue efficiently to create a self-sustained, growing economy less dependent on the oil sector.

The evaluation of utility of oil export revenues as major sources for economic plans will be discussed in some detail in the following sections. An attempt will also be made to evaluate and analyse the economic plans 1970-1975, and 1975-1980.

Table 3.1 Development programmes and plans for the period 1951-1969 (in millions I. D and percentage)

Economic sectors	A		B		C		D		E		F		G	
	I.D	%	I.D	%	I.D	%	I.D	%	I.D	%	I.D	%	I.D	%
Agriculture	30.0	45.7	53.4	34.4	114.4	38	168.1	33.6	47.6	12.2	113.0	20.0	142.0	25.9
Transport & Communication	15.9	24.2	26.8	17.2	74.2	24	124.4	24.9	101	25.7	136.5	24.1	91.0	16.5
Industries	-	-	31.0	19.2	43.6	14	67.1	13.4	48.7	12.4	166.8	29.4	157.0	28.0
Building & Housing	72.6	19.2	18.0	11.6	60.9	20	123.2	24.6	191	48.7	140.1	24.7	108.7	20.2
Miscellaneous expenditure	7.2	10.9	26.2	16.9	11.4	3.7	17.3	3.5	4.0	1.0	10.0	1.8	65.5	9.4
Total	125.7	100	155.4	100	304.3	100	500.1	100	392	100	566.3	100	561.2	100
Revenues	Est	%	Est	%	Est	%	Est	%	Est	%	Est	%	Est	%
Oil	29.4	86.7	164.6	97.6	215.0	100	385.0	98.7	-	-	315.8	55.8	390.0	69.5
Other revenues	4.5	13.3	4.0	2.4	0.7	0.3	5.0	1.3	-	-	250.6	44.2	171.0	30.5
Total	33.9	100	168.0	100	215.7	100	390.0	100	-	-	566.4	100	561.2	100

Note: A = Planned expenditure in first five year development programmes, 1951/52-1955/56. B = The six years general programme, 1951/52-1956/57. C = Planned expenditure, the five years programmes, 1955/56-1960/61. D = Planned expenditure, the revised six years programmes, 1955/56-1960/61. E = The provisional economic plan, 1959/60-1962/63. F = The expenditure of the detailed economic plan, 1961/62-1965/66. G = The expenditure of the economic development plan, 1965-1969.

Sources: 1. International bank for reconstruction and development, the economic development of Iraq, Baltimore Hopkins Press, 1955, p. 182, 168. 2. Lord Salter, the Development of Iraq, London, Caxton Press Ltd., 1955, pp. 137-142. 3. Europe Publications Limited, The Middle East, 1958, London, Staples Printers Limited, p. 186. 4. The five-years detailed Economic Plan 1961/62-1965/66, pp. 44-45. 5. Quarterly economic review of Iraq, annual supplement, The economist intelligence united limited, August, 1981, p. 8.

3.2.2 The economic development plan 1970-1975

During the 1970-1975 plan period, Iraq entered a new era in the history of development planning. There were two main reasons for this: first, a new political regime was in power, second, a development methodology had been adopted as a vehicle, not just for social change and economic prosperity but for political stability as well (Edith and E.F. Penrose, op. cit., p.479).

Table 3.2 Actual development expenditure, planned and actual development revenue for the period 1951/1952-1969/1970

Fiscal years	A	B	C	D %	E %
1951/52	3.1	10.5	7.5	29.52	41.33
1952/53	7.5	20.5	24.0	36.59	31.25
1953/54	12.0	33.8	35.3	35.50	33.99
1954/55	20.5	34.9	40.7	58.74	50.37
1955/56	31.2	44.8	60.7	69.64	51.40
1956/57	42.4	65.8	51.1	64.44	82.97
1957/58	56.8	65.8	35.9	86.32	158.21
1958/59	51.6	65.8	61.7	78.42	83.63
1959/60	49.6	65.8	43.4	75.38	114.29
1960/61	75.5	66.8	47.7	71.11	99.58
1961/62	66.7	84.7	66.7	78.75	100.00
1962/63	58.8	84.7	70.0	69.42	84.00
1963/64	53.5	84.7	67.6	63.16	79.14
1964/65	74.2	84.7	76.4	87.60	97.12
1965/66	59.8	112.2	75.0	53.30	79.73
1966/67	82.8	112.2	70.8	73.00	116.93
1967/68	68.9	112.2	81.8	60.41	84.23
1968/69	64.4	112.2	88.9	51.40	72.44
1969/70	91.4	112.2	89.8	81.46	101.78

Note: A= Actual expenditure, B= Planned revenues, C= Actual revenues, D= Actual expenditures as a percentage of planned revenues, E= Actual expenditure as a percentage of actual revenues.

Sources: Republic of Iraq, Ministry of Planning, Annual Abstract of Statistics, 1970, pp. 329-30.

Table 3.3 Planned and actual development expenditures by main economic sectors and actual development expenditure during the period 1951-1969

Economic sectors	1951/52-1955/56				1956/57-1960/61				1961/62-1964/65				1965/66-1969/70			
	A		E		A		E		A		E		A		E	
	I.D	%	I.D	%	I.D	%	I.D	%	I.D	%	I.D	%	I.D	%	I.D	%
Agriculture	60.7	44.5	23	43.3	124.3	25.6	62.2	25.1	87.5	19.8	28.8	11.4	142.3	27.3	49.2	15.1
Industries	18.1	13.3	6	7.4	66.0	13.6	36.1	14.6	121.7	27.5	43.5	17.2	160.3	30.8	99.7	30.6
Transport	30.0	22.2	20	27.1	136.6	28.2	56.6	22.9	115.0	26.0	67.2	26.5	98.2	18.8	59.9	18.4
Building & housing	27.5	20	17	22.2	157.9	32.6	92.4	37.4	118.4	26.7	113.7	44.9	120.3	23.1	117	35.9
Total	136	100	75	100	484.8	100	247	100	442.6	100	253.2	100	521.1	100	326	100
Revenue:																
Oil			159	92.3			234	97.0			230.7	82.2			372	91.5
Others			9	7.7			7.0	3.0			50.1	17.8			33.6	8.5
Total			168	100			241	100			280.8	100			406	100

Note: A= Allocations, E= Expenditures.

Source: This table calculated from Table 3.2.

Table 3.4 Planned and actual development expenditure by economic sectors for the period 1951-1969

Economic sectors	Allocation (1)	Expenditures (2)	Ratio ½
Agriculture	414.8	172.4	41.6
Transport & Communications	379.8	203.9	53.7
Industries	366.1	184.8	50.2
Building & Housing	424.1	339.7	80.1

Note: All figures in millions I. D.

Source: This table derived from Table 3.2.

The result of this was a new development plan for the five years 1970-1975 announced by the Ministry of Planning on March 29, 1970 as a National Development Plan (Law No.70 for 1970). This plan was the most ambitious and the most advanced of all the ones previously proposed. The government objectives of the development policy implicit in the plans were to increase the productive capacity of the economy and to raise the standard of living, the wealth and the welfare of the people of Iraq. At the same time the plan intended to provide for national security and to maintain economic and social stability along the path of development. The specific objectives of this plan were:

i.   To raise the rate of growth of the gross national income.
ii.   To diversify the economy and to reduce the country's dependence on oil by increasing the contribution of the commodity sector, especially agriculture and industry, to the national products.
iii. To lay the foundation for sustained economic growth.
iv.   To develop human resources so as to enable different elements of society to contribute more effectively to the growth of the economy and to participate more fully to the process of development (ibid.).

The plan projected an increase in the national expenditure from about I. D 826 million in 1969 to about I. D 1162.6 million in 1974, i.e. a compound annual growth rate of 7.1 per cent (ibid.).

To achieve the above target and other objectives, the plan projected an outlay of I. D 536.9 million of the central government and 321.8 million of the public business sector. In addition, emphasis was given to the private sector to increase its ability to participate in the process of development, with a distribution of I. D 285 million, that is 25 per cent of total allocation (Table 3.5).

In order to diversify the economy and to reduce its dependence on oil, the plan aimed at increasing the contribution of the other productive sectors, in particular agriculture and industry, to the national product. However, the amount allocated to these sectors was 35 per cent of total outlay to agriculture, and the industrial sector received only 24 per cent of the total project outlay, followed by transport and communication with 11.5 per cent, the building and housing with 12.5 per cent respectively (Table 3.6 and Figure 3.1). In other words, the emphasis was shifted back once more to the agricultural sector.

It seems that with regards to the development of both agriculture and industry, the plan relied heavily upon the public sector. In this respect, it might be said that Iraq differs to a certain extent from some other developing countries where the government has put too much faith in the private sector's ability to contribute to investment and its overall participation in the economy.

Iraqi planned expenditure for 1970-1974 was based on the assumption that at least 50 per cent of the expected revenues would come from the export of crude oil. The 50 per cent of oil revenue was estimated to a round I. D 425 million and the rest was to be raised from international loans and other sources of government revenue (National Development Plan, 1970-1975, p.154). It was to be allocated towards financing the five year development plan, but in reality, the contribution of oil export revenues amounted to 79.2 per cent, foreign loans contributing 11.9 per cent and the remaining 9.6 per cent coming from the various sources presented in Table 3.7 and Figure 3.2.

The 1970-1974 plan was, however, amended in 1971 and again in 1974, with an increase in oil revenue expected during 1970 and 1974; the government increased planned investment in the development plan from I. D 536.9 million to I. D 952 million in 1971, and then to the astounding figure of I. D 1169.0 million in March 1974 to cover development plans for 1974/1978 alone. The main reasons for that amendment, which provided increasingly for the capital investment in development projects were as follows:

a. The direct exploitation of Iraqi oil revenues by the Iraqi company (INOC) after nationalisation of the oil industry.
b. The increase in the international demand for crude oil, which frequently augmented both the oil prices and revenues of all the oil exporting countries which improved gradually, beginning with the Tehran and Tripoli agreements between (OPEC) and the international company in 1971 (W.B. Fisher, 1981, pp.101-102).
c. Political instability. Iraq's revenue from crude oil exports increased from I.D 186.1 million 1970 to I. D 2123.214 million in 1975, and this new revenue was used towards the finance of the development programme. The remaining capital came from foreign loans 7.2% and other sources 5.8% (see Table 3.7 and Figure 3.2).

It can be seen from Table 3.8, that generally speaking, actual expenditure did not suffer seriously from any financial constraints during the period of the development plan 1970-1975, the reason being primarily an increase in oil revenue for the country. This situation was not confined to Iraq, the self-same thing happened in all the major oil exporting countries where oil revenues were used to finance economic development. For instance, the ratio of government expenditure to gross domestic product (GDP) in major oil exporting countries jumped from 24 per cent in 1972/1973 to 40 per cent in 1975, and it has continued to rise (David R. Morgan, Vol. 26, 1979).

3.2.2.1 Specific sector targets of the plan

As was mentioned earlier in this chapter the best way to evaluate the utilisation of oil export revenues as a major source of economic plan revenues is by attempting to analyse and evaluate the economic plans and developments that were adopted in Iraq during the period 1970-1980.

The investment criteria models are either the *"Big-Bush"* Balanced growth model spreading the available resources over the production of many commodities or the unbalanced growth model (involving staggering economic development, so that net or gross investment output grows faster in one sector than in other), but at the same time, the process of developing a less developed economy gives rise to an imbalance mainly because of basic structural characteristics such as rigidities and sluggishness of response.

Therefore, if adjustment is to be achieved, a system of co-ordinated planning must be adopted. It is also held that there is no assurance that the strategic sectors will be able to pull those unresponsive sectors (Paul Streeten, 1970, pp. 366-371).

It is axiomatic, therefore, that the Iraqi planners were dependent on the oil export sector, so that it is an implicit feature/characteristic of their plan to have an unbalanced allocation of the investment expenditure. Therefore, economic planning was adopted to strengthen and co-ordinate the ratio between the oil sector and other sectors of the economy in the modern plans, especially in 1970-1975, and 1976-1980. The figures in Table 3.8 show that the allocation of actual versus planned expenditure in the main sectors of the economy was as follows.

The Industrial Sector the facts indicate that the industrial sector figures larger in this plan than in previous ones, indeed more so in this plan than in previous ones, particularly in the public industrial sector which, included the completion and expansion of the construction operation at the following industrial factories; in *'Hillah'* a textile factory at Babylon, which cost I.D 7 million, in *'Basrah'* a paper factory which was completed in 1971 at I. D 11.3 million and in 1974, a further I. D 70 was spent on its expansion. Another project was *'Iskandariah'* an agriculture large assembly factory which was completed in 1972, at a cost of I. D 10.3 million. Another one was in *'Summarrah'*, a drug factory that was completed in 1971 at a cost of I. D 7.0 million and yet another was the sulphur and natural gas factories in *'Kirkuk'*, completed in 1971 at a cost of I. D 10.7 million. Indeed many new factories were established during the plan period of 1970-1975, for example the chemical fertiliser factory in *'Basrah'*, which was completed in 1974, at a cost of I. D 9.5 million and its expansion in 1975 at a cost of I. D 28 million. There were other projects with construction costs not less than I. D 5 million each, such as in cement, footwear, tomato paste, cigarettes ... etc. In other parts of Iraq, ten heavy projects were undertaken with Soviet aid for the production of steel and electric equipment, sugar and the building of three hydra electric power stations and ten transmission stations feasibility studies were also initiated for establishing further estates in different parts of Iraq (The Middle East and North Africa Journal, 1974/1975-1977/1978).

It can be seen from Table 3.8 that actual expenditure in this sector was considerably higher than in any of the other main sectors; overall expenditures during 1970 and 1975 amounted to I. D 620.0 million, more than 40.9 per cent of total actual expenditure on the whole economy. As a result of the projected investment, as well as the availability of both skilled and semi-skilled manpower (U.N., 1967.p.11), the contribution of manufacturing industries was estimated to have increased from about 643.9 million at the end of it, implying an average annual rate of the growth sector of 39.7 per cent for the period of the plan (see Chapter 2, section 3 and Table 3.9).

In the agricultural sector the plan aimed at achieving an annual compound rate of growth. The plan had to give first priority to agricultural development. An amount of I. D 336.5 million was allocated for the current expenditure outlay (Table 3.6). The plan recommended expansion and implementation in irrigation and drainage projects, for instance, in 1970, the USSR agreed to provide considerable technical and financial assistance towards the realisation of these various projects. The Soviet experts were consulted in the preparation of the plans for the '*Bakhma, Hadithah, Mosul, Hirmreen*' and '*Kirkuk*' irrigation projection, and in 1975 when the '*Hadithah*', '*Himreen*' and '*Alakarh*' dams were completed, together with the *Tharther-Euphrates* canal. Other irrigation projects were also completed during this time. The plan, therefore, recommended expansion in services and programmes that would encourage private investment in agriculture and allied industries with an emphasis on research programmes, studies and statistics, and the provision of agricultural loans and credit (see Chapter 2).

A sound infrastructure base is essential if output is to be enhanced, substantial funds were also committed over the years by Iraq to this sector with the aim of removing all potential bottlenecks to increased output.

The availability of oil financing influenced expenditure in this sector in the following way: one, there were massive efforts to increase the volume of the infrastructure; two, the government became increasingly concerned about the quality of Infrastructure facilities; three, the government diversified their shipping activities to include oil tanker fleets, with a view to participating in downstream oil trade. In this section the discussion will cover transport facilities, roads, railways, port and shipping lines, and communication facilities like the telephone and postal system during the 1970-1975 plan period.

With a view to creating the necessary physical infrastructure for sustained economic growth, this sector continued to receive the largest share of public investment. As compared with the preceding period; the total expenditure allocated to the transport and communication sub-sector increased in the first year of the plan from I. D 7.4 million to I. D 138.0 million in the last year (Table 3.9). A total of 33.763 km of main roads was earmarked for construction during the five-year period (Ministry of Planning, 1984). An expansion scheme for the *OM-Qassir* port with new facilities built for loading sulphur, and an adjacent oil terminal was completed at *'Khor-Amaiyah'* and Loa (cost I. D 3617) together with the new port of *'Al-Bakar'* at *'Basrah'* port (cost over 5617) (S. *'Mohsin'*, July 1982). As regards the airport, the plan necessitated substantial improvement and expansion in air facilities; it advocated and effected a new civil international airport in Baghdad, developed the *'Mousal'* and *'Basrah'* airports to take international services as well as other projects costing the planning council over I. D 6514 (Middle East and North Africa Journal, op. cit.). At the same time, outlay emphasis for the railways meant that the principal lines from Baghdad would have to go through *'Mosual'* to *'Telkotcket'* (529Km) and from *Basrah* to *Baghdad* (569 Km). These were completed with Russian assistance in 1971, the latter line being realigned and converted to standard gauge. A line was also built to link *'Shaiba'* and *'Om Qassir'*, whilst work on the line from *'Kirkuk'* to *'Sulimaniya'* was almost completed in 1975. The total actual expenditure of these projects was I. D 22 million during the period 1970-1975 (Ministry of Planning, Iraq, 1975, pp. 37-38). The plan for communication systems quality improvement involved the establishment of 12 automatic telephone exchanges, a radio and wire communication network and a microwave project.

The plan also recommended the setting-up of a department of electrical services to be responsible for initiating and carrying out the necessary changes in the electricity sector to enable it to meet growing demands and execute programmes for supplying electricity to the largest part of the country; consequently, during the period of plan 1970-1975, the government built (with some assistance from the Soviet Union) many electric power stations in Baghdad and in other parts of Iraq, to expand and renew the old electric power station. For the purpose of achieving this target, the planned allocation for this sector was 26.9 million, that is 2.5 per cent of total expenditure in the plan.

With regard to human capital and social development, a sizeable target was set in the plan. In an attempt to develop a manpower programme which would reduce the shortage of both skilled and semi-skilled labour, education and vocational training facilities were given priority, because Iraqi planners saw education as an instrument for effecting national development.

Oil financing has influenced expenditure in this sector as well. It has made it possible for the Iraqi economy to rapidly expand educational services at all levels. So, the objective of the 1970-1975 plan was to raise the number of students, at all levels of education, substantially during the period of the plan's implementation. There was also increased emphasis on technical education throughout the education system now that the necessary funds were available to meet the high cost of such education (Edith L. Penrose, op. cit., p.486). The number of universities also rose from 2 to 5 and new ones were established in the provinces '*Mosul, Basrah, Sulimanya Moustansaray, Kawfa*'.

In the public sector, health service and public health care were boosted; the plan aimed to raise the level of health in the rural and uban areas; the number of public hospitals increased from 150 in 1970 to 167 in 1975, and that of physicians from 2908 in 1970 to 4477 in 1975 (Ministry of Planning, Annual Abstract of Statistics, for a number of years). These new health institutions were equipped with the most modern equipment and personnel were trained in different parts of the world.

As it turned out, and as we shall see in the next section, one lesson was certainly learnt and put into practice: there is a positive correlation between oil export revenues and a plan size. In spite of the plan size, do not depend solely on the capacity to finance the plan; in the case of Iraq, where finance is no constraint, the relevant factors which should collectively determine the size of a plan are those other than finance.

Table 3.5 Distribution of investment by economic activities in national economic development plan 1970-1974

Economic sectors	Government	Public sectors	Total	%	Private sector	Total	%
Agriculture	185000	8000	193000	24.5	18000	211000	19.7
Industry	106600	55950	162550	20.7	50000	212550	19.8
Mining & quarrying	1000	153550	154550	19.6	-	154550	14.4
Electricity	24400	2500	26900	3.5	-	26900	2.5
Commodity sectors	317000	220000	537000	68.3	68000	605000	56.4
Transport & comm.	6000	54290	114290	14.5	35000	149290	13.9
Trade & finance	-	17500	17500	2.2	15000	32500	3.0
Total distribution sectors	60000	71790	131790	16.7	50000	181790	16.9
Housing	1000	9250	10250	1.3	150000	160250	15.0
Other services	74000	20750	94750	12.0	17000	111750	10.4
Services sector	75000	30000	195000	13.3	167000	272000	25.4
Other investments	13601	-	13601	1.7	-	13601	1.3
Total sectors' investment	465601	321790	(b) 787391	100.0	(e) 285000	1072391	100.0
Loans and international obligations:							
Loans for Government departments	37300	-	27300		-	27300	
International obligations	44000	-	44000		-	44000	
Grand Total	536901	321790	858691		285000	1143691	
Percentage (%)	46.9	28.1			25.0		100

Note: (a) Inclusive of the mixed partnership sector. (b) Investment in building and construction are in different economic sectors. (c) Inclusive of investment of contractor's sector (building and construction). (d) All figures in thousands I.D.
Source: Adapted from the National Development Plan, 1970-1974, p.151.

Table 3.6 Expenditures outline in Iraqi economic development plan 1970-1975 and 1970-1975 (amended)

Economic sectors	The first five years National Development Plan 1970-1975		The first five years National Development Plan 1970-1975 (amended)	
	%		%	
Agriculture	185.0	35.0	336.5	35.5
Industry	132.0	24.0	207.2	21.8
Transportation & Communication	6.0	11.5	96.6	10.2
Building & Housing	67.0	12.7	120.1	12.6
Others	92.0	17.0	192.1	20.1
Total	536.9	100.0	952.5	100

Sources: Ministry of Planning, National Economic Development Plan, Law 70 of 1970, Ministry of Planning, C.S.O., Annual Abstract of Statistics, various volumes, 1970 to 1977.

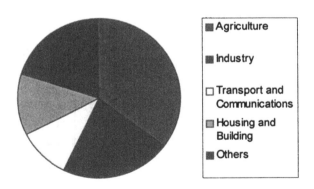

Figure 3.1 Expenditure in the first five years development plan 1970-1975 (amended)

**Table 3.7 The revenue allocated in the Iraqi economic development plan
1970-1975**

Sources of revenues	The first five years National Economic Development Plan 1970-1975		The first five years National Economic Development Plan 1970-1975 (amended)	
		%		%
Crude oil export	452.0	79.2	828.9	87.0
Foreign loans	60.0	11.9	69.0	7.2
Domestic loans	10.0	1.9	10.0	1.1
International payments	0.06	-	0.3	-
Government's profit	11.4	2.0	11.5	1.2
Cash balance	-	-	31.8	-
Other revenues	30.0	5.6	1.0	3.4
Miscellaneous	0.5	-	1.0	0.1
Total	536.9	100.0	952.5	100.0

Source: Ministry of Planning, C.S.O., Annual Abstract of Statistics, Volumes
1970-1977.

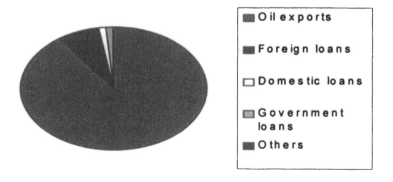

Figure 3.2 Revenues allocated in the Iraqi development plan 1970-1975

Table 3.8   Planned and actual development expenditure and revenues during the period of plan 1970-1975

Year	Expenditures			Revenues			
	Planned (1)	Actual (2)	½	Planned (3)	Actual (4)	¾	2/4
1970	116.5	78.1	67.0	116.5	115.5	95.5	70.2
1971	202.0	153.8	76.1	202.0	189.3	93.7	81.3
1972	134.5	128.5	95.5	89.5	135.8	151.7	94.6
1973	310.0	244.0	78.7	250.0	441.8	176.7	55.2
1974	1169.0	576.4	49.3	169.0	661.8	56.6	87.1
1975	1076.0	916.2	85.2	1076.0	1089.3	101.2	84.0

Sources: 1. Statistical pocket book, 1986, Ministry of Planning, Baghdad, 103-111, Table 6.5.   2. Ministry of Planning, Iraq, C.S.O., Annual Abstract of Statistics, 1970-1977.

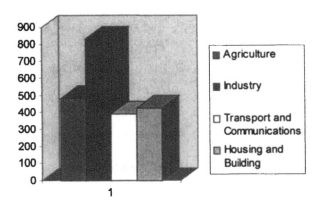

Figure 3.3   Actual expenditure on economic sectors plan (1970-1975)

3.2.3   The second economical development plan 1976-1980

Unlike the first plan, the second development plan for the period 1976-1980 embodied the efforts of the government to develop in a manner unconstrained by finance, especially foreign exchange. Since nationalisation and the increase in oil prices in 1973 raised the foreign exchange resources of Iraq, the major economic problem had been that of finding domestic avenues for absorbing the so called "surplus funds".

In this plan, again, the long-term policy of Iraq was to diversify the economy so as to reduce its dependence on the primary exhaustible resource, oil. In this respect, an important goal of the plan was the diversification of the Iraqi economy based on the efficient utilisation of human and natural resources. This involved the shifting of resources to agriculture, industry and mining to expand these important sectors of the economy. There is no doubt that it is in the expansion of these sectors that the participation of private entrepreneurs would have been most needed and welcomed by the Iraqi government.

In spite of the fact that the goal of diversification of the Iraqi economy is an indication of judicious foresight on the part of Planners, one wonders whether the emphasis which an industrialisation programme places on the Petrochemical industry, Fertiliser, Gas, Iron and the Oil refining sector, will serve only to sustain the dependence of the economy on oil (Europe publication, 1983/1984). If this happens, then the economy may be in trouble when the crude oil in a country like Iraq has been exhausted. Unless the oil-based low cost housing, extending the welfare system, and making a credit system readily available to poor people in need of financial help.

The plan also saw the indispensable role which infrastructure plays as the basis upon which any meaningful policy should be executed. This role is especially important in a "surplus-funds" country in which an abundance of foreign exchange resources is likely to create port facilities, transportation, communication and housing and to develop existing municipalities and establish new ones.

The government of Iraq believed that achieving the objectives of the 1976-80 plan would establish other public sector as the dominant one in the economic field. The government, therefore, supports the private sector and encourages it to invest in light industry and construction.

The rest of the plan, after an outline of the goals, consists essentially of the specification of policies and the necessary allocations which would achieve the stated broad goals. The specific nature of each goal is expressed in terms of objectives or forecasts of output in the various sectors of the economy: manufacturing, human resources, agriculture, infrastructure.

Before a detailed discussion of the plan, it must be noted that, like most comprehensive plans, it conforms to the criteria enunciated by Professor Arthur Lewis, 1969, who writes:

A Development plan may contain any or all of the following parts:
i.   *A survey of current economic conditions;*
ii.   *A list of proposed public expenditures;*
iii. *A discussion of likely development in the private sector;*
iv.   *A macroeconomic projection of the economy;*
v.   *A review of government policies.*

The Iraqi plan contains all of the above, but in addition, it devotes space to plan implementation and management, aspects of planning which are as important as any of the above five points. It is hoped that the following discussion will show the extent to which these parts do interact, as well as elucidating the details of each aspect of the planning process.

3.2.3.1 Development strategies and pattern of development

The second plan is certainly an ambitious one. This, however, is not so pie-in-the sky as to make its finance unfeasible. On the other hand, from the point of view of the physical and manpower constraints existing in Iraq, the 1976-1980 plan could be seen as far larger a project than its predecessor.

This plan had an original outlay of about I. D 15193.3 million and oil revenues were expected to finance over 98 per cent of the total plan's requirements. The seemingly over ambitious goal of the original second plan called for a 16.8 per cent annual increase in GNP (Edith and L. Penrose, op. cit.).

In addition, larger oil revenues were naturally expected and these have presumably tempted the authorities to disregard the strains that existing rates of spending have placed on the economy. During the time-span of the plan, these amounted to about I. D 13219 million of which over 92 per cent come from oil (see Figure 3.4 and Table 3.10) of the total projected expenditure of about 15193.6 million about I. D 12255 million was earmarked for the public sector.

As shown in Figure 3.4, the principal noteworthy features of the revised second plan are the importance of oil export sector revenues as principal suppliers of funds for the government, and its small contribution to foreign borrowing. On the payments side, fixed-capital formation constituted the largest share being about I. D 1060 (1975 constant prices) during the period of the plan (ibid.).

The second plan had total expenditure larger than that of the first plan 1970-1975. The size of the second plan development is only one of the features that distinguishes it from the first plan as can be seen from Tables 3.9 and 3.11 which give expenditure breakdown of the two plans; some very interesting shifts of emphasis can be observed.

At an aggregate level it can be seen from Table 3.9 that, whereas, the first plan allocated 66.9 per cent of total expenditure to be expended on the development sectors, the current plan made provision for 62.2 per cent of the total expenditure for the purpose of development (Table 3.9). On that basis alone, one may conclude that the second plan is more development-oriented. This characteristic is important because it is a measure of the emphasis the government places on the development of natural and human resources, and the extent of the diversification programmes. The plan also took into account expenditure as advised by feasibility studies carried out before the plan was formulated.

Table 3.9 Planned and actual expenditure on economic sectors with their rate of percentage during the years of economic national development plan 1970-1975*

Years	Agriculture			Industry			Transportation & Communication			Building & Housing			Total		
	P	A	%	P	A	%	P	A	%	P	A	%	P	A	%
1970	28.0	14.1	50.4	28	21.2	75.8	15.3	7.4	48.3	13.0	9.9	76.1	84.3	52.6	62.3
1971	60.0	49.3	82.1	50	35.9	71.8	28.0	17.0	60.7	28.0	18.0	62.8	166	120.0	72.2
1972	23.2	29.3	126	28	22.2	79.3	16.0	19.9	124.3	22.0	17.0	76.0	89.2	88.1	98.8
1973	65.0	37.9	58.3	60	66.4	10.3	40.0	27.6	69.0	45.0	37.0	81.1	210	168.4	80.2
1974	190.0	78.0	41.0	225	184.1	82.0	120.0 ·	105.6	88.0	175.0	91.0	51.7	710	458.3	64.5
1975	207.5	99.9	48.1	448	290.2	64.8	166.0	138.0	83.1	188.0	101.0	53.7	1010	629.7	62.3
Total	573.7	308.5	53.8	838	620.0	74.0	384.3	395.3	100.0	471.0	263.0	55.7	2269	1517	66.9

Note: P = Planned, A = Actual, % = A / P % . * All figures in millions I. D.

Sources: 1. Ministry of Planning, Iraq, Economic Department, Indicates of developed Iraqi economy for the period 1970-1976, April, 1976. 2. Ministry of Planning, Iraq, C.S.O., Annual Abstract of Statistics, Volumes 1970 to 1978.

Table 3.10 The revenues allocated in the Iraqi economic development plan 1976-1980

Economic sectors	The revenues allocation in the plan 1976-1980	%
Crude oil export	13219	92.0
Domestic loans	-	-
Foreign loans	351	2.4
Interest payments	-	-
Government's profits	645	4.5
Cash balance	66	0.5
Revenue from other sources	8	0.1
Miscellaneous	78	0.5
Total	14367	100.0

Source: Ministry of Planning (1984), Indicates of Iraqi economic development for the period 1970-1980.

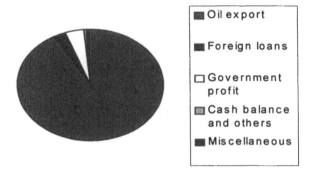

Figure 3.4 Revenues allocated in the Iraqi development plan (1976-1980)

From Table 3.11 and Figures 3.5 and 3.6, it can be concluded that the development strategy under the second plan was for the plan to give priority to the industrial sector. However, in this case, the Iraqi planner did not ignore the agriculture sector. In fact the plan was instrumental in its expansion, thus providing some diversification in the Iraqi economy. Another strategy was to expand both the quantity and quality of manpower resource. Thirdly, the plan made provision for the fair and efficient regional distribution of economic and social programmes.

The principal objective of a diversification strategy is as indicated in the broad goals of the 1976-80 plan, to reduce the over dependence of the economy on oil. This is the kind of economic vision which the Iraqi planners hoped to achieve in the long run, adopting the expedient of the expansion of investment in different industrial exports (Europe publication, op. cit.).

The creators of the 1976-80 plan placed emphasis on the importance of a large supply of efficient manpower through education and recommended that training should be given practical recognition by the plan, and at the same time, increase the size of the labour force. The labour force grew from 25.26 per cent of the total population of Iraq in 1976 to about 26.02 per cent in 1980 (Ministry of Planning, April 1982).

The growth of the gross domestic product of Iraq was projected in real terms at 10 per cent annually, that of the oil sector at 15.5 per cent, while the non-oil sectors such as manufacturing, agriculture, distribution, services, had 32.9 per cent, 7.1 per cent, 16.9 per cent and 10.4 per cent respectively (Penrose, op. cit. p.485). The growth differential between oil and non-oil sectors of the economy reflected the goal of the government to reduce the over dependence of the Iraqi economy on oil. However, the composition of projected (GDP) at the end of the plan period was not significantly different for that estimated for the first plan. Oil remained the major component of GDP, accounting for almost 97.6 per cent at the end of the plan, and continued to be the principal foreign-exchange earner (Ministry of Planning, op. cit.).

With the financial constraints lifted in the Iraqi case, during the period of the second plan 1976-1980 the crucial problem was that of optimising the Utilisation of deplorable oil revenues. In order to meet both the short and long term objectives of development, monetary and fiscal policies received different emphasis from policies which sought to increase financial resources for these various development projects, at the time they were needed and in the right quantities.

Manufacturing to meet the target envisaged for industry, policies have been devised to generate an expansion in this sector which is a major alternative to crude-oil exports if over dependence is to be reduced (The Law of 1976-1980 plan, 1977). In an economy which has such an overwhelming dependence on a single product for foreign financial resources and thus for development, diversification cannot be completed over-night. Indeed, initial industrialisation efforts are bound to be concentrated on oil-related manufacturing industries; after all, this is the area in which Iraq has a comparative advantage. Several important plans were thus envisaged in order to gather and treat gas, most of which is flared during the process or crude-oil production. Also petrochemical plants, refineries, fertiliser, iron sponge, steel, as well as some non-oil industries were to be constructed to produce exports (Europe publication, op. cit., p.353).

Of the planned expenditure for the manufacturing industries, about I. D 4490 million was generated during the period of the second plan. Thus, the actual expenditure allocated to the manufacturing sector expansion was about I. D 2687.1

million, i.e. seven times more during the second plan compared with the actual expenditure of this sector for the period of the 1961-1964 plan, as can be seen from Table A. One cannot stress enough the importance of the industry sector in Iraqi Development plans, especially in the second plan, where it frequently forms the major part of the oil export revenue.

Table A The actual expenditure investment for the manufacturing industry sector 1961-1980 (in million I. D)

Economic Plans	Actual Expenditures
1961-1964	36.3
1965-1969	103.9
1970-1975	219.8
1976-1980	2687.1

Source: Ministry of Planning, Iraq, development of Iraqi economy during the period 1976-1980, and 1984.

As a result of this there followed a sizeable allocation to the industrial sector, the annual rate of growth become 11.3 per cent (in constant Prices 1975 year), as well as the value in this sector increasing from about I. D 339.9 million in 1976 to about I. D 513.1 million in 1980.

Other manufacturing industries were also to be expanded. These included the foodstuffs, chemical, oil, textile and footwear industries, and machine equipment. Amongst other things, the capacity of cement production was increased from 2.77 ton in 1977 to 5.20 ton in 1980 (Europe publication, op. cit.). Likewise for the other important industries such as construction materials, paper and cigarette factories.

In the area of social investment, the revised second plan paved the way for a substantial improvement in the general welfare of the country. Education, housing, family planning, health and regional development were given top priority in the period of the second plan's welfare programmes. Examples of this were free education, free schooling, social security, and free basic medical services. Furthermore public affairs allocation had been geared towards more decentralised decision-making. It proposed the district and city councils for urban and rural development, and the period identified some amendment to worker's profit-sharing principles as a means of increasing labour productivity for the allocation of the second plan total fixed investment.

Qualitatively, the most important socio-economic goals were in the following order of priority:

1.   To raise the standards of living of every social stratum, and provide equal economic, political and cultural opportunities for all individuals and groups.
2.   To maintain a rapid and sustained rate of economic growth, together with price stability and achieve a more equitable distribution of income.

3. To improve the quality, and increase the supply of skilled labour force in order to raise labour productivity and overcome the main development bottleneck.
4. To put pressure on, rehabilitate, and improve the environment with particular emphasis on the over populated cities.
5. To develop the level of science and technology, and promote creativity.
6. To preserve and revise the country's valuable culture heritage and enhance the quality of life.

Agriculture although the need for a strong agricultural sector has long been recognised and supported by the government, progress in agriculture to date has not been particularly good. In the second plan, agriculture's real growth rate at approximately 3.5 per cent annum, compared with the projected annual rate of growth of 7.1 per cent for the period of second plan. The governmental ideal was to attain a prudent level of self-sufficiency in food production and provide opportunities for reasonable agricultural income; this self-sufficiency has so far been elusive, because food still plays a big part in the allocation of the bill of imports.

Nevertheless continued striving for progress in the agricultural sector was important as demand for food increased rapidly in response to an ever-swelling population and its related income. Alternatively, the government's aim was to attain some sectoral balance in the economy by decreasing its dependence on the oil sector; the total project expenditure in the second plan was 2162.9 million i.e. 14.2 per cent in the total expenditure of the second plan (see Table 3.11).

The ambitiousness of the government's programme in this sector and the effect of the increase in the oil revenue for expenditure for the agricultural sector in the second plan, compared with previous plans, can be seen from Table B below.

Table B   Actual expenditure investment for the agriculture sector (1961-1980)

Years	Actual expenditures (million I. D)
1961-1964	19.6
1965-1969	54.8
1970-1975	708.5
1976-1980	1411.2

Source: Ministry of Planning, Iraq, development of Iraqi economy for the period 1976-1980, and 1984.

Thus, as the government expected the private sector to contribute significantly to the country's agriculture process, provision was made for direct government involvement, and to develop its forms further, attention was given to the private sector in the form of supporting services, mainly agricultural credit, by the Iraqi agricultural bank. This played an important role in the development of this sector and the improvement of productivity by promoting investment in agriculture. In the second plan this increased from 13.9 million in 1976 to 98.6 million, i.e. with a rate growth 63.2 per cent per annum (Ministry of Planning, op. cit.).

Physical infrastructure the development of a physical infrastructure, which was given top priority in the second plan was stressed further in that of 1981-1985. In the second plan, there was a sizeable sum available to infrastructure development which assisted in the continued diversification of the economy and supported both the industrialisation and the agriculture that was planned for the period 1976-1980. The specific areas receiving attention in this were transport, communication and municipal and residential development.

Transportation and communication the second plan's aim was to attain a rate of growth of 16.7 per cent per annum, with a real added value growth of I. D 166.4 million in 1976 to I.D 386.5 million in 1980. The roads system represents a vital component in the transportation infrastructure of Iraq, as more than 64.0 per cent of domestic inter-city passenger conveyances are by high-way. So, at the termination of the second plan, the road system comprised 3750 km including highways, main roads, secondary and rural roads. Moreover, the plan took into account the construction of the main arterial roads running between Iraq and both Arab countries and neighbouring countries, for example, the motorway networks across the country, to provide road links with Syria, Jordan, Kuwait and Turkey (Lloyds Bank Group, 1983, p. 7).

Railways make a significant contribution to the available transportation in Iraq. The second plan emphasised the development of the railway transportation; it increased the capacity of transport at the same time, as well as that of the '*Baghdad-Maakel-Amcaser*' metric line from three million ton in 1975 to 11 million/ton in 1980, and the '*Baghdad-Musal*' metric line from 1.5 million/ton in 1975 to five million/ton in 1980. The second plan also presented feasibility studies for several railway systems consisting of the '*Baghdad-Kirkuk*-Erbil' metric line of 461Km/the *Baghdad-Mousal-Yurubiyab* standard line of 528 km, which links the Turkish system with the Baghdad '*magal-Umm Qas*' standard line of 582 km which was built with assistance from the USSR. 200 km of the 400 km Syrian border railway was completed and work was finished on the remaining permanent line, while a 155 km line was undertaken to link '*Hsaiba*' with '*Akkasha*' to transport phosphates (Lloyds Bank op. cit., p.7). The ultimate aim of the railway administration was the elimination of all the load metric gauge lines. In 1976 it was reported that 704 million passengers/km and 2252 mn/km of freight were carried by Iraqi railways with an increase of 818.000 passenger/km and 298 mn/km in 1979 (Ministry of Planning, 1980).

The Iraqi port system has a heavy trade link with the rest of the world; the importance of this port system to the economic development of the country was felt very acutely during the early and middle 1970 when bottlenecks in supply were caused by insufficient port capacity. The construction of an additional nine berths was scheduled during the second plan. These additional berths would serve the port in increasing the transport capacities to 545 thousand/ton in the plan period; particular attention in the plan was also given to improving the efficiency and safety in the ports.

Air transport is highly developed in Iraq compared to other models of transportation; the second plan emphasised improvement of the international airports, giving special attention to Iraq; air traffic and ancillary support facilities, including fire and rescue equipment and maintenance programmes.

As more emphasis is placed on the development of the productive sector so adequate communication becomes more vital. In the first plan, this sector received a much improved microwave network consisting of a 960 channel system, and the available requirement of the labour in this sector, major emphasis in the second plan was on augmenting these services to meet the demands of a developed countries (Quarterly Economic Review of Iraq, op. cit., p.16).

Migration to the cities and towns, for example, urban population increased from 63.7 per cent in 1976 to 66.4 per cent in 1980-caused strain on the infrastructure i.e. on housing. This compelled the second plan to turn its attention to available accommodation for the population, but housing remained and still remains a critical area in need of attention in Iraq. This was indicated by the housing construction ruining the second plan for both the public and private sectors. Approximately 19.872 dwellings were constructed in 1976, and these increased to 35.781 dwellings in 1980. Emphasis in the public sector shifted to make residential accommodation available to lower income families. The private sector was dependent upon the loans of the mortgage bank which financed I. D 191,478 million in 1979, i.e., an increase of more than 385 per cent in 1979 compared to the 1976 of private sector houses (Ministry of Planning, 1982).

All in all, the second plan period was one of considerable progress in Iraq. favourable growth rates were attained, inflation was reduced, absorptive capacity was increased, and infrastructure was improved, it was all in a period of relative social stability. As can be seen from the tables above, the second plan paid more attention to the promotion of the industrial export sector compared with previous plans. Yet the Iraqi economy still depends heavily on the oil export sector.

3.3 The benefit of oil revenues for ordinary budgets for the period 1968-1980

Oil revenues continued to dominate the government revenue sector despite the government's diversification policy. Also, the government continued to use tax relief as a weapon against inflation. This increased the share of the oil sector in the revenue of the government, especially, during the nationalisation period which was completed in 1973, when all oil companies became nationalised.

In Iraq, government revenues increased rapidly during the thirteen years of study, i.e. they rose from I. D 220.7 million in 1968 to I. D 597.4 million in 1973, to I. D 2714.7 million in 1979 and to I. D 6262 million in 1980 (see Table 3.13).

The rapid growth in government revenue as well as in the absolute level of national income was dominated by a single source oil.

The relative share of various sources of government other than oil in the total budget revenue remained not only relatively insignificant, but was in general declining; Direct Tax income contributed about 9.2 per cent of estimated total government revenues in 1968, falling to 6.4 per cent in 1973 before a recovery during the second plan period to 2.1 per cent in 1979. The government policy of diversification that had been in effect during both the first and second plans should continue to increase the share of the non-oil sector in the future of the Iraqi economy.[4] It is worth mentioning here that during the 1965-1969 plan, the oil revenue allocated to the economic plan was more than 50 per cent, and less than 50 per cent to the ordinary budget. During the 1970-1975 plan 79 per cent of oil revenue was allocated to the economic plan and 20.8 per cent to the ordinary budget. These ratio of allocation to economic plan were 92.0 per cent and 8.0 per cent from the others resources, for the 1976-1980 period plan. As can be seen from Table 3.13, the ordinary budget share of oil revenues increased from 91.6 million in 1968 to 5227.2 million in 1980.

However, from the increased incomes will emerge increased pressures on the government to spread the oil revenue around. The human capital, infrastructure, administrative and technical bases of the Iraqi economy will therefore be stretched to their limits (maybe beyond their limits) in the years ahead, unless the recognition of the inflationary consequences of the governmental expenditure expansion can in still more produce into the fiscal measures of the government. Thus there may be certain disadvantages (such as instability in profit) connected with the revenue coming from outside the domestic economy while the opposite will occur if the revenues are created the domestic economy.

So far, have been concerned with the quantitative aspects and availability of financial resources in Iraq. One must also consider the decision of how to allocate the available resources of the ordinary budget among various users, as efficiently as possible. In other words it is not enough to analyse the size of the budget but it is also necessary to investigate aspects of governmental budgetary-expenditure.

In developing countries, the problem of allocating investment resources involves, in general, several choices amongst a number of alternatives: amongst various projects within sector, and amongst techniques which might be applied to a given project. Various hypotheses have been developed and suggestions made regarding these choices, G. M. Miel, op. cit., Chapter 7. In a developing country, the choice is very complex, due to the inadequate working of the market system and because of the structure of the economy in such countries.

In the case of Iraq, the problem of allocation as it confronts public finance, is centred mainly around the aim of attaining economic diversification and structural change within a balanced development programme. Since 1970 Iraq has launched two five-year development plans. The first covering 1970-1975, the second 1976-1980. The general objectives of the plans, their performance, as well as the sectoral allocation of their development expenditure have been presented and analysed in detail in the last two sections.

It can be seen from Table 3.12 that the ordinary budget expenditure has increased over the years from the modest sum of I. D 303.4 million in 1970 to 748.4 million in 1978 and an estimated I. D 1761.5 million in 1980. We have shown that the largest proportion of the budget expenditure was allocated to national defence and security, for the selected years, accounting for 47.3 per cent in 1970 to 48.6 per cent in 1980 of the total expenditures. Economically speaking, these expenditures make a relatively small contribution to economic growth, particularly if we know that most of the military equipment is imported and not produced domestically (Cedric Sandford, 1984).

Most of the expenditure was allocated into the provision of overhead facilities and infrastructures; the creation of these facilities and services, such as education, health and communication was essential for the initial inducement to economic growth. In fact, it is well-known that the general policy of the government has been, as defined by the annual budget data, to accelerate investment outlays with a view eventually to putting the economy on a self-sustained growth path. This has meant diversification of the economy. The strategy has been to create an infrastructure and other physical developments and to expand human and social development activities. The upshot of this was that of the total budget the proportion of allocation in favour of principal development parts (for instance, expenditure on education) accounted for I. D 59.5 million in 1970 and increased to about I. D 245.7 million in 1980, but otherwise, the relative importance to the total expenditure of the ordinary budget declined from 19.6 per cent in 1970 to 13.9 per cent in 1980 (see Table 3.12).

However the expansion of the above services and infrastructures will require more expenditure; with increasing expenditure, more revenue will have to be found. In the Iraqi case, one way of doing this would be to raise the ratio of oil revenues devoted to budget expenditure, a policy which would reduce the capital allocated for development projects, thus reducing the growth rate of the economy. To avoid this situation, more revenues will have to be found elsewhere, in order to decrease the dependence on oil revenues, for instance, direct and indirect tax and other sources of revenues (indirect tax accounted on average for only 17.5 per cent of total budget revenues for the period 1968-1980) (see Table 3.13). If more non-oil revenues could be collected, a higher ratio of proceeds from oil can be allocated towards expanding development expenditure, thereby raising the rate of economic growth, diversifying the economy and making the country less dependent on oil revenues.[5]

Table 3.11 Planned and actual expenditures on economic sectors for the period of second plan 1976-1980, and its performance

Economic sectors	(1)	(2) %	(3)	(4) %	3/1 %
Agriculture	2162.9	14.2	1411.2	14.5	21.6
Industry	4490.0	29.6	2687.1	27.5	59.8
Transport & Communication	2318.1	15.2	1484.6	15.2	64.0
Housing & services	2458.3	16.2	1352.8	13.9	55.0
Education	681.9	4.5	540.3	5.5	79.2
Total	12111.2	79.7	7476.0	79.6	61.7
Others	3082.4	20.3	2279.9	23.4	74.0
Grand Total	27304.8	100.0	9755.9	100.0	35.73

Note: 1= Planned expenditures 2= Relative importance as a percentage of planned expenditure 3= Actual expenditure 4=Relative importance as a percentage of actual expenditures.

Sources: Ministry of Planning, 1980, C.S.O., Annual Abstract of Statistics, Iraq. Ministry of Planning (1984), Indicates of Iraqi economic development for the period 1976-1980.

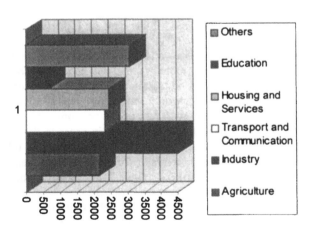

Figure 3.5 Planned expenditure on economic sectors (1976-1980)

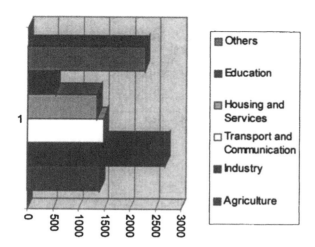

Figure 3.6 Actual expenditure on economic sectors (1976-1980)

Table 3.12   Actual expenditure of the ordinary budget for selected years

Sectors	1970		1975		1976		1980	
	Value	%	Value	%	Value	%	Value	%
Defence	143.6	47.3	346.5	46.3	792.9	54.0	856.9	48.6
Education	59.5	19.6	107.3	14.3	162.7	11.0	245.7	31.9
Social affairs	1.9	0.6	8.1	1.1	4.5	0.3	14.3	0.9
Health	13.4	4.4	25.7	3.4	44.7	3.0	56.6	3.2
Information	1.1	0.4	11.8	1.6	6.0	0.4	22.2	1.3
Finance	34.3	11.3	127	17	261.9	17.8	352.6	20.0
Transport	0.6	0.2	2.1	0.3	0.6	0.1	2.8	0.2
Interior & Justice	4.6	1.5	6.5	0.9	16.9	1.2	40.9	2.3
Municipal affairs	14.4	4.8	6.8	0.9	30.4	2.1	51.8	2.9
International obligations	0.4	0.1	28.7	3.8	84.9	5.8	35.3	2.0
Pensions & Gratuities	22.0	7.3	34.3	4.6	51.4	3.6	74.9	4.3
Others	5.4	1.8	42.8	5.7	3.9	0.3	5.7	0.3
Total	303		748.4		1467		1762	

Sources: 1. Ministry of Planning, Iraqi economy for the period 1970-1977, part three,   Money and Finance, January 1978. 2. Central Bank of Iraq Bulletin, Iraq Statistical Department, Series, from January to December, 1978.

Table 3.13 Source of revenue in Iraqi ordinary budgets, for the period 1968-1980**

Sources	1968	1969	1970	1971	1972	1973	1974	1975*	1976	1977	1978	1979	1980
Share of oil revenue	91.6	84.5	114.5	179.3	109.3	412.9	1123.3	584.0	964.0	839.2	1160	2017.1	5227
%	41.5	33.5	39.1	52.0	40.4	68.9	80.2	65.8	69.5	64.4	68.7	74.3	83.5
Direct taxes	20.3	23.7	27.6	30.7	33.4	38.1	30.7	40.5	103.7	60.3	56.7	56.3	75.8
%	9.2	9.4	8.9	12.3	6.4	6.4	2.2	4.6	7.5	4.6	3.4	2.1	1.2
Indirect taxes	50.9	59.5	66.1	74.0	72.4	76.9	72.9	162.9	249.4	251.7	263.9	336.4	479.3
%	23.1	23.7	22.6	21.5	26.8	12.9	5.2	18.3	17.9	19.3	15.7	12.4	7.7
Non-oil revenue	57.9	82.9	84.4	60.8	55.4	70.8	173.4	100.5	70.6	152.5	206.2	304.2	479.2
%	26.2	33.1	28.9	17.6	20.5	11.8	12.4	11.3	5.1	11.7	12.2	11.2	7.6
Total	220.7	250.6	292.5	344.8	270.5	597.4	1400.3	887.9	1388.0	1304.0	1686	2714	6262
%	100	100	100	100	100	100	100	100	100	100	100	100	100

Note: * Revenues for 1975 covered 9 months only. ** All figures in million I.D.

Sources: 1. Iraqi economy for the 1968-1980 period. Ministry of Planning, economic office, December 1978. 2. Status of Iraqi economy, 1970-1980, Ministry of Planning, 1983.

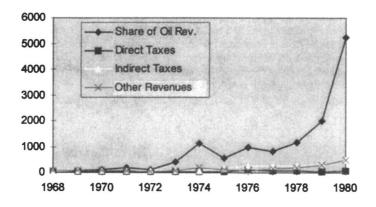

Figure 3.7   Source of revenues in Iraqi ordinary budget 1968-1980

Notes

1. Rascheed O. Khalid, *Fiscal Policy, Development Planning and Annual Budgeting, International Monetary Fund Staff Paper*, Vol.16, No.1, March 1969, p.65. The construction of a publicly-owned steel mill (to be operated at a loss) may produce more external economies and, in the long-run, although indirectly, more government revenue than the construction and operation of a self-liquidating toll-bridge (ibid., p.471).
2. The new economic literature provides a survey of some new developments in international economics concerned with the general equilibrium effects and policy implications of a sectoral boom in the traded goods producing part of an economy. It is concerned, for example with the effect of an export revenues boom in an OPEC country. This sort of boom is liable to give rise to problems that have been called the Dutch Disease. Thus one often refers now to *a Dutch Disease literature*. See W.M. Corden (1982) and Mckinnon (1976). There is no Dutch Disease problem for Britain. It should be added that the resource movement effect can probably be ignored in the case of oil, since the use by the oil industry of domestic inputs, including labour, would be low in relation to their use by the rest of the economy. See W.M. Corden (1981), Forsyth and Kay (1980).
3. It also needs to be emphasised that spending refers to expenditure on consumption and investments (i.e. for absorption) so that the extent to which it exceeds or falls short of income and output does not just reflect dissaving and saving. Furthermore, the spending effect, which initially creates excess demand for non-tradable, and then gives rise to a real appreciation and de-industrialisation does not depend on the current account outcome (see W.M. Corden 1982).
4. One can think of many cases where there have been sectoral export booms with adverse general equilibrium effects on other producers of tradable, for example, Gregory (1976). He pointed out that the earlier growth of mineral exports had at least as adverse an

effect on Australian import-competing manufacturing industry and agricultural export as well, see for example, Maddock and Mclean (1982), Forsyth and Nicholas (1981).

5. In Corden (1981) the case is considered where the boom rise pre-tax and, even more, post-tax real wage and an attempt to reverse the Dutch Disease (through spending reduction brought about by tax increase) then leads to unemployment. The cause is real wage resistance designed to keep real wage at the boom level. See also for more detail Van Wijnbergen (1982).

4 The fiscal (direct) effects of the exports sector on the economics sectors in the Iraqi economy

While the last chapter discussed the indirect effects of the exports sector on the machinery of planning the Iraqi economy, it now seems reasonable to turn to the direct impact of the export sector. To do this, it is necessary to discuss the principle of direct benefits derived from the oil export sector during the period under study.

Possibly the best way to do this is by studying the following:

1. The backward and forward linkages are the fluid inter-dependency between the oil sector and the rest of the economy.
2. Employment effects.
3. The direct benefits of Iraq's non-oil exports.

The lack of overlap between different parts of the economy is a typical characteristic of under-developed economies. This is most readily seen in agriculture and mining where there is little or no common ground economically, which is characterised by a scarcity of linkages effects.

However, it should be mentioned that the lack of interdependence among different sectors of the economy is one of the most typical characteristics of less developed economies (Hirschman 1958). Chapter 1 will examine the impact of the Iraqi oil sector the rest of the economy through the linkages effects.

The above seems to advocate that a discussion on the direct influence of the oil sector on the economy of Iraq may best take place within the scope of the vital notion of the flow of resources to and from the indigenous sectors. A kind of reciprocal movement may be perceived: on the one hand, the non-oil sector has its demand for the products of the oil industry, that are the forward linkages. On the other hand, the oil sector has its demand for various products and services, such as capital equipment, labour and supplies, which the non-oil sectors are apt to provide, i.e. backward linkages.

The primary binding force between the sectors has been the indigenous demand for petroleum products. The fact is that numerous new industries in Iraq are making a wide use of low cost fuel so that. In general, the non-oil sector can absorb the products from the oil sector much sooner, and more readily, than it can supply the latter with its highly sophisticated requirements.

4.1 The measurements of backward and forward linkages

The impact of the oil export and non-oil export sectors on the economy and the characteristics of the economy can be summarised in input-output tables.

Method one: direct measurement of linkages in order to make the picture more clear we have used two kinds of quantitative measures to confirm the position of interrelationships among the economic sector. Chenery and Watanabe (1958) suggest as direct linkage indicators the share of intermediate sales and inputs in total output. Thus the proportion of an industry's total output coming from demand is used as the backward indicator, whilst the proportion of an industry's output going to intermediate users is used as the index of forward linkages.

Thus if *A* is the Leontief technical coefficient matrix, the direct unweighted backward linkages indicator for the j th column, i.e. A j, where:

$$A_j = \sum_{j=1}^{n} A_{ij} \qquad (j = 1, 2, ...n) \qquad [4.1]$$

Direct forward linkages the direct unweighted forward linkages could be measured by the following equation:

$$A_i = \sum_{j=1}^{n} A_{ij} \qquad (i = 1, 2, ... n) \qquad [4.2]$$

Combined unweighted direct backward and forward linkages the following equation has been used in order to estimate the combined unweighted direct backward and forward linkages for 11 sectors in the Iraqi economy:

$$A_j + A_i = \sum_{i=1}^{n} A_{ij} + \sum_{j=1}^{n} A_{ij} \qquad (i,j = 1,2,....n) \qquad [4.3]$$

However, the unweighted direct measures of linkages ignore the indirect effects which the Leontief inverse captures, this is usually considered a major objection against using direct measures to identify key sectors.

Method two: Direct and indirect measure of linkages within the framework of the open static input-output model sector of gross production is the sum of output for intermediate demand plus exogenously determined final demand. Thus, the gross output level X required to sustain a given vector of final demand Y is determined in the input-output model by the following equations:

$$X = AX + Y \qquad\qquad\qquad [4.4]$$

$$X = (1 - A)^{-1} Y \qquad\qquad\qquad [4.5]$$

Where;
X= sector gross output;
A= matrix of input--output coefficients;
Y= final demand;
$(1 - A)^{-1}$ = Leontief inverse.

Denoting the elements of $(1\text{-}A)$ by K_{ij}, the sum of the element of any column represents backward linkages and is given by:

$$K_j = \sum_{i=1}^{n} K_{ij} \qquad (j = 1, 2, ...n) \qquad\qquad [4.6]$$

While unweighted direct and indirect forward linkages, could be measured by the following equation:

$$K_i = \sum_{j=1}^{n} K_{ij} \qquad (i = 1, 2, ...n) \qquad\qquad [4.7]$$

Method three: the weighted direct and indirect measures of linkages in the economy the average $(1/n)$ K_j is interpreted by Rasmussen* as "*an estimate of all the direct and indirect increases in output to be supplied by an industry chosen at random if the final demand for the products of industry j is increased by one unit*".
These averages can be normalised by obtaining the ratio of each to the average of the averages, giving as an index of indirect plus direct backward linkages:

$$U_j^b = \frac{\dfrac{1}{n} K_j}{\dfrac{1}{n^2} \displaystyle\sum_{j=1}^{n} K_j} \qquad (i , j= 1,2, ...n) \qquad\qquad [4.8]$$

Measures of Ubj for the 11 sectors of the Iraqi economy are shown in Table 4.3. It should be noted that each of the Kjs is the corresponding Ubj multiplied by a constant. See in J.A. Haji (1987).

The sum of the elements in the *ith* row of K, Kj, is given by:

$$K_i = \sum_{j=1}^{n} K_{ij} \qquad (i = 1, 2, ...n) \qquad [4.9]$$

This shows the increase in the output needed in sector i to cope with a unit increase in the final demand of all industries. Equivalent to the definition of Equation 6, the following has been suggested (ibid.) as an indication of direct and indirect forward linkages:

$$U_i^f = \frac{\frac{1}{n} K_i}{\frac{1}{n^2}} \sum_{i=1}^{n} K_i \qquad (j = 1,2, ...n) \qquad [4.10]$$

Measures of Ufi for the 11 sectors of the Iraq economy the indices Ubj and Ufi, which have been used as measures of backward and forward linkages (Thorbum, 1971), have been termed by Rasmussen "the index of power of dispersion and the index of sensitivity of dispersion", respectively.

Ubj> 1 indicates that industry j draws more heavily on the rest of the system than the average sector, whilst

Ufi > 1 means that industry I will have to increase its output more than the average industry for a unit increase in final demand in each sector.

The indices, Ubj and Ufi, are based on averages. Averages do not fully describe a set of numbers hence the indices do not fully describe the structure of a particular industry. For instance, the same value for Ubi, could arise if industry j calls (i) very heavily on one industry and not at all on others, or (ii) equally and moderately on all industries.

To overcome this difficulty, a measure of variability is available. Hence the coefficients of variations are used as additional indices:

$$V_j^b = \sqrt{\frac{\frac{1}{(n-1)} \sum_{i=1}^{n} \left(K_{ij} - \frac{K_j}{n} \right)^2}{\frac{1}{n} K_j}} \qquad (j=1,2,...n) \qquad [4.11]$$

$$V_i^f = \sqrt{\frac{\frac{1}{(n-1)} \sum_{j=1}^{n} \left(K_{ij} - \frac{K_i}{n} \right)^2}{\frac{1}{n} K_i}} \qquad (i=1, 2, ...n) \qquad [4.12]$$

A high Vbj can be interpreted as showing that a particular industry draws heavily on one or a few sectors and a low Vj shows an industry draws evenly from all sectors. The Vfis have similar interpretations. Hirschman defines a key sector as one that has high forward and backward linkages. Hence key sectors are identified here as those with both Ufj and Ufi greater than unity, with, in addition, Vj and V relatively small.

4.2 The effects of the oil export sector

4.2.1 Backward and forward linkages of the oil sector

A. Backward linkages the demand in the oil sector is of a dual nature; its two components, however, are not at odds with each other but may, as they form the foundation of the Iraqi oil consortium operate conjointly.

There is, in the first place, demand for fixed assets required for the expansion of industry. The second kind of demand is for current resources to meet the routine requirements of the industry for a certain level of operations, once desired capacity has been reached.

The special significance of this classification for the present purpose calls for further clarification. Backward linkages, with regard to capital goods, are negligible, almost nil in fact, owing to the fact that oil operations are highly capital-intensive and especially diverse. Actually, the trends that have been observed in recent times in the Iraqi oil industry tend toward a greater degree of automation and capital intensiveness. So the oil industry sector imports most of its needs, and, in particular, capital goods, because if the high capital-intensity of the oil industry and the fact that Iraq, like many developing countries, was not in a position to supply capital goods. Furthermore, the non-oil sector has so far been unable to provide such heavy capital goods for the oil industry sector. In fact, the only major response of the domestic economy to the needs of the oil sector industry has been the construction of buildings and pipelines. In parts of the country, given that economic progress and versification entail similar advances and diversification in the economy's capacity to supply the capital needs of the industry, such a situation may not carry on forever. When the country achieves such a level of development, those characteristics, typical of a dualistic economy, will become less and less pronounced.

Current expenditures, including labour wages, office equipment and furniture, purchase of supplies, and of some industrial ports provided by the domestic sectors, have thus been the most important aspects of backward linkages.

However, as far as the pre-nationalisation period is concerned, the nature of the actual transactions between oil companies was such that it had very little direct influence on the Iraqi economy (UN, 1968, p. 4). During the same period, no major strategic industry for production or processing (other than oil) developed: there was little demand on the part of the foreign companies for consumer goods and services, due to the fact that oil companies imported part of their current consumption needs from abroad; they also run many services such as medical services that were available locally or could have been produced competitively in Iraq. At the same time, there was no demand, on the part of the company, for local capital, because of the high capital-intensity of the oil industry and the fact that Iraq, like many developing countries, was in no position to supply capital goods. In other words the size of demand was not sufficiently large to encourage the development of supply industries. Hence, the backward linkage is very small and equal to less than one (see Table 4.3).

Furthermore, all oil companies in Iraq, had their refineries abroad. This was the other main reason for the diminution of the oil companies' expenditure and the requirement of employment in Iraq.[1]

During the post-nationalisation period, a wide range of non-basic operations such as those related to health, housing, social service, training and road construction. (which are not directly related to oil production and refining) have accounted for a sizeable share of the INOC domestic purchases These activities were financed by the consortiums but carried out by (INOC). These expenditures had a positive effect on aggregate demand and the level of economic activity as a whole, but their relevance to the input requirement of oil production exploration or refining was quite limited. It is, in fact, unlikely that they contributed to an expansion of such industries whose input is directly linked with the oil sector.

The non-basic operations mentioned above constitute an increase in the real wages of the workers and can best be considered as one of the national income multiplier effects which is introduced by the fact that a portion of the required supplies comes from foreign sources as imports.

At the same time, during the period of post-nationalisation, the oil industry had only a minimal effect on overall labour employment, as can be seen from Table 4.3. Hence the backward linkages are still very small, equal to less than one during the post-nationalisation period.

The Iraqi input-output tables for the years 1976 and 1980 shows that the percentage of locally produced inputs used in the oil industry were 0.4 and 0.3 per cent respectively, which indicate the continuance of the very weak backward effects.

B. Forward linkages, in general, as a measure of the forward linkages, the proportion of oil output purchased by the domestic economy to total oil output are estimated. In other words, forward linkages embody those influences which stem from an abundance of low-cost raw materials produced in the oil leader sector. When large quantities of cheap raw materials are produced in the oil sector, it tends to encourage the consuming elements of the domestic economy to acquire these inputs in more quantities, by intensifying their activities related to the products that use the oil industry products. Forward linkages unlike backward ones, are likely to play a significant role in augmenting the inter sector flow of resources.

As the economy becomes more and more industrialised, a demand for certain basic products will be created, which the oil sector will be able to meet, in part. The fact that oil products are relatively cheap will encourage the economy to substitute oil for other energy resources and to create petroleum based industries. The expansion of the domestic economy, in turn, is likely to generate an increase in the flow of resources from the oil sector into the rest of the economy.

However, as far as forward linkages during the period of pre-nationalisation are concerned, again the oil companies influence seems to have been insignificant In fact, almost non-existent - oil companies did not establish, nor help to establish, any by-product industry linked to oil production and refining. It also failed to develop the domestic financial and credit institution since it kept most of its foreign exchange earnings, reserves and deposits in foreign banks. In fact, some of the companies were registered in London and their activities have been extended far beyond the Iraqi borders, their only contribution being the sale of oil for domestic consumption; and even here, no effort was made to encourage these uses of oil. The growing crude oil production in Iraq has been highly oriented to the export market, with less than seven per cent of crude oil produced being used at home during the period 1956-1969 (Ministry of Planning, C.S.O.). That means that oil was developed in response to changes in the energy position of industrial countries, while local consumption constituted a tiny fraction of the total output.

It can be ascertained from the above that the period of pre-nationalisation gave rise to the non integration of the oil industry with the local economy, both being attributes of the under development of the economy and of the slow process of mechanisation. Very little use was made of petroleum products by the industry.

The above mentioned reasons explain why no strong demand-supply links evolved between the oil sector and the remainder of the Iraqi economy. The upshot being that the oil sector did not become an integral part of the Iraqi economy.

The available facts on the consumption of oil and its products during the post-nationalisation period indicate that petroleum products constituted a major proportion of the total energy consumption in Iraq. In 1980, the consumption of oil in the form of a variety of products amounted to 9.43 million metric tons, in comparison with 3.2 million metric tons in 1968 (Ministry of Planning, years 1968, 1980). This signifies that a considerable increase in demand has taken place, over a period of about 13 years.

Among the various products consumed, fuel oil has consistently (since 1972) been the most important for industries such as manufacturing, transport and similar concerns. For example, the manufacturing industry allocated expenditure on fuel oil amounting to I. D 3.9 million. As well as gas, oil directly related to the energy supplies needs of important indigenous industries such as transport in order to import different machines in the country.

Among forward linkages, important industries, based on petroleum products were developed. These included the petrochemical industries, and fertiliser plants, and attempts were also made to utilise natural gas.

The several petrochemical plants constituted a conspicuous example of forward linkages where a low cost source of supply generated a whole new line of activity, even though it occurred as a result of the direct action of the government. The production of a variety of products for both export and internal consumption began in most of these firms. The emergence of this new kind of industrial activity was principally due to the abundance and cheapness of the natural gas supply. The local demand for fertiliser was rising so rapidly that by early 1979, it was estimated that it would make up a sufficient and adequate economic foundation, on the sole basis of which it would be possible to set up and operate additional large plants.

The whole Iraqi economy thus began to feel the widespread, compounded effects of the oil industry through forward linkages. It is quite likely that the most significant effect of oil on the Iraqi economy will be derived from forward rather than backward linkages, see Table 4.3 and Table 4.4.

For instance, there are previous studies on this subject Puttrus (1978), Salman (1985), which depend on the most accepted method of measuring sectoral linkages, namely the inverse of matrix of an open static input-output table, for 1960, 1968 and our measurement, which depends on The input-output table for 1976 and 1980 as well. These studies have found that the most significant effects of the oil sector on the remaining economic sectors would be derived from forward linkages rather than backward linkages.

The reasons for the above relation of linkages of the oil sector with other sectors, are not hard to find. At the onset of the industrialisation phase of the economy, the large available supply of low-cost raw materials in the oil sector should generate a tendency in the domestic sector to intensify the production of the goods that use these cheap raw materials; also industrialisation and adaptation to changing supply-demand conditions should induce an increase in the flow of these resources. With regard to backward linkages, the domestic economy is likely to remain unable to meet the oil sector's demand for its requirements of sophisticated and complicated equipment for a long time, being able only to provide perhaps minor component need and labour.

To recapitulate; until 1969, the direct benefits of the oil industry in Iraq were not particularly advantageous to the economy as a whole; the benefits affected a minority of the population and a relatively small section of the economy, the domestic sale of the oil products sector. Thus, the integration between the oil industry and the remainder of the economy, was not achieved during that particular time; this was due to the fact that the growth of the oil industry did not result in an increase in the production capacity of the economy, and neither domestic factors nor any entrepreneurial class existed to exploit the newly discovered product. In terms of direct contribution, the development of the oil industry neither induced sizeable investment in the remaining fields, nor did it act as a highway of learning and technology for the economy as a whole. Even when the problems of geographic isolation were solved (by a transportation break through with the north-south highways and railways), an almost complete economic isolation of the oil industry remained. Moreover, although Rollin's (1956) pessimistic argument came true, i.e. the oil industry did not really become integrated into the rest of the economy to the extent that would have stimulated the economic growth, none of Lewis and Hirschman,[2] predictions were realised as far as the impact of the oil industry on the Iraqi economy during the period 1960-1978, is concerned.

The oil export sector in Iraq played a far different role from that played by export in certain other countries. For example, in Japan, the export sector was an integral part of the domestic economy and was a vital and influencing factor on the whole economy with different requirements. The reasons for Iraq's situation were the following. First, the economy in underdeveloped countries is characterised by a high degree of capital and labour immobility with resulting institutional barriers. In addition to that there is the nature of underdevelopment itself. Despite this a most important benefit to the Iraqi economy or development of the oil industry occurred especially during the period under consideration, 1968-1980.

The indirect benefits could best be seen in the boost to economic development provided by the petroleum industry through foreign exchange.

As regards direct influences, while the forward linkages become increasingly important through the supply of low-cost raw materials to the domestic economy, the total contribution of the backward linkages was insignificant during the post-nationalisation period. The reasons for that were:

1. The highly capital intensive nature of the oil industry,
2. The isolation of the oil industry, in that it did not provide a market for domestic industries, and;
3. The indigenous economy was not in a situation to provide the requirements of the oil industry. Generally speaking, these problems can be viewed as typical for underdeveloped countries (Hirshman, 1966, p.109).

Unlike the pre-nationalisation period, the period of post-nationalisation was marked by a complete change in the Iraqi petroleum industry. In fact, in the case of Iraq, given the nature of the leading industrial sector, indirect influences were the most significant factors in the development of the economy.

Thus, it was the forward linkages, rather than the backward linkages, as Hirshman tends to believe, which were the prime factor in the development of Iraqi economy.

4.2.2 The effects on employment

The oil industry as a capital-intensive industry employs a tiny proportion of the total labour force in most oil states, including Iraq. In other words, because the oil industry has the characteristic of a very high capital-labour ratio, the number of persons employed in this industry is relatively small. Furthermore in the early 1950s foreigners accounted for a significant proportion of the labour force as a result of the lack of a trained local supply of labour.

Table 4.1 reveals that the percentage of foreign employment classified as "staff" was 90 per cent, in the early 1950s of the total staff in Iraq. This percentage fell to 46.8 per cent in 1960 and this decline went on to reach 8.2 per cent of total staff in 1968. In contrast, the number of the Iraqi staff leapt from 81 persons in 1952 to 608 persons, or 91.8 per cent of the total in 1968 leaving only 54 non-Iraqis. This has been the result of the willingness and the pressure of the Iraqi government to substitute a national cadre for foreigners and the acquisition of experience by the local workers by both training on the job, and by formal training.

Statistics from the Iraqi Ministry of Oil and Minerals show that the rate of increase of Iraqis in the oil industry was about 34 per cent. Immediately after the nationalising of the oil industry in June 1972, all foreign staff left the country, to bring the manpower in the Iraqi company for oil operation (I.C.O.O.), previously IPC and its affiliates, to 100 per cent Iraqis.[3]

The following table shows the employment, productivity and the ratio of value added in the oil sector to GDP in Iraq.

It is clear from Table 4.2 that the number of employed workers decreased throughout the 1960s from 11,368 persons in 1963 to 8,366 persons in 1969. The number of employees in the oil sector has increased from 12,700 persons in 1972 to 25,075 persons in 1980. This increase was achieved after the nationalisation of the oil industry. Although the oil industry accounts for about one-third of the GDP before the nationalisation of the oil industry and more than a half of the Iraqi GDP after nationalisation, it still employs only a very small fraction of the total labour force. In 1980, the total workers employed in the oil industry numbered 25,075, equal to 0.69 per cent of the total labour force in the country. This indicates the weak backward effects, in spite of the fact that the oil industry can provide experience for supervisory and management personnel to be transferred to other sectors of the economy.

Thus, it can be said that the employment opportunities offered by the oil sector are very limited and hardly growing with the growth of the oil output.

Table 4.1 The number of staff: nationals and foreigners engaged by the foreign oil companies "*IPC, BPC* and *MPC*" in Iraq 1952-1968

Year	Iraqis	Foreigners	Total	2/3 Percentage
1952	81	677	758	89.3
1954	196	674	843	80.0
1956	235	708	943	75.0
1958	295	609	906	67.2
1960	564	494	1060	46.8
1962	620	239	859	27.8
1964	625	150	775	19.4
1966	626	79	705	11.2
1968	608	54	662	8.2

Sources: 1. Ministry of Planning, report about the foreign oil companies in Iraq, 1969. 2. Ministry of Planning, statistical handbook for 1957-67, pp. 74-77.

Table 4.2 The employment, productivity and ratio of value added in the oil sector to GDP, for the period 1963-1980

Year	Number of employment	Productivity employee	Ratio of employment in crude oil sector to total labour force	Ratio of value added in crude oil to GDP (%)
1963	11368	102.2	0.59	36.1
1965	11128	117.9	0.52	33.7
1967	10910	112.5	0.46	29.2
1968	8527	176.2	0.25	32.6
1969	8366	181.8	0.33	31.6
1972	12700	151.9	0.38	29.5
1974	17000	115.9	0.59	60.4
1980	25075	105.7	0.69	64.5

Sources: 1. Central Organisation of Statistics, handbook, 1960-70. 2. Annual Abstract of Statistics, C.S.O., Ministry of Planning, Baghdad, Iraq, 1980.

4.3 The direct influence of the non-oil export sector

In the first instance, it is very important, when analysing the direct effect of Iraq's non-oil export sector during the period under considerations that any difficulties must be first pin-pointed and then smoothed out. The most significant difficulty here was that the relevant data concerning employment, output, inputs and source of inputs (i.e. domestic or foreign) of most of these products were not available for consideration at the time of study. In such circumstances, it is impossible to give a true picture of the forward linkages and backward linkages of these exports. All we can do in this case, is to use the input-output tables for the Iraqi economy, available for 1968, 1976 and 1980 in analysing these linkages for the non-oil sector.

In this section, I shall explain the direct influence of the non-oil export sector on the economy, and shall demonstrate the comparisons between the direct influence of the non-oil export sector with those of the oil export sector. The respective direct influences of individual non-oil export can be vastly different. It is beyond the aim of this study to analyse each group separately.

A. Integration for various historical and structural reasons, economic development in many countries (including Iraq) has been handicapped by the inadequate linkages between sectors. The links between capital-intensive and non-capital intensive industries, and agriculture on the one hand and the urban informal sector and the rest of the rural economy on the other have been tenuous. As regards the non-oil export sector, this consists of agricultural products (food mainly and raw materials, and manufactured products (non-oil products) in Iraq. This sector is different from the oil-sector, in that it is integrated, to a higher degree with the economy of the country as a whole; this is a special feature of the non-oil sector which needs to be discussed at some length.

Let us consider employment effects first - while the oil sector is highly capital-intensive, the non oil sector, is a sector characterised by a much lower ration of capital per worker or a high ratio of labour per unit of output than oil-enterprises (Hans Singer, 1977 and A.S. Bhalla, 1978). One can see from Table 2.12 that the agriculture sector, and the non-oil industries both engaged a large number of workers, as compared with the oil sector. Therefore, in general, as enterprises using relatively labour-intensive technologies tend to generate higher rates of surplus in relation to the capital input than more capital-intensive enterprises, and as a higher surplus per unit of capital input leads to higher saving and investment, the promotion of a small-scale and informal sector would result in simultaneous increase in the growth rates of output and employment.

Further the transport facilities required by the non-oil export sector are totally different from those demanded by oil exports. A wider network of feeder roads and railways are likely to be found in the case of the former, whereas a pipeline may be sufficient for the latter. Thus, the direct effects of an export industry on the Iraqi economy, in terms of transport facilities, will be greater in the former case than in the latter. In this case, a non-oil export industry, such as the agriculture sector, induces the development of a complex road and/or railways system over a large part of the country, encouraged by the relatively cheap and available fuel for transport and increases the opportunities for further growth. The lower transport costs make it more feasible to establish other export industries, to develop industries directly supplying the export industry or to create industries supplying commodities demanded by those employed by the export sector. The development of these industries in turn stimulates further growth. Moreover, increased growth, coupled with employment expansion (backward linkage) and appropriate change in the product mix, enhances industrial development and harmonises it with the development of other sectors. On the other hand, as regards transport in the Iraqi oil industry, as was mentioned earlier, there exists a dependence on the pipelines which transport the oil, so that transport has little impact on stimulating other industries.

As was mentioned in the last section, until 1972 the Iraqi oil industry had belonged to another country; so the various stages of oil sector activities (production, transportation and marketing) were undertaken by foreign oil companies, while the non-oil sector was an integral part of the economy which, unlike the oil industry, could not operate independently of the local economy.

B. The non-oil sector linkages as was mentioned earlier, export has a significant direct effect, and it must operate in an economic environment that is responsive to the demand for intermediate input for the export 00A industry. There should also be opportunities for processing the 0A export sector's products for domestic use or for export. If the economic conditions are suitable, the direct effects on an export sector tend to be substantial.

The picture, as regards the significance of the direct effect of the non-oil sector, becomes clearer if we use two kinds of econometric measurement of forward and backward linkages for those sectors based on the inverse coefficients matrix of input-output tables 1968, 1976, and 1980.

The highest two linkages are recorded in the years 1976 and 1980 for the following sectors: mining and manufacturing and the highest two linkages recorded in the 1968 table were for the following sectors: manufacturing and construction. This means that the gross value added in these sectors is high, i.e that income produced in these sectors involves little application of intermediate inputs.

Table 4.4 shows total forward linkages of the 11 sectors in the Iraqi economy. The two economic sectors are mining and manufacturing in the years 1968 and 1976, while the two highest weighted total forward linkages for the Iraqi economy for the year 1980 are mining and services, which means that these sectors are producing predominantly for final demand.

Sectors having relatively high weighted direct plus indirect backward linkages, with a low coefficient of variation, are considered to be key sectors of the Iraqi economy. Out of 11 sectors, all the sectors have backward linkages with a value greater than one. In the top rank order come mining, manufacturing industries, the construction and service sector.

4.4 Conclusion

Iraq's efforts to develop economically have been primarily designed to diffuse the benefits of its major growth centre (i.e. oil) throughout the economy. Iraqi development planning has aimed at increasing the direct and indirect influences of the oil industry sector on the economic sectors. This strategy has been partly aimed at providing some of the missing structural elements in the economy while lengthening the economy's other promising sectors. In this sense, it may be said that the Iraqi development plans have thus far been concerned with the first phases of attaining self-sustained growth through public investment financed by the oil income providing substantial indirect influences. The establishment of such new projects as petrochemicals, natural gas, and fertilisers that have a direct and relatively high linkage with oil may be taken as an indication that the planners are approaching self generating development.

However the oil sector remains classic example of an enclave export-oriented industry superimposed on an entirely different type of economy without any significant economic linkages between it and the rest of the economy. From the analysis in this Chapter, we are able to follow the following important conclusions relevant to the Iraqi situation, namely that the oil sector in a dualistic economy has very little impact. Its main influence lies in its fiscal contributions.

The linkages between the crude oil sector and the other sectors of the economy are very weak. The forward effects have resulted only in building of some oil refineries which are publicly owned. The percentage of locally produce inputs used in the crude oil industry is very low, indicating the weak backward effects. This situation is characteristic both of the pre- and post-nationalisation periods in the Iraqi economy. While, it appeared from Tables 4.3 and 4.4 that Iraqi economy is more responsive to the non-oil export sector than to the oil sector, and the non-oil industry has proven to be a more integral part of the economy.

Since the crude oil sector has failed to play a leading role through these effects in accelerating economic development and that the magnitude of direct influences both forward and backward of the oil industry during the period 1968-1980 has been little and that the industry has remained fragmented and virtually isolated from the rest of the Iraqi economy, more emphasis should also be placed on the non-oil export industries since, as can be seen from Tables 4.3 and 4.4, these provide important linkages for the Iraqi economy.

Table 4.3a Direct and indirect index of backward linkage for Iraqi economy for input-output table of 1968

Economic sectors	Aj	U_j^b
Mining	1.0789	2.4438
Manufacturing	0.6163	2.0618
Wholesale & Retail trade	0.961	2.0566
Banking & Insurance	0.4493	1.9019
Electricity, Water & Gas	0.3747	1.7040
Transport & Communication	0.3644	1.6587
Public Administration	0.3900	1.6356
Services	0.2963	1.4447
Agriculture	0.2463	1.4432
Construction	0.1228	1.1870
Crude oil	0.0111	1.0229

Note: This table calculated from Table 4.6 in appendix to Chapter 4.

Aj = Direct backward linkage, U_j^b = Direct and indirect backward linkage

Table 4.3b Direct and indirect index of backward linkage for Iraqi economy for input-output table of 1976

Economic sectors	Aj	U_j^b
Manufacturing	0.8128	2.7000
Services	0.6715	2.5930
Wholesale, Transport	0.6160	2.3787
Mining	1.0607	2.3557
Electricity & Water	0.3901	1.9657
Banking & Insurance	0.4017	1.8830
Agriculture	0.3511	1.8085
Construction	0.0655	1.0841
Sulphur	0.0248	1.0251
Crude oil	0.0036	1.0097

Note: This table calculated from Table 4.8 in appendix to Chapter 4.

Aj = Direct backward linkage, U_j^b = Direct and indirect backward linkage

Table 4.3c Direct and indirect index of backward linkage for Iraqi economy for input-output table of 1980

Economic sectors	Aj	U^b_j
Services	0.9033	3.3330
Banking & Insurance	0.8291	3.0840
Transport & Communication	0.7758	2.7799
Manufacturing industries	0.841	2.7022
Mining	1.0806	2.4464
Wholesale & Retail trade	0.4610	2.1238
Agriculture	0.3397	2.0687
Electricity & Water	0.3326	1.7961
Construction	0.0730	1.1109
Sulphur	0.0318	1.0860
Crude oil	0.0032	1.0087

Note: This table calculated from Table 4.11 in appendix to Chapter 4.

Aj = Direct backward linkage, U^b_j = Direct and indirect backward linkage

Table 4.4a Direct and indirect index of forward linkage for Iraqi economy for input-output table of 1968

Economic sectors	Ai	U^f_i
Construction	0.6263	2.2130
Manufacturing	0.6320	2.1001
Transport & Communication	0.4115	1.6997
Public administration	0.3863	1.6294
Mining	0.3595	1.5964
Agriculture	0.2942	1.4456
Wholesale & Retail trade	0.2469	1.4157
Service	0.2166	1.4090
Electricity, Water & Gas	0.1421	1.2800
Banking & Insurance	0.0408	1.0681
Crude oil	0.0126	1.0243

Note: This table calculated from Table 4.5 in appendix to Chapter 4.

Ai = Direct forward linkage, U^f_i = Direct and indirect forward linkage

Table 4.4b Direct and indirect index of forward linkage for Iraqi economy for input-output table of 1976

Economic sectors	Ai	U_i^f
Mining	0.8266	2.4532
Manufacturing	0.6751	2.4067
Service	0.5531	2.2513
Construction	0.4899	2.1548
Sulphur	0.5567	2.1033
Agriculture	0.3901	1.6971
Wholesale, Retail trade, Transport & Communication	0.3052	1.6356
Electricity & Water	0.2024	1.4572
Banking & Insurance	0.1850	1.3137
Crude oil	0.0110	1.0123

Note: This table calculated from Table 4.7 in appendix to Chapter 4.

Ai = Direct forward linkage, U_i^f = Direct and indirect forward linkage

Table 4.4c Direct and indirect index of forward linkage for Iraqi economy for input-output table of 1980

Economic sectors	Ai	U_i^f
Mining	1.8775	3.9041
Construction	0.5486	2.4646
Manufacturing	0.6696	2.3913
Service	0.5624	2.2789
Sulphur	0.5454	2.0901
Transport & Communication	0.3500	1.7625
Agriculture	0.3830	1.6840
Wholesale & Retail trade	0.2647	1.5405
Electricity & Water	0.1715	1.3783
Banking & Insurance	0.1619	1.3100
Crude oil	0.00140	1.0260

Note: This table calculated from Table 4.9 in appendix to Chapter 4.

Ai = Direct forward linkage, U_i^f = Direct and indirect forward linkage

Notes

1. All refineries in Iraq were government owned and their main purpose was to satisfy domestic demand for refined products; see for more details; Schurr, S. and Homan, P., "Middle Eastern Oil and the Western World, prospects and problems", N.Y. Am Publishing Co., 1971, p.105.
2. Hirschman in his unbalanced growth theory, argued that a leading sector through its forward and backward linkages would eventually pull up the remaining sectors of the economy. For details see Albert O. Hirschman (1958) and also W.A. Lewis (1954).
3. Ministry of Oil and Minerals, second annual book, Iraq, 1973.

5 The macroeconomic model of the Iraqi economy

The objective of this chapter is to examine the structure of the macro model of the Iraqi economy and to discuss the specification and estimation issues of the individual equation constituting the model. Model validation and policy simulation based on the constructed model are presented in a separate chapter.

5.1 Purpose of the model

The objective of the model is to provide a consistent framework in which policy analysis can be carried out in quantitative terms. Without a complete framework showing how major economic variables interact with each other in the economy, any policy analysis could at best be partial. Much too often, important aspects of a policy change have been ignored. One of the most important contributions of econometric modelling is to allow the policy makers to examine the full impact of a proposed policy change on the entire economy and to compare it with various other policy alternatives before deciding on the optimal package to adopt in order to achieve certain desired results. With this purpose firmly in mind, we designed the structure of the macro model of Iraq.

The interest in policy analysis has grown in recent years mainly due to the increasingly large role assumed by the public sector in its pursuit of the new economic policy.

The constructed model will be used to study the impact of export fluctuation and short-term stabilisation policies. In particular, the impact of changes in external prices on the domestic economy.

5.2 An overview of the model structure

The earlier approaches taken by economists towards a model for a developing economy were cast mainly in the framework of Harrod Domar aggregate growth models and Chenery-Strout two gaps models. These models are completely supply-orientated with capital stock and foreign exchange reserves acting as constraints. Since economic growth alone is seen to be the most important objective for a developing economy, the simultaneous determination of income through demand and supply is considered to be of limited value. As a result, the constructed models are more concerned with long term issues such as the optimal rate of investment, the size of external borrowing and the savings rate and thus they are ill equipped to deal with short-run stabilisation problems. However, events in the decades of the 1960s and 1970s had demonstrated that the economic performance of a large number of developing economies and could be significantly improved with the judicious use of short-run stabilisation policies. The use of stabilisation policy measures would not only help to dampen undue economic fluctuation and thus minimise the loss of output and employment but also help to ensure that short-run fluctuations do not adversely effect the attainment of long-run term economic objectives. This is particularly true for countries that are pursuing long-term economic development plans to deal with such pressing economic problems as poverty, unequal income distribution and the development of a modern industrial sector. If for instance, the general income level were to be depressed over a long period of time, widespread under utilisation of existing capital stock would most likely exist, which would in turn prevent further investment in productive capacity stock and thus make the attainment of long-term development objectives all the more difficult. If, on the other hand, aggregate demand were so be raised to such a level that it is incompatible with the available productive capacity of the economy, severe inflation would result unless some portion of that aggregate demand could be siphoned off by one of the following: raising taxes; increasing the cost of borrowing; or reducing the level of public spending. Therefore, short-run stabilisation policies have important roles to play in the economic management of a developing country despite the theoretical criticism by Lucas (1976) about the impotency of public policies in the developed economies. The reason can be found in the fact that the public sector plays such a prominent role in an LDC economy.

While the growing interest in short-term stabilisation problems had given rise to the growth of a large number of Keynesian-inspired econometric models for the developing economies, many of these aggregate demand models however failed to incorporate the special conditions and features of the developing economies (Adams, F.G. and Behrman, J.R., 1980).

5.2.1 Some of the more serious shortcomings include

1. As national income is determined only by aggregate demand in a Keynesian model; constraints due to the lack of capital stock, land and other factors of production were often ignored.
2. A distinction between the agriculture and non-agriculture sectors as seldom made clear.
3. The direct foreign investment as well as retained earnings in the real investment process not was captured.
4. The importance of the foreign trade and balance of payment in the economy were often treated in much too aggregative terms so that important consequences of variations in any specific commodity prices were lost.

102

5. Public policies were not adequately represented. An attempt is made to incorporate the following features in our model:

   a. This model combines demand and supply factors in the determination of sectoral outputs. Output of agriculture sector, for instance, is supply determined. Output of the other sectors, such as the manufacturing sector and the services sector are determined by input-out relationships.

   b. The production sector is disaggregated.

   c. The emphasis of the model should be on a disaggregated foreign trade and balance of payment sector which examine both the exports and imports of different categories of goods as well as financial flows.

   d. In this model we provide for the possible channels through which monetary variables may influence the economy, and trade and payments can influence monetary variables.

   e. In this model we make a distinction between different classes of national income in the economy and explain their determination.

   f. As we may conclude from Chapters 3 and 4, one of the most distinct characteristics of the Iraqi economy is the presence of a dualistic economic structure which consists of highly developed, capital intensive industry and agriculture which is mostly traditional and labour intensive. All the dualistic models are constructed only from the supply side and the equilibrium condition is the equality of saving and investment which is always assumed to hold (S. K. Singh, 1975, F. Adams and R. Behrman, 1982). So the dualistic models based on dualistic conditions and emphasising the historical process of transformation from backward agriculture economy to a highly developed and industrial economy, reflect several vital social and economic distinctions in the dualistic nature of the economy concerned. Thus, the construction of a macroeconomics model for Iraq should take into account this feature of the economy as well as the above mentioned five conditions.

The macroeconometric model of Iraq can be viewed as a disaggregated multi-sectoral dynamic model. The level of disaggregation is aimed at reflecting both the structure of the economy and the optimal use of the available information. The model explains the demand and supply of goods, and factor inputs, the processes of price and wage formation, the performance of the balance of payments account and the operation of the government budgets. For further exposition, the model is treated as consisting of the following seven interrelated blocks:

1. The production or value added block
2. Aggregated demand block
3. Employment, wage and factor income block
4. Foreign trade and balance of payments blocks
5. The price block

6. Government activities
7. The financial sector.

Within each block further disaggregations are made in order to examine the structure of the component parts in some detail. As a result, each block is made up of a number of behavioural and technical relationships as well as accounting identities. The behavioural equations are specified according to accepted theoretical concepts, while the technical relationships are governed mainly by legal regulations. Accounting identities, on the other hand, are used to reflect the adding up constraints.

To capture the dynamic adjustment process of the variables, a polynomial distribution lag structure is widely applied. In addition, the model attempts to incorporate all the important characteristics of the Iraqi economy. In particular, the role of the oil export sector and the government sector have been expanded and emphasised. Some elements of the disequilibrium theories, as expanded by Clower (1965) and Barro and Grossman (1976), have been introduced into the model, especially in the determination of employment and sectoral output. It is assumed that markets do not clear and thus the short-side (either demand or supply) determines the output in each sector.

5.3 Method of estimation of the macro model

Two different methods of estimation have been used to estimate all the coefficients of the models, namely ordinary least squares (OLS), and a modified version of two stage least squares (TSLS).[1]

In fact the application of OLS technique in estimation of the structural parameters in a simultaneous structural linear model, is an inappropriate one. It leads to biased or even inconsistent estimates and also raises the problem of multicollinearity. Hence, to avoid these problems alternative techniques that yield at least consistent and possibly efficient estimates, such as TSLS, limited information maximum likelihood (LIML), three stage least squares (3SLS) and full information maximum likelihood (FIML) should be adopted, which takes us too far away from the modest purpose of this study.

In fact, there still exists disagreement over the precise technique of the parameters, estimation and given the likely existence of data errors and inaccuracies, one has to decide what particular gain is to be achieved by applying one technique rather than another.

According to P. Dhrymes (1970), one of the criterion in choosing the appropriate method is that of specification. He argues that in any techniques, such as TSLS, LIML, the main emphasis would be on the explicit specification of the particular equation under study, while the application of methods, such as FIML, 3SLS, require a greater reliance on the specification of every individual equation in the system. This would lead to a considerably high risk of miss specification error and hence to some very complicated problems and more computations.[2]

However, given our main purpose (policy analyses) and the data limitation the estimation of the proposed model by OLS with correction for serial correlation where necessary and TSLS is likely to be an appropriate method in estimating equations in the model employing annual data. In fact, as can be seen in the course of following sections, and as far as the empirical results are concerned, the OLS and TSLS estimates are very close. This given the existence of data error and the small number of observations does not seem to be surprising.

Moreover, despite a very small difference in the estimated parameters of each individual equation, the simulation results using the two different estimates of coefficients were quite different. The simulation results obtained by the OLS estimates seemed to give a more realistic picture of the Iraqi economy during the period of study, and to trace the post economic trends more closely. Hence, given the purpose (simulation) in constructing the model, the application of OLS, though least desirable (Goldberger, 1964) seems quite reasonable.

All the stochastic equations estimated by OLS and TSLS are given below.[3] Presented in brackets below the right hand side coefficients is their respective t values, R^2 is the coefficient of multiple correlation adjusted for degree of freedom, dw statistics,[4] indication the presence of absence of serial correlation of error is shown at the end of each equation. The problem of serial correlation could not be avoided in the model, although the researcher tried very hard to minimise its effects. In some equations the problem could not be eliminated completely. This is in fact due to the nature and characteristics of the data used in estimating the equations. It is worthwhile to note that developing countries (of which Iraq is one) utilise in comprehensive and inefficient data gathering procedures. SEE is the standard error of estimate that is defined as $\sqrt{e`e/n-k-1}$, where e is the vector of residuals, n is the number of observations and k represents the number of explanatory variables.

The main criteria for selecting the reported estimates are that the relevant coefficients have the expected signs, estimated coefficients are statistically significant and there is a satisfactory overall level of explanation (high R^{-2}). Hence whilst the most equations were augmented by oil price and the government policy dummies at the estimation stage these were only retained where significant.

The package used for estimation were the SPSSX and the Time Series Processor (TSP version 4.0E) mounted on the UWIST 'Cardiff Business School' University of Wales regional computer centre.

The estimation periods for the equations are not uniform. They differ considerably depending on the length of data period available on variables. Hence, whilst some equations were estimated over the period 1962 to 1980 (19 observations), most were estimated over the period 1963 to 1980 (18 observations), and very few equations were estimated over the period 1968-1980 (13 observations).

It should also be noted that a number of equations in the model used a natural logarithm transformation. This was done in order to obtain linearity for the relationships and it was also thought that it is more appropriate for particular equations in the model.

5.4 Previous studies of the models for Iraq

Many research efforts have been devoted to the specification and for estimation either in part or complete of macroeconomics models in both developing and developed countries.

In Iraq, there have been some attempts to specify and estimate an adequate structural model for the economy. In this exercise, we have divided these attempts into two broad categories, namely partial and to complete models. There are two complete empirical macroeconomic models for this country.

These are the UNCTAD staff model (1968),[5] and that of A. Kader (1974). Even these models completely ignore the wage, prices sectors, employment, as well as the financial sector, rationalising this exclusion as due to lack of data.

The partial works in this area involve specification and estimation of the behavioural relationship of some of the major components of the economic structure. Some of the components that have received attention in the Iraq context include the production function for manufacture, transport and agricultural sector as well as demand for import. We consider each of the single equation estimates one after the other. We will discuss the two full macroeconometric models briefly.

5.4.1 UNCTAD staff and A. Kader's models

These two models due to UNCTAD staff (1968) and Kader (1974) are the only full attempts in specifying and estimating macroeconometric models for Iraq. The common feature of both models is that they have concentrated on the real side of the economy.

The UNCTAD econometric model in Iraq, which was based on the two-gap approach, i.e. resources gap measured by the excess of investment requirements over savings for a given level of income; and trade gap measured as the difference between imports and exports consistent with same level of income, disaggregates the economy Into three major sectors, namely oil, construction and manufacturing. The chief concern of this was to explain the behaviour of the national aggregates and foreign trade components of the economy of Iraq, and in turn to give the rates of growth of gross domestic production.

This model consisting of in total 14 equations with annual observations numbering eight (1956-1963) was estimated by the ordinary least squares (OLS) method using deflator prices for the national income and capital formation. As regards foreign trade using current prices, no deflators are available for use and, for the purposes of study, special indices have had to be constructed from foreign trade quantity and value data to deflate the principal categories of imports and exports, the data being limited in number and low in quality. However, through this model provides some insight into the development needs and a reasonable basis for projections, it does not incorporate the effects of alternative development policies because of its theoretical and measurement limitations (R.J. Ball, 1973).

The A. K. Kader model of 1974 was less disaggregated than that of the UNCTAD staff. In the A. K. Kader model, there are 11 behaviour equations and four identities. The model was estimated OLS over the period 1953-1969 employing annual data. This model is essentially similar to the model developed by Thorbeck and Condos for the Peruvian economy in 1966 and to the model developed by Fardi for the Iranian economy in 1972. The model also draws on previous work by Klein.

In Kader's study, the model consists only of aggregate demand and its main components. Nothing is said about the economy's capacity to meet the desired level of aggregated demand. The consumption equation estimated was based on Friedman's permanent income hypothesis. This hypothesis differentiates between measure income (the income actually received) and permanent income (the income on which the consumers are assumed to base their behaviour). The behaviour specification behind this hypothesis is that consumption is a function of permanent income and so may rise even when current income is falling. Kader's estimated equation, however, was slightly modified by including a constant term and time trend to take account of autonomous growth in consumption.

In the foreign trade sector, the import demand equation was specified with total import volume depending on GNP. The export was divided into oil export and non-oil export, oil export was treated as an exogenous variable. Non-oil export related to an aggregate of non-oil export. The total volume of non-oil export is related to gross value added of non-oil sector (Vnoil).

Kader's model was also closed by estimating a number of government tax equations. As in the case of the UNCTAD staff model, Kader's model also concentrated solely on the real side of the economy and neglects the monetary sector.

Another limitation of both models is the exclusion of price, employment and wage's equations. Our model will attempt to remedy these limitations by considering both the price and wage determination equations as an integral part of the model. Also, we shall incorporate the employment of agricultural sector and non-agricultural sector.

Furthermore, Kader's model does not seem to be applicable to the post 1970 period. The Iraqi economy as a whole had begun to undergo a tremendous change as a result of early 1970s economic events, of which the most important was the nationalisation of all Iraqi oil industries (most notably there had also been the unprecedented increase in the country's foreign exchange receipts). Hence, Kader's specifications in some equations were eroded. It needs major modification to become more suitable for the current situation of the economy.

Finally, Kader's study ignores the important equations of model stability and provides no discussion of system-wide dynamic multipliers.

Furthermore, because of the continuous revision of the official data, we might expect that the estimated coefficients of Kader's model are no longer valid. Therefore a more complete and up-to-date macroeconometric model of Iraq is greatly needed.

5.4.2 The partial work

The partial work in this field, the model which was developed and evaluated by N. Z. Ahmed 1976, consisting of annual observations numbering 17 (1953-1970) by the ordinary least squares (OLS) methods, disaggregates the economy into three major sectors; manufacturing, transport and communication; and agricultural sector. The chief concern of this study was to trace the impact of the development expenditure financed by oil revenues on the economic growth within the above mentioned sectors during the period 1953-1970.[6]

This study is essentially based on the Irving Fisher (see, M. Koyck 1954). However, this study has many shortcomings. The major one is that it consists only of the supply side of the non-oil sectors only for the three sectors mentioned above and it ignores all other components.

Among other recent studies, is Al-Sofy's, 1980. This study consists of in total five equations with a number of 23 annual observations 1953-1975 and its structural relationships measuring all variables in current prices, are estimated by the OLS method. This work is neither an aggregate economic model for Iraq, nor is it a study of her development policy. It is essentially an investigation of the role of exports in economic growth and development.

An estimation of partial work based on both approaches is given by E. Leamer, which takes the above frame, and the logarithmic approach of T. Murray and F. Ginman (referenced to Al-Sofy, 1980).

This work reckons the impact of the export (oil and non oil) sector to be variable on economic growth; it is highly aggregated as far as the exports study is concerned with only a single equation, which consists of the effect of agricultural, manufacturing and crude oil exports on the whole economic growth. However, in the process of constructing our own model, steps have been taken to correct the shortcomings of previous studies of Iraqi.

The period of analysis in our study is 1963-1980 for which the Ministry of Planning and Central Bank of Iraq have published a set of tables with data for a relatively large number of economic activities.

5.5 Specification of macro models

The purpose of this area is to formulate a relatively small macroeconomics model that is relevant to the economy in question. The logical structure of the model is based on our a priori knowledge about the economy. That is, in contrast to the economies of other developing countries that depend primarily on agriculture, the distinguishing feature of the economy in the short and medium term is the rapid development of its oil-producing sector, which is providing a considerable degree of relief from balance of payments pressures and resource mobilisation difficulties. Also, we have allowed for the influence of the nationalisation of oil industries and the sudden oil wealth to be reflected in the model specification on the speculation that these events have caused some structural breaks in the performance of economic activities.

The supply of output is divided into real output and into seven major sectors: agriculture, manufacturing, oil, other mining, construction, transport and communication, and service sectors. The sum of value added to these seven sectors determines the level of the real gross domestic production (GDP).

5.6 The supply or value added (production) block

5.6.1 The agriculture sector (AGR)

Agriculture remains one of the most important sectors compared with other sectors in Iraq both in terms of employment and in supplying the need for food. Even with rapid economic growth and diversification in the previous two decades, the agriculture sector still employed close to 33.6 per cent of the active labour force in 1980. There is no doubt that private investment exists in the agriculture sector, but it is small and one doubts that it has a significant impact. Most of the investment is public in nature and like most public projects, completion is spread over a long time (for example, dams). In Iraq, most public projects have been completed. As the agriculture sector is also the area where the highest incidence of poverty occurs, large amounts of public funds have been consistently directed to this sector in an effort to raise the living standards of the farmers. A variety of agricultural programmes and numerous other rural development projects have been undertaken by the government. In addition, a number of specialist institutions have been set up to deal with the particular needs of farmers. The problems of the agriculture sector particularly were explained in Chapter 2, and are likely to occupy a great deal of government attention in the future as well as influencing the direction of public sector spending.

Initially, the value added in the agriculture sector is constrained by the major factors of production, i.e. physical capital, labour, amount of fertiliser used, soil condition, area under cultivation and a dummy variable representing weather conditions. Hence, on the basis of the available data, several possibilities have been attempted, i.e. we have examined the various relationships between dependent variable and several of the explanatory variable such as: laggard investment expenditure in the agriculture sector, lagged in the value added of the agricultural sector, lagged development plan expenditure, agricultural employees, rural population, and investment in agriculture. Only one equation based on statistical results, turned out to give satisfactory results, that is the relationship between the dependent variable and explanatory variables such as: the lagged development plan expenditure in agriculture and lagged dependent variable. The equation for estimation of value added of the agriculture sector is:

$$VAgr=63.5+ 0.914\ DEAgr_{t-1} + 0.585\ Vagr_{t-1} \qquad\qquad [5.1]$$
$$\quad\ (2.75)\ (2.41) \qquad\qquad (2.52)$$

$$R^{-2} = 0.974,\ \ SEE = 30.79,\ \ d\,w = 2.33, \qquad (1960\text{-}1980)$$

Where;
DEAgr   = lagged development plan expenditure
VAgr   = value added in agriculture sector.

    In general, this study included the production function of each major crops in the agricultural sector. A similar approach has been used by Behrman and Varges (1979) in their model on the agriculture sector of the Panamanian economy.

    In this case, the supply function is expressed as a function of the yield of the crop, productive capacity and the real commodity price which is expressed as the ratio of the producer prices of the commodity to the general level in the case of perennial crops, and to the prices of its competing crop in the case of annual crops (see Nerlove, Marc, 1950 and Behrman, Jere R., 1968, and also Hansen, Lars P. and Sargent, Thomas J., 1980 and Eckstein, Zui, 1984). The producer price of commodity is defined as the export price of a commodity deflated by its export tariff rate. That is:

Producer price of commodity X = export price commodity/$(1+ te)$ [5.2]

Where;
te = export tariff rate.

Thereby, the value added in the agriculture sector is related to an aggregate agriculture production of the crops, that is: Agrt = f (Tpct)   [5.3]

Where;
Tpct = total production of crops agriculture.

5.6.1.a Agrarian agrarian cultivation such as wheat, barley, rice are important occupation in the agriculture sector. The output of grain is very sensitive to weather conditions and large percentages of farmers are burdened by land tenure problems as well as generally result, uneconomic sizes of land holdings. As a result, there was little incentive for the farmers who work on the land to improve the condition for the land in order to raise its productivity. Realising the existence of these problems, the government has, since the 1950s, focused a great deal of attention on improving the conditions of the farmers, through various land resettlement schemes, direct subsidy of fertilisers, and price support as well as extensive research aimed at improving the yield of the crop. A large number of specialised institutions such as the general organisation of grain, agriculture bank and Farmers Association were set up to cater to the needs of the farmers. As a result of these measures there has been a substantial improvement in the productivity of the farmers.

Since it has been the government's stated policy to expand the fields of grain output, the field of grain output is simply a function of time (time), relative prices of grains to the alternative crop (Xprice/XpToB) and a dummy variable to reflect the droughts which rendered some land uncultivable under plans, and another dummy that reflects the civil war in the North of Iraq, which ended in 1975. However upon estimation it was found that the coefficient for the dummy variables did not give the correct sign. It was therefore decided to drop the dummy variables from the equation. The final equation estimated is:

$$LnYgrain = 5.73 + 0.05Ln\ TIM + 0.614Ln\ Xprice/XPoT \qquad [5.4]$$
$$\quad\quad\ (10.2)\quad\quad\ (2.99)\quad\quad\quad (1.53)$$

$R^{-2} = 0971$, SEE = 37.81, d w = 1.61, (1963-1980)

5.6.1.b Vegetable oil the supply of vegetable oil is a function of current and lagged values of the relative price of the GDP deflator (XPoil veg/PDGDP), the volume of the previous year's vegetable oils exports (Xvo Loilveg $_{t-1}$) and a dummy variable to reflect the importance of government policy to support vegetable oil production (DL) is used as an anticipatory variable to reflect the producer's expectation of the current period's demand of vegetable oil.

The estimated equation is given by:

$$Ln\ Veg\text{-}oil = 2.19 + 0.194\ Ln\ DL + 0.595Ln\ XvoLoil + 0177Ln\ Xpoileg/PDGDP$$
$$\quad\quad\quad (2.02)\ (1.85)\quad\quad\quad (9.71)\quad\quad\quad\quad\quad (1.82)$$
$$\quad\quad + 0.237\ Ln\ Xpoilveg/PDGDP_{t-1} + 0.177\ Ln\ Xpoilveg/PDGDP_{t-2}$$
$$\quad\quad\quad (1.82)\quad\quad\quad\quad\quad\quad\quad (1.83)$$
$$[5.5]$$

$R^{-2} = 0.902$, SEE = 129.97, d w = 1.94, (1963-1980)

All the estimated coefficients give the correct signs. The short-run and long-run supply elasticity with respect to the relative prices are 0.18 and 0.59 respectively which seem plausible due to the time lag involved between cutting down trees and making the finished product for the market place.

The equation also shows that the export volume of vegetable oil in the previous year was an important influence in terms of rising the output level of vegetable oil in the current period.

5.6.1.c Date palm the output of Dates in the model is related to the real current price of Dates (XpDate*/PDGDP) which is the producer price of Dates deflated by the GDP deflator, the level of real palm output price of about five years and the matured palm (Apalm). The current real price of Dates is introduced to capture the effect of variations in output prices on production decision. The five year lagged price's term is introduced to capture the effect of price on the investment decision. The average gestation period for the palm is about five years, as a planting decision undertaken five years ago would have an effect on current output. Beside the above variable there are another two variables, which are explained by the current and lagged yield of the palm (Ypalm), and the dummy variable (DL), to reflect the role of the government in boosting the production and marketing of Dates, as a result of this attention the government established the General Organisation of Dates.

The lagged yield of the palm (Ypalm) was initially introduced in the equation but it resulted in negative coefficients and was therefore left out in the final estimation. The estimated equation is given by:

$$\text{Ln outp Date} = -4.514 + 0.205 \text{ Ln XpDate*/PDGDP} + 0.194 \text{ Ln XpDate*/PDGDP}_{t-5}$$
$$(-7.82) \quad (2.31) \qquad\qquad\qquad (2.22)$$

$$+ 1.915 \text{ Ln Ypalm} + 0.334 \text{ DL} \qquad\qquad\qquad [5.6]$$
$$(4.49) \qquad\qquad (2.01)$$

$R^{-2} = 0.979$, SEE $= 58.44$, d w $= 1.13$,   (1963-1980)

5.6.2 The manufacturing sector

The manufacturing sector has been the fastest growing sector in the Iraqi economy. Its share of the total gross domestic product, which was only 5.9 per cent in 1970, grew to 7.7 per cent by 1980. At the same time, its share of total employment had also grown from 8.6 per cent in 1970 to 12.7 per cent in 1980. This rapid growth can be attributed mainly to the efforts of governments in fostering industrial growth in Iraq. Various investment incentives and assistance were given to attract both domestic and foreign investors to invest in the manufacturing sector. The more direct forms of assistance provided by government to promote the growth of manufacturing industry is: industrial loans at preferred rates of interest; assisted programmes for the development of basic industrial skills; accelerated depreciation allowance tariff, protections; there were also further fiscal incentives. Furthermore, exchange control regulations are relatively liberal, and there are agencies to advise on investments in this sector.

As we have seen from Chapter 2, the manufacturing sector of Iraq produces a wide range of consumer products, such as processed foods beverages, tobacco, textiles. Iraq produces intermediate goods also, like chemicals, fertilisers, building materials and petrochemical derivatives, steel and iron and capital goods too, in the forms of electrical machinery and transport equipment, etc. This is because of the

112

government's industrialisation policy, especially in those industries that make use of local materials and are highly capital intensive. As is well-known, Iraq has not suffered during the period of study from financial constraints in covering the costs of establishing new industries depending on imported capital equipment. At the same time, the unemployment level was down to three per cent of the total work force in 1980.

However, recently, after the increasing of government revenues from oil export, the government has made greater investment in the manufacturing of certain categories of capital goods as well as petrochemical products. This is indicated in the investment allocations in the last three economic development plans that cover the period 1970-1986.

One of the most significant stimuli provided by the government to promote, the growth of the manufacturing sector is made available to the manufacturers both short-term and medium-term industrial finances on favourable terms: the manufacturing industrial finance (MIDF), with substantial government equity. Participation was set up in 1964 especially to cater for the financial needs of the manufacturers. Meanwhile, the industrial bank has been constantly urged to extend a larger fraction of their loans to the manufacturing sector for different industrial purposes. As we mentioned in the last chapter, the government placed its emphasis on growth and increased investment in the industrial sector. This policy comes from the desire of Iraqi planners to reduce dependency on oil exports as the source of revenues for the economy.

There are three variables which can be identified in the manufacturing sector. They are: the manufacturing sector's potential output; the real output of the manufacturing sector; and a capacity utilisation index of the manufacturing sector (George, F., National Institute Model II, Discussion Paper, No. 10A).

5.6.2.a The potential output (PO) of the manufacturing sector is derived from the production function. We assume that the production function is of a fixed coefficient type, with capital stock and real working capital acting as limited by inputs.

Potential output is thus expressed as a function of capital stock in the manufacturing sector ($KMAU_{t-1}$) and the availability of short-term working capital to manufacturing which is the level of short term credit extended by the commercial banks and the finance institute to the manufacturing sector deflated by the Import Prices Index (MP).

Import price index is chosen as a deflator. The inputs in the manufacturing sector are derived from imports. The equation is that:

$$PoMAU = -4.51 + 0.84*KMAU_{t-1} + 0.14\ CRAMAU/MP + 0.97\ LMAU \quad [5.7]$$
$$(-2.25)\ (5.15) \qquad\qquad (2.94) \qquad\qquad\qquad (5.81)$$

$$R^{-2} = 0.983,\ SEE = 61.89,\ d\,w = 2.29, \quad (1963\text{-}1980)$$

113

Where;
PoMAU   = potential output of manufacturing sector
$KMAU_{t-1}$ = lagged capital stock
RCAMAU/MP = real capital working
LMAU   = real employees in manufacturing sector.

Real Output (value added in the manufacturing sector), on the other hand, is estimated as a function of components of final demand. This specification can be interpreted as transformation of an input-output type of production process. In an input-output framework, the vectors of gross output and final demand are related by the following identity:

$$(I-A). \, Yt \; = \; Ft \tag{5.8}$$

Where;
Ft   = final demand sector
Yt   = gross output vector
I   = identity matrix
A   = matrix of input-output coefficients.

For this identity, gross output can be obtained by inversion:

$$Yt = (I-A).^{-1} \, Ft \tag{5.9}$$

Again, if we assume that the ratios of gross outputs to value added are approximately constant, that is; $Vt = Byt$ [5.10]

Where;
Vt   = value added
B   = a diagonal matrix with all of diagonal elements equal to zero, and the diagonal elements equal to the ratio of value added to gross output in the respective producing sectors;
Vt $= B.(I-A)^{-1} \, .Ft$ [5.11]

However, not all final demand components are expected to be equally important in the determination of value added in every sector.

5.6.2.b   Real output of the manufacturing sector depends on consumer expenditures adjusted for the import of consumer goods and manufactured exports (CP + XMAU -MCG), gross investment including both private and government investment (TINV),[7] and a dummy variable, represented the effect of the nationalisation of the oil industries and its effects in this sector. The function for the value added for the manufacturing sector is:

$$VMAU = 32.7 + 0.131(CP+XMAU-MCG) +0.0932TINV + 0.113DL \quad [5.12]$$
$$\quad (1.58) \quad (3.42) \qquad\qquad (2.84) \qquad\quad (2.20)$$

$$R^{-2} = 0.968, \ SEE = 27.63, d \ w = 2.04, \quad (1963-1980)$$

Where;
VMAU = real output of manufacturing sector (value added)
(CP+MAU-MCG) = real consumption of domestically produced manufactured goods. This aggregate is derived by adding real private sector consumption expenditure to real exports of manufactured good and subtracts from it real import of consumer goods.

Where;
YINV   = total real gross investment
DL   = dummy variable, represents the effects of nationalisation of the oil and increasing the government revenues and its role in economy. This equation was also estimated by TSLS. See appendix to Chapter 5.

5.6.2.c   The capacity utilisation in the manufacturing sector is constructed from the identity:

$$CAUT = [VMAU/PoMAU]*100 \qquad\qquad\qquad [5.13]$$

Where;
CAUT   = capacity utilisation in manufacturing sector
VMAU   = real output (value added) in manufacturing sector
PoMAU   = potential output in manufacturing sector.

5.6.3   The value added in the mining sector

The most important mineral produced in Iraq is petroleum. Other minerals such as sulphur, phosphates, iron and copper ores are produced on a very much smaller scale.

To estimate the real value added in this sector, we are separating the petroleum products function from the other minerals produced function. The main reason for separating the oil production function from other mineral products, is because of the importance of petroleum in the Iraqi economy, and, on other sides the factors determining the production function or real value added in this product will be different. So we have two equations to estimate value added.

The coefficients and t ratio for the variables were respectively:

$$-0.037VMAU_{t-1} - 0.49MINT - 0.0004EMployMAU$$
$$(-0.24) \qquad\qquad (-0.62) \qquad (-0.076)$$

5.6.3.a Value added in oil sector the objective of the government's long-term policy is to achieve the necessary balance between the use of oil revenues for the financing of development plans on the one hand, and the conservation of an exhaustible natural resource on the other hand, and creating other sources to finance the needs of the Iraqi economy, as well as the crude oil export, which is the source of almost all the country's foreign exchange earnings and government revenues. Value added in sector is related to the country's need for foreign currency rather than to any other factor, such as productive capacity, fixed investment and the level of labour. Therefore, value added in this sector can be either a function of crude oil exports or grow according to an exogenous specified growth rate.

Exports of crude oil were chosen as a good proxy for the country's need for foreign exchange, simply because oil revenues are the country's major source of foreign income. It should, however, be mentioned that in the later stage of development when both the forward and backward linkages (see Chapter 4) of the oil sector with the rest of the economy, become significant, value added in this sector then will also be affected by domestic consumption. Moreover, it has been argued that production function for oil should take into account the effect of oil prices, total oil consumption by importing countries, and political factors. However, on the basic of the situation during the period of study, the new oil discoveries and price structure will not seriously affect the world's demand for oil in the mid-1980s As for political factors, developments in Iraq have shown that they are not so effective any more in keeping prices down, but has, on the other hand, a considerable influence in dictating the level and direction of the outflows.

Thus, the value added from the oil sector must be seen as a function of the lagged value added of oil. At the same time, we have further incorporated a 0.1 dummy variable for the nationalisation of oil industries in Iraq in 1973 to take account of possible structural breaks due to this event. The dummy variable taking the value 1 for the period after the nationalisation process during the years (1973-1980) and zero for before the nationalisation period is an out model. Hence the equation is given by:

$$Voil = 71.7 + 0.34Voil_{t-1} + 0.18DL73 + 0.10Tim \qquad [5.14]$$
$$(-1.87) \quad (1.87) \qquad (1.83) \qquad (3.69)$$

$$R^{-2} = 0.997, \ SEE = 34.74, \ d\,w = 1.40, \qquad (1965\text{-}1980)$$

Where;
Voil   = value added in oil sector
Xoil   = value of oil export
DL73   = dummy variable.

This equation is highly significant at almost all levels. The coefficient of determination R^2 which measures the proportion of the total variance accounted for by the relation fitted is, in equation very high, providing evidence of a good fit. The (d w) statistics showed absence of serial correlation in the disturbance terms, at 1 per cent level of significance, in almost all equations. Only in this case, the test for autocorrelation in the residual yields inconclusive results.

5.6.3.b The other mining besides oil, Iraq has other minerals mined including sulphur, phosphates, iron and copper ... etc. Since these groups of minerals are mined in small quantities if compared with the quantities of oil produced, and their production is not expected to expand rapidly in the near future, they are treated as exogenous variables in the model as well. To derive the value added in the other mining sector from its gross output, a national income determinant between the value added and the gross sale of the industrial sector is often used. The relationship can be expressed as:

$$NVDi \quad = SLi - INi - Tri \tag{5.15}$$

Where;
NVDi   = nominal value added of industry
Sli   = gross sales of industry
Tri   = transportation and other services used by industry.

Real value added is then derived by deflating the nominal value added by its sectoral deflator as well as intermediate input and services absorbed by the mining industry. This approach is not directly applicable to Iraq. Instead, we adopt a simpler approach in the model. Our approach hinges on the strong assumption that the ratio of value added to gross output is relatively stable over time, so that value added can be reasonably approximated as a direct function of output. Indications are that this has been the case for other mining sectors in Iraq. As a result, real value added in sulphur and phosphates ... etc., are estimated as a total function of their output in 1975 prices which is chosen as the base year. So, the value added in other mining is treated as exogenously determined. Output of this sector is derived from the sum of the two value added components of oil value-added and other mining value-added. The estimated value added equation for other mining sector as follows:

$$VothMin= -19.60+ 1.95OPothMin*OthMin \tag{5.16}$$
$$(-3.36) \quad (6.83)$$

$R^{-2} = 0.838$, SEE = 5.38, d w = 1.55,   (1965-1980)

Where;
VothMin   = value added in their mining sector
OPothMin*XPothMin = value of other mining sector in 1975 prices.

The value added in the mining sector is the total sum of the value added to its components; Vmin = oil value added + other mining value added. [5.17]

5.6.4   The construction sector

The construction industry in Iraq consists of residual housing, government building projects and the construction of industrial and commercial buildings. This is an important and fast growing sector of the economy. The rapid growth registered in this sector can again be attributed to the role played by the government in promoting its growth. Especially after 1970, the government has been strongly committed to improving housing conditions. The government began to actively promote home ownership. This is done through an expansion in public housing programmes which provide housing facilities to the lower income group and also making available housing loans at an extremely favourable rate of 5 per cent per annum to people for purchases of residential homes. At the same time, the mortgage bank has also been active in financing people and companies to grant more housing loans to private individuals.

The rapid economic growth experienced in the country, particularly in the 1970s, also gave rise to a rapid increase in the construction of industrial and commercial buildings. Value added in the construction sector, is determined by the current and lagged level of real gross investment expenditure (TINV) which included both private and public investment and a dummy variable to reflect the occurrence of a construction increase in 1975 and 1976 following the upturn in government revenues from oil exports and economic activities. The estimated function is given by:

$$Vconst = -18.40 + 0.327 \text{ TINV} + 104 \text{ DL7576} + 0.04 \text{ Tim} \qquad [5.18]$$
$$ (-2.08) \qquad (48.47) \qquad (5.55) \qquad (2.41)$$

$$R^{-2} = 0.992, \text{ SEE} = 24.73, \text{ d w} = 2.22, \qquad\qquad (1965\text{-}1980)$$

The estimated coefficients indicate that the elasticity with respect to real investment, and dummy variables are 1.11 and 0.39 respectively.

This equation was also estimated by TSLS. See appendix to chapter 5.

5.6.5   Value added in transport and communication

Value added in this sector would be primary in response to the country's demand for such services rather than the factor of production. In fact, an attempt to estimate the supply function based on some factors of production (such as investment) was a failure [5.19*]. Therefore, transport and communications value added is assumed to be a function of lagged adjusted GDP (ADJGDP), (i.e. normal constant price GNP adjusted for the terms of trade changes) which represents the demand for the

118

above mentioned services. The demand equation that is taken to represent a good proxy for the value added in this sector is:

$$VTRC = 96.6 + 0.273 VTRC_{t-1} + 0.053\ TGIN_{t-1} \qquad [5.19*]$$
$$\quad\ (4.10) \quad\ (4.99) \qquad\quad (0.73)$$

$$R^{-2} = 0.992,\ SEE = 24.73,\ d\,w = 2.22, \qquad (1968\text{-}1980)$$

$$VTRC = 52.50 + 0.0569\ ADJGDP_{t-1} + 1.10 Tim \qquad [5.19]$$
$$\quad\ (2.31) \quad\ (2.31) \qquad\qquad (9.81)$$

$$R^{-2} = 0.888,\quad SEE = 57.63,\ d\,w = 2.1, \qquad (1968\text{-}1980)$$

5.6.6   The service sector (value added)

The shares of the services sectors as a percentage of total GDP has been relatively unstable over the sample period. In 1968, it accounted for 13.5 per cent of total GDP, and by 1980, the share had only grown marginally to 12.76 per cent. The main components which constitute the services sector are electricity and water supply, trade and finance, and public administration and defence. The growth in both categories of services was the direct consequence of a rapid expansion in public development expenditure during this period.

Value added in the services sector (Vserv) is related directly to real aggregate expenditure (AER). AER is defined to include consumption and investment expenditure of both the private and public sectors as well as the level of real exports. This specification can be interpreted as an input-output transformation (Behrman and L.R. Klein, 1970). It should be noted that this equation suffers from serial correlation. It may be due to the small number of observations for this equation (13 years). For more details see section 5.4.

$$Vserv = 101 + 0.157\ AER \qquad [5.20]$$
$$\quad\ (2.54)\ (17.21)$$

$$R^{-2} = 0.964,\quad SEE = 89.67,\ d\,w = 0.92, \qquad (1963\text{-}1986)$$

This equation was also estimated by TSLS. See appendix to Chapter 5. The elasticity coefficient with respect to real aggregate expenditure is 0.74.

5.7   Definitions of gross domestic production (GDP)

The real gross domestic production is determined by summing up the seven value added in sectors, which is explained in the following equation:

$$GDP = VAgr + Vman + Voil + Vomin + Vconst + Vtran + Vserv \quad [5.21]$$

Where;

Vagr	=	value added in the agriculture sector
Vman	=	value added in the manufacturing sector
Voil	=	value added in the oil sector
Vomin	=	value added in the other mining sector
Vconst	=	value added in the construction sector
Vtran	=	value added in the transport sector
Vserv	=	value added in the service sector.

5.8 Aggregate demand block

This section describes the structure of aggregate demand of the economy. The components explained by the model are: private consumption expenditure (C), public consumption expenditure (GC), private sector investment (I), and public sector investment (GI). The exports of goods (XG), and imports of goods (MG) are determined in the later section dealing with foreign trade and balance of payments.

Several interesting developments have taken place in the composition of the expenditure components of real GDP during the period of study. In particular, it is noted that the growth of public sector expenditures (both consumption and investment) far outpaced the private sector counterparts. The fastest growth rate among the components is the public investment which grew at an average annual rate of 15.3 per cent (see Chapter 2), derived, again from the increasing government income from the oil sector, and this took place after the introduction of the new economic policy in the seventies, when the government began to participate strongly in every aspect of economic activity. It is also shown that within the private sector, the share of investment as a percentage of total private sector expenditure has grown. The shares of exports and imports as a percentage of total GDP have relatively increased over the sample period.

5.8.1 Private consumption

Several competing theories have been developed to explain the consumption functions of developed countries. Some recent studies seem to indicate that these theories are generally applicable to the developing economies as well (F. Modigliarli and E. Taratalli, 1975). However, in order to incorporate the structural characteristics of Iraq into the consumption function, it is necessary to modify these theories.[8]

The most popular consumption theories are those expounded Keynes (1936), Duesenberry, Friedman (1957), and Modigliani-Ando-Brumberg. All these theories shared in common the belief that most significant explanatory variable for the consumption function is some measure of aggregate income. What distinguishes one theory from the other is choice of the aggregate income available (E. P. Davis, 1984). Thus Keynes formulated his absolute levels of personal income hypothesis by making aggregate consumption a function of aggregate income, both variables having been deflated by the wage index.[9] The relative income hypothesis proposed by Duesenberry attempted to explain the consumption-income ratio in terms of the ratio of current income to the previous peak Income. Finally, the permanent income hypothesis of Milton Friedman and the life cycle hypothesis of Modigliani, Ando and Brumberg postulated that consumption expenditure is best explained by some long-term aggregate income. As a result, Friedman made a distinction between the permanent and the transitory components of income and stated that the relevant income variables should be the permanent income component while Modigliani and Brambery preferred to use the average of expected life time income as the representative income measure.

While the reasoning of these earlier theories is useful, they failed to capture the important features of the less developed countries (LDCS), which are characterised by small capital markets, low per capita income, a relatively large rural sector and a rapid pace of industrialisation and urbanisation.

One of the most distinct characteristics of the LDCS is the presence of a dualistic economic structure which consists of a rural traditional, and a urban modern sector within the same economy,[10] and at in the same, we could see very clearly this fracture in the oil exporting developing countries, such as Iraq which has a modern oil sector beside other traditional sectors. The consumption and savings behaviours in these sectors are very different. For instance, the spending unit in the rural sector is often the extended family unit that is not the typical spending unit in the urban sector.

Furthermore, the consumption and saving decisions in the rural sector are directly linked to the plans for future farm expansion and other production decisions. This is due mainly to the underdeveloped nature of the credit market, which does not adequately provide for the financial needs of the rural sector. In addition, the income and consumption time horizon of the two groups may also be vastly different. Farmers in general, have a longer time horizon, as long as one year for some single crop farmers whereas in the case of the urban wage earners the time horizon may be as short as one month. The farmers are also more likely to be faced with fluctuations in their earnings than the city dwellers. Tastes and habits too may be different between the two groups. In particular, the rural dwellers tend to spend less on housing, clothing, transportation and entertainment than their urban counterparts.

This, therefore, necessitates the development of a new consumption function for the dual economy. Ideally, we should have two consumption functions one for the rural sector and another for the urban sector. However, due to the unavailability of data to permit such an undertaking, we are forced to take a different route. The origin of this concept is attributed to Klein (1950) and is developed further in Kaldor (1955).[11]

Klein made a distinction between wage and non-wage income in the consumption of one of his earliest econometric models, while Kaldor constructed a theory of consumption based on the income distribution of different socio-economic classes, in particular, he hypothesised that the marginal propensity to consume (MPC) of the capitalists is smaller than that of the workers. Therefore, it is useful in our model to express private sector consumption as a function of the disposable incomes of the rural and urban sectors separately. The urban sector is not a homogeneous area; instead it consists of two quite distinct social classes: the urban workers whose incomes are derived from wages and salaries; and the urban business entrepreneurs whose MPC is expected to be much lower than the MPC of the wage earners. There is, in fact, a great deal of evidence showing that the retained earnings of businesses (non-wage and non-agriculture income) are important sources of domestic savings in the LDCS, implying that the business community has a low MPC.

Another important issue which confronts the specification of the consumption function is with respect to the relevance of the concept of long-run income or permanent income to an LDC economy. Empirical results from a number of studies seem to indicate that consumption behaviour in the LDC is largely influenced by current income (Byung-Nak Song, 1981, John W. Hill and Stuart A. Low, 1982).

Several reasons were offered to explain this observation. Capital market and consumer credit are relatively undeveloped in LDC economics. Unemployment compensation schemes are virtually non-existent. In addition, there were very little social welfare provisions to smooth out income fluctuation. Behrman and Hanson (1979) also observed that due to the fact that a large number of individuals are living at subsistence income level, consumption may not be proportional to income even in the long run. As such, the concept of permanent income may not be applicable for the consumption to income even in the long-run. As such, the concept of permanent income may not be applicable for the consumption function of a developing economy.

Finally, it is also suggested in the development literature that certain financial variables such as interest rates or loans may be used to indicate the effects of financial liberalisation of the previously controlled financial system on savings and consumption (Veber, W.E., 1971, S.V. Wijnbergen, 1982).

Based on the above discussion, private sector consumption expenditure in the model is expressed as a function of disposable income in explaining private urban income and rural income, and the real rate interest rate (RINTR) which is the commercial banks lending rate minus the expected rate of inflation (Easton, W.W. 1985). A distinction is made among three sources of disposable income which are namely: non-wage, non-agriculture income, agricultural income and wages and salaries.

The real interest is introduced to capture the effects of the financial system in the 1970s on aggregate savings. We can show this in the equation which includes all explanatory variables:

$$PCon = -114 + 0.621WSSR + 4.50 \ Wagr -2.13RINTR_{t-1} \qquad [5.22]$$
$$ (-0.78) \ (1.96) \qquad (3.34) \qquad (-1.88)$$

$$R^{-2} = 0.976, \ SEE = 170.1, \ dw = 2.16, \quad (1963\text{-}1986)$$

In addition, several other alternative specifications were tried. They include the incorporation of the permanent income hypothesis, liquid assets (Patternson, K. D., 1986, Hendry, D.F. and Von Undern-Sternberg, T., 1981), as well as the imports of consumer goods, total disposable income, and dummy variables to take account of the government's decision on improving the standard of living in Iraq and absorbing unemployment from the labour market in 1976 after increasing the crude oil exports.

To incorporate the permanent income hypothesis into the consumption function, it is often assumed that permanent income is some function of past incomes. The most commonly used hypothesis is to estimate permanent income as the same distributed lags of current and past incomes.

A geometric lag scheme in which the weights on past incomes decline with the length of the lag, in particular, has found wide application in this context.

After appropriate substitutions, the permanent income consumption function can be expressed as:

$$CON \ t = \alpha + \beta Yt + \gamma \ CON_{t-1} \qquad [5.23]$$

Where;
CON   = consumption
Y   = disposable income
α, β, γ = parameters.

From this equation, the estimated coefficient of the consumption function specified in this form, it is possible to derive the short-run and long-run marginal propensity to income. The short-run MPC is given by β while the long-run MPC is given by $\beta/1-\gamma$.

An attempt was also made to incorporate liquid assets into the consumption function. As the market for financial assets is relatively undeveloped in Iraq, it was decided that the real money supply, broadly defined MS might be an appropriate measure of liquid assets.

Our inclusion of GDP and imports of consumer goods into the consumption function, however, requires a great deal of justification. It was in accordance with the fact that the force of development in Iraq is mostly directed towards higher consumption. The share of private consumption in GDP rose from 28.7 per cent in 1960 to 52.0 per cent in 1970 and reached 24.7 per cent in 1980. In the case of Iraq, the creation of demand for consumer goods in Iraq by the government during the period 1965-1980, through increasing wages, increasing the money supply and higher crude oil prices, led the country's total imports to rise, since the domestic supply could not meet the demand. It would be appropriate to assume that in a developing country, demand is related to the additional capacity. In fact, through imported capital and intermediate goods the capacity to produce in Iraq vas expanded during the period of examination and, therefore, total imports in general and imports of consumer goods in particular have some explanatory power in determining the private consumption. The share of imports of consumer goods in total imports increased from 26.9 per cent in 1968 to 32.9 per cent in 1968, and rose to 90 per cent in 1971.

The alternative equations estimated are:

$$Pcon = -9.2 + 0.0256 \, WSSR + 0.304 \, WAgr + 0.078 \, CMBLR_{t-1} + 0.968 \, Pcon_{t-1}$$
$$\quad (22.92) \qquad\qquad (-0.38) \quad (0.44) \qquad\quad (1.07) \qquad\qquad (0.33)$$
$$[5.24]$$

$R^{-2} = 0.999$, SEE $= 27.43$, d w $= 1.96$,   (1963-1980)

$$Pcon = 11 + 0.558 \, WSSR + 2.52 \, WAgr + 3.78 \, CMBLR_{t-1} - 1.82 \, MS + 0.399 Pcon_{t-1}$$
$$\quad (0.04) \quad (4.08) \qquad\quad (0.75) \qquad\quad (1.75) \qquad\quad (-0.80) \quad (1.80)$$
$$[5.25]$$

$R^{-2} = 0.946$, SEE $= 236.8$, d w $= 2.27$,   (1963-1980)

$$PCON = 192 + 0.471 \, WSSR + 0.61 \, WAGR - 3.52 Ms + 0.703 PCON_{t-1} \quad [5.26]$$
$$\quad (1.14) \quad (5.75) \qquad\quad (0.25) \qquad\quad (-1.67) \quad (2.19)$$

$R^{-2} = 0.944$, SEE $= 233.5$, d w $= 2.19$,   (1963-1980)

The final estimated of private consumption is:

$$PCON = -21 + 3.39 \, IMGC_{t-1} + 0.654 \, GDP_{t-1} + 874 DL76 \qquad [5.27]$$
$$\quad (-1.31) \quad (8.13) \qquad\qquad (1.99) \qquad\qquad (2.19)$$

$R^{-2} = 0.986$, SEE $= 132$, d w $= 2.19$,   (1963-1980)

Equation [5.24] was not satisfactory on several grounds. First, it gives the wrong sign for the real interest rate variable. Secondly, neither the short-run nor the long-run MPC for the different groups are plausible. It was thus rejected.

Equation [5.25]; it was found that the estimated result of this equation was not satisfactory either. Firstly, both the real interest rate and the real liquid assets terms have the wrong signs. Secondly, the speed of adjustment term was much too large implying that it takes 18 years to adjust to the desired consumption. Moreover, it implied the long-run MPC for all groups are far greater than 1.0, that seem highly implausible.

Compared with equations [5.24] and [5.25] equation [5.27] still has the wrong sign estimated. Also, the agriculture income and the real asset term continue to have the wrong sign.

Considering all factors, it has therefore been decided that equations [5.22] and [5.21] are the right signs. According to the estimate of equation [5.21], the marginal propensities to consume with respect to wages and salaries WSSR and agriculture income, WASR are respectively 0.6 and 4.5. The marginal propensity to consume out of agriculture income is higher than either wages and salaries. This can be explained by the behaviour of most farmers who spend not only what they earn but also a portion of what is granted to them by the government through development plan expenditures for improving their methods of production and increasing the quantity and quality of their agriculture products, e.g. by spending these funds on fertilisers and butter seeds. It can also be argued that many farmers in Iraq have other sources of income such as casual employment in the towns near their villages during a certain period of the year. The farmer's income, earned by casual employment, is neither taxed nor recorded properly in the national accounts.

The coefficient on the real interest term implies that the interest rate in the 1970s has a significant positive effect in raising aggregate saving and thus led to a reduction in consumption. The effect of interest rate changes can also be seen from the rapid growth of fixed and savings deposit, particularly in the latter part of the 1970s.

As far as equation [5.27] is concerned, since it was not possible to obtain a reliable data on disposable income,[12] we have made use of gross national product GDP as a proxy for consumer's income with the imports of consumer goods and dummy variables, which explained the importance of both the previous variables above in determining private consumption function in Iraq. All of these three variables have correct signs in equation [5.27]. Moreover, the coefficient of imports of consumer goods lagged one year has the correct sign, meaning that it is theoretically plausible. In other words, given the imbalance in domestic supply and demand and based on the empirical results, it is correct to hypothesis in the Iraqi economy, where domestic supply lags behind domestic demand, that demand is a function of both domestically produced and imported goods. Thus imports of consumer goods which are chosen on priori grounds are now accepted as an explanatory variable in explaining private consumption.

Moreover, GNPt $_{t-1}$ appears to be the significant effect in determining the private consumption. This was a natural choice because of a strong correlation between the dependent variable and GDP lagged one year. Finally the dummy variable, has a high sign of significance, this was actually because of a strong correlation between the dependent variable and dummy variables (DL 1976). The coefficient of determination R^2 is quite high in this equation, that is above 90 per cent, implying a good fit. Also there is no evidence of autocorrelation in the residuals in any of the equations.

5.8.2 Government consumption

From section 4 in Chapter 2 we have seen a clear picture of increasing government consumption expenditure, and the important role it plays in overall economic activities. This is reflected in the payment of wages and salaries to public servants which is the most significant component of government consumption. In order to complete the picture, there are other items which have become increasingly important in recent years: the transfer of funds to the states and statutory authorities, as well as to a statutory fund for emergency spending by the government.

The explanatory variable which is used to explain the behaviour of public consumption (GC) is the real government revenues adjusted for transfer to the household (GR-TFR), and the level of the previous year's real government consumption expenditure (GCt_{t-1}). It has always been the case that the government has not been able to spend all its revenues; the government might need to increase its resources through tax and non tax measures. Since government consumption expenditure is of a recurrent nature, the previous year's government consumption is included as an explanatory variable for the reason that commitments made by government in the previous year are most likely going to affect the current period's consumption. For instance, the creation of new positions in the civil service or a rise in the public servants wages, salaries and subsidies in the previous year would, made a strong impact on the level of government consumption. In the economic literature, Brown (1952), interpreted the introduction of the lagged consumption term in the consumption function as including a kind of habit-persistence behaviour. This explanation seems appropriate in the determination of this function. The equation is given by:

$$GC = 122.56 + 0.72051 \, GC_{t-1} + 0.615 \, (GR\text{-}TFR) \qquad [5.28]$$
$$(2.8367) \quad (3.6369) \qquad \qquad (4.161)$$

$$R^{-2} = 0.979, \, SEE = 35.57, \quad d \, w = 2.05, \, H = 0.1968 \qquad (1963\text{-}1980)$$

The explanatory variables which were used to explain the behaviour of the public sector has a highly significant coefficient and the right sign. Additionally, the estimated coefficients indicate that the short-run marginal propensity to consumption of GC_{t-1} and (GR-TRE) are 0.72 and 0.62 respectively. Additionally, the estimated coefficients indicate that the long-run propensity to consume out of total adjusted revenue is 0.66. This seems to confirm the observation that public saving is an important source for the financing of development projects. However, public consumption may also be treated as exogenously determined in the policy simulation exercises.

5.8.3 Investment function

All investment functions in the model are expressed in real terms. Investment functions include public sector investment (GIN), private sector investment (PIN), and inventory investment. However, attempts to endogenous the demand for

126

inventory investment have not yielded any satisfactory result, as such it is treated as an exogenous variables.

5.8.3.a   Private sector investment this section relates the development of the theory of investment in the advanced economies to the investment function of the less developed countries and, at the same time, presents the estimated results of the investment functions of Iraq.

Several theories of investment function that have provided some basis for the statistical models are those most often used in modelling the economy of the developed countries. The most famous theory of investment function is the general theory, Keynes introduced on the concept of the marginal efficiency of capital. The marginal efficiency of capital was defined as that rate of discount which equates the present value of the stream of net revenues associated with a given capital good to the purchase prices of that good. Keynes asserted that investors would purchase capital goods until the marginal efficiency of capital equals the rate of interest. Assuming that the flows of future income of all investment projects are known, it would be possible to trace out an investment schedule for the entire economy by varying the rate of interest. Some modification has included the possibility of technical innovations embodied in the new investment goods and renamed it Marginal Efficiency of Investment (Abba. Lerner, 1944). R.G.D. Allen later formalised this notion, and proposed a specification of the investment function, as given by (R.G.D. Allen, 1967):

$$I = f(r^{-}, k^{-}, x^{+})$$
[5.29]

Where;
I   = investment
r^{-} = rate of interest
k^{-} = initial capital stock
x^{+} = shift parameter.

This equation expounds the determinants of the investment function, which the investment function has negatively related to the rate of interest and the initial stock of capital, and positively related with other determinants, which raise the marginal efficiency of investment. The shift parameter is assumed to include such variables as the level of national income, the rate of unemployment or other factors which may influence expected future profits. The parameter is often taken to correspond to Keynes expectation elements. While this specification did provide a good first approximation of the investment function, it was found to be lacking a strong theoretical foundation. The specification with a strong theoretical foundation is the specification proposed by Dale Jorgenson. In fact, most investment functions in the current models of the industrialised economies can be traced directly or indirectly to Dale Jorgenson's new neo-classical theory of investment demand. Jorgenson assumed that a typical enterprise adjusts its outputs

127

and inputs in such a way as to maximise its present discounted value, V (Dale W. Jorgenson, 1965). See also K. F. Wallis (1979).

$$V = \int_0^a e^{-rt} \left[PX - SL - qI - T(t) \right] dt \qquad [5.30]$$

Where;
T(t)=   tax bill at time t
I   =   level of gross investment
S   =   unit labour cost
Qi =   purchase price of 1 Unit of Capital
P   =   price of the firm's output
X   =   level of output.

By making a further assumption about the rate of change of the capital stock and by approximating the production function with a Cobb-Douglas production function: X=A.K L, such that x + B < 1, Jorgenson was able to demonstrate that the optimal level of capital stock for the firm is:

$$K^* = \frac{\alpha Px}{UCC} \qquad [5.31]$$

Where;
UCC   = the user cost of capital.

Included in the user cost of capital term are such parameters as the purchase price of capital, the rate of depreciation, the interest rate, the rate of capital gains or losses and the tax rates.

To translate the desired level of capital stock into an investment function, the flexible accelerator mechanism is often used. The use of this accelerator mechanism is justified by the fact that due to cost consideration and structural rigidities in the economy, adjustment of the existing capital stock to its desired level can only take place gradually over time. Finally, to complete his theory of investment demand, he assumed that replacement demand for capital is proportional to its initial stock. With all these additional assumptions, Jorgenson's formulation gives rise to an investment function of the form:

$$I_t = \sum_{i=0}^{n} a_i \Delta K_{t-1}^* + \int K_{t-1} \qquad [5.32]$$

Besides Jorgenson's model, there are many other models of investment behaviour which attempt to explain the determination of desired capital stock in terms of variables such as capacity utilisation, internal fund, cost of external finance, sales or real output.

It has been observed in the development literature that the investment functions of some advanced developing countries could be satisfactorily modelled along this line. For example the studies by Behrman and Lasaga on the investment functions of Chile (Jere R. Behrman, 1972 and Manuel Lasaga, 1979). In general however for most LDCs, certain modifications are required.

Two strong objections raised against the use of the Jorgenson's model for Iraq are with respect to his assumption about the maximisation of discounted value of the value and the implied marginal conditions for investment. Both of which are likely to be violated. Also other difficulties make this model fail to recognise those business firms in the LDCS are differently organised and the environments in which firms operate are different from that in developed countries. The objectives of the firms are more likely governed by such considerations as the maximisation of the pay-off period of investment and the growth of market shares. In the case of Iraq, for those government sponsored private enterprises, their objectives may very well be dominated by such socio-economic considerations as: maximising the participation of the Iraqi and other indigenous people in businesses; increasing the employment of the Iraqi in the modern sector; stepping-up the training of technical skill through learning by doing: assuring that the Iraqi and other indigenous people acquire a certain fraction of the equity capital in the corporate sector and capturing a certain fraction of the market share. Moreover, due to the imposition of various government regulations, quotas, licensing requirements and a large number of other protective measures, businesses are on the whole, less competitive in the LDCs than in the developed economies.

Furthermore, in Iraq, due to the existence of a small and underdeveloped capital market, the prevalence of public sector controls which affect almost every aspect of private sector investment as well as the dependence of the economy on the external sector for the supply of capital goods, the private sector's investment criteria are expected to be very different from that of the developed countries.[13] In particular, the marginal conditions for investment in the neo-classical model are not likely to hold true. Jorgenson's framework assumed the existence of an efficient capital market and a perfectly competitive capital goods market. In such an environment, the firm can borrow as much money as it needs to supplement its own resources, without effecting the market rate of interest. In addition, it can also buy and sell as many capital goods as it desires without effecting the price of capital goods. These conditions obviously do not exist in Iraq.

Like most LDCs, the capital market in Iraq is still very much underdeveloped and at the same time, it is highly regulated. Numerous requirements are imposed on a company that plans to raise its equity capital through the stock market. In addition, there also exist certain amounts of credit rationing in the forms of lending guidelines on the extension of credit by commercial banks and finance companies. As a result the bulk of domestically financed investment expenditure originates not from the capital market, but from past retained earnings of the firms and loans extended by the public sector, and the commercial banks. To capture this feature in the investment function, a real credit variable should be used as an explanatory variable.

The Iraqi government plays a very significant role in stimulating private sector investment. It acts through a wide range of agencies and instruments which include both direct measures such as the issue of licenses, price control on goods manufactured and tariff protection, and indirect measures which deal with the formulation of trade, financial, tax and labour policies. However, direct interference by the government on private sector investment decision is minimal. Rather, entrepreneurs are guided to invest in certain desired industries through the use of various incentive schemes which are aimed at affecting the profitability of investment projects. Investors are also urged to observe certain socio-economic requirements such as the desired racial balance in the labour force and the desired ratio of local equity participation. Due to the paucity of information, it has not been possible to quantify the effects of these requirements of private sector investment. On the whole, it has always been the intention of government to create favourable conditions for private sector investment.

The role played by social and physical infrastructure in the process of economic growth is often emphasised in development literature as follows; Rosenstein Rodan (1961), for instance maintained that because of the external economies social infrastructures brings, the government should continue to increase its investment in them in order to induce a rapid growth in private investment. Birnberg and Resnick (1973) were also able to show that historically, social infrastructure development was an important factor for bringing about rapid export growth in the developing countries. As such, in the determination of investment function, due consideration ought to be given to the role of social overhead development by the government.

External conditions also effect private sector investment in the LDCS as following: firstly, direct foreign investment in the modern sector is an important component of total private sector investment, financial and economic conditions abroad may influence the inflow of foreign investment.[14] Secondly, as the bulk of machinery and equipment in the LDCS, are derived from imports, both the exchange rate policy and import policies have important influences in the determination of the cost of capital. The availability of imported machinery and equipment constrained investment in developing countries. Being a small open economy, both fluctuations in export earnings as well as in commodity prices are expected to have a significant impact on the investment climate in Iraq.

Based on the above discussion, several alternative specifications of the real investment of private sectors were explored. The variable chosen as explanatory variables include profits, real output, availability of credit, export receipts, the availability of external reserves, and the lack of a developed capital market. Considering that a system of liberal exchange control was followed in Iraq and also there was the existence of a favourable attitude of the government towards private sector investment together with the availability of large reserves of foreign exchange, it is evident that external reserve had not been a constraint on private sector investment in the sample. Among the list of factors considered, four variables emerged as the most significant in explaining the movements of the private sector investment. They are the real export of goods (EXG), the real interest rate (RINTR), the real investment extended to the private sector (RINVCR/MP),[15] that is defined as the total investment credit extended by the Government and the financial sector deflator by the import price index. The import price index is chosen as the deflator because the bulk of inputs in the manufacturing sector comes from imports. Both (RINTR) and (RINVCR/MP) are used to reflect the conditions in the financial market. It has been observed in several other LDC models that both credit availability and the cost of credit are important determinants of private sector investment. Similar approaches were followed by Wijnbergan (1982) and K.L. (1984). Real export and commodity prices are used to capture the general economic conditions of the economy. Being largely an export-dependent economy, the economic conditions of Iraq can be well gauged by the performance in the export sector. An attempt was also made to introduce the index of capacity utilisation of the manufacturing sector (AUT) as an exogenous variable. The introduction of the current and past levels of total investment, and other variables, such as the gross disposable non-wage income and the real commodity prices into the equation did not yield plausible results and were consequently dropped from the list of variables chosen. The estimated equations are shown below:

$$PINV = 57.20 - 0.0829RINTR + 0.468EXG + 0.848RINVCR/MP \quad [5.33]$$
$$(7.31) \quad (-1.95) \quad (6.57) \quad (14.07)$$

$$R^{-2} = 0.983, \ SEE = 21.03, \ d \ w = 1.96, \quad (1963\text{-}1986)$$

The elasticity coefficients with respect to the real rate of interest (RINTR), real export receipts (EXG) and the real investment credits (RINVCR/Mp) are -0.083, 0.047 and 0.90 respectively. This equation was also estimated by TSLS. See appendix to Chapter 5. The estimated results of two other alternative specifications are also presented below:

$$PINV = 45.80 - 0.0779 \ RINTR + 0.589 \ RINVCR/MP + 0.0195 \ EXG + 0.0227GDP$$
$$(3.49) \ (-1.83) \quad (2.39) \quad (1.08) \quad (0.97)$$
$$[5.34]$$
$$R^{-2} = 0.983, \ SEE = 20.90, \ d \ w = 2.08, \quad (1963\text{-}1986)$$

In equation [5.34] the elasticity coefficients with respect to the real interest rate and real commercial prices and real export receipts are 0.08 and 0.59 respectively.

$$PINV = 38.40 - 0.102 \ RINTR + 0.468 \ EXG + 0.848 \ RINVCR/MP \quad [5.35]$$
$$(2.57) \ (-2.19) \quad (6.83) \quad (14.64)$$

$R^{-2} = 0.984$, SEE $= 20.22$, d w $= 2.10$, (1963-1980)

Equation [5.34] used the real interest rate RINTR, real export receipts, real investment credit to the private sector (RINVCR/MP), and real Gross Domestic Product (GDP) as explanatory variables. While equation [5.35] used the real interest rate, real export receipts, real investment credit and the capacity utilisation index of the manufacturing sector (CAUT) as the explanatory variable. While the CAUT was used in equation [5.35] with the correct sign, it was not statistically significant.

Amongst these three estimated equations, it appears that equation [5.33] with the correct sign, was statistically significant. So, equation [5.33] is the preferred equation and thus it will be used in the model.

5.8.3.b Public investment in real terms (GIM) the determinants of government investment in our model are the rate of growth of domestic output (CHGDP), real sectoral development expenditure (RDPE), lagged government investment, and the intermediate capital goods imports (MINTKG). The estimated equation is given by:

$$GINV = -107 + 0.122 CHGDP + 0.334 MINTKG_{t-1} + 0.488 GIN(-1) + 0.392 RDPE_{t-1}$$
$$(-3.30) \quad (4.74) \qquad (5.26) \qquad\qquad (4.14) \qquad\qquad (3.24)$$
[5.36]

$R^{-2} = 0.994$, SEE $= 60.26$, d w $= 2.09$, (1963-1986)

The RGDP is used to reflect the use of the counter cyclical fiscal policy stance adopted by the government. while in the previous period government investment is used to reflect the 'habit persistence' hypothesis, it is reasonable to assume that the fraction of current period investment is to service, replace or maintain the capital stock invested last year. Current and lagged development investment expenditure measures the financial resources made available for spending through the investment budgetary process of economic development. Finally, the import of intermediate and capital variable in the government investment equation reflected the dependence of a country on foreign countries to make this equipment for the development process. It is also noted that public investment expenditure could be treated as exogenous in the simulation exercises.

The elasticity of coefficients of the rate growth of domestic output (CHGDP) and the real sectoral development expenditures (RDPE) are 0.12 and 0.29 respectively.

5.9 The employment, wages and factor income block

In this point we will discuss the level of employment, wage rate and the level of factor incomes. To account for the existence of a dualistic economic structure, total employment is divided into employment in the agriculture sector and employment in the modern sector.

The employment equations estimated in most econometric models are treated either as labour requirement equations or factor demand equations. As such their specifications depend on the assumptions made about the underlying production function. The type of production functions, commonly used for this purpose are fixed coefficients, Cobb-Douglas, CES and VES (Naiem A. Sherbiny, 1981). In addition, the producers are either assumed to be profit maximises or cost minimises. A further assumption is usually made about the sluggishness of firms in adjusting their labour force.

In our model, we assume that the output in the agriculture sector followed a fixed coefficient function, with only capital stock acting as the limiting constraint. While in the non-agriculture sector some substitution between labour and capital is assumed.

5.9.1 Employment in the agriculture sector (EMAgr)

In 1981, close to 33 per cent of the employment labour force in Iraq were still engaged in the agriculture sector. However, its share as a percentage of total employment has been declining steadily. Within the agriculture sector, there exist two distinct sub-sectors: modern agriculture and traditional subsistence agriculture.

The government has played an important role in creating the modern agriculture sector, for instance, the government investment allocation has increased from 143 million I. D in 1968 to 3192.3 I. D million in 1980. The modern agriculture sector consists of the large Cotton, Rice, Wheat and Barley Crops as well as the 'government-sponsored' land development schemes. While in the new land schemes, the government has allocated sufficiently large areas of Cotton and Wheat and Barley land to the participants to assure that they are profitably employed. The extent of unemployment in the modern agriculture sector is small. In fact, in recent years, some rice estates in remote areas have already been facing persistent labour shortages due to the accelerated pace of rural urban migration. Employment in the modern agriculture sector is expected to be influenced by the level of output and real wage (i.e. the ratio of wage to commodity prices). The level of output is used to measure the work-force needed in the production of such an output, while the real wage rate indicates the real cost of employing labours. There are indications that producers in the modern agriculture sector are quite sensitive to variation in labour cost in their production decisions.

The subsistence agriculture sector, on the other hand, consists of the fishermen, vegetable and fruit gardeners, and other small farmers. There is a substantial amount of surplus labour within this sub-sector (G. Meier, 1979 and Squire, Lyn, 1981). As such in the subsistence sector, employment opportunities are created largely through the opportunities to expand output. The wage rate is not a relevant determinant.

Unfortunately, a separate set of employment figures for the modern agriculture sector and the subsistence agriculture sectors are not available. Instead, we are required to estimate overall employment in the agriculture sector.

Based on the above discussion, the most appropriate variable for explaining employment variations in the agriculture sector appears to be agriculture output; a dummy variable to reflect the enforcement of Employment Restriction Act in 1972, which severely affected the employment of non-citizen workers, and the real wage rate (WR/Prcom) which is the ratio of wage rate index to the prices of primary commodity. WR/Prcom is used to measure the real cost of labour to the producers in the modern agriculture sector. Three alternative equations were estimated and they are expressed below:

$$\text{Ln EMAgr} = 4.33 + 0.511 \text{ Ln Agr} - 0.491 \text{ Ln DL972} \qquad [5.37]$$
$$\quad\quad\quad (6.78) \ (4.16) \quad\quad\quad (-3.01)$$

$$R^{-2} = 0.495, \text{ SEE} = 0.1578, \text{ d w} = 0.95, \qquad (1963\text{-}1980)$$

$$\text{Ln EMAgr} = 7.45 + 0.007 \text{Agr} - 0.988 \text{ DL972} - 0.988 \text{ER/Prcom}_{t-1} - 0.522 \text{WR/Prcom}_{t-2}$$
$$\quad (46.86) \ (5.57) \quad\quad (-4.53) \quad\quad\quad (-3.55) \quad\quad\quad\quad (-5.05)$$
$$\qquad\qquad\qquad\qquad\qquad\qquad\qquad\qquad\qquad\qquad\qquad\qquad [5.38]$$
$$R^{-2} = 0.64, \text{ SEE} = 0.1324, \text{ d w} = 1.53, \qquad (1963\text{-}1980)$$

$$\text{Ln EMAgr} = 1.89 + 1.15 \text{ LnAgr} - 0.457 \text{ LnDL972} - 0.586 \text{ LnWR/Prcom}_{t-1}$$
$$\quad\quad\quad (3.34) \quad (8.54) \quad\quad (-4.81) \quad\quad\quad (-3.42)$$
$$\quad\quad -0.675 \text{ WR/Prcom}_{t-2} - 0.390 \text{ Ln WR/Prcom}_{t-3} - 0.580 \text{ Ln WR/Prcom}_{t-4}$$
$$\quad\quad (-4.57) \quad\quad\quad\quad (-1.93) \quad\quad\quad\quad\quad (-1.76)$$
$$\qquad\qquad\qquad\qquad\qquad\qquad\qquad\qquad\qquad\qquad\qquad\qquad [5.39]$$
$$R^{-2} = 0.95, \text{ SEE} = 0.01644, \text{ d w} = 1.97, \qquad (1963\text{-}1980)$$

Equation [5.37] used only agriculture output (Agr) and an employment restriction dummy as explanatory variables, while equations [5.38] and [5.39] incorporated the lagged real wage terms WR/Prcom. The difference between equation [5.38] and equation [5.39], is that equation [5.38] is estimated in linear form while equation [5.39] is estimated in log-linear form.

Comparing the estimated results of these equations, it is seen that in all three case the output elasticity ranges are 0.51 and 1.15 respectively, and in every case the dummy variable appears to be significant since there exists a significantly high level of underemployment in the subsistence agriculture sector, as such, although the coefficient for agriculture output seems to be low in equation [5.38], nevertheless is not totally unreasonable. The negative sign on the dummy variable signifies the effect of the enforcement of the employment (restriction) act in 1976 reducing employment in the agriculture sector. There are however some difference with respect to the output agriculture terms. While the signs of the coefficients for the output agriculture terms in equation [5.38] are correct, they have an extremely low coefficient value. However, equation [5.39] is statistically significant and has the correct signs, thus equation [5.39] is the preferred equation.

5.9.2 Employment in other sector (non-agriculture) (EMoth)

Employment in the non-agriculture sector is also modelled as labour demand function. In this section, there are more opportunities for factor substitution in the non-agriculture sector. As such, the explanatory variables are lagged real output of non-agriculture sector (GDP non-agri), and relative factor prices (WR/RCML) which is the commercial bank's lending rate. Lagged relative factor prices are used to reflect the adjustments of employment to past variations in relative factor prices (Sushil B. Wadhwani, 1987). The lagged real investment expenditure in the non-agriculture sector (RINV non-agri), reflects the effects of increasing government revenues from oil export and its effects on the size of employment in Iraq. Labour productivity (NProDT), and non-agriculture wages were initially introduced as explanatory variables, but neither gave a plausible coefficient estimate and were subsequently dropped from the equation:

$$\text{EMoth} = 658 + 0.199 \text{GDPnon-agri}_{t-1} + 0.517 \text{RINVnon-agri}_{t-1} - 0.149 \text{ WR/RCML}_{t-2}$$
$$\quad\quad (8.87) \quad (1.91) \quad\quad\quad\quad (3.71) \quad\quad\quad\quad\quad\quad (-2.81)$$
$$\quad\quad -0.337 \text{WR/RCML}_{t-3} \quad\quad\quad\quad\quad\quad\quad\quad\quad\quad [5.40]$$
$$\quad\quad (-2.81)$$

$$R^{-2} = 0.951, \text{ SEE} = 122.70, \text{ d w} = 2.01, \quad\quad (1963\text{-}1980)$$

These estimated results indicate that the factor of the real investment expenditure in the non-agri sector (RINVnon-agri) has a higher statistical significance the long-run elasticity with respect to the real investment expenditure in the non-agriculture sector is 0.53 while the elasticity coefficient with respect to the non-agriculture output is 0.21.

5.9.3 Total employment (TEM)

$$\text{TEM} = \text{EM agri} + \text{Emoth} \quad\quad\quad\quad\quad\quad\quad\quad [5.41]$$

The total employment is equal to the total sum of employment in the agriculture sector (EM agri) and the other non-agriculture sector (EMoth).

5.9.4 Wage rate index (WR)

A general wage rate series for Iraq is not available, the wage rate index used here is a constructed series. The estimation of the wage rate series is based on the available information about the share of wages and salaries as a percentage of the total GDP and the level of total employment.

Usually in econometric models of developed countries some modified version of the Phillips curve proposition is used, to determine the rate of wage variables.[16] Moreover, these models are mainly concerned with explaining the rate of change of wage rate and not the wage rate per person.[17] The Phillips curve relationship postulated that the Rate of change in wages is determined by the level of unemployment rate. In order to make use of this basic construct in econometric models, further refinements were often necessary. In the Brooking model, for instance, Schultz and Tryon (1965),[18] determine the rate of change in compensation per man hour in a given industry as a function of the level of general unemployment, the ratio of profits to income originating from that industry and the rate of change in consumer prices. In addition, they hypothesised that wage change followed a lagged adjustment process that resulted in the introduction of a one period lagged wage change as an explanatory variable. Their formulation can be expressed as:

$$\Delta W/W = f(U_1\ X/Y,\ \Delta P/P,\ \Delta W/W_{-1}) \qquad\qquad [5.42]$$

Where;
$\Delta W/W$	=	rate of change of the wage rate
U	=	unemployment rate
X/Y	=	the relative share of profit in the industry's income
$\Delta P/P$	=	rate of change of the consumer price.

The unemployment rate was used to capture the central proposition of Phillips curve which hypothesises that the rate of change in wages would be affected by the access demand for labour. In order to reflect the non-linear relationship between the rate of changes of the wage and the unemployment rate, the reciprocal of the unemployment rate is sometimes used.

Relative profit share in the industry's income introduced to indicate that in an environment of largely oligopolistic firms, an increase in profits above same long-run 'normal' for that industry would ultimately find its way into wage increases. Various studies have argued that oligopolistic firms found it advantageous to share part of increase in profit with the employees in the form of wage increases. This would be used to boost the workers morale as well as to build up a high quality work force. Moreover, oligopolistic industries often deliberately avoid showing an excessively high profit margin for fear of attracting new entries.

The rate of change of consumer price is used to reflect the fact that wage bargaining is aimed at affecting the real wages (Artis, M.J., D. Leslie and G.W. Smith, 1982), and therefore, a rise in consumer prices will most likely lead to a higher wage settlement. For longer term wage contracts, expected inflation (that is the rate of change of consumer prices expected in the future) was likely to play a significant role in the demand for higher wages in the new negotiations.

Besides the Schultz and Tryon's formulation, there have also been numerous other modifications (A. Bradley Askin and John, 1974). Other determinants generally considered to be significant in affecting the rate of change of the wage rate include the rate of change of the employment rate, the legislated minimum wage, the extent as well as the rate of change in labour union strength and other labour-related legal and institutional changes.

An attempt is made here to fit the Schultz and Tryon model to the Iraq data. Two separate equations were estimated. In the first equation, the exogenous variables used to explain the rate of change in wages ($\Delta W/W$) were the unemployment rate UN), the relative share of corporate income to the total national income (YS/TNY), rate of change in consume price index ($\Delta cP/CP$) and one period lag in the rate of change in wage rate ($\Delta W/W$). In the second equation, the same set of exogenous variables was used with the exception that the unemployment rate was being replaced by its own reciprocal. That is:

INUN = 1/UN.

The estimated equations are shown as follows:

$$\Delta W/W_t = -109 + 0.141 YS/GDP + 4.55 \Delta P/P - 0.609 \Delta W/W_{t-1} - 0.342 \; UN \quad [5.43]$$
$$\quad (-1.49) \; (6.96) \qquad \quad (5.92) \qquad \quad (-2.76) \qquad \qquad (-1.31)$$

$$R^{-2} = 0.993, \; SEE = 19.48, \; d\,w = 2.20, \qquad (1963\text{-}1980)$$

$$\Delta W/W_{t-1} = -13.20 + 13.40 INVUN + 0.47 YS/TNY - 0.662 \Delta W/W_{t-1} + 0.439 \Delta cp/cp$$
$$\quad (1.48) \quad (1.73) \qquad \quad (2.25) \qquad \quad (-1.93) \qquad \qquad (0.58)$$
$$\qquad \qquad \qquad \qquad \qquad \qquad \qquad \qquad \qquad \qquad \qquad \qquad \qquad [5.44]$$

$$R^{-2} = 0.61, \; SEE = 6.150, \qquad \qquad (1963\text{-}1980)$$

The estimated results indicate the existence of a short-run trades off between unemployment and rate of change in wage increase, and thus render support for the pursuit of stabilisation policies (Pesaran, M.H., 1986).

Recently, there have been several attempts at the level of wage rate directly instead of the rate of change in wage rate. This is particularly true for the LDC models. For instance, Priovolis (1980), Malgrange, P. and Muet, P.A. (1984), Olarnchaipravat, Kanitta Meesook and Siri Ganjarendee (1979), have all estimated the wage rate variable in the level form. The major determinant of the wage rate equation includes such variables as the unemployment rate, legal minimum wage rate, labour productivity, price expectation and the wage rate of the leading sectors. As an alternative, we have also estimated a wage rate equation in the level form. The explanatory variables of the nominal wage rate function are the unemployment rate (UN), consumer prices (cp), TIM, and labour productivity (LPROD). LPROD is measured as the ratio of real GDP to total employment. The GDP is in the non-oil sector (non-oil GDP divided by the level of employment). The oil sector in spite of its high share in GDP, is extremely capital intensive and employs a small proportion of the total labour force. We would thus get a misleading measurement of average productivity if we measure it using total GDP (oil and non-oil).

The employment rate is introduced to capture the Phillips curve phenomenon, while the consumer price index is used to reflect the demand by workers for higher wages in response to prices increases.

In view of the weak bargaining power of the workers in Iraq, the wage rate is expected to adjust only gradually to higher prices. Moreover, it seems that some kind of marked up mechanism seems to work in the determination of the wage rate as well. In addition, the lagged terms can also be interpreted as the formation of price expectation based on current and past prices. Based on the neo-classical proposition that the margin wage depend on productivity, labour productivity was introduced as an exogenous variable. The estimated equation is shown by:

$$\text{Ln W} = -2.05 - 0.229 \text{ Ln UN} + 0.561 \text{ Ln LPROD} + 0.107 \text{ Lncp}_{t-1} + 0.0351 \text{Tim}$$
$$(-4.43) \qquad (4.52) \qquad\qquad\qquad\qquad (2.05) \qquad\qquad (1.88)$$
$$[5.45]$$
$$R^{-2} = 0.991, \text{ SEE} = 0.05622, \text{ d w} = 2.37, \qquad (1963\text{-}1980)$$

The elasticity coefficient with respect to labour productivity is 0.56, while the elasticity coefficient with respect to consumer price index is 0.11. It is also shown that the level of unemployment does exert a significant downward pressure on the movement of the wage index. Judging from the errors generated by each of these three alternative equations it is shown that the equation in level form performed better in tracking the movement of wage rate variable than the other two equations and thus equation [5.45] will be used in subsequent simulations.

5.10 Factor income block

All factor incomes in this model are expressed in nominal terms. Three income categories are identified in the model. They are: sectoral incomes (exception crude oil income) (TD value); oil income which is determined by the level of oil sector output (Voil); and direct tax and net of subsidies (INDTAX). Thus the model will be expressed in two equations, the first equation determines the identity of the real (GDP); which is explained by the given equation.

The second equation expresses the nominal GDP. As we know sectoral incomes are determined by the level of value of sectoral output and the cost of production that is proxied by the overall GDP deflator (PGDP). Therefore the equation which explains GDP in nominal terms is:

$$\text{NGDP} \;=\; \text{RGDP} * \text{PGDP} + \text{Voil} *(\text{PCoil})/100 \qquad\qquad [5.46]$$

Where;
Poil   =   the deflator of crude oil (1975=100)

The nominal aggregate domestic demand components given by the equation:

$$NADD = GC + GINV + Pcon * Consup + PINV * PDTINV + XG + S - MG + S$$

$$[5.47]$$

Where;

GC   =   government consumption in millions of current dinars
GINV   =   government investment in millions of current dinars
Pcon   =   private consumption
Prcon   =   consumer price index (1975=100)
PINV   =   private investment
PDTINV=   price deflator of total investment (1975=100)
XG+S   =   nominal export of goods
MG+S   =   nominal import of goods.

5.11 The price block

This section deals with the determinants of consumer prices, export prices, import prices, overall non-oil GDP deflator; the crude oil output deflator, plus the price deflator for investment and consumption expenditure. There exists a large body of literature on the equation price determination and causes of inflation in the less developed countries.[19] Broadly, this literature can be classified into two main groups.

There exists a large body of literature on the equation price determination and causes of inflation in the less developed countries.[20] Broadly, this literature can be classified into two main groups.

The two alternative theories of output price determination are namely, the monetarist view and the structuralism view. Each theory is based on a different perception about the workings of the economic system. In the structuralism view, the structure of the economy system is ever evolving and as such it could generate certain disequilibria in the process. These disequilibria may take the form of balance of payments deficits/surpluses, public sector deficits, unemployment and inflation. In explaining the growth of the price level the structuralist makes a distinction between the causes of inflationary pressure and the propagation mechanism through which a price spiral may develop.

The main cause of inflationary pressure according to the monetarist view, is that the economic system is inherently stable, and inflation is caused mainly by excess demand for goods and services generated through an excessive expansion of money supply in the economy. The tool of their analysis lies in the exchange equation or the quantity theory of money, first proposed by Irving Fisher. The monetarist therefore would recommend the control of the money supply as the most effective means of bringing inflation under control.

Structuralism, however, holds a very different view with regard to the causes of inflationary pressure. This is due mainly to the failures of some sectors in the

139

economy to adjust quickly to changes in the level and composition of aggregate demand; distortions of the price system caused by the price control policies associated with inflation and miss-allocation of past investment funds. Therefore, in the structuralist view, inflation cannot be eliminated until these structural limitations are overcome.

The propagation mechanism of inflation, on the other hand, works at two levels. Firstly, there is the continuous struggle among the different economic groups to improve their share of total income. This is manifested in the struggle between the wage earners and the non-wage earners. Secondly, there is the struggle between the private and public sector to increase their share of real resources. This works through an ever increasing level of Government expenditure, taxes and the financing need of government deficits.

With regard to the rate of inflation of Iraq, until the first oil price shock in 1973, the economy enjoyed remarkable price stability. Since then, prices have begun to move upwards at a faster pace. However, compared with the rest of the world, inflation is relatively mild. In most years with the exception of 1973 and 1974 inflation was kept at below 5 per cent a year. Price stability was most remarkable during the years from 1960 to 1971 when critical prices grew by about 1 per cent a year, while during the same period, the inflation rate in the industrial countries was almost four times higher. Several factors were thought to have contributed significantly to price stability during these years.[21] Chief among them was the sluggish oil export sector. Being an export-dependent economy, a depressed export sector affected directly the growth of the national income and money supply.

The second contributory factor was considered to be the conservative fiscal and monetary policies pursued by the government. From 1960 to 1970, the budget deficits averaged about 7.69 per cent of the GDP.

Finally, there was the government's free trade policy which encouraged effective import competition and resulted in shifts of imports from 'high cost' countries like the United Kingdom and the USA to the 'low cost' countries such as Japan, West Germany and the socialist countries. This had led to a smaller increase in import prices. The import price index grew by only 1.5 per cent during this period, despite the significantly higher inflation rates of the OECD countries.

The signs of inflationary pressure in Iraq first emerged in 1970 when the consumer price index rose by an unprecedented rate of 5.3 per cent. It was then followed by two rather bad inflation years of 1971 to 1973 when the consumer price index grew at 16.7 points, at an average 4.6 points annually. While the inflation rate increased at an average 9.3 points annually during the period 1973-1976. Since then, the price situations improved significantly and inflation was brought under control. However, recently price pressures seem to be building up again. The rate of growth of consumer prices was close to 8.5 per cent in 1981. Although this largely reflected the worldwide double digit inflation following a significant increase in oil prices and the increase in oil exports, the price situation was nevertheless viewed with serious concern by the authorities.

140

A significant portion of the total supply of goods and services in Iraq is derived from imports. Import prices are expected to have widespread influence on the domestic price situation. It was estimated that an increase in consumer prices accounted for about 30 per cent of the growth in consumer prices in 1973 and 1974 in the first round. The direct import of import prices took the form of higher import food prices at a ratio equalling 11.3 per cent and higher prices for imported raw material and capital goods. Indirectly, higher import prices also enabled the manufacturers of import industry substitutes to raise their prices.

The substantial increase in commodity prices in the 1973 and 1974 commodity boom had resulted in a sharp growth in aggregate demand. Because of the existence of supply bottlenecks in certain industries and in the agricultural sector, and at the same time, particularly in the housing and construction industries, prices for these commodities began to rise sharply. Thus, property values in certain urban areas appreciated by more than 50 per cent in 1974/1975 and again in 1979/1980. In fact, the main reason for change in the prices of 1979/1980 was due to the increase of oil production and oil revenues by the Iraqi government. This resulted in a government inspired additional spending policy and then the aggregate demand and prices increased again.

In addition, excessive public sector spending may have generated inflationary pressure too. In particular, large government spending would stimulate the growth of aggregate demand and if capacity utilisation was already at a relatively high level, this added demand would contribute to worsening supply shortages. There was substantial evidence that in 1973, many key industries, particularly those in the manufacturing and construction sectors were operating close to their productive capacities, and that the added government spending had contributed to a widespread scarcity and longer delays in delivery. Such a situation, it was easy for producers to raise prices.

As mentioned above, the increasing government revenues from the oil export sector, meant more foreign exchange. This resulted in an increase in external reserves and thus the money supply, narrowly defined, grew at an annual rate of 63 per cent in 1973. However, inflation due to a significant inflow of capital has not been repeated since, and also this appears to be unlikely in the future.

As well as the above mentioned factors, there are other factors contributing to the change in the inflationary expectation such as price expectation and wage adjustments (Harvey, A.C., 1983 and 1980) of unionised labour are also expected to exert an important influence on the movement of consumer prices. In order to take into account the effects of shortages in productive capacity on prices and the index of capacity utilisation (CAUT) was developed. The capacity utilisation factor was measured as the ratio of actual to potential output multiplied by (100). The higher the capacity utilisation index, the larger would be the pressure on productive capacity. Meanwhile, potential output is viewed as the level of output the economy is capable of producing if all the productivity factors were fully utilised in a normal production pattern. The level of potential output is measured in the model as the underlying growth trend in real output. The equation is:

$$LNPOTGDP = 7.80 + 0.27\ GRGDP * Time \qquad [5.48]$$

Where;
POTGDP = Potential real GDP
Time   = Time index 1970 equal 1.0 this index is increased by 1.0 every year
thereafter.

$$CAUT = (GDP/POEGDP) * 100 \qquad [5.49]$$

From the discussion above, clearly inflation in Iraq has its origin in both domestic and foreign resources. In addition, both excess demand and higher production costs are likely to exert an equal influence on the movements of the consumer price index. As such neither the monetarist nor the structuralism model alone is able to adequately explain the process of price determination in Iraq. Rather hybrid of the two approaches would be more appropriate.

5.11.1 Consumer prices

A number of alternative specifications for the consumer price equation were explored. The list of variables used in these equations include wage rate (W), real rate of wages, import prices PM), export prices index (PEX), the money supply (MS), direct development expenditure of the public sector (GDT), and index of capacity utilisation (CAUT), wage rate, import price and index of capacity utilisation are closely associated with cost-push inflation, while export prices, the money supply and direct development expenditure of the government are viewed as demand-pull factors. The oil effect was initially introduced as an explanatory variable. Meanwhile, it did not give a plausible coefficient estimate and was subsequently dropped. Of all the specifications explored, the following three estimated equations appeared to be most satisfactory in explaining variations in consumer price index.

$$Ln\ cp = -175 + 55.70\ Ln\ CAUT + 0.0037\ Ln\ GDP + 0.0167 Ln\ MS \qquad [5.50]$$
$$(-8.25)\quad (10.87)\qquad\quad (5.52)\qquad\quad (3.38)$$

$$R^{-2} = 0.998,\ SEE = 1.099,\ d\ w = 1.26, \qquad (1963\text{-}1980)$$

$$Ln\ CP = 42.7 + 0.141\ Ln\ PM + 0.0463\ Ln\ MS + 0.800\ Ln\ MS_{t\text{-}1} \qquad [5.51]$$
$$(12.89)\ (4.19)\qquad (6.89)\qquad\quad (2.11)$$

$$R^{-2} = 0.992,\ SEE = 2.456,\ d\ w = 1.63, \qquad (1963\text{-}1980)$$

$$LnCP = -186 + 57.0 LnCAUT + 0.350 LnMP + 0.211 LnMS + 0.455 LnW + 0.760 LnW_{t\text{-}1}$$
$$(-8.28)\quad (10.17)\qquad (2.26)\qquad (6.30)\qquad (3.48)\qquad (5.78)$$
$$[5.52]$$

$R^{-2} = 0.999$, SEE = 0.7948, d w = 2.59,   (1963-1980)

Equation [5.50] used capacity utilisation index (CAUT), direct development expenditure of the public sector (GDT) and the money supply narrowly defined as explanatory variables, while the import price index (MP) and the current, previous year money supply were used in equation [5.51]. Finally, equation [5.52] used the capacity utilisation index (CAUT). Import prices (MP) and the normalised money supply which is the ratio of money supply to real output MS/GDP were used as variables in equation [5.52].

Judging from the estimated results of the three equations, it appears that [5.52] performs best in terms of both Durban-Watson and R^{-2} value and equation [5.52] will be used in the model. According to the estimated coefficients in equation [5.52], the elasticities in long-run with respect to the MP and MS/GDP are 0.35 and 0.21 respectively.

5.11.2   Aggregate demand price deflator

There are four deflators for the components of aggregate demand. They are the deflators for private consumption, government consumption, private sector's gross fixed investment and government investment.

5.11.2.a   Private consumption deflator (PDC) private consumption deflator is a function of the consumer price (CP) index.   The estimated equation is:

Ln PDCon = 1.04 + 0.830 LNCP   [5.53]
          (4.5)   (16.32)

$R^{-2} = 0.957$, SEE = 0.0469, d w = 1.02,   (1963-1980)

This equation was also estimated by TSLS. See appendix to Chapter 5.

5.11.2.b   Government consumption deflator (PDGC) the public consumption deflator is a function of the wage rate index (W) and the consumer price index (CP). Since salary payment to civil servants forms the bulk of Government consumption expenditure, it is therefore expected that a rise in wage rates will have the effect of raising the level of the public consumption deflator. Beside wages and salaries, public consumption also includes numerous consumption goods purchased by the Government. The consumer price index is thus used to reflect the source of price increases due to consumer prices.   The estimate equation is given by:

Ln PDGC = 0.84 + 0.167 Lncp + 0.717 LnW   [5.54]
          (2.26) (2.04)   (3.96)

$R^{-2} = 0.988$, SEE = 0.035, d w = 0.75,   (1963-1980)

This equation was also estimated by TSLS. See appendix to Chapter 5.

5.11.2.c Private sector gross fixed investment deflator (PDI) PDI is related to the import price index for investment goods (PMKI), and unit labour cost (UNLCOL). PMKI is used to reflect material cost while UNLCOT captures the labour cost:

$$\text{Ln PDPINV} = -0\ 239 + 0\ 506\ \text{Ln PMKI} + 0.545\text{Ln UNCOL} \qquad [5.55]$$
$$\qquad\qquad (-1.09)\quad (10.16)\qquad\qquad\quad (6.26)$$

$R^{-2} = 0.983$, SEE = 5.678, d w = 0.96,   (1963-1980)

5.11.2.d Public sector investment deflator (PDGIN) PDGIN is related to the import price index for investment goods and unit labour cost.

$$\text{Ln PDGIN} = 5.39 + 0.034\ \text{Ln PMKI} + 0.907\ \text{Ln UNCOL} \qquad [5.56]$$
$$\qquad\qquad (1.64)\quad (1.92)\qquad\qquad (20.29)$$

$R^{-2} = 0.997$, SEE = 5.069, d w = 2.18,   (1963-1980)

In equation [5.56] PMKI is used to reflect material cost, while UNCOL reflects the labour cost.

5.11.3 The implicit GDP deflator (PDGDP)

PDGDP is a summary of the overall price performance in the in the economy. It consists of the consumption of the private and public sector and the private and public investment deflators as well as import and export prices weighted by their relative share in the gross domestic expenditure. That is [5.57]:

$$\text{PDGDP} = (\text{NGDPT/GDPT})*100 \qquad\qquad [5.57]$$

Where;
PDGDP = implicit GDP deflator
NGDPT = nominal gross domestic expenditure in millions of current Iraqi Dinar
GDPE = gross domestic expenditure in 1975 prices.

Since both GDPT and GDPE are determined in the model, the implicit GDP deflator can be derived from the above identity.

5.11.4 Export prices

This section will determine the prices of the pattern of export, which divided into oil export prices and non-oil export goods that are categorised into the export price of the primary goods and the export prices of the manufacturing goods.

Therefore, in this section we will estimate the oil export (as then determined) as a function of the world price of that commodity, converted into local currency Iraqi Dinar (I. D). Because the price of this commodity is determined in the international market and it has been observed that like most international commodity areas Iraq exerts very little influence on the prices of her exports, in our model we assume that Iraq is a price taker for almost all her primary exports. The domestic export of crude oil is then price determined as a function of the world price of that commodity converted into local currency I. D.

5.11.4.a Export price of crude oil exports (XPoil) XPoil is a function of world prices of crude oil export converted into I. D:

$$\text{Ln XPoil} = 2.4265 + 0.9514 \text{ Pxoil*EXCH} \qquad [5.58]$$
$$\qquad\qquad (16.21) \quad (26.34)$$

$R^{-2} = 0.996, \text{ SEE} = 0.5424, \text{ d w} = 1.70, \qquad (1960\text{-}1980)$

Where;
Pxoil	= world price of oil
I.D	= Iraqi Dinar/US$ exchange rate.

5.11.4.b Export price of the manufactured exports (PXMANU) unlike the primary commodities, manufactured goods are highly differentiated. As such it is expected that the manufacturers of these products may exercise some influence on the product prices. It is further assumed that the export price of manufactured goods in Iraq is influenced largely by the cost of production which includes both labour cost and material cost. Since the bulk of manufactured goods produced in Iraq are low-technology and labour intensive goods, an increase in both labour cost and intermediate imports would certainly have a significant effect in raising the cost of production. The export price of manufactured goods is thus made a function of the unit labour cost (UNCOL) and the import price index for intermediate goods (MPINTG). UNCOL is used to reflect cost of labour, while MPINTG the cost of material in the production of manufactured goods.

The estimated equation is:

$$\text{Ln PXMANU} = -1.7545 + 0.271 \text{Ln MPINTG} + 1.1092 \text{ Ln UNCOL} \quad [5.59]$$
$$\qquad\qquad\quad (-3.18) \qquad (3.56) \qquad\qquad (5.93)$$

$R^{-2} = 0.973, \text{ SEE} = 5.57, \text{ d w} = 1.52, \qquad (1962\text{-}1980)$

5.11.4.c Export price of primary commodities (PXPRIM) PXPRIM is constructed as a weighted export index of the major primary commodities exported. The weights used are derived from the relative share of each commodity in the 1970 total primary exports. The year 1970 is chosen because it is a base year for all price indices.

PXPRIM=0.10 XP Date+0.78 XP Leather +0.03 XP veg-oil+0.80 Xpgrain [5.60]

5.11.5   The general non-oil export price index (XP)

The general export price index is also a constructed price series. It consists of the export price index for the primary commodities and manufactured goods weighted by their relative share in 1970 gross exports.

$$GXP_{non\text{-}oil} = 0.75* XP \text{ Prim} + 0.25*XPMAU \qquad [5.61]$$

5.11.6   The import prices (MP)

MP is the price of all the categories of imports such as, the consumer, intermediate, and capital goods. In this section we will express each category individually.

The import prices of consumption, investment and intermediate goods are directly related to the corresponding world price indices. Furthermore, since the government is able to influence the import prices through import tariffs (MT) in the conversion of world prices into comparable local currency terms, variations in import tariffs have to be taken into account.

5.11.6.a   Import price of consumption goods (PMGC)

$$\text{Ln PMGC} = 0.686 + 1.127 \text{ Ln WPMC*TM*EH} \qquad [5.62]$$
$$\qquad\qquad (-3.90)\quad (31.47)$$

$R^{-2} = 0.942$, SEE = 4.71, d w = 1.57,   (1962-1980)

Where;
WPMC*MP*EH = import tariff adjusted
WPMC   = the world prices of consumer goods
TM   = average import tariff rate
EH   = ID/US exchange rate.

5.11.6.b   Import price of intermediate goods (PMINT) MINT is related to PWMINT * TM * EH. The estimated equation is:

$$\text{MINT} = 0.4601 + 0.883 \text{ Ln PWMINT*TM*EH} \qquad [5.63]$$
$$\qquad\quad (6.49)\qquad (6.19)$$

$R^{-2} = 0.93$, SEE = 0.319, d w = 1.10,   (1962-1980)

5.11.6.c   Import price of investment goods (MPKG) MPKG is a function of PWMK*TM*EH. The estimated equation is:

$$MPKG = 0.198 + 0.9357 \, Ln \, PW * TM * EH \qquad [5.64]$$
$$(0.933) \quad (2.0)$$

$$R^{-2} = 0.933, \, SEE = 8.43, \, d\,w = 0.76, \qquad (1962\text{-}1980)$$

5.11.7   The general import price index TMP

We estimate the function of price imports for all their categories together. By assuming that the prices of goods and services move together, the general import prices can be expressed as a function of the prices of all import commodities (MPG). The estimated equation is given by:

$$Ln \, TMP = 1.77 + 0.469 \, Ln \, MPG \qquad [5.65]$$
$$(6.19) \quad (11.06)$$

$$R^{-2} = 0.883, \, SEE = 0.1704, \, d\,w = 1.20, \qquad (1962\text{-}1980)$$

Where;
MPG = is a weighted price index, consisting of the export prices of consumption, intermediate and investment goods.

5.12   The balance of payments block (BP)

The balance of payments account is modelled through the identity of the overall balance.

$$BP = XG + S \, (oil + Nonoil \, commodity) - (MG + S) + NGT + NPT + NGB + NFI + EMTF + SDRS + IMF \qquad [5.66]$$

Where;
BP   = overall balance of payment account
XG + S   = export of goods and service in current prices
MG+S   = import of goods and services in current prices
NGT   = net government transfer abroad
NPT   = net private transfer abroad
NGB   = net public sector borrowing abroad
NFI   = net long-term foreign capital movements
EMTF   = net errors and omissions and short-term capital movements
IMFPC   = operations of the IMF financing facilities.

It is noted that, in the above identity both SDRS and IMFPC are jointly determined by the interaction between the government and the IMF on the other side. As such they are treated as policy variables. An attempt was then made to endogenous EXG+S, MG+S and NFI. Due to the difficulties of explaining NGT, NGB and EMTF satisfactorily, they are treated as exogenous variables in the model.

The relationship between the surplus and deficit in the balance of payments and the central bank's external reserves (NFABNI) is represented by the identity:

$$NFABNI = NFABNI_{t-1} + OBM \qquad [5.67]$$

Where;
NFABNI = net external reserves position of Central Bank of Iraq
OBM = overall balance of the balance of payment.

5.12.1 Merchandise imports

The imports are further disaggregated by economic classification into imports of consumption goods (MCG), imports of intermediate goods (MIM) and imports of investment goods (MINV). All imports functions are specified as domestic demand equations. As such, relative price terms are widely used to reflect either relative competitiveness of imported goods compared with domestic goods or in the case of non-competitive goods the relative *dearness* of imports. Of the three categories of merchandise imports, imports of consumption goods, imports of intermediate goods and imports of investment goods are being modelled as endogenous variables.

5.12.1.a Volume of consumption goods imports the demand for the imports of consumption is explained by private sector real consumption expenditure (Pcon), and relative prices of imported consumer goods to domestic price level (PMCG/PGDP). Private sector real consumption expenditure (Pcon) is used as an explanatory variable because in Iraq a significant portion of the private sector consumption is derived from imports. They are mainly in the forms of manufactured goods which include a wide range of products from toys and clothing to imported liqueurs and expensive foreign cars. Through the Government's import substitution industrialisation policy, some of these consumer products are now being manufactured locally. However, it is difficult to influence the taste and performance of the consumer to switch from foreign to domestically manufactured substitute, particularly those in the higher income brackets. It is therefore expected that imports of consumer goods will continue to constitute an important component of the private sector's consumption expenditure.

The relative price terms measure the degree of substitution between domestically produced consumer goods and imports, while the dummy variables are introduced in the equation to account for the sudden jump in the value of imports of this category in 1974 (DL74). However, we introduced the import tariff in the equation to reflect the effects of variation in export duties on the demand for imported consumer goods.

$$MCG = -29.10 + 0.140 \, Pcon - 118 PMCG/PGDP - 82.1 PMCG/PGDP_{t-1} + 61.70 DL74$$
$$\quad (-0.57) \quad (10.48) \quad (-1.95) \quad (-2.50) \quad (2.16)$$
$$\quad -0.837 TRM \qquad\qquad\qquad\qquad\qquad\qquad [5.68]$$
$$\quad (-3.21)$$

$R^{-2} = 0.97$, SEE $= 28.69$, d w $= 2.73$, \qquad (1964-1980)

The elasticity coefficient for real private sector consumption expenditure is 0.95, while the short and long-run elasticities with respect to the relative prices is 0.59. The import of consumption goods appears to be very sensitive in effect of oil revenues for the country, with an elasticity of 1.29. Meanwhile, the import tariff has a high coefficient in the equation with right sign and is significant statistically, with an elasticity of 0.15 which reflects mainly the effects of the import substitution policy pursued by the government in order to shift demand from imports to locally manufactured goods. This equation was also estimated by TSLS. See appendix to Chapter 5.

5.12.1.b Volume of imports of intermediate goods (MINT) the demand for the imports of intermediate goods is explained by the lagged values of manufacturing output (MANU) the relative prices (the ratio of import price index of intermediate goods to the investment expenditures deflator), ($MPINT_{t-1} / PDINV_{t-1}$), import tariffs (TRM100), and dummy variable (DL74) to account for the liberal import policy the government adopted in 1974. MANU is used to measure the level of effective demand for intermediate goods by the manufacturing industry. The reason for introducing (TRM100) as an explanatory variable has been explained in the earlier equation specifications. The estimated equation is:

$$MINT = 268 + 1.30 MAU_{t-1} + 328 DL74 - 2.95 TRM - 1.42 MPINT_{t-1} / PDINV_{t-1} \quad [5.69]$$
$$\quad (1.33) \ (3.53) \qquad (7.49) \qquad (-1.41) \quad (-2.59)$$

$R^{-2} = 0.959$, SEE $= 37.96$, d w $= 2.13$, \qquad (1964-1980)

The estimated coefficients indicate that in the long-run, imports of intermediate goods are sensitive to the long-run elasticities for MANUF and $MPINT_{t-1}/PDINV_{t-1}$ are 0.64 and -0.14 respectively, while the elasticity coefficient for import tariff is 1.03.

5.12.1.c Volume of investment goods imports (MINVG) the demand for the imports of investment goods depends on the level of real total investment activity (TRINV), relative prices $PMINVG_{t-1}/PDINV_{t-1}$, which is the ratio of the import price index of capital goods to the investment expenditure deflator, and the dummy variables (DL 74) to account for the value of the import policy the government adopted in 1974. Real current investment activity (TRINV) and its lagged values are used because most of the nation's investment goods come from imports. These variables serve the purpose of linking the level of imported investment goods to the level of investment activity. Relative prices on the other hand measure the relative 'dearness' of imported goods in relation to the locally produced investment goods. The imports of tariffs were introduced into the equation but its estimation gave a wrong sign, thus we dropped it from the equation of imported investment goods:

$$MINVG = -146 + 0.477\ TRINV + 59.7 TRINV_{t-1} + 227 DL\ 74 - 147 PMINV_{t-1}/PDINV_{t-1}$$
$$\qquad (-6.55)\quad (61.55)\qquad\quad (14.49)\quad (8.60)\qquad (-8.60)\qquad [5.70]$$

$$R^{-2} = 0.998,\ SEE = 17.56,\ d\,w = 2.38,\qquad (1964\text{-}1980)$$

Again all the estimated coefficients have the correct signs. Moreover, it is shown that in the long-run demand for imports of investment goods is sensitive to both real investment activity and prices. This equation was also estimated by TSLS. See appendix to Chapter 5.

5.12.2 Import of goods and services (TMG + Mser)

The total imports of goods and services are determined in the model through identity (69). Meanwhile, the real merchandise imports of services mostly travel and expenditures of embassies and military missions are taken to be exogenous.

The identity is given by; TMG + MSer is derived from the sum of its component parts:

$$TMG + mSer = MG + Mser \qquad\qquad\qquad [5.71]$$

Where;
MG   = imports of merchandise in current value
Mser   = imports of services in current value.

5.12.3 Merchandise exports (Xoil)

In this model, export has been divided into export of non-oil goods and oil exports. It is important to note here also that the non-oil goods consist mainly of agriculture goods and manufacturing goods.

The distinction between oil and non-oil export is made in order to bring out the importance of the oil sector in terms of its huge contribution to foreign exchange earnings in the country.

The export of oil is assumed, among other things, to be influenced by the volume of world economic activity represented in this analysis by the level of industrial production. This seems a reasonable assumption in the sense that petroleum is largely regarded as an input. Hence, we postulate that if the level of world economic activity rises, demand will rise and vice-versa. Also given that Iraq produces a large quantity of this commodity, we have assumed that the demand for Iraqi oil is affected by the relative price of Iraq oil to the world price of the same commodity. Although the existence of OPEC has almost cancelled out the differences in the oil prices of exporting countries coupled with the fact that there are differences in quality, we speculated that the Iraqi (an OPEC number producing an high grade of oil), oil prices can differ from the world's average price of the same commodity. It, therefore implies that if the export price of Iraqi oil falls relative to the world price for the commodity, more Iraqi oil will be in demand and vice versa.

Hence, the function of the demand for Iraqi oil export was determined by the exogenous variable such as the relative prices (the ratio of Iraqi oil exports to the world's prices), the industrial production index of the OECD countries, and two dummy variables, first to account for the impact of the nationalisation of foreign oil companies operating in Iraq, and the other is used to account for the effect of oil price rises on the volume of oil exports. All the above determinants of the equation are exogenous to the model. The problem of simultaneity bias does not arise and also is expected to give an unbiased and efficient estimate of this equation:

$$\text{Ln Xoil} = -8.7 - 1.13 \text{ Ln (PXoil/PW)} + 1.81 \text{ Ln INP} + 0.34 \text{ Ln Xoil}_{t-1} + 0.32 \text{DL } 73$$
$$\qquad\qquad (-1.19)\quad(-1.92)\qquad(2.03)\qquad\quad(2.66)\qquad\qquad(1.85)$$

$$+0.31 \text{DL } 72$$
$$\quad(1.79)\qquad\qquad\qquad\qquad\qquad\qquad\qquad\qquad\qquad\qquad [5.72]$$

$$R^{-2} = 0.98, \text{ SEE} = 0.03, \quad d\,w = 1.59, \qquad\qquad (1963\text{-}1980)$$

Where;
PXoil/PN = the ratio of Iraqi oil prices to the world prices of oil
INP   = industrial production index of the OECD countries
Xoil_{t-1} = lagged export prices
DL   = dummy variable to reflect the oil price rises in 1973
DL   = dummy variable to reflect the success of nationalisation of all oil industries in Iraq from foreign companies in 1972.

The equation [5.72] given the correct signs and significant statistically.

The result shows that the long-run elasticities of Iraqi crude oil export with respect to price and world activity (proxied by the OECD industrial production index), are -1.71 and 2.74 respectively. These elasticities seem quite high. They indicate how sensitive Iraqi oil exports are to these variables. The size of these elasticities seems consistent with Iraqi experience.

The oil dummies had significant effect, whereas the nationalisation of Iraqi oil had a positive effect on oil exports, the simultaneous mass oil discovery and oil price hike of 1973 indicate a positive effect.

5.12.3.a   The non-oil merchandise exports this section is divided into two categories: the first is the primary commodity exports, and the second is manufactured commodities exports.

5.12.3.a.i   The primary commodity exports (non-oil) (XPriMnoil) the export of primary commodities was influenced by both demand and supply conditions. Accordingly, this function will be accounted for by two estimations. First, we have postulated that this category of exports is determined by the ratio of the price of exports to the domestic price of these commodities, which is taken as a measure of the relative profitability of selling abroad to selling at home. The higher the ratio, the higher will be the incentive to export and vice-versa, and we introduced the per capita income (Pincom) in urban areas to account for the impact of the level of life in urban areas on the size of export and on the level of employment in agriculture sector.

In Iraq, there are organised marketing boards which announce the price of each commodity in advance, and the sales volume responds to this pre-announced price. Hence, we have allowed for this to be reflected in the specification of this equation by lagging the relative price variables by one period.

$$\text{Ln XPrim} = 19.4 - 0.0979 \text{ Ln Pincom} + 0.0166 \text{ Ln PXno}/P_{t-1} + 29.9 \text{ Ln WY}$$
$$(4.82) \ (-2.83) \qquad\qquad (2.03) \qquad\qquad (5.18)$$

$$+ 0.530 \text{ Ln Xprim}_{t-1} \qquad\qquad\qquad [5.73]$$
$$(2.70)$$

$$R^{-2} = 0.821, \text{SEE} = 5.149, \text{d w} = 1.95, \qquad (1963-1980)$$

Where;
PXno/P = the ratio of export price of non-oil goods in domestic currency to the
        domestic price level
WY   = the level of the world's economic activity: in analysis it is proxied by
        the OECD income
Xprim $_{t-1}$ = lagged of the primary goods exports.

From the above result, it can be seen that all the coefficients have the right sign and are statistically significant at the 5 per cent level. The coefficient of determination R^{-2} indicates that the equation has a good fit and *d w* obtained is also satisfactory.

With regard to the second estimation, primary commodity exports are directly related to the volume of commodities produced after taking into account the restocking or restocking of commodities, the volume of domestic consumption and the volume of import of the commodities for re-export.

Hence, the basic determinant of the relationship between production and export of commodities is identified by:

$$Vx_t = Vo_t - \Delta K_t - Cx_t + M_t \qquad [5.74]$$

Where;
Vx = volume of commodities produced
ΔK_t = change inventory
CX_t = volume of commodity consumed domestically
M_t = volume of commodity imported for re-exported.

In Iraq, in the case of the primary commodity, it is reasonable to assume that the above variables, which constitute the volume of commodity exports equation are relatively small and stable, and thus one can explain the factors which have an effect on the supply of Iraq's exportable which are equally important to explain export commodities.

Hence, the ability of the country to export such commodities depends on domestic production. Cairncrose and Maclean have argued that developing countries have failed to increase their exports because they have not produced enough (Yadav. Ram, Prakash 1975). Thus the hypothesis is examined that domestic production is a significant explanatory variable in export function. Theoretically, other things remaining constant, a positive relationship between export and domestic production is expected. Therefore, we will see in the following equation the test of the hypothesis, the impact of the domestic equation on the volume exports.

5.12.3.a.ii   Volume of primary commodities exports (XPrimG) XPrimG is a function of the output level of primary commodities exports. The estimated equation is given by:

$$Ln\ XPrimG = 0.609 + 0.921\ Ln\ PrPrimG \qquad [5.75]$$
$$(0.84)\quad (15.86)$$

$$R^{-2} = 0.958,\ SEE = 0.1813,\ d\ w = 2.18,\qquad (1963\text{-}1980)$$

In this case, the export price for this commodity is assumed to be determined in the world commodity markets. Moreover, it is assumed that demand for these commodities is perfectly elastic and thus the export supply functions determine the level of exports. The export prices do not enter the export supply functions directly but they have already been taken into account in the determination of output of this commodity.

5.12.3.b   The manufactured goods exports (XHAU) exports of manufactured goods have been growing rapidly since the early 1970s. This is due largely to a gradual shift in the industrialisation policy from import substitution to export promotion. Attractive incentive and generous financial assistance are provided by the government to promote the growth of manufactured exports. Among them are the refinancing facilities for export bills at favourable interest charges and the provision for tax deductible expenses incurred by companies in their export promotion missions abroad. However, the range of manufactured goods currently exported by Iraq is relatively small. The exports of manufacturing goods mainly are oil products, electrical machinery, footwear, and food. Although there is scope for further expansion for many other categories of manufactures, whether or not Iraq will succeed in increasing her export of manufactured goods depends mainly on its competitiveness in the international market as well as the intensity of the projectionist policy pursued by industrial countries where most of Iraq's manufactured goods are sold.

XMANU is treated as a demand equation in our model. The explanatory variables are the level of world real income (UY), the relative prices of Iraq's manufactured export's to the rest of the world price (PXMANU/PU), and a dummy variable to indicate the beginning of an active government's export promotion policy (DLPX), such as the expansion of export credit financing and exemption of duties in the import of certain materials to facilitate the growth of manufactured exports.

Two estimated equations for volume of manufactured exports: the first excludes the dummy variable (DLPX), and the second is estimated including a dummy variable (DLPX).

$$\text{Ln XMANU} = -3.19 + 1.01 \text{ Ln WY} - 0.689 \text{ Ln PXMANU/PW}_{t-1} \qquad [5.76]$$
$$\qquad\qquad (-7.17) \quad (14.31) \qquad (-1.87)$$

$$R^{-2} = 0.958, \text{SEE} = 0.2161, \text{d w} = 2.23, \qquad (1963\text{-}1980)$$

$$\text{Ln XMANU} = -2.90 + 0.955 \text{ Ln WY} - 0.664 \text{ Ln PXMANU/PW}_{t-1} + 0.126 \text{ Ln LPX}$$
$$\qquad\quad (-4.50) \quad\quad (7.39) \quad\quad (-173) \quad\quad\quad\quad\quad\quad (1.54)$$
$$\qquad\qquad\qquad\qquad\qquad\qquad\qquad\qquad\qquad\qquad\qquad\qquad [5.77]$$

$$R^{-2} = 0.946, \text{SEE} = 0.2241, \text{d w} = 2.18, \qquad (1963\text{-}1980)$$

From equation [5.77], the dummy variable term has a small 't' value, the estimated coefficient is correct with sign. The dummy variable term is retained in order to give us an indication as to the effect of the government's export promotion policy in the exports of manufactured goods.

The estimated coefficients in equation [5.76] indicate that the manufactured exports are the most sensitive to world demand condition with an elasticity coefficient of 1.01. The price elasticity of demand at -0.69 tends to be on the low side.

154

5.12.3.c Exports of goods at current value (TXG) TXC is obtained by summing up all the components determinants:

$$TXG = XPrim + XManu + Xoil \qquad [5.78]$$

Where;
Xprim   = current value of primary goods exports
XMANU = current value of manufacturing goods exports
Xoil   = current value of crude oil exports.

5.13 The government activities block

This section deals with the determination of the public sector's revenue and development expenditures. The financing of the public sector's development expenditures is also treated.[22]

5.13.1 Development expenditure

The level of development expenditure in nominal terms is determined in the model by the growth rate of the nominal gross domestic production (GRGDP), and the targets set in the development plans (PLANTARG) GRGDP is used to capture the responsiveness of the government's spending decisions with respect to the state of the economy. PLANTARG is used to capture the relationship between the planned and actual level of development expenditure. The estimated equation is:

$$DET = 981 - 11.3\ GRGDP + 0.350\ PLANTARG \qquad [5.79]$$
$$(2.67)\ (-2.18) (5.97)$$

R^{-2} = 0.80, SEE = 2992, d w = 1.20,   (1968-1980)

All estimated coefficients have the correct signs and are statistically significant. It is shown that the actual level of spending of the development expenditure is closely related to the planned level. The government does however seem to take a counter cyclical role in the implementation of its development spending. The elasticity coefficients for GRGDP and PLANTARG are 0.30 and 0.53 respectively.

This equation was also estimated by TSLS. See appendix to Chapter 5.

5.13.2 Total government revenues (GR)

The major sources of Government revenues spanning the period 1968-1980 are mentioned in Chapter 3.

In the case of Iraq, the financial policy was designed as an instrument to attain socio-economic objectives. Therefore, the tax structure in Iraq is not designed for the purpose of generating revenues, but also for the purpose of achieving certain socio-economic aims. For example, the government has been especially successful in the promotion of investment in the modern sector through such fiscal incentives as the accelerated depreciation-allowance, tax exemption on the creation of new imports, particularly crucial raw materials and machinery; and import duties on certain goods which are also locally produced. At the same time the tax policy has been used to encourage the growth of private savings; for reducing the pressure of import inflation; and for raising the income levels of the poorest farmers through direct subsidies.

Since 1970, Government revenues have grown very rapidly, especially from oil exports, it averaged 37.2 per annum for the period 1970-1980, compared with a growth 27.2 per cent in nominal GDP over the same period. As a result, the share of the public sector's claim on total economic resources has expanded. This development is quite commonly observed among developing countries as the Government sector widens its activities. The main reasons that account for the rapid growth in revenue are: a significantly high rate of growth of real output, an increase in the oil revenue sector, and the developed tax-collection machinery.

In this model, total Government revenue is divided into oil revenues (OilR), direct taxes (DTX), and indirect taxes (INDTX), and finally other revenues (OTHTX). Within these categories, the oil revenues are the largest component (see for more detail, Chapter 3). The total government revenues are:

$$TGR = OiLRN + DTX + INDTX + OTHTX \qquad [5.80]$$

Where;
TGR = Total Government Revenues
OilR = Oil Revenues
DTX = Direct Tax
INDTX = Indirect Tax
OTHTX = Other Tax.

5.13.2.a Oil revenues in this model, we treated the oil revenues as an exogenous variable.

5.13.2.b Direct tax (DTX) DTX is included on the personal tax, company tax and income tax of the petroleum companies; therefore the estimate of these three categories of tax are given by three equations:

$$Per\ DTX = tw * (WS_{t-1}) - NCPWS_{t-1} \qquad [5.81]$$

Where;
PeDTX = personal tax
Tw = tax parameter on wage and salaries
NCWS = non-taxable component of wages and salaries.

$$COMDTX = tc *(Ycs_{-1}) - NCCWS_{-1} \qquad\qquad [5.82]$$

Where;
tc   = tax parameter for company tax
Ycs   = corporate sector's income
NCCWS = non-taxable component of corporate income.

5.13.2.c   Income tax payment of petroleum companies (oilcomTX) the revenues collected by the Iraqi government until 1973, when the government nationalised most of the foreign oil companies:

$$OilcomTX = tpc * PCFIT_{t-1} \qquad\qquad [5.83]$$

Where;
tpc   = tax parameter for petroleum companies.

Both profit tax rate, tpc, and company tax rate, tc, are uniformly applied to all companies. While tax parameter on wages and salaries, tw, is computed by taking a weighted average of average tax rated across different income categories. The weightings are derived from the relative shares of each income category in the total taxable income.

5.13.2.d   Indirect tax (INDTX) this category of tax includes import duties and excises duties and others. Historically, export and import duties were the only sources of government revenue, but rapid economic growth and structural diversification. Since the early 1950s has alternated this resource of revenues. As noted above, direct taxes are most likely going to replace indirect tax as the major source of government revenues in the near future, but indirect tax will remain an important source of government revenue in the immediate future. As a result, the government is now less dependent on the export and import duties to fund its expenditure programs. This means that more options are now available to the government in its design and execution of both the export and import tariffs structure to achieve other more pressing socio-economic objectives such as raising the income level of the small holders through a reduction in export duties of some goods or a reduction in import duties on the essential imports in order to reduce the pressure of imported inflation on the lower income group.

The revenue from indirect taxes is further disaggregated into export duties (EXDU), import duties (IMDU), excise duties (CISDU), sales tax, road tax, cash payment by foreign oil companies ... etc., other indirect taxes. Both export and import duties are expressed as the product of the tax base and the related tax parameters. While excise duties are a function of value of output of the manufacturing sector and the rate of growth of nominal GDP, sale tax is made a function of the level of nominal GDP. The other components of indirect tax are treated as exogenous variables.

5.13.2.e The indirect taxes (INDTX)

INDT = IMDU + EXDU + SALDU + CisDU +THDU   [5.84]

Where;
IMDU   = import duties
EXDU   = export duties
SALDU   = sale duties
CisDU   = excise duties
THDU   = other duties.

5.13.2.f Import duties (IMDU)

$$IMDU = tm * (MG * MPI)/100 \qquad\qquad [5.85]$$

Where;
tm   = import tax rate.

5.13.2.g   Excise duties (CisDU) CISDU is a function of value of the manufacturing sector's output of manufacturing sector (MAU), and the growth rate of nominal GDP (RGGDP). The MANU is used as excise duties are collected mainly from manufacturing industry, while the RGGDP is always used as an indicator for the level of economic activities. The estimated equation is given by:

CisDU = 3.55 + 0.0510 MAU + 0.044 RGGDP   [5.86]
      (1.23)   (8.74)   (2.30)

R^{-2} = 0.98, SEE = 4.939, d w = 2.18,   (1963-1980)

The estimated coefficients show that the elasticity coefficients with respect to MANU and RGGDP are 0.79 and 0.063 respectively. This equation was also estimated by TSLS. See appendix to Chapter 5.

5.14 The financial sector block

In this section, we shall only be concerned with the determination of the supply of high powered money and reserve money which was taken as exogenous in the monthly model. It is assumed that when in equilibrium, the demand of money would be equal to the supply of reserve money. Algebraically,

RM = qR + CiR + NFsstB + NCG + LPS + OTH   [5.87]

Where,

RM   = reserve money or 'high-powered' money
qR   = required reserve
CiR   = currency in circulation
NFsstB   = net foreign assets of the central bank
NCG   = net credit to the government
LPS   = leading to the private sector
OTH   = other items.

The components to the left of the identity are associated with the demand for reserve money while the terms to the right are identified with the determinants of the supply of reserve. It is observed that in the case of an open economy supply of reserve money is strongly influenced by the balance of payments as reflected by net foreign assets of the Bank (NFsstB), and by the Central Bank's net lending to the government (NCG).

In our model, the equation explaining reserve money is treated as a linkage equation relating variations in reserve money to its sources. That is, reserve money is made a function of net foreign assets of the Central Bank (NFsstB), net credit to the government (NCG) and other financial changes initiated by the Central Bank (OTF).

$$RM = 22.2 + 0.958 \ NFsstB + 1.02 \ NCG + 1.89 \ (OTF) \qquad [5.88]$$
$$ (0.54) \quad (43.43) \qquad (21.45) \quad (2.90)$$

$$R^{-2} = 0.999, \ SEE = 20.94, \ d \ w = 0.85, \qquad (1965\text{-}1980)$$

This equation was also estimated by TSLS. See appendix to Chapter 5.

The elasticity coefficients for NFsstB, NCG and OHF are 0.51, 0.22 and 0.31 respectively. As expected the inflation of payments through the net foreign asset position of the central bank is found to have the most powerful influence on the reserve money. This equation suffers from serial correlation. The reason behind this problem lies in the incomplete set of data available to the researcher. In estimating this equation, the Central Bank definition of equilibrium in reserve money was used and it is thought that it caused the equation to behave in the manner reported above.

Notes

1. The total number of predetermined variables in our model exceeds the total number of observations, or, there is insufficient degree of freedom to estimate the first stage equations. In view of this information, the TSLS method is modified as follows; in the first stage the explanatory endogenous variable is estimated by using a selection of only those predetermined variables that are most closely related to the endogenous variables in the equation rather than using the full set of predetermined variables. Having replaced the explanatory endogenous variable by its estimated value, the second stage least-squares once again to estimate the structural form equation.

2. For a detailed discussion on the alternative methods of estimation, see the following: C. F. Christ, 1966, *Econometric Models Methods*, John Wiley and Sons, Inc.; Dhrymes, 1970, *Econometrics: Statistical Foundation and Application*, Harper and Row Publisher; A.S. Goldberger, 1964, 'Econometric Theory', New York; John Wiley and Sons, Inc; J. Johnston, 1972, op. cit.; H. Theil, 1971, 'Principles of Econometrics', Amsterdam North Holland Publishing Company.

3. See Johnston, J. (1977), pp.312-13.

4. All the estimation by TSLS method in appendix to Chapter 5.

5. UNCTAD, 'Trade Prospects and Capital Needs of Developing Countries', *United Nations Publication*, Sales no. E.68.II. D.13, 1968, reprinted in 'The International Linkage of National Economic Models', edited by R. J. Ball (1973).

6. Abdul Kadur, Ahmed 1974, *The role of the oil sector in the economic development of Iraq*, PhD thesis, unpublished, West Virginia University.

7. NAFI, Zuhair Ahmed, 1976, *A Description Of The Impact Of Crude Oil Export On The Economic Growth Of Iraq 1953-1970*, PhD thesis, unpublished, University of Graduate Studies, School of Business Administration, USA.

8. In fact, the attempt to include both lagged value added in manufacturing, imports of intermediate goods and employment in this sector was a failure. From the regression analysis, the following results have been obtained from the equation; the coefficients and ratio for the variables were respectively:

$$(-0.037 \ VMAU_{t-1} - 0.49 \ MINT - 0.00046 \ Employ \ MAU)$$
$$(-0.24) \qquad\qquad (-0.62) \qquad\quad (-0.076)$$

9. The studies on estimating consumer demand for developing countries based on flexible econometric techniques are rather scant. See Ray (1980) for India, Strauss (1982) for Sierra Leone, and Ahn, Singh and Squire (1981) for Korea.

10. Keynes' macroeconomics theory was expressed in terms of wages units, hence consumption function was: $(C/W) = a + (Y/W)$.
    Where; C= Consumption, Y= Income, W= Nominal Wages.

11. Dale W. Jorgenson (1961), 'The Development of A Dual Economy', Economic Journal 71, pp.309-34. J.C. Fel and G. Ranis (1961), 'A Theory of Economic Development', American Economic Review, 51, pp.533-4. A.C. Kelly, J.G. Williamsons and R.J. Cheetham (1972), 'Dualistic Economic Development: The Theory and History', University of Chicago Press and Peter, James and Jameson, Kenneth (1981), 'Economic Development: Competing Paradigmst', Washington, DC, University Press of America. Meanwhile, recently, many studies to estimate consumer theory in developed countries depend on the concept duality in consumer theory, see, Lau (1977). Also see Christensen, Jorgenson and Lau (1975), Christen and Manser (1977), Caves and

160

Christensen (1980), Berndt, Darrough and Diewert (1977), Simmons and Weiserbs (1979).

12. J.H.F. Schilderinck (1978) and Jere R. Behrman and James A. Hanson (1979).
13. Systematic tax collection in Iraq is still at its early stage of development. Apart from civil servant's income, which is recorded and taxed systematically, the private sector's and self-employed incomes are not well recorded and declared incomes though often inaccurate are not taxed properly.
14. For these arguments see, in particular Coghlan (1981), Laidler and O'Shea (1980) and Laidler and Bentley (1983).
15. Because of the unavailability of data about activity of foreign investment in Iraq, the model will not include the external private investment equation.
16. Wijnbergen (1982), op. cit. and Gupta, K. L. (1984), for example, estimated investment functions for a number of developing countries, current interest rate as explanatory variable, and see also, the sensitivity to the rate of interest in estimating the investment function, Van Wijnbergen (1983).
17. The wage rate series is estimated from the wages and salaries and total employment figures obtained from various issues of the Ministry of Planning, Department of Statistics National Account. Wage rate is defined as the average wage per man year. That is:
    WR = (WSSR/TEM)
    Where; WSSR = wages and salaries, TEM = total employment.
18. A. W. Phillip (1958) and, see also, Michael Summer (1984).
19. Charles L. Schultz and Joseph L.Tryon (1975) and Charles L. Schultz (1985).
20. Adam, F. and Behrman, R. (1982), Olivera, J.H.G. (1979), Canavese, A.J. (1982), Thompkinson, P. (1978), and Watcher, S. M. (1976).
21. Organisation of the petroleum exporting countries (1978) (OPEC), Annual Report, p.8.
22. See Chapter 3 for details about the important role of the government sector in economic development and the determinants of the expenditures of public sectors.

Further reading:

Cuthbertson, Hall and Taylor (1992), Carlin and Soskice (1990), Carlin and Soskice (1990), Hall (1994), Layard, Nickell and Jackman (1991), Mckibben and Sachs (1991) and Whitley (1992).

6 Historical dynamic simulation test 1968-1980

The purpose of this chapter is to examine the overall tracking performance of the Iraqi model. The results of the dynamic historical simulations for the period 1968-1980 are represented. The causes and effects of the simulation errors are also examined in order to reveal the important structural linkages in the model.

Before one can decide whether to accept or to reject a newly constructed model as a useful policy tool, the constructed model has to undergo a series of tests. In general, a good model should be able to track or predict the movements of the endogenous variables reasonably well, that is, within an acceptable margin of error. In addition, a good model should be able to respond to changes in the policy or exogenous variables in a manner which conforms to both economic theory and empirical observation. We shall assess the performance of the Iraqi model first by examining its tracking ability and then its sensitivity to policy changes. This chapter concentrates on the tracking ability of the model while the next chapter will examine the sensitivity of the constructed model when subject to various policy shocks.

6.1 Dynamic simulation path: 1968-1980

The tracking performance of the model is assessed by comparing the 'model solution' with the actual historical values for the most important variables in the model. The 'control' or 'base' solution of the Iraqi model is obtained by solving the values of all endogenous variables for the given values of exogenous and lagged endogenous variables. The constructed model is treated as a simultaneous equation system made up of n equations and n unknowns. However, due to the presence of non linearities in some of the equations, it is not possible to use the method of matrix inversion in solving the equation system. Instead, the solutions to the system are calculated through the use of Gauss-Seidel iterative procedures. Thus, with given initial conditions and for each period, the system iterates until successive values converge within a limiting amount for all endogenous variables in the system. In addition, the dynamic characteristics of the equation system are fully incorporated into the solution by using the system solutions for the earlier periods whenever lagged endogenous variables are encountered. Through this solution procedure, it is possible to analyse the secondary effects as well as the intertemporal response patterns of an initial 'shock' to the system.

However, one of the important requirements of a dynamic econometric model that purports to show the impact of macroeconomics variables (such as that presented above) relates to its tracking ability. That is, the extent to which the model is able to replicate the historical data. In order to accomplish this exercise, the parameter estimates obtained for all the behavioural equations, within the help of the identities, were solved dynamically. That is, the lagged values of the dependent variables were themselves generated by the model over the sample period. This method of evaluating and validating system like models may be very important because even when each individual equation may have a very good statistical fit (a conventionally measured), the whole model when put together may fail to reproduce the historical time series satisfactorily. Also, the individual equations of a model may perform poorly on standard statistical criteria and yet the model as a whole may be capable of generating the historical data rather closely. This may be so because,

"the single-equation model does not explain that the interdependencies that may exist between the explanatory variables are related to other variables. In addition, the single-equation mode explains causality in one direction, i.e. explanatory variable determine a dependent variable but there is no feed back relationship between the dependent variable and the explanatory variables" (Pindyc and Rubinfeld, 1981, p. 317).

To compare the dynamic solution values with the actual values, number of descriptive statistics have been devised. In order to examine how closely each endogenous variable tracks it's corresponding data series, some of the common techniques of assessing a model in this way are summary measures such as:

1. Mean absolute percentage error (MAPE)
2. Arithmetic means of the actual value of the predicted value
3. Root mean squared error (RMSE)
4. Root mean percentage squared error (RMPSE), and
5. Theil's inequality statistics U1 and U2.

The first measure MAPE is to take into account the size of average deviation of the solution from the true value while the second measure is used to capture the extent to which the model solution would overestimate or underestimate the true value. For this purpose we prefer to use the RMSE and or RMPSE which by constructions do not distinguish between negative and positive errors and indicate more accurately the true size of the errors. These measures are defined as follows:

163

1. Mean absolute percentage error (MAPE)

$$\text{MAPE} = \frac{1}{T}\sum_{t=1}^{T}\left|\frac{Y_t^s - Y_t^a}{Y_t^a}\right|*100 \qquad [6.1]$$

Where;

T_t = is the number of period of simulation

Y_t^s = is the solution value at time t

Y_t^a = is the actual value at time t.

2. Mean of actual, Mean of predicted values

$$\text{Mean of actual} = \frac{1}{T}\sum_{t=1}^{T}Y_t^a \qquad [6.2]$$

$$\text{Mean of predicted} = \frac{1}{T}\sum_{t=1}^{T}Y_t^s \qquad [6.3]$$

In Table 6.1 we present the summary statistics with respect to the performance of the endogenous variables in the model, while the graphical comparisons of the actual values and the base solutions for some of the endogenous variables as shown in Figure 6.1 (see appendix to Chapter 6). These graphs give indications of the ability of the model to capture turning points. In addition to graphical presentation, the actual values, the dynamic simulation values (denoted by 'predicated' in the figures), the difference as well as the percentage deviations between the two series are also shown.

From the summary statistics of Table 6.1, it is shown that the results of the base simulation are on the whole quite reasonable. Except for a few variables whose mean absolute percentage errors (MAPE) exceed 10 per cent, the error terms for most variables in the model are tolerable. Since there does not exist a standard performance benchmark against which the calculated summary statistics can be compared, it is extremely difficult to judge the 'goodness' of a model based on the error statistics alone. Moreover, in assessing the performance of a model, two major factors have to be taken into account. First, a model should only be compared with the other models of similar size, type and class, and secondly, the importance attached to the error statistics and the predictive ability of a model varies with the use the particular model is intended for.

Although, we depend on the MAPE measure to examine our model, it is useful to mention that there are many other statistics tests that can be used to examine how closely each endogenous variable tracks its corresponding data series. First there are root mean squared error (RMSE) and root mean squared percentage error (RMSPE). These measures are defined in 3. and 4. equations as shown below:

$$3. \quad \text{RMSE} = \sqrt{\frac{1}{T}\sum_{t=1}^{T}\left(Y_t^s - Y_t^a\right)^2} \qquad [6.4]$$

Equation 1 measures the deviation of the simulated variables from its historical time path. The magnitude of this error must be evaluated relative to be the mean value of the variable in the equation. This measure often gives a larger error more than MAPE.

With regard to the second measure RMSPE, Priovolos (1979) made a comparison of the RMSPE for the real GDP and consumer price index CP of the five similarly constructed developing country's models for a simulation period of 10 to 13 years. All the models selected by him were well constructed and displayed desirable properties. He found that for this model the RMSPE for the real GDP and CP were in the regions of 2.9 per cent - 5.3 per cent and 2.1 per cent - 9.1 per cent respectively. Against these figures, the RMSPE for real GDP and CP for the Iraqi model are 4.5 per cent and 0.007 per cent respectively. We can thus say that the Iraqi model compares favourably with those of other developing country models of similar size, the simulated results of using the RMSPE to examine the other variables of model are provided in Table 6.3. The measure of the root mean square percentage error is the same as RMSE but in percentage terms. It is defined as:

$$4. \quad \text{RMSPE} = \sqrt{\frac{1}{T}\sum_{t=1}^{T}\left(\frac{Y_t^s - Y_t^a}{Y_t^a}\right)^2} \qquad [6.5]$$

It is also recognised that a model which is intended primarily for policy simulations, need not necessarily have the same kind of tracking performance as a forecasting model. Sometimes it may even be desirable to sacrifice tracking ability for the sake of achieving better simulation properties. Since our model is intended mainly for policy analysis, we should not be unduly concerned if the error statistics in a few variables appear to be fairly large.[1]

In the value added block, the MAPE for agriculture, oil, other mining, construction, manufacturing, transportation and service are 7.18 per cent, 1.12 per cent, 9.81 per cent, 0.59 per cent, 1.56 per cent, 8.59 per cent and 9.58 per cent respectively. The solution value of the real GDP for each simulation is determined by the sum of the sectoral value added. In theory, the value of real GDP determined in this manner should be equal to the sum of the components of aggregate demand. However, in practice, the real GDP determined from the production side of the national accounts and that determined from the expenditure side of the national accounts are bound to differ. Therefore, in our model, a statistical discrepancy between the value of GDP (defined as the sum of supply components) is calculated. This statistical discrepancy can be treated as a measure of the compatibility of the national data and of the performance of the model when simulated (Adam, F.G. and Jonosi, P.E., 1966).

As shown in Table 6.2 below, the size of the statistical discrepancy in real and current terms as a percentage of real and nominal GDP is very small. This speaks well of the internal consistency of the model.

The MAPEs for the real and current GDP are 4.7 per cent and 4.1 per cent respectively, while the control solution tracks closely the historical values of both real and current GDP as earlier.

Table 6.1 Results of dynamic simulation: error statistics, means of actual and predicted values of selected variables

Variables	Actual	Predicted	MAPE
Agri. (value added in agriculture sector)	362.28	358.45	6.92
V oils (value added in oil sector)	2110.20	2110.20	1.12
V manuf. (value added in manufacturing)	289.05	293.05	9.81
V min. (value added in mining sector)	18.45	18.72	0.59
V cont. (value added in construction sector)	166.21	167.47	1.57
V tran. (value added in transportation sector)	211.28	211.28	8.59
V serv. (value added in service sector)	623.09	630.78	9.58
P cons. (private consumption)	667.01	670.70	0.99
GC (Government consumption)	599.93	593.00	5.21
P inves. (private investment)	79.13	81.30	4.10
G inves. (Government investment)	312.92	214.24	7.03
Pot manuf. (potential manufactured product)	697.37	697.37	6.39
Em. Agri. (employment in agriculture sector)	1221.0	1201.0	6.83
Em. Oth. (employment in other sectors)	1437.20	1437.30	5.23
W (wage rate)	347.48	347.48	0.16
CP (consumer prices)	82.32	82.39	0.31
Dpcon. (deflator of private consumption)	127.33	126.01	1.89
DGC (deflator of Government consumption)	119.59	118.84	0.48
PD inves. (deflator of private investment)	163.97	163.79	1.29
PDGinves.(deflator of Government investment)	166.78	166.78	1.85
X P oil (export of oil)	186.27	186.27	3.88
Xpmanuf. (export prices of manufactured goods)	151.40	152.10	6.30
XP prim. (export prices of primary goods)	151.40	157.30	4.00
PM CG (import prices of consumer goods)	149.90	149.20	3.90
PMINT (import prices of intermediate goods)	145.90	143.60	6.70
PMINV (import prices of investment goods)	194.70	194.50	2.10
TMP (import prices)	172.70	168.10	9.85
MCG (imports of consumer goods)	110.98	109.28	5.97
MINT (imports of intermediate goods)	180.20	181.69	2.95
MINV (imports of investment goods)	154.04	151.28	1.57
TMG (total imports)	1495.60	1496.40	0.8
X oil (oil export)	467.73	466.73	1.89
X prim. (exports of primary goods)	29.06	29.06	2.30
X prim. (export of primary goods)	12.09	12.09	1.22
X manuf. (exports of manufacturing goods)	25.08	24.87	1.86
DET (development expenditure)	646.68	646.72	65.70
CISDU (the excise duties)	45.46	45.46	8.98
RM (reserve money)	767.16	591.83	6.37
Y grain (the output of Grain)	1207.30	1215.50	12.60
Y oil vegt. (the output of vegetable oil)	2217.80	2155.30	7.80
Y date (the output of date)	1156.90	115.20	5.50

Table 6.2 Statistical discrepancy as percentage of GDP, control solution

Year	In real terms	In current terms
1968	2.08	2.00
1969	2.00	2.03
1070	1.84	2.40
1971	1.71	2.11
1972	1.65	2.05
1973	1.80	2.48
1974	1.36	1.38
1975	0.99	0.88
1976	0.87	0.95
1977	0.84	0.97
1978	0.80	1.03
1979	0.69	0.97
1980	0.53	0.80

In the simulation period, since 1974 the model seems to have consistently underestimated the true values. This could be due to the fact that the model had underestimated the growth of both the real and nominal GDP in 1974 and had also over predicted their declines in 1975. Due to the built-in dynamic structure in the model, the errors committed in these two years were then transmitted to the subsequent periods. The model is nevertheless able to keep the size of the error term from growing.

An examination of the simulated path of the GDP components reveals that the underestimation of the GDP during the period 1975-1980 is due mainly to the underestimation of value added in the oil sector, other mining, manufacturing and agriculture sectors. The extent of the underestimation, however, has been quite uniform from year to year. In the agriculture sector, the MAPE for the production of grains, and vegetable oil is particularly large. This is very much due to the volatile nature of the production of agriculture commodities.

A glance at the simulated analysis figures in Table 6.1 shows that for aggregate domestic demand and its components, the MAPE for private consumption and private investments are 0.99 per cent and 4.10 per cent respectively. The simulated path for private consumption is also successful in predicting its decline in 1973 and for three years in 1978, 1979 and 1980. The reason for this is found in the underestimation of the real disposable income of the wage earners in the same period, which in turn can be traced to the underestimation of employment in both agriculture and non-agriculture sectors. Tracing a further step backward, we end up in the underestimation of the real GDP output and real value added in the agriculture sector. We have thus completed a full cycle beginning and ending in the value added in the agriculture sector. In addition, this is an example which illustrates the intimate relationships that bind variables together in a simultaneous

168

equation model. There are too many loops and cycles in the model to be traced individually. However the effects of their interaction are all captured in the simulation results.

The MAPEs for Government investment and consumption expenditure are 7.03 per cent and 23.8 per cent respectively. While the simulated path for Government investment appeared to have traced out the historical values reasonably well, the solution values have consistently underestimated its true value by a small margin for the initial simulation periods. Except for the latest periods, the simulation path of the Government consumption MAPE is relatively high, this was mainly due to the large errors committed in 1974, 1975 and 1977.

The MAPE for export of goods is divided into the oil export and non-oil export, which is made up of two principal components, which are the exports of primary commodities and the exports of manufactured goods. The MAPEs for each of these two components are 2.30 per cent and 1.86 per cent respectively while the MAPE for the oil export is 1.86 per cent.

The components of real imports of goods that is being recognised include real imports of consumption goods, investment goods, and the imports of intermediate goods. The MAPE for these variables are 5.97 per cent, 1.57 per cent and 2.95 per cent respectively. The reason for a smaller MAPE for the total real imports of good than its component parts is due to the presence of offsetting errors. All the components of imports of goods appear to have performed reasonably well.

In the wage block, the MAPE for the wage rate is 0.15 per cent, while the MAPE for the employment in the agriculture and non-agriculture sectors are 1.0 and 6.83 per cent respectively. The simulation path for employment in the agriculture sector displays some volatility associated with the output of the agriculture sector, while the solution appears to have marginally underestimated its historical values since 1974.

In the price block, the MAPE for consumer price's index, the exports' prices of oil and imports' prices' index are 0.31 per cent, 3.88 per cent and 9.85 per cent respectively. The MAPE for the other deflator as well as the components of export and import prices appear to be performing well too.

In the Government sector, the MAPE of total public sector revenue such as excise duties is 8.99 per cent, while the development expenditure is 65.70 per cent. The large MAPE for the development expenditure is due to the fact that the error term was particularly large in 1974 and 1977, when the percentage deviation between the solution and the historical value represented 128.0 per cent. The MAPE for reserve money is 6.37 per cent, which displays a good tracking property too.

Bearing in mind the above mentioned tracking ability for the model, for this purpose most people prefer to use RMSE and/or RMSPE which by constructions do not distinguish between negative and positive errors and indicate more accurately the true size of the errors. These measures are defined in equations 3 and 4. As can be seen from Table 6.3, which provide the RMSE and RMSPE values of the variables reported, the simulation period is 1968-1980.

169

From Table 6.3 both measures have turned out low values indicating that the simulated values of all the variables considered (except very few variables), do not deviate too much from the actual or historical time path. This signals the fact that, in general, the model has been able to track the historical value of the endogenous variables reasonably well.

While, low RMSPE is one desirable measure of assessing the 'goodness of fit' of a model, a more decisive (important) criterion is how well the model simulates turning points in the historical data. In this case, a modeller is concerned with the ability of the model to track periods which correspond to turning-points in the endogenous variables. This criterion is considered to be more decisive than those discussed above because even when a model has a low RMSPE and/or, MAPE most economic investigates would, probably, reject it in favour of one which might have a higher RMSPE and /or MAPE if the better had a greater capacity to capture turning-points.

Table 6.3 Results of dynamic simulation: root mean squared error (RMSE) and root mean percentage squared error (RMSPE) for selected variables in model

Variables	RMSE	RMSPE
Value added in agriculture	29.5797	0.08907
Value added in oil	31.9594	0.14990
Value added of mining	0.02154	0.01068
Value added in manufacture	24.7750	0.0135
Value added in construction	16.1891	0.11750
Value added in transportation	53.0048	0.19506
Value added in service	81.6084	0.11270
Private consumption	11.4835	0.01159
Government's consumption	38.7039	0.06569
Private investment	52.8939	0.38830
Government's investment	62.5487	0.07238
Employment in agriculture	109.6142	0.08646
Employment in non-agriculture	102.0956	0.06121
Wage rate	11.8249	0.04850
Consumer price	0.5008	0.00540
Deflator of private consumption	2.2999	0.03137
Deflator of Government consumption	2.5073	0.02070
Deflator of private investment	20.6526	0.2442
Deflator of Government investment	4.44716	0.03213
Import of consumption goods	20.72623	0.22352
Import of intermediate goods	19.80434	0.2474
Import of investment goods	10.01402	0.07842
Export of oil	3.46470	0.0700
Export of primary goods	4.03811	0.14578
Export of manufacturing goods	2.80578	0.19965
Import prices of consumption goods	6.96637	0.04552
Import price of intermediate goods	3.94669	0.02660
Import price of investment goods	12.89233	0.08035
Export price of oil	3.46470	0.02725
Export price of primary goods	6.53240	0.04469
Export price of manufacturing goods	2.43460	0.06934
Expenditure of development	225.6200	2.10217
Non-oil Government revenues	4.3307	0.11454
Revenues of money	19.1816	0.07138
GDP implicit	2.4608	0.01830

However, we have also considered the other measure for use. Theil's Inequality statistics (U1 and U2) are always presented both in levels and changes. U1 is expected to take any value among zero and unity. The closer to zero the value of U1 is, the better the predictive ability of the model. However, because the normalisation in U1 is influenced by the predictions in the deflator, U2 has always been regarded as a better indicator than U1. U2 itself can take any value among zero and infinity. The smaller this statistic is, the better the tracking ability of the model. Even for this U2 statistic, the uses of changes have a better interpretation than when the levels are used to assess the predicting power of a model. This is because there is no measuring rod (in a quantitative sense) with which to compare the figures generated (when U2 in levels are used) in order to ascertain whether or not the model predicts well. For instance, how small should U2 (in levels) be before a model can be taken to predict its historical path well? The use of changes, on the other hand, allows one to compare the model with the naive-no-change model. It then implies that if the value of U2 (using changes) obtained is equal to 1, our model performs as well as a naive-no-change model and indicates a correspondingly poor predicting ability. If U2 (using changes) is greater than 1, it signifies that our model is worse than a naive model in predicting that particular variable for which the value of U2 (using changes) is greater than 1 and vice versa.

Thus Theil's inequality statistics (U1 and U2) are (for variable Y) calculated as follows:

$$0 < U_1 \text{(levels)} = \frac{\sqrt{\sum_{t=1}^{T} \left(Y_t^s - Y_t^a\right)^2}}{\sqrt{\sum_{t=1}^{T} \left(Y_t^s\right)^2} + \sqrt{\sum_{t=1}^{T} \left(Y_t^a\right)^2}} \leq 1 \qquad [6.6]$$

$$0 < U_2 \text{(changes)} = \frac{\sqrt{\sum_{t=1}^{T} \left(\Delta Y_t^s - \Delta Y_t^a\right)^2}}{\sqrt{\sum_{t=1}^{T} \left(\Delta Y_t^s\right)^2} + \sqrt{\sum_{t=1}^{T} \left(\Delta Y_t^a\right)^2}} \leq 1 \qquad [6.7]$$

$$0 < U_2 \text{(levels)} = \frac{\sqrt{\sum_{t=1}^{T}\left(Y_t^s - Y_t^a\right)^2}}{\sqrt{\sum_{t=1}^{T}\left(Y_t^a\right)^2}} \leq \infty \qquad [6.8]$$

$$0 < U_2 \text{(changes)} = \frac{\sqrt{\sum_{t=1}^{T}\left(\Delta Y_t^s - \Delta Y_t^a\right)^2}}{\sqrt{\sum_{t=1}^{T}\left(Y_t^a\right)^2}} \leq \infty \qquad [6.9]$$

Where,

$Y^a =$ is actual value of variable Y

$Y^s =$ is simulated value

$T =$ is number of period of simulation, and

$\Delta =$ is first difference operator.

Presented below in Table 6.4 are Theil's Inequality statistics (U1 and U2), both in levels and changes for most of the endogenous variables of our model. Judged by these statistics, it can be seen that the model performs well. Even U2 (using changes) has all its values less than unity indicating that the model is significantly better than the naive-no-change model in predicting all the variables. However, it can be seen that the model has been able to predict some variables better than some others. If we take U2 (using changes) development expenditure and the deflator of private investment seems to be the most poorly predicted, but even in this case, the model performs better than the naive-no-change model.

6.2 Conclusion

Based on the above discussion of graphs and tables on the performance of simulation of the model for the period 1968-1980, we can conclude that the model seems to be able to track most of the endogenous variables reasonably well.

Table 6.4 Theil's inequality statistics of the simulation exercise for the period 1968–1980

Economic Sectors		U(1) Statistic 0< U(1) <1		U(2) Statistic 0< U(2) <INF	
Name	Last Data	Levels	Change	Levels	Change
V. oil	1980/81	0.0073	0.0396	0.01432	0.0801
V. mining	1980/81	0.0039	0.0198	0.0078	0.0396
V. manuf.	1980/81	0.0330	0.1767	0.0661	0.3479
V. contra.	1980/81	0.0334	0.1053	0.0672	0.2033
V. trans.	1980/81	0.0997	0.5022	0.1975	0.8196
V. service	1980/81	0.0535	0.2159	0.1068	0.4193
Privet. Con.	1980/81	0.00316	0.0168	0.0063	0.0336
G. con.	1980/81	0.029367	0.24822	0.05855	0.4587
P. inv.	1980/81	0.0844	0.1847	0.1671	0.3698
G. inv.	1980/81	0.0242	0.1273	0.0484	0.2637
EM. Others	1980/81	0.03385	0.2230	0.0676	0.4983
Det.	1980/81	0.1432	0.4227	0.02802	0.9151
Reserve M.	1980/81	0.0127	0.0275	0.0254	0.0546
G. revenue	1980/81	0.0395	0.1577	0.0788	0.3173
PC	1980/81	0.0029	0.0422	0.0059	0.0858
PDGC	1980/81	0.0104	0.1954	0.0207	0.3637
PDP con	1980/81	0.04189	0.3111	0.0365	0.5550
PDG invt	1980/81	0.0120	0.0565	0.0241	0.1135
Mining	1980/81	0.0194	0.0429	0.0382	0.0843
Mintm	1980/81	0.0530	0.1101	0.10428	0.2294
MCG	1980/81	0.0707	0.1646	0.1385	0.3375
Poil	1980/81	0.0227	0.1206	0.0456	0.2332
Tmp	1980/81	0.0021	0.0108	0.0041	0.0217
W	1980/81	0.0144	0.0760	0.0288	0.1511
PDPINV	1980/81	0.1218	0.3906	0.2492	0.9466
XPRIM	1980/81	0.0647	0.2179	0.1289	0.4139
XMAU	1980/81	0.0398	0.1210	0.0791	0.2348
PotMAU	1980/81	0.0323	0.1551	0.0645	0.2956
Xoil	1980/81	0.0020	0.0005	0.0004	0.0006

Note

1. All satisfactory equations in the model are then subjected to simulation within the sample period so as to assess the validity of the model in terms of its response to certain exogenous shocks. Other simulation exercises will be approached adopting standard counterfactual simulation techniques.

Further reading:

Artis, M.J., Bladen-Hovel, R. and Zang, W. (1992), Britton and Pain (1992), Granger and Newbold (1986), Hendry and Clements (1992), Keating (1985a), Litterman (1986), Mcnees (1991, 1982, 1986), Osborn and Teal (1979), Turner (1990), Wallis (1989) and Wallis and Whitley (1991b).

7 The impact of the multiplier and sensitive analyses on the macroeconomic model of the Iraqi economy

The examination of the macro-econometric model is not complete until multiplier analysis is explored. Multiplier analysis examines the path that the system follows, when it is subjected to an exogenous shock, and sees whether it corresponds to a priori information derived from economic theory. The dynamic multiplier provides a measure of both the magnitude and time response pattern of endogenous variables to changes in an exogenous variable. Dynamic multiplier-analysis also checks on the stability of the model. The system is provides considered stable if the dynamic multipliers become smaller and smaller in absolute value and converge to some finite over time, i.e., the sum of the dynamic multiplier is finite.

The purpose of this chapter is to examine the sensitivity of the Iraqi model when subjected to alternative policy shocks. In this chapter a number of simulations are carried out in order to determine the behavioural characteristics of the model as well as to see if the individual variables in the model behave properly under different perturbations. To compare the effect of the various policy shocks on the model, the dynamic historical period solution for the period 1968-1980 was used throughout the study as the base solution or 'bench mark' for comparison.

Policy changing can be imposed on the model through various means. Some of these techniques used are:

1. By changing the value of an exogenous variable while keeping all other exogenous variables unchanged; or
2. By first exogenousing or endogenous variable and then assigning to the variable a different set of values from its base solution. In our study, we will be using both methods in affecting changes, to show the effects of policy change.

Furthermore, as the focus of the constructed model is mainly on the short-run stabilisation policies, the following exogenous shock and policy measures are being considered:

1. A one-period 15 per cent increase in oil export in 1970

2. A sustained 10 per cent increase in the money supply for the period 1970-1980
3. A sustained 10 per cent increase in government consumption for the period 1970-1980
4. A sustained increase in the direct taxes by 5 per cent for the period 1970-1980
5. A sustained 5 per cent point increase in the export duties for the period 1970-1980
6. A sustained 15 per cent reduction in the export prices for the period 1970-1980
7. An sustained 15 per cent increase in the export prices for the period 1970-1980.

The results of the above simulation tests are presented and analysed separately.

7.1 A one period 15 per cent increase in oil export in 1970

Since the 'export of oil' variable is endogenous in the system, we first exogenous it and then solve the model under this condition. This solution is considered to be the original solution. We then assumed that increase in the volume of oil exports in 1970 by 15 per cent and solved the model to obtain the control solution. The increase in the volume of oil exports causes nearly every variable in the system to increase. See Table 7.1. The 15 per cent increase in oil exports results in about a 13.51 per cent increase in total GDP in the first year. In the second year, the percentage increase in the total GDP declined sharply to about 1.31 per cent and continued in this direction in the years after. These results are due to the fact that the 15 per cent increase in the volume of oil exports in 1970 is a non-sustained one; it caused oil-GDP to increase by about 22.51 per cent in the same year and declined sharply in the subsequent years. Consequently, the 13.51 per cent increase in total GDP in the first year came mainly from the 22.51 per cent increase in value added in the oil sector. The small percentage increase in total GDP in the subsequent years came solely from non-oil GDP. The response of non-oil GDP to the increase in oil exports is very small; it increased by only 5.28 per cent and by the third year the increase was only 0.25 per cent. Import and prices increased because of the increase in domestic demand. These results indicate that the oil sector in general, and oil exports in particular, have little effect on domestic non-oil economic activities and the major part of the gain from these exports comes through their effect on domestic demand. The implication of this simulation experiment is that in order for Iraq to benefit from a sharp stimulus and enter an era of sustained growth, it must launch an attack on the limits that restrict its absorptive capacity and use its oil revenues more efficiently.

Comparing the effects of the 15 per cent increase in the price of oil with the 15 per cent increase in the volume of oil exports, we can say that both have expansionary and inflationary effects on the economy, but the effects are larger in the case of the increase in the volume of oil exports; even though the increase in both government consumption and government investment resulting from both shocks (the increase in oil exports and the increase in oil prices) are almost of the

Table 7.1 A one-period sustained 15 per cent points in oil exports in 1970

Economic sectors	1970	1971	1972	1973	1974	1975	1976	1977	1978	1979	1980
Total G.D.P.	13.51	4.33	1.03	1.31	0.97	0.32	0.53	0.17	0.34	0.57	0.00
Real G.D.P.	5.28	0.97	0.25	0.56	0.24	0.31	0.23	0.10	0.18	0.22	0.00
V. add. agriculture	0.04	0.04	0.09	-0.08	0.03	0.04	0.05	0.02	0.01	0.00	0.00
V. add. oil	20.4	0.00	0.00	0.00	0.00	0.00	0.00	0.00	0.00	0.00	0.00
V. add. mining	0.00	0.00	0.01	0.00	0.00	0.01	0.00	0.00	0.00	0.00	0.00
V. add. oil	22.51	0.27	0.24	0.25	0.74	0.01	0.33	0.10	0.16	0.48	0.00
V. add. construction	2.78	2.11	1.03	1.02	0.81	0.94	0.85	0.25	0.30	0.30	0.00
V. add. manufacturing	2.06	1.01	0.55	0.23	0.04	0.05	0.05	0.03	0.02	0.02	0.00
V. add. transport	1.81	1.71	1.23	0.00	0.79	0.73	0.23	0.03	0.02	0.03	0.00
V. add. services	2.24	2.04	1.78	0.94	0.48	0.35	0.20	0.20	0.15	0.10	0.00
Gov. consumption	3.15	2.99	0.34	0.16	0.16	0.20	0.09	0.04	0.11	0.09	0.00
Gov. investment	12.84	9.05	6.47	6.45	1.01	0.00	0.00	0.00	0.00	0.00	0.00
Private consumption	3.60	0.01	-0.22	0.27	0.32	0.05	0.15	0.26	0.01	0.05	0.00
Private investment	0.85	3.84	1.99	1.19	1.21	0.24	0.15	0.12	0.12	0.14	0.00
Import	7.62	4.12	2.03	1.05	0.83	0.36	-0.12	0.06	0.04	0.00	0.00
Export	8.54	6.29	4.22	0.40	0.84	0.14	0.13	0.03	0.22	0.40	0.00
Aggregated demand	9.44	1.09	1.09	0.77	0.46	0.77	0.36	0.19	0.39	0.14	0.00
Price index '75=100	1.67	1.47	0.99	0.85	0.36	0.20	0.20	0.15	0.13	0.08	0.00
GDP deflator	3.77	1.17	0.37	0.05	0.40	0.30	0.25	0.21	0.11	0.09	0.00
Employment in agri.	0.19	0.64	-0.60	-0.11	-0.04	-0.06	-0.08	-3.33	0.00	0.00	0.00
Employment in others	0.06	0.07	0.09	0.16	0.09	0.14	0.13	0.05	0.03	0.07	0.00
Real wages and salaries	8.66	6.06	2.11	1.05	0.43	0.10	0.06	0.05	0.09	0.06	0.00
Rate of wages index	7.07	4.91	2.03	0.91	0.35	0.22	0.12	0.09	0.02	0.03	0.00
Gov. revenues	12.15	8.24	1.29	0.98	0.52	0.05	0.29	0.08	0.19	0.48	0.00
Money supply	115.85	7.30	2.81	1.18	-0.23	-0.11	-0.16	-0.33	-0.28	-0.13	-0.0
Balance of payments	543.71	-60.20	-43.20	-39.60	1.00	-6.21	-18.50	-20.11	-14.20	-7.31	-2..0

Note: per cent deviation from control solution.

same magnitude, the increase in GDP which resulted from the former shock is much larger than that resulting from the latter shock. The reason is that oil export affects GDP in two ways: first, through its effect on the oil revenues, which directly affects both government consumption and government investment; secondly, more export of oil means more production of oil, which also means higher value added in the oil sector and hence, higher GDP.

7.2 A sustained 10 per cent increase in the money supply for the period 1970-1980

This simulation is carried out by raising the level of the nominal money supply by 10 per cent for the entire simulation period 1970-1980. The effects of this policy change on the most significant variables in the model are summarised in Table 7.2.

The initial impact of raising the level of the money supply was to stimulate the growth of bank credit. As expected both the bank's credit and the loan rate were affected. There was a rise in the commercial bank's loans and advances to the private sector as well as a decline in the loan rate. The availability of credit then stimulated the growth of private investment. Private investment. in 1970 was raised by 2.41 per cent from its base solution. The reduced loan rate was also a stimulant to both private consumption and investment. However, the initial impact on private consumption was relatively small. It nevertheless gathered momentum in 1974 and 1975, but declined after 1975 as a result of an increase in the domestic inflation rate. Thus by 1980 private investment was only 0.57 per cent high compared to its base solution value.

The impact of raising the level of money supply was to stimulate the increase of government investment. As expected the consumption of the government was affected. Government investment in 1970 was raised 9.79 per cent from its base solution. However, the initial impact on government consumption was relatively small compared with the government investment.

Meanwhile, there was a marginal improvement in the real export of goods which was mainly the result of an increase in manufactured exports. Real imports on the other hand rose even more rapidly, mainly stimulated by a higher level of aggregate demand. This situation then generated a decline in the balance of payment account which in turn created a drain on the 'high-powered' money. This is one of the reasons why the expansion of the money supply became less of a stimulation in the later part of the simulation period. In addition, the expansion of the money supply also brought about a higher inflation rate. Both the consumer price index and the GDP deflator were substantially raised.

As a result of the policy change, the total GDP and real GDP were raised. In 1970, real GDP was 1.79 per cent higher than its base solution, while total GDP was 2.34 per cent. However, as the inflation rate rose, the growth of real GDP was severely dampened. Thus by 1980, real GDP was 0.59 per cent higher than its base solution.

Compared with their base solutions, the employment in the non-agriculture (others) sectors were moderately higher. This was due mainly to an expansion of output for the non-agriculture sector. Meanwhile, employment in the agriculture sector was for most years lower than its base solution values, this was due to the decrease in output and the increasing immigration from rural to urban areas. Within the production sector, the output of the construction, manufacturing transportation and services sectors received a strong boost, while the production of the agriculture and the mining sectors were only marginally higher. This is because the level of output in construction, manufacturing, transportation and the services, was closely linked to the level of aggregate demand and the availability of credit. On the other hand credit only effected the agriculture sector indirectly through an improvement in crop yield and an expansion increase; both of which take a long time to effect output.

As a result of a higher level of economic activity wages and salaries received a strong boost. As a consequence of higher rates of domestic inflation, the wage rate variable in the model has also been raised.

7.3 A sustained 10 per cent increase in government consumption for the period 1970-1980

This policy simulation is carried out by increasing government consumption by 10 per cent for the entire period of the simulation. Government consumption is assumed to be financed completely by the Central Bank.

The effects of this policy change on the most important variables in the model are summarised in Table 7.3.

The initial impact brought about by a higher level of public consumption expenditure was an increase in the level of aggregate demand. Stimulated by higher real income, both private consumption expenditure and private investment were substantially raised. In 1970 for instance, private consumption was 4.38 per cent and 7.89 per cent respectively higher than their base solution. At the same time, the higher level of aggregate demand stimulated the growth of imports. Imports picked up quickly to reach a peak in 1975, but grew more slowly thereafter due to a smaller increase in real income, beside the government depended on the restriction of imports. Higher aggregate demand however, also brought about an increase in the inflation rate. Both the consumer price index and GDP deflators were higher than their base solution. A higher inflation rate then eroded the growth of real income. Thus, both real and total GDP began to follow a dampened growth path soon after the policy change was effected. Another reason for the growth of real GDP tapering off was due to the leakage of imports. This was noted with a higher inflation rate and assuming that the commodity prices which were determined in the world market were unaffected by the policy change, a reduction in real export price had occurred. This would then adversely affect the production decisions of the agriculture producers and thus, lead to a smaller volume of exports of goods. In

Table 7.2 A sustained 10 per cent increase in the money supply for the period 1970 -1980 for selected variables

Economic sectors	1970	1971	1972	1973	1974	1975	1976	1977	1978	1979	1980
Total GDP	2.34	2.79	3.06	3.67	6.62	4.87	2.67	2.86	2.60	4.74	3.56
Real GDP	1.79	1.71	1.47	1.15	1.71	1.68	1.09	0.43	0.89	0.60	0.59
V. add. agri.	0.07	0.09	0.19	-0.20	0.24	0.23	0.24	0.18	0.07	0.06	0.05
V. add. mining	0.00	0.00	0.00	0.00	0.01	0.03	0.01	0.00	0.00	0.00	0.00
V. add. construction	1.42	2.04	3.01	2.05	2.36	1.59	0.27	1.10	1.18	1.07	1.02
V. add. manufacturing	2.13	3.01	2.10	2.08	2.10	1.25	1.24	1.13	0.48	0.13	0.03
V. add. transport	0.12	0.04	0.03	0.01	0.13	0.18	0.13	0.07	0.01	0.01	-0.04
V. add. services	1.20	2.10	2.10	1.12	1.46	0.28	0.39	0.19	0.11	0.03	0.04
Gov. consumption	0.36	1.14	1.33	1.59	2.45	2.83	1.66	1.13	0.40	0.29	0.13
Gov. investment	9.79	9.99	8.49	5.43	5.19	4.10	4.42	3.18	3.54	3.05	2.23
Private consumption	0.42	1.03	1.43	1.72	2.28	2.29	0.73	1.74	0.71	0.98	0.92
Private investment	2.41	4.11	4.89	3.90	3.11	2.01	1.93	1.78	1.49	0.95	0.53
Import	1.29	1.30	2.06	3.15	1.85	1.85	1.58	1.27	1.19	1.20	1.03
Export	0.27	0.73	0.43	1.08	6.05	0.79	0.64	0.16	1.07	0.29	0.22
Aggregate demand	1.84	2.48	2.27	3.20	3.30	4.21	2.76	2.90	2.93	2.29	2.00
Price index '75=100	1.02	1.01	1.12	1.27	2.02	2.03	1.11	1.95	1.61	1.46	1.15
GDP deflator	2.62	2.73	2.71	2.61	2.62	2.71	2.90	2.79	3.40	3.29	3.18
Employment in agri.	0.42	1.61	-1.15	-0.29	0.26	-0.33	-0.36	-1.30	0.00	0.00	0.00
Employment in others	1.23	1.68	1.28	0.45	0.65	0.82	0.66	0.23	0.16	0.54	0.10
Real wages and salaries	1.41	1.15	1.22	1.55	0.96	0.54	0.37	0.28	0.45	0.46	0.39
Rate of wage index	0.67	0.97	1.62	0.76	0.34	0.14	0.94	0.85	1.20	0.75	0.32
Gov. revenues	1.00	1.60	1.55	2.65	3.77	1.25	1.43	1.36	0.95	1.49	1.15
Money supply	10.00	10.00	10.00	10.00	10.00	10.00	10.00	10.00	10.00	10.00	10.0
Balance of payments	-61.90	-166.8	-217.9	-273.1	-348.6	-363.7	-383.0	-410.2	-394.2	-440.6	-501.1

Note: per cent deviation from control solution.

the case of manufactured exports, on the other hand, a higher inflation rate caused a rise in both the costs of production and the selling prices of manufactured goods. These rendered manufactured goods less competitive in the world markets. The combined effect was a reduction in the volume of real exports. A small decline in exports coupled with a sharp increase in imports implied the balance of payment account had been adversely affected. The current account of the balance of payments suffered a significant reduction. For instance, in 1970 the current account balance of payments was I.D 179.4 million lower than its base solution. Moreover, the decline in this balance appeared to be worsening over time. Thus by 1980, the fall in current account had reached I.D 823.8 million.

The decline in the components of the balance of payments then set in motion a drain on 'high-powered' money, which in turn led to a reduction in the money supply and bank credit as well as an increase in the loan rate. All these exerted a powerful brake on the growth of real output.

With the exception of the mining and transportation sectors, output in all other sectors of the economy were raised. The stronger initial impact was on the production of the manufacturing sector. However, due to a decline in the exports of manufactured goods and slower growth in aggregate demand, the growth of manufactured goods soon tapered off. Thus, while in 1970, the output of the manufacturing sector was 3.92 per cent above its base solution, it was only 0.23 per cent higher in 1980. The output of the construction sector also followed a very similar time response pattern.

In response to a smaller volume of agriculture output, employment in the agriculture sector declined, except in the first year, growth of real output in other sectors of the economy stimulated an increase in non-agriculture employment. Similarly, the earnings of the agriculture sector were depressed, while the wage earners benefited from the policy change. Meanwhile, the acceleration in domestic inflation rate as well as the gains made in labour productivity triggered an increase in the wage rate.

In addition, the size of the impact multiplier of the policy change on the real output was calculated by using the following expression:

$$\text{Impact multiplier} = \frac{GDP_t^a - GDP_t^b}{GC_t^a - GC_t^b} \qquad [7.1]$$

Where;

GDP_t^a = Real GDP for (t) 'disturbed path'

GDP_t^b = Real GDP for control path

GC_t^a = Government consumption for year (t) 'disturbed solution'

GC_t^b = Government consumption for year (t) 'control solution'.

Table 7.3 A sustained 10 per cent increase in government consumption for the period 1970-1980

Economic sectors	1970	1971	1972	1973	1974	1975	1976	1977	1978	1979	1980
Total GDP	4.68	5.59	5.33	4.73	2.35	6.81	2.04	2.47	2.92	2.17	1.89
Real GDP	1.88	1.68	3.17	0.86	0.76	0.59	0.42	0.52	0.48	0.86	0.23
V. add. agri.	0.10	0.06	0.10	-0.10	0.08	0.09	0.07	0.01	0.04	0.04	0.00
V. add. mining	0.00	0.00	0.00	0.00	0.00	0.00	0.01	0.00	0.00	0.00	0.00
V. add. construction	1.29	1.61	2.60	0.53	0.32	0.25	0.15	0.01	0.10	0.04	0.09
V. add. manufacturing	3.92	2.01	1.07	1.05	1.03	1.10	1.07	1.06	0.43	0.40	0.23
V. add. transport	0.00	0.04	0.02	0.01	0.04	0.07	0.05	0.04	0.06	-0.10	-1.70
V. add. services	4.36	2.17	2.07	2.07	2.19	1.99	1.94	1.71	1.49	1.37	1.36
Gov. consumption	10.0	10.0	10.0	10.0	10.0	10.0	10.0	10.0	10.0	10.0	10.0
Gov. investment	5.81	4.01	3.03	2.25	1.40	1.45	1.17	1.11	1.30	1.37	0.92
Private consumption	7.89	2.19	2.01	1.33	0.73	1.05	0.89	0.67	0.55	0.88	1.04
Private investment	4.38	5.02	2.29	2.41	1.77	2.11	2.29	2.73	2.04	1.21	1.11
Import of goods	2.91	5.21	3.03	2.01	3.62	4.96	2.24	1.16	1.11	1.16	1.14
Export of goods	-0.50	-0.80	-0.29	-0.62	-2.04	-1.31	-1.26	-0.92	-0.59	-1.54	-0.91
Aggregate demand	6.58	4.33	3.14	4.12	11.11	2.65	2.71	5.34	1.60	2.53	2.47
Price index '75	1.14	1.98	1.10	1.80	1.10	1.70	1.07	1.50	1.10	1.01	0.97
GDP deflator	2.62	3.07	3.65	2.98	2.70	2.82	2.28	2.06	2.65	1.90	1.84
Employment in agri.	1.10	2.84	-0.77	-1.68	-0.90	-1.29	-1.49	-0.92	0.00	0.00	0.00
Employment in others	0.97	1.22	1.21	2.57	2.19	3.22	2.69	1.40	0.39	-2.30	-0.77
Real wages and salaries	9.65	10.00	10.42	8.40	3.22	2.13	1.54	1.46	2.48	2.39	1.50
Gov. revenues	5.23	9.07	5.71	5.04	2.67	2.00	5.82	2.10	5.35	2.84	2.61
Money supply	7.88	5.10	6.81	5.11	1.97	0.89	0.49	0.37	0.29	0.51	0.77
Balance of payments	-179.4	-339.9	-404.3	-512.3	-505.2	-568.6	-587.6	-529.0	-623.7	-628.7	-823.8

Note: per cent deviation from control solution.

7.4 A sustained increase in the direct tax by 5 per cent for the period 1970–1980

This policy simulation is carried out by raising the income taxes of the wage earners, business corporations and companies, each by 5 per cent for the entire simulation period from 1970 through to 1980. The additional revenue collected in is then channelled to raising the level of public investment. Due to a difference in the tax rates paid by each income group, the extent of the increase as a percentage of the existing tax rates was not uniform, rather the increase is greater for wage incomes than for either petroleum companies profits or corporate income. We have chosen, in this hypothetical simulation, to raise each tax rate uniformly by 5 percentage points purely for the ease of manipulation, to take into account the importance of wage incomes, and also to create a hypothetical situation whereby it is possible to trace the full impact of this policy change. An increase of a smaller magnitude is not appropriate for our study because it not only has the tendency of producing only a small change that is difficult to detect but also because the effects generated by such a change could be quickly submerged by other sectors in the model. The results of this simulation should provide a good indication as to the effects of a 'balanced-budget' operation on the economy. Moreover, it would also indicate the response of the economy where resources are being channelled from the private sector to the public sector. Table 7.4 summarises the effects of this policy change on the most important variable in the model.

The immediate impact of this policy change was a reduction in the income of the private sector, the real wages of income earners suffered a decline; they fell by 43 per cent for instance in 1970; furthermore, the fall continued to worsen over time until 1974. Thus by 1972, it was 0.05 per cent higher than its control solution. However, after that it began to recover gradually and was only 0.20 per cent higher than its control solution in 1980. The recovery in real wage income towards the latter part of the simulation period was due to an expansion of the income base which partially offset the increase in the tax rate.

In response to a reduction in the real disposable income of wage earners, private consumption expenditure declined. As shown in Table 7.6, it was 0.16 per cent higher than its base value in 1970. Thereafter, private consumption declined through out the entire period to reach 0.65 per cent below its base value.

As noted earlier, it was assumed in this simulation that the increase in income tax collections derived from the imposition of higher tax rates was directly channelled to raise the level of public investment expenditure. Consequently, government sector investment was 3.27 per cent higher than its base value in 1970. Thereafter, the level of government investment grew to reach a high of 8.89 per cent in 1979. The growth was dampened slightly in the last years of the simulation period.

Moreover as a result of higher government revenues the level of public consumption was also raised above its control solution, for instance government consumption was 1.27 per cent higher than its control solution in 1970. Thereafter, it was to reach only 5.35 per cent higher than its control solution in 1980. The major sources of finance for the higher public consumption expenditure came from the increase in indirect and direct tax revenues.

Thus, despite the fall in private consumption, total aggregate demand was slightly raised, due mainly to higher public sector spending. Furthermore, in response to a higher level of real output, private sector investment expenditure was correspondingly raised.

In the price indices, a reduction in the disposable income of the private sector created a slack in the demand for consumer goods and contributed directly to relieving the price pressure on consumption goods. Consequently, the consumer price index experienced a marginal reduction in 1970. Thereafter, it continued to fall reaching a level of 0.2 per cent by 1980. Since the consumer price index exerted an important influence on the components of the GDP deflator, the fall in the consumer prices index led directly to a fall in the GDP deflator, by about the same magnitude.

The decline in GDP deflator, with unaltered commodity prices inferred that real commodity prices had improved. A rise in real commodity prices then stimulated the production and export of primary commodities. Meanwhile, the exports of manufactured goods were also more competitive through a fall in their prices. Consequently, value added in the agriculture sector initially showed an increase, but began to decline towards the end of the simulation period. The experiences of the mining and manufacturing sectors were very similar too. Only the construction, transport and services sectors showed consistently higher growth rates throughout the simulation period. By adding up the value added in all the productive sectors, it was shown that real GDP was consistently higher than its base solution. The increase in real GDP was also fairly uniform throughout the simulation period.

As a result of higher investment expenditures in both the private and the public sector, the demand for imports as raised. For instance, imports rose from 0.84 per cent in 1970 to 1.18 per cent above their control solution in 1980. In fact, as indicated in Table 7.6, the increase in imports was much higher than the marginal increase in exports. Consequently, the balance of payment position worsened, at first, marginally and later at a more rapid pace as the policy change was being sustained. Thus by 1980, the balance on the current account of the balance of payments had fallen by 254 million below the control solution. The decline in turn contributed to reducing the level of the money supply. The fall in the supply of bank credit coupled with a higher real rate of interest then adversely effected the further expansion of output in the agriculture and manufacturing sectors.

As a result of this policy change, employment in the agriculture sector and the non-agriculture sectors in the initial periods was higher than the base solutions. However, towards the later half of the simulation period, in response to a decline in agriculture output, employment in the agriculture sector fell below the control solution.

Meanwhile, except for 1979, employment in the other sectors remained to stay above the control solution for the entire simulation period.

Table 7.4 A sustained increase in the direct rate of tax by 5 per cent for the period 1970-1980

Economic sectors	1970	1971	1972	1973	1974	1975	1976	1977	1978	1979	1980
Total GDP	0.51	0.61	0.73	0.85	2.12	0.56	0.48	0.34	0.83	2.80	2.30
Real GDP	0.39	0.36	0.69	0.62	0.93	0.53	0.46	0.63	0.59	0.65	0.73
V. add. agri.	0.43	0.59	1.15	1.14	1.89	1.74	1.07	1.06	-0.84	-1.00	-1.50
V. add. construction	0.55	0.84	0.40	0.28	2.74	4.40	1.16	1.03	2.32	1.95	3.58
V. add. manufacturing	0.79	0.47	0.66	0.40	0.78	1.89	1.05	-1.32	-0.98	-1.90	0.52
V. add. transport	0.68	0.23	0.61	0.46	0.78	1.89	1.05	1.30	0.98	1.91	0.52
V. add. services	0.69	0.23	0.16	0.76	0.99	1.32	0.59	0.69	1.30	2.96	1.68
Gov. consumption	1.29	1.51	1.89	2.91	3.36	4.32	4.72	4.78	4.82	5.04	5.35
Gov. investment	5.27	5.61	6.21	7.81	7.36	7.32	7.11	8.17	9.73	9.39	8.93
Private consumption	-0.06	-0.03	-0.26	-0.29	-0.11	-0.05	-0.09	-0.40	-1.69	-0.75	-0.65
Private investment	0.95	0.87	0.39	0.59	0.96	0.22	0.28	0.25	0.27	0.38	0.64
Import	0.84	0.92	0.34	0.33	0.69	0.70	1.13	1.13	1.12	1.22	1.28
Export	0.02	0.12	0.08	0.21	0.14	0.18	0.09	0.05	0.41	-1.28	-1.20
Aggregate demand	0.36	0.33	0.40	0.36	0.48	0.35	0.48	0.59	0.65	0.61	0.73
Employment in agri.	0.56	2.33	1.60	0.38	0.48	0.51	0.37	-0.57	0.00	0.00	0.00
Employment in others	0.43	0.11	0.10	0.20	0.48	0.59	0.48	0.72	0.99	0.88	1.97
Real wages and salaries	0.43	0.36	0.52	0.20	0.30	0.16	0.06	-0.11	-0.23	-0.21	-0.20
Rate of wage index	0.16	-0.23	-0.21	-0.33	-0.28	-0.35	-0.88	-0.79	-0.52	-0.76	-0.87
Consumer's prices	-0.11	-0.07	-0.11	-0.10	-0.19	-0.2	-0.17	-0.98	-0.31	0.30	-0.23
Gov. revenues	3.06	3.30	4.20	4.12	4.24	5.02	5.05	5.30	6.11	6.43	6.55
GDP deflator	-0.01	-0.22	-0.13	-0.23	-0.31	-0.4	-0.24	-0.16	-0.15	-0.11	-0.09
Money supply	-1.61	-3.29	-3.36	-3.19	-4.29	-5.05	-4.60	-5.04	-4.88	-5.16	-5.59
Balance of payments	-16.11	-48.70	-61.40	-78.11	-87.11	-98.98	-118.1	-178.3	-197.3	-220.2	-255

Note: per cent deviation from control solution.

In the case of wage income although there had been a marginal improvement in the employment situation, its positive contribution to total wage income was partially offset by a decline in the wage rate. The wage rate declined largely in response to falling consumer prices.

The results of this policy simulation are, on the whole, plausible. It indicated the possible consequences of a shift in the use of resources from the private sector to the public sector in the form of income tax. In particular, such a policy would result in a marginally higher level of output and employment; a marginally lower consumer price index, a higher interest rate and lower level of money supply as well as a lower level of bank credit in the private sector. It is also shown that after a period of time the initial positive output effect on a number of sectors quickly diminished due to the existence of a tighter credit condition. Moreover, the initial simulative effects brought about by lower consumer prices and GDP deflator are quickly eroded away.

7.5 A sustained 5 per cent points increase in export duties for the period 1970-1980

In the 1970s, export duties made a small contribution to total government revenues. However, in order to highlight the effects of variations in export duties on the other sectors of the economy and to explore all possible channels of transmission of this policy change, the export tariff rate on all primary commodities is hypothetically raised by 5 percentage points for the entire simulation period from 1970 through 1980. The change is deliberately kept at a high level in order to ensure that the policy change has an opportunity of being fully manifested in all sectors of the economy. The effects of only a small change in the export tariff rate has been shown to dissipate quickly, thus making the task of tracing the effects of variations in the export tariff rate through various channels of influence impossible.

For the purpose of this simulation, it is assumed that both the public sector and the monetary authorities are pursuing a passive policy of non-intervention. Therefore, other than the direct link between public sector consumption expenditure, investment expenditure and revenues that has been earlier established in the model, no new discretionary policy change is assumed.

Two main channels through which changes in export duties are transmitted to the other sectors of the economy are commodity prices and government revenues. The effects of this policy change on the most important variables in the model are summarised in Table 7.5.

The production prices of all export commodities are adversely affected by the increase in export duties. Each declines by about 5 per cent compared with its historical value. As prices fall, both production and exports of these commodities decline. The extent to which production and exports are being adversely affected by falling prices depends on the prices sensitivity to the supply function concerned. Thus, the production of Dates, Wheat and Leather, which were shown to be particularly sensitive to price variations experienced the sharpest decline. Output of

186

dates falls by 1.3 per cent in 1970 and the rate of decline accelerates in the subsequent years to reach 12 per cent by 1980, output of leathers falls by 4.3 per cent in the first year. Moreover, the decline worsens progressively during the subsequent period to reach 13.9 per cent, below its control solution by 1980. Since all the major agricultural crops were adversely effected, the value added in the agriculture sector was therefore lower than the control solution. For instance, in 1970 the first year in which this policy change was affected, the value added in the agriculture sector fell by 0.66 per cent compared with its control solution. Moreover, the dynamic effects of the price change caused the initial negative impact on the value added in the agriculture sector to worsen further. Thus by 1980, the value added in the agriculture sector had fallen to 1.1 per cent below its control solution.

In the mining (excluding oil) sector, due to the prices' elasticities in the production function, the majority of its production was only marginally lower than the base solution values. Also, the output of petroleum was only slightly depressed as a result of a decline in the producer's price of petroleum. Therefore, except for the first few years, when the decline in output was relatively large, the fall in output of the mining sector was uniformly small throughout the simulation period.

The output of the manufacturing sector initially suffered only a marginal decline of 20 per cent in 1970 as a result of a small decline in aggregate demand. However, in response to a large decline in national income as well as a large fall in aggregate demand in the subsequent periods, manufacturing output began to plunge more steeply.

The effects of the policy change on the construction, transportation and service sectors which were transmitted mainly through the components of aggregate demand, were relatively mild. Value added in the construction sector, for instance, declined by 0.84 per cent in 1970 and slid further to 2.41 per cent below its control solution in 1980. Meanwhile, the value added in the service sector also declined. It fell from 1.72 per cent in 1970 to 4.40 per cent below its base solution in 1980. In addition, the value added in the transportation sector declined from 1.0 per cent in 1970 to below 1.2 per cent in 1980.

The sum of the value added in the production sector constitutes the real GDP. Since all the sectoral values added were adversely affected by the policy change, they resulted in a lower level of real GDP. The level of real GDP first declined by 0.59 per cent in 1970. It then slid further to 1.53 per cent below its control solution in 1980.

The effects of the policy change on real GDP as well as on the value added in the production sectors appeared plausible. The agriculture and manufacturing sectors in particular, were most severely hit by the increase in export duties, while output of the other production sectors was affected to a lesser extent. Since employment was directly related to output in the model, a fall in real output of both the non-agriculture and agriculture sectors resulted in a decline in overall employment. As shown in Table 7.7, the level of employment in the non-agriculture sector declined first by 0.64 per cent in 1970, and then accelerated to

5.93 per cent in 1976. Thereafter, it declined to about 1.42 per cent below its control value. The level of employment in the agriculture sector was also consistently below that of its control solution.

Within the government sector, the increase in the export tariff rate significantly boosted the level of export duties. These due to the negative impact of such a policy change on imports, output, income and development, government revenues from the other sources declined marginally. However, on balance the increases in export duties more than offset the combined effects of the decline in income tax, excise duties and import duties. Consequently, total government revenue increased. As shown in Table 7.8, total government revenue was raised by 6.48 per cent from its base value in 1970. It then followed an upward trend to reach 7.60 per cent in 1980.

As a result of a higher level of government revenue, the level of government investment and consumption was significantly raised. This was brought about largely by the fact that public revenue was the major source of funds for investment and consumption. In 1970 for instance, both real government consumption and investment was about 2.8 per cent, 1.04 per cent above its base value respectively. It then followed an upward trend to reach 4.99 per cent, and 4.49 per cent in 1980 respectively.

In the balance of payment sector, since both the real output and aggregate demand were depressed by the policy change, the demand for various categories of imports of goods, the imports of consumption goods, capital and intermediate goods was most severely affected by higher export duties. Imports of consumer goods fell in response to a fall in private consumption which in turn was caused by a decline in real disposable income. The decline in the imports of investment goods on the other hand was caused mainly by a decline in total investment expenditure, while the decline in the imports of t intermediate goods were the result of a decline in manufacturing output. Import of consumption goods fell by 0.2 per cent in 1970 but declined further to reach 1 per cent below its control solution in 1973. Thereafter, the rate of decline moderated so that by 1980 it was only 0.8 per cent below its control solution. The imports of intermediate goods initially declined by 0.5 per cent in 1970. It continued to fall over the simulation period so that by 1980 it was 1.97 per cent below its control solution. The real import of goods was consistently lower than its control solution over the entire simulation period. For instance, in 1970, the real import of goods only declined by 0.06 per cent. Therefore, it generally followed a declining trend so that by 1980, it was 0.2 per cent below its control solution.

Compared with the fall in the real import of goods, the decline in the real export of goods was considerably larger. This was due to the reason that with declining production prices of major commodities, a smaller volume of these commodities would be produced and exported.

In 1970 for instance, the real export of goods declined by 0.32 per cent and the rate of decline worsened over the simulation period. By 1980 the real export of goods was 3.11 per cent below its control solution.

As the level of exports had fallen more severely than imports, the combined effect was a substantial reduction in the balance of payment account.

The decline in the balance of the balance of payment account directly implied a reduction in the country's foreign reserves. Since net foreign assets constitute the most important component of money base in Iraq, a fall in the overall balance also implied a drain on the monetary base, this situation would develop into a reduction in the money supply. Consequently, the level of the money supply was lower than in the base solution, while the real rate of interest was raised marginally. In 1970 the money supply was 1.47 per cent below its base solution. The fall in money reserve also pulled down the level of bank credit.

In response to both a lower level of aggregate demand and a smaller money supply, both the consumer price index and GDP deflator declined marginally compared to the base solution values. The decline in the consumer price index appeared to be slightly larger than the decline in the GDP deflator, mainly due to the influence of the money supply variable in the determination of the consumer price index. Their time response patterns over the simulation period were however, very similar.

In the aggregate demand sector, with the exception of public consumption all the other components of aggregate demand were lower than in the base solution. Private investment expenditures declined. Furthermore due to a fall in private sector income (for instance real wages and salaries), private consumption expenditure was also adversely affected. As shown in Table 7.8 private consumption was about 0.18 below its control solution in 1970. Moreover, the rate of decline also accelerated over time, and thus by 1980, private consumption were about 3.2 per cent of its base solution.

Finally real wages and salaries were adversely effected by the policy change. The decline in wages and salaries was due to a simultaneous reduction in the wage rate and the level of employment. While the fall in agriculture income was accounted for by a simultaneous reduction of agriculture output and commodity prices.

The simulation results produced by the model appear plausible, in particular, they pointed out the areas which would be most effected by the kind of policy change examined here.

7.6 A sustained 15 per cent reduction in export prices for the period 1970-1980

The purpose of this simulation is to test whether there is any significant asymmetry between an increase and decrease in export prices when the extent of price variation in either direction is maintained at the same level.

This simulation is carried out by reducing all export prices by over 15 per cent over the entire simulation period from 1970 through 1980. The effects of this

Table 7.5 A sustained 5 per cent increase in export duties for the period 1970-1980

Economic sectors	1970	1971	1972	1973	1974	1975	1976	1977	1978	1979	1980
Total GDP	-0.42	-0.54	-0.50	-0.38	-0.37	-1.59	-1.64	-1.33	-1.25	-3.13	-1.54
Real GDP	-0.59	-0.58	-0.14	-0.30	-0.34	-0.51	-2.37	-1.16	-2.46	-1.42	1.53
V. add. agri.	-0.66	-0.97	-2.35	-1.70	-2.04	-2.94	-2.20	-1.21	-1.78	-1.68	-1.07
V. add. mining	-0.05	-0.10	-0.16	-0.27	-0.60	-0.39	-0.60	-0.69	-0.40	-0.90	-0.40
V. add. construction	-0.84	-0.14	-0.85	-0.43	-2.95	-2.43	-2.39	-1.18	-2.14	-0.44	-2.41
V. add. manufacturing	-0.20	-0.78	-1.22	-0.67	-0.84	-3.20	-2.16	-1.51	-0.90	-0.35	-1.29
V. add. transport	-1.02	-0.39	0.33	-0.89	-1.07	-2.24	-1.22	-0.80	-1.21	-0.46	-1.99
V. add. services	-1.72	-1.03	-1.30	-1.04	-4.74	-3.55	-0.85	-2.14	-2.41	-3.26	-4.40
Gov. consumption	2.76	1.42	4.08	13.23	3.68	2.78	5.92	3.03	4.62	2.89	4.99
Gov. investment	1.04	1.79	5.14	3.57	9.76	13.74	3.75	2.70	6.20	6.81	7.49
Private consumption	-0.18	-0.18	-3.53	-3.89	-3.72	-3.38	-4.49	-3.78	-0.82	-3.77	-3.17
Private investment	0.29	0.27	-0.52	0.03	-0.22	-0.77	-0.81	-0.78	-0.59	-0.47	-0.18
Import	-0.06	-0.15	-0.04	-0.01	-0.75	-1.19	-0.26	-0.15	-0.11	-0.14	-0.20
Export	-0.32	-0.29	-1.64	-2.70	-1.53	-3.15	-1.75	-1.54	-3.79	-3.58	-3.11
Aggregate demand	-0.83	-0.55	-0.21	-0.17	-0.46	-1.74	-0.18	-0.72	-1.54	-1.19	-1.93
Price index '75	-0.08	-0.06	-0.02	-0.02	-0.20	-0.59	-0.18	-0.11	-0.25	-0.11	-0.23
GDP deflator	-0.08	-0.07	-0.13	-0.41	-0.12	-0.05	-0.05	-0.13	-0.15	-0.18	-0.15
Employment in agri.	-0.88	-3.74	-3.29	-0.57	-0.52	-0.95	-0.77	-0.41	-0.80	-0.97	-1.12
Employment in others	-0.64	-1.78	-2.20	-3.70	-5.33	-1.20	-5.93	-2.65	-1.87	-1.22	-1.14
Real wages and salaries	-0.30	-0.33	-0.75	-1.18	-1.44	-1.67	-0.84	-0.92	-1.29	-2.45	-1.25
Rate of wage index	-0.05	-0.06	-0.11	-0.50	-0.33	-0.28	-0.14	-0.27	-0.25	-0.18	-0.11
Gov. revenues	6.48	5.70	5.81	5.88	6.82	6.00	6.11	3.49	9.70	7.91	7.60
Money supply	-1.47	-2.69	-2.68	4.16	-3.08	-2.18	-3.43	-3.51	-2.27	-3.20	-4.30
Balance of payments	-22.2	-18.7	-51.1	-72.6	-98.4	-151	-120	173	146.4	201.5	251.4

Note: per cent deviation from control solution.

exogenous shock on the most important variables in the model are summarised in Table 7.6.

Both the public sector and the monetary authorities are once again assumed to pursue a passive policy of non-intervention in this simulation. They could, of course, pursue a number of policy measures to offset the effects of a decline in export prices. However, since our purpose is to achieve a better understanding of the consequences of a sustained decline in export prices, it is more appropriate at this stage to focus our investigation on export prices alone.

By comparing the results of this simulation with a later simulation in Table 7.7 where export prices were raised by 15 per cent for the entire duration of the simulation period, it was evident that while the immediate impact of an exogenous shock whether it was due to an increase or a decrease in export prices as very similar, although in opposite directions, they nevertheless exhibited significant differences in their response pattern over time. In general, the decline in real output appeared to deepen the longer the fall in export prices was sustained. Moreover, the loss in real output arising from a prolonged decline in export prices was far larger than the gain in real output associated with a sustained increase in export prices. The main reason for this asymmetry was found in the behaviour of the prices and the wage rate variables. While a large increase in aggregate demand due to an increase in export earnings, even without the accompanied growth in productive capacities, would certainly lead to a higher inflation rate and eventually to a dampening of the simulative influences of the increase in export earnings; a reduction in export earnings. however, is seldom accompanied by a fall in prices and wages of the same proportions. This feature is partially captured by the capacity utilisation index in the price equation. However, the full extent of this asymmetry has not been adequately captured. As such it may be necessary to introduce a dampening factor on the fall of consumer prices in order to reflect the real life situation. This is an illustration of how sound judgement can be combined with the econometric model in producing plausible simulation results. A mechanical use of the model may give rise to answers very different from reality.

This asymmetric behaviour in prices and wages is particularly true in the case of Iraq, where the productive capacity for most of her industries is rather small. Thus, whenever there is a sudden increase in aggregate demand, the productive capacity would quickly be pushed to its limits, leading to an overall increase in product prices. The increase in the prices of both intermediate goods and final goods would ultimately lead to an increase in the consumer prices index. Furthermore, any attempt by producers to expand their productive capacity or the suppliers to import from abroad to satisfy domestic demand would be likely to require a long time to complete, especially when we consider that the bulk of machinery and equipment is imported. The mere process of planning for an expansion of capacity would require a long time to finalise when it involves foreign technology and expertise. Therefore, once inflationary pressure has been built up, the chances of bringing it down quickly are often remote. Instead, the likelihood is for prices to spiral upwards, as the increase in prices spill over to the demand for higher wages and profit margins, both of which contribute indirectly to the higher cost of material inputs. Meanwhile, inflationary expectation would almost certainly be formed too. This expectation element would then influence pricing behaviour in both the product and labour market. The cost of borrowing in such a setting would be likely to be raised too. Furthermore, in an inflationary environment, it is often easier for the entrepreneurs and the producers to pass on their costs in the form of higher product prices. The increase in prices would then quickly drain away the positive effects on real output, employment and the balance of payments. This observation has been confirmed by the experience of the 1974/1975 inflation in the Iraq economy.

The effects of a sustained increase and a sustained decrease in export prices produce two major contrasting characteristics; First, while the real benefits of a sustained increase in export prices appear to peter out after a lapse of a few years, the negative impacts arising from a sustained decrease in export prices appear to linger on for a much longer period and moreover the effects had the characteristics of being entrenched into the system in the form of negative influences. Secondly, while the strongest influence of a sustained increase in export prices appears to be on the price level, the most important influence arising from a sustained decrease in export prices seems to be on real output.

With significantly lower export prices, both export receipts and the output of commodities were adversely affected. For instance, while real exports of goods and services fell by only 2.7 per cent compared to its base solution, the export of goods in nominal terms had fallen by more than 16 per cent. The decline in export volume was brought about by a decline in the production of commodities which was in turn caused by a decline in the real export prices. While commodity prices had fallen by 15 per cent in 1970, the GDP deflator fell only by 5.6 per cent and the consumer price index by 1.5 per cent when compared with their respective base solution. Had the decline in GDP deflator been able to reach the same level as the decline in commodity prices, the level of real commodity prices on which production decisions were based, would have remained unaltered. However, as indicated by the simulation results, this was not the case in reality. Instead, the decline in both the GDP deflator and the consumer price index were very much smaller than the decline in commodity prices. As a result, the decline in real export price was severe. The fall in real export prices in turn acted as a strong disincentive, for instance, for farmers to increase their output level both in the current period as well as in the subsequent periods through the lagged price effects.

As a result of the decline in export prices, the output of all the commodities in the agriculture sector was lower than their base solution values. So the value added in the agriculture sector was therefore depressed. Thus, in 1970 the fall in export prices was 2.2 per cent below its control solution. The fall in value added in agriculture, however, continued to deepen with the prolonged decline in export prices, although to a smaller extent.

The output of the mining sector at first fell by 1.16 per cent below its control solution. After that its decline was more gradual, and, by the end of the simulation period in 1980, value added in mining sector was only 1.3 per cent below its control.

In response to a decline in both the real income and the aggregate demand, the output of construction, the manufacturing, transports and the services sectors were all lower than their respective base solutions. The manufacturing sector in particular appeared to have suffered the most severe decline in output. As shown in Table 7.6, the value added in the manufacturing sector first declined by 7.4 per cent in 1970. It was also consistently lower than its base solution in the subsequent period. The initial declines in the value added in both the construction and service sectors as well as the transport sector were relatively small. The cumulative effects of a prolonged decline in export prices soon brought about a steeper decline in the output of these sectors. Thus by 1980, the values added in the construction, service and transport sectors were 6.7 per cent, 8.7 per cent and 6.11 per cent respectively lower than their respective base solution value.

Since the output of every productive sector of the economy was adversely affected, the level of GDP as the sum of sectoral value added was naturally lower than its control solution. For instance, real GDP showed a decline of 4.76 per cent. The fall in real GDP also continued to worsen with a sustained decline in export price. Consequently, by 1980 the gap between the disturbed solution and the control solution had widened to 8.3 per cent. As can be seen from Table 7.6, every component of the aggregate demand was adversely affected by this external shock.

In the balance of payments sector, both the real export and real imports of good were adversely affected. The fall in real exports or the volume of exports especially non-oil exports was largely the result of a decline in the output of commodities, while the fall in the major categories of imports accounted for the decline in real imports of goods. In response to the lower level of commodity prices, output of the commodities declined. Since export volume is closely related to the output level, export volume fell too.

All the major components of imports were adversely affected by the sustained decline in export prices. Imports of consumption goods declined in response to a lower level of private consumption expenditure as well as to higher relative prices. As import prices were unaffected by the change in export prices, while the GDP deflator declined due to a fall in aggregate demand and a reduction in excess liquidity, the price ratio of the import price index for consumption goods to the GDP deflator was significantly raised. As a result of the increase in relative prices, import demand for consumption goods declined as the prices of imported consumption goods were more expensive. At the same time, higher import prices stimulated home production of import substitutes.

The decline in the imports of investment goods, on the other hand, was caused by a reduction in real investment activity and an increase in relative prices, while the decline in the import of intermediate goods was the result of a reduction in manufacturing output and a raise in relative prices.

Moreover, in response to a fall in total trade volume and a higher level of native prices for all categories of imports, the demand for foreign services declined too. A sustained decline in commodity prices indirectly implied a reduction in the payments of factor income abroad and affected the profitability condition of the output. Even then their profitability in these new ventures was dependent on the level of aggregate demand, and therefore was closely related to the performance of the export prices.

When the negative influences of the components of imports were disaggregated, they produced a significantly lower level of real imports of goods compared to the base solution. The real import of goods fell by 4.1 per cent in 1970. From then on, the decline worsened to reach a low of 13.4 per cent in 1976. Therefore, the decline in total imports recovered somewhat and ended up in 1980 at 11.7 per cent below its control solution.

Since import prices were determined in the world market and with Iraq being a small economy, they were assumed to be unaffected by changes in Iraq's export prices. By virtue of this assumption, the percentage decline in both the real and nominal imports from their base solution was almost identical. This was however not the case for exports. For all the commodities the decline in nominal exports was much steeper than the fall in export volumes. The difference between the two was accounted for by the decline in export prices. Therefore, a familiar situation in which a large decline in nominal exports was accompanied by a less than proportionate decline in imports emerged. This situation then resulted in a larger current account deficit as well as a larger deficit in the overall balance of the balance of payment account and the deficit occurred in the current account too. This was the result of the decline in net foreign long-term capital inflow brought about by a decline in investors income. Therefore, the fall in the overall balance then generated a drain on the money reserve which in turn created a decline in the money supply. The money supply declined by 12.6 per cent in 1970. In subsequent periods, the decline in the money supply fluctuated between 12.6 per cent and 15.3 per cent below its base solution value. The decline in the money reserve also resulted in a fall in the level of bank credit as well as a higher rate. The fluctuation path in the money supply was partly due to the use of the complicated lagged price structure in production and the import functions in the model, and partly due to the large fluctuations in export prices experienced during the simulation period. For the same reasons, the simulated time path for the overall deficit of the balance of payments was not smooth but exhibited some fluctuations. These fluctuations were however limited to within reasonable bounds and thus did not adversely affect the simulation results of the model.

The general sluggishness in aggregate demand as well as the absence of excess liquidity pressures in the economy then resulted in a decline in both the consumer price index and the GDP deflator. The decline in the GDP deflator was, however, much larger than the decline in the consumer price index as the export price index entered directly into the identity which determined the GDP deflator, while export prices only influenced the consumer price index indirectly through changes in aggregate demand and the money supply.

An important assumption was made in this simulation about the behaviour of the consumer price index in an environment of a sustained decline in export prices. In particular, the consumer price index was assumed to be relatively sluggish in its downward adjustments. The reasons for making this assumption are discussed below.

It is by now a well-known fact that the price level does not react to both an upswing and a downturn in aggregate demand in the same fashion. In particular, an increase in aggregate demand pressures are likely to cause the price level to rise faster than a corresponding slack in aggregate demand sends prices tumbling and the extent of the variation in both directions is identical. Although the existence of downward rigidity in the price variable is well recognised, this phenomenon has rarely been modelled adequately. Even with the use of a non-linear relationship between the consumer prices index and some measures of excess demand, the estimated coefficients are seldom able to capture this asymmetry adequately. Unfortunately, this is the case with our price equation. To overcome this problem, we applied a dampening factor directly on the consumer price equation in the current simulation. The dampening factor is computed based on our knowledge about the price behaviour in Iraq. The effect of this dampening factor is to slow the rate of decline in consumer prices. Of particular relevance to our simulation study was the experience of the Iraq economy in the 1976 recession when there was a severe decline in export prices. With falling export prices, the rise in the consumer price index moderated in that year to ? per cent compared with an increase of ? per cent in the previous year. However, in that same year, real GDP grew only marginally by 7.44 per cent and total GDP actually declined by 13.11 per cent. The index of capacity utilisation showed a sharp decline too.

If we compare the result in Table 7.6 with the results reported in Table 7.7, it can be seen that in export prices decline hypothesis is a slow effective decline when combined with a prices and rate of wages. In particular, Table 7.6 reveals that the magnitude of the decline was much smaller than that of the increase when there was a sustained increase in export prices. Moreover, since, the consumer price index appeared as an important explanatory variable directly in the equations for the determination of private investment and consumption deflator and indirectly in the equations for government consumption deflator and government investment deflator through the wage rate and unit labour cost, the influence of the consumer prices index on the GDP deflator as well as the wage rate was evident.

Employment in both the agriculture and non-agriculture sectors was adversely affected by the decline in real output. Moreover, due to the larger decline in the output of the non-agriculture sector, the fall in non-agriculture employment appeared to be steeper than the fall in agriculture employment. The simulation results thus indicated the sensitivity of the employment situation to variations in the export prices.

The categories of income earners in the model appeared to be more severely affected by the adverse consequences of a prolonged decline in export prices. The wage earners on the other hand, appeared to have only suffered a minor setback set in their earnings. The depressed state of corporate earnings was due to an all-round reduction in output and income. The fall in wage income was relatively smaller than the corporate income due mainly to a smaller decline in the wage rate and also because the fall in employment had been less severe than the fall in output.

On the whole, the simulation results appeared reasonable. The variables most sensitive to a prolonged decline in export prices were revealed. In particular, it appeared that a prolonged decline in export prices would result in a progressively lower level of income, output and employment. The relative share of income however, showed some improvement in favour of the wage earners, although in absolute terms all categories of income were depressed. Meanwhile, the balance of payment situation worsened. Finally, due to our assumption about the downward rigidity of the consumer price index, the wage rate variable and the GDP deflator were significantly lower than the decline in real output or income.

7.7 A sustained 15 per cent increase in export prices for the period 1970-1980

The only difference between this simulation and the earlier one in (1) is that in this simulation the price increases for all export commodities are maintained for the entire simulation period. The effects of this sustained export price increase are summarised in Table 7.7.

As a result of this exogenous shock, there was a significant growth in both real and total GDP. However, due to the significant increase in the GDP deflator, real GDP rose more slowly than total GDP. For instance, total GDP was raised by 16.19 per cent from its base solution, while the percentage deviation of real GDP from its base solution was only 6.32 per cent.

The export of goods also showed a significant increase. The increase was due mainly to a higher production of crude oil and other goods. The supplies of the primary commodities while fairly inelastic in the short-run were moderately sensitive to real price changes in the longer run. The exports of manufactured goods, however, suffered a significant decline which was the result of emerging unfavourable terms of trade for manufactured exports. Moreover, due to the rapid increase in the domestic price level, particularly the implicit GDP deflator the initial simulative effects of the higher real exports were quickly eroded over a short span of time. As a result, by 1980, the 'disturbed' solution for the export of goods was only marginally higher than the base solution.

The higher level of real income brought about by higher production in turn stimulated the growth of private sector expenditure. Both private consumption and investment were substantially raised. Real imports of goods were similarly given a strong boost. It was raised from its base solution by 7.6 per cent in 1970 and further by 14.5 per cent in 1972. The growth of imports however, begun to dampen thereafter as the level of real income began to be adversely effected by the higher inflation rate.

The level of government revenue also benefited substantially both from the increase in export receipt and the increase in income level. Higher government revenue was channelled to raise the level of public sector consumption.

The output of all the seven productive sectors of the economy was significantly raised from their base solutions in the first few years. However, since 1974, a marginal decline in the output of the manufacturing sector began to emerge. This occurrence could be attributed to the fact that as a result of the higher inflation rate, domestically produced manufactured goods became less competitive in the world market and thus foreign demand for manufactured exports had fallen off. Meanwhile, in the domestic market, the existence of a higher domestic price level with the import prices being held unchanged implied that imports had progressively cheapened. This change in the relative prices between the domestically produced and imported manufactured goods had resulted in widespread substitutions between domestic and foreign manufactured goods in favour of imports. Consequently, the demand for the locally produced manufactured goods was depressed, resulting in a decline in the value added in the manufacturing sector.

In response to the higher levels of aggregate demand and export prices, both the consumer price index and the GDP deflator were significantly raised. The wage rate was also raised in response to both the increase in prices and labour productivity.

Although all the categories of income: corporate income and wages and salaries were substantially improved as a result of the increase in export prices, the corporate income seemed to benefit the most. Thus observation supported the contention that businesses tend to reap the greatest benefits in a booming economy.

A sustained increase in export prices also benefited the balance of payment account. There was therefore an increase in the supply of 'high-powered' money, which in turn led to growth in the money supply and credit as well as a marginal decline in the loan rate.

Table 7.6 A sustained 15 per cent reduction in the export prices for the period 1970-1980

Economic sectors	1970	1971	1972	1973	1974	1975	1976	1977	1978	1979	1980
Total GDP	-8.10	-11.97	-12.58	-13.58	-13.65	-10.05	-17.12	-14.30	-13.11	-14.08	-15.84
Real GDP	-4.76	-5.93	-7.84	-9.03	-6.10	-7.24	-8.14	-7.40	-7.09	-7.34	-8.30
V. add. agri.	-2.19	-3.24	-4.15	-5.72	-4.42	-4.97	-6.21	-6.51	-5.42	-5.36	-7.61
V. add. mining	-1.16	-2.51	-2.79	-2.58	-1.78	-1.16	-1.08	-1.19	-1.12	-1.29	-1.31
V. add. construction	-2.25	-4.74	-5.47	-6.33	-6.91	-8.15	-8.95	-7.57	-7.21	-7.01	-6.74
V. add. manufacturing	-7.35	-6.91	-6.69	-8.40	-6.97	-7.36	-6.62	-7.11	-7.84	-8.45	-8.93
V. add. transport	-3.11	-3.35	-4.65	-5.11	-5.89	-6.30	-5.45	-5.31	-4.61	-5.73	-6.11
V. add. services	-3.51	-4.95	-5.46	-7.36	-8.46	-7.21	-7.80	-8.72	-8.53	-8.08	-8.74
Gov. consumption	-0.91	-6.70	-7.57	-8.12	-10.93	-12.88	-13.70	-14.77	-15.59	-15.99	-16.19
Gov. investment	-10.61	-12.30	-12.98	-10.13	-10.51	-13.98	-15.20	-16.19	-14.78	-14.18	-14.78
Private consumption	-5.65	-4.05	-6.50	-8.88	-6.71	-5.50	-9.56	-8.10	-7.61	-9.09	-9.80
Private investment	-8.63	-8.78	-14.39	-11.61	-10.83	-14.98	-13.95	-13.69	-12.71	-12.06	-11.86
Import	-4.10	-6.96	-12.20	-11.32	-10.41	12.84	-13.38	-13.00	-11.92	-11.22	-11.72
Export	-2.72	-3.93	-7.11	-7.71	-6.74	-5.72	-5.90	-5.98	-6.11	-6.51	-6.40
Aggregate demand	-10.31	-10.11	-10.90	-14.43	-13.33	-10.49	-12.64	-12.13	-11.94	-14.32	-15.44
Consumer price index	-2.21	-2.08	-2.23	-2.41	-2.55	-2.71	-3.06	-3.13	-3.30	-3.37	-3.49
GDP deflator	-5.37	-4.97	-3.69	-5.70	-7.71	-5.90	-6.32	-6.90	-5.77	-7.06	-7.32
Employment in agri.	-0.25	-0.81	-0.99	-1.26	-1.56	-1.89	-2.41	-2.56	-2.39	-2.22	-2.64
Employment in others	-3.10	-3.34	-4.80	-6.10	-4.63	-4.75	-6.63	-5.95	-6.11	-6.80	-7.73
Corporate income	-24.92	-20.39	-16.08	-14.71	-19.37	-15.73	-21/33	-19.35	-17.08	-25.20	-27.12
Real wages and salaries	-3.75	-5.16	-6.29	-5.66	-6.96	-8.15	-7.89	-7.87	-7.83	-7.90	-8.05
Rate wage index	-2.77	-3.81	-3.99	-4.35	-4.76	-4.40	-4.93	-4.43	-4.68	-5.06	-5.38
Gov. revenues	-9.84	-30.76	-18.68	-21.25	-25.84	-25.96	-18.71	-23.11	-21.18	-19.71	-25.90
Money supply	-12.61	-12.11	-10.51	-15.31	-18.49	-6.03	-13.16	-14.78	-11.61	-11.11	-12.34
Balance of payments	-396.1	-242.2	-225.9	-790.1	-271.6	-647.5	-710.9	-114.8	-1454	-2147	-290.0

Note: per cent deviation from control solution.

Table 7.7 A sustained 15 per cent increase in the export prices for the period 1970-1980

Economic sectors	1970	1971	1972	1973	1974	1975	1976	1977	1978	1979	1980
Total GDP	16.19	17.11	15.50	12.90	12.90	12.90	11.40	11.40	11.50	12.00	12.00
Real GDP	6.32	5.85	4.10	3.89	2.82	2.07	2.96	2.61	1.83	3.00	3.15
V. add. agri.	0.41	1.60	1.93	1.99	1.34	1.34	1.43	1.65	1.45	1.48	2.11
V. add. mining	1.15	2.18	2.50	2.50	2.46	1.72	1.14	1.06	1.16	1.05	1.00
V. add. construction	4.54	7.11	6.55	2.57	2.39	3.50	3.19	3.19	3.21	3.19	3.18
V. add. manufacturing	8.21	6.40	2.14	1.74	0.64	-1.21	-1.64	-0.89	-1.03	-0.93	-0.98
V. add. transport	4.81	4.11	4.51	3.20	2.33	1.87	1.20	1.05	1.85	2.03	1.88
V. add. services	6.00	5.76	4.43	3.80	2.18	2.20	2.74	2.49	2.33	3.73	3.83
Gov. consumption	0.50	4.79	7.07	7.18	8.18	8.92	8.88	8.30	8.67	8.99	9.71
Gov. investment	8.69	7.72	6.35	7.87	8.11	8.82	9.79	10.49	9.61	9.99	10.09
Private consumption	5.88	7.89	3.37	4.20	3.61	2.23	1.68	2.78	2.99	4.10	4.45
Private investment	7.99	5.38	5.12	4.40	2.23	4.11	3.64	5.01	5.97	5.50	5.25
Imports	7.61	14.53	17.02	15.10	12.55	10.96	11.35	10.40	9.63	8.79	8.53
Exports	0.54	2.76	2.98	3.06	2.21	1.31	1.58	1.80	1.94	0.68	0.31
Aggregate demand	15.33	13.82	11.35	12.71	12.72	11.58	10.22	10.31	10.61	11.00	11.43
Consumer price index	5.82	5.89	5.97	5.43	4.91	4.72	4.41	4.23	4.08	3.38	3.48
GDP deflator	10.18	10.70	11.41	11.24	11.70	10.66	10.59	10.30	10.41	10.45	10.51
Employment in agri.	0.20	0.33	0.43	0.61	0.48	0.40	0.35	0.49	0.58	0.62	1.11
Employment in others	4.00	3.63	1.16	1.14	1.18	1.11	0.99	0.46	0.70	0.40	0.09
Corporate income	20.00	17.79	9.89	10.64	13.59	14.35	13.06	13.39	14.70	19.90	19.53
Real wages and salaries	11.10	10.19	15.42	14.21	15.00	15.90	9.83	8.92	7.81	7.96	7.79
Rate wage index	9.11	11.42	12.74	11.94	11.03	10.30	9.52	8.89	8.05	7.74	7.32
Gov. revenues	6.90	28.71	18.69	13.60	18.31	20.56	17.96	16.49	16.31	16.21	16.39
Money supply	12.99	8.84	6.81	7.30	6.97	7.59	7.18	8.98	10.82	9.54	8.97
Balance of payments	43.10	448.18	85.04	162.24	11.91	130.00	189.11	311.89	494.90	595.43	678.20

Note: per cent deviation from control solution.

7.8 Conclusion

The simulation exercises carried out in this chapter appeared to produce plausible results. The results also conform quite closely to a priori expectation as well as empirical observation. Moreover, the policy simulation had also revealed some useful insights into the linkages of variables in a simultaneous equations model. Of particular interest was the role played by imports of goods. Since imports formed close to more than 50 per cent of total GDP in Iraq, and because they are highly sensitive to variations in aggregate demand (furthermore, due to a liberal trade policy pursued by the Iraqi authorities), it was not surprising to find the existence of substantial import leakages whenever stimulative economic policies were applied.

Another interesting observation was the relative sluggishness of export volume to change in stimulative policies. The increase in export receipt was mostly due to higher export prices rather than higher volumes.

Based on the results of the above stimulation tests, we conclude that the constructed model is sufficiently reliable to be used as a tool for the analysis and design of short-run stabilisation policies.

It must nevertheless be pointed out that the numerical results of the simulation are not meant to be a mathematically precise valuation of the effects of various policies. They should rather be treated as indicative of the relative impact on the important variables. This type of analysis is most useful in identifying the problem areas and the beneficiaries of a specific policy change.

Further reading:

Blackburn (1987), Fisher and Wallis (1990), Fisher (1992), Hall (1985), Hendry (1993), Hendry and Richard (1993), Hendry and Brown (1991), Hendry, Karakitsos and Savage (1982), Hughes Hallett (1992), Mariaano and Brown (1991), Mackie, Miles and Tylor (1989), Wallis and Whitley (1989) and Walliss et al. (1987).

8 The effects of the instability of export prices on the Iraqi economy (export sector simulation)

As a small open economy, the performance of the Iraqi economy is dependent to a large extent on its export sector. Since the 1950s as we mentioned in Chapter 3, Iraq has experienced several periods of booming economic activity which occurred during the economic development plans for the periods 1960-1969, 1970-1975 and 1976-1980. It has also been shown historically that the swings during economic activity are closely correlated with the fluctuations in the major commodity exports.

With the export sector playing such an influential role in economic fluctuations, it is only natural that the central concern of stabilisation policies was to dampen the large swings in aggregate demand brought about by export fluctuations. As elsewhere, the objective of the stabilisation policy in Iraq is aimed at ironing out short-run fluctuations so that the economy may be guided along a smooth, sustainable long-term growth path. Undue fluctuations in the export sector are thought to be detrimental to the economic life of the economy, particularly during a period of a severe downturn in export earnings when large unemployment of the labour force may result. This could bring with it widespread human suffering. In addition, a depressed export sector may reduce further the already meagre income of the small farmers whose livelihood very often depends on a single crop. As a result, more people are being pushed into poverty. Widespread human suffering would also generate social and political instabilities. It is in this context that undue fluctuations in economic activity must be seen as best to be avoided.

Indirectly, undue fluctuations in economic activity may also affect the achievement of a long-term growth objective, since its occurrence brings about an increase in political uncertainties and social unrest, both of which are bound to affect the perception of the investors with respect to the future course of the economy and would therefore adversely influence their decision to invest in the country.

Moreover, a sustained period of low economic activity may result in valuable machines, skilled workers and other factors of production being laid idle, thus contributing to a loss of output, time and energy as well as human resources. The existence of high unemployment may also put a severe strain on the political system to produce quick results. In addition unduly large short-term fluctuations in aggregate demand may cause the economy to alternate between economic recession and hyperinflation, with the accompanying familiar social ill effects. The use of stabilisation policies in Iraq is therefore both necessary and desirable in order to achieve a smooth long-term growth. There exists, however, a number of alternative routes through which this objective may be achieved.

Another problem which is related to export fluctuations is that of the implementation of public development programmes. These programmes had been found effective in overcoming some of the fundamental economic problems of Iraq, namely, the lack of infra-structure facilities to support a large industrial base, etc. It is essential that the public development programmes be smoothly implemented according to plan. However, a smooth execution of these development programmes would require the availability of financial resource. A downturn in export earnings would choke off significantly the flows of financial resources to the public sector in the form of a lower contribution to the provident fund which is the main source of development financing. Lower tax revenue and higher foreign debt-servicing burden may also cause a drain on foreign reserves and thus reduce the ability to import essential capital goods. All these contribute to delaying the implementation of the public sector programmes. Moreover, projects which had already begun may have to be postponed or even abandoned due to lack of funds.

One of the available policy options to deal with the problems of export fluctuations appears to be for the authorities to smooth out export fluctuations at the source, possibly at the level of the individual commodities. This could only be achieved with the existence of international commodity agreements which are capable of stabilising commodity prices. Furthermore, these commodity agreements may have to be supplemented by the establishment of a large stabilisation fund as well as a buffer stock scheme which would help domestic producers to adjust to the changing conditions in the commodity markets. It should also be recognised that stability in commodity prices, besides being difficult to attain, need not automatically guarantee stability in export earnings.

The second policy option to deal with export fluctuation consists of manipulating the other components of aggregate demand in order to offset the effects of export fluctuation on the economy. This could be carried out in the following ways:

1. Through an expansion or contraction of public sector spending;
2. Through manipulating the producer prices by raising or reducing the level of commodity or other taxes and subsidies and;
3. Through increasing or decreasing the level of the money supply, bank credit or interest rates.

Yet another policy action would be for the government to set up marketing boards which would guarantee fixed prices to the producers and to neutralise export earnings in commodity booms through higher commodity taxes.

The objective of this chapter is to broadly explore, through the use of model simulations, the problems involved in pursuing the first policy option in the conduct of stabilisation policies. This chapter will thus include an examination of the influence of the export sector on the other sectors of the economy within the framework of the complete macroeconometric model. In particular, it attempts to answer the question: what are the effects of export fluctuations on the rate of economic growth, the level of employment, the degree of price instability, the direction of income distribution and equilibrium in the balance of payments account, and whether price stability would contribute to higher economic growth.

Moreover, there has also been a growing interest on the part of the Iraqi government at stabilising the prices of such other commodities like dates and grains. In such a setting, it is appropriate to examine the possible consequences of export price stabilisation as a policy stance in terms of the attainment of economic goals such as growth of output and employment, domestic price stability and the performance of the balance of payments account. So far, studies as these have produced mixed results. In some countries these studies, the results seem to indicate that with greater stability in export prices, the rate of economic growth would be raised. However, there are other studies that show that the effects of export fluctuations are quite inconsequential to economic growth. More importantly, it was shown in all of these studies that the extent to which economic activities of a country would be influenced by export fluctuations depends very much on the size of the export sector in the economy as well as the relationship between the export sector and other sectors of the economy (see the discussion in Sanders (1982), Nurkse (1958), Glezakos (1973) and Sebastian (1988)).

Various simulation studies carried out in this chapter beside serving as tests for the possible effects of export fluctuations on the economy, will also contribute to a better understanding of the characteristics of the export sector and thus improve the formulation and execution of stabilisation policies in general.

Finally, this chapter can also be viewed as a test for the validity of the variability hypothesis in the case of Iraq.

Two dimensions of the commodity problem dealt with in this chapter are instability and variations in the secular trends of commodity prices. The variability in earnings from primary commodity exports would bring about large fluctuations in the balance of payments account with a consequent impact on the rest of economy. The impact of export instability could also be manifested in the form of increased fluctuation of economic variables as measured by the standard deviations of the variables concerned or the change in the growth path of the economy.

The methodology for testing the variability hypothesis consists of two alternative model simulations for the historical period 1970-1980. One simulation is carried out with smooth export prices the other with fluctuating export prices. By comparing the time path of the important variables of these two simulation results, it is possible to identify the earnings most severely effected by export price instability. These areas would include the rate of economic growth, the composition of sectoral output, the balance of payment account, the public sector budget and the overall price level. The results of the simulation study will also indicate the kind of policy measures which are most appropriate in offsetting the negative consequences of price instability of the primary commodities and manufacturing commodities.

The consequence of variations that is the secular trends of export prices, on the other hand, is studied in the forecast period 1981-1995. Three alternative assumptions with respect to the growth path of export prices in the future are used. Under each price assumptions, for forecasting the most important variables in the model. By comparing the time paths and mean value of the forecast variables, it is possible to get an indication of the impact of changes in the secular trend of export prices on the equilibrium in the balance of payment account, the level of employment, the overall price level and the rate of economic growth.

Most of the empirical investigations on the issues of export instability have adopted either a cross-section approach or a time series approach.

The cross-section analysis involves the collection of a homogeneous group of countries, while the time series analysis deals with one particular country over time. A general conclusion drawn by most of the recent studies seems to support the contention that the country-specific approach yields more fruitful results. Maizels (1968), Rangarajm, and Sundararajan (1976) and Adams (1981) all pointed out the need to analyse the relationship between export instabilities and the other macroeconomic aggregate in a disaggregated macroeconomics framework which allows for the establishment of significant linkages between the export sector and the other sectors of the economy.[1]

Cross-section studies are generally less satisfactory for the reason that such an approach implicitly assumes an identical economic structure across countries. Since in reality, economic structures and institutions, differ widely across countries, the use of cross-section data to estimate the correlation between export instability and economic growth does not provide any conclusive evidence either in support of or in refutation of the existence of such a relationship. In fact, the regression results are difficult to interpret meaningfully. Even if the regression results are difficult to interpret meaningfully and even if the regression results happen to be statistically significant it could very well be due to the presence of series relationships which are unrelated to the export instability.

8.1 Previous studies on the importance of the export sector

Since the export sector plays such a prominent role in the Iraqi economy, it is obvious that the policy makers have shown a deep interest in exploring the characteristics of the Iraqi export sector. Consequently, a substantial body of literature on Iraqi export has merged. These earlier studies were however either purely descriptive in nature or used only the single equation or "reduced form" approach in explaining the relationship between the export variables and the rate of economic growth (Al-Sefou, 1980; A. Samara,1981).

While the descriptive approach does provide a wealth of insights and careful reasoning as well as numerous untested hypotheses as to the relationship between the export sector and the other sectors of the economy, these hypotheses nevertheless remain conjectures at best. Moreover since no consistent economic framework was provided in many of these studies, it would be extremely difficult to apply these piecemeal reasoning to any policy analysis in a consistent manner.

The quantitative studies, on the other hand, were largely concentrated on obtaining the single equation estimates and were mainly centred around the issues of prices elasticities of demand and supply as well as the export instabilities. Thus far, no attempt has been made to analyse the export within the framework of a complete macroeconometric model in order to study the linkages of the export sector with the other sectors of the economy and to assess the impact of the export sector in influencing factors such as macro variables, the level of employment, output and price. Furthermore, the single equation approach is fraught with problems. The methodological flaw of using such an approach in dealing with the export sector was severely criticised by Adams and Behrman, 1981. One of their main objectives was the lack of specification of the structural relationship among the variables in the model. As a result, such an approach would almost always encounter the problems of estimation with omitted variables.

The current study attempts to overcome the weaknesses of the earlier studies. In particular, this is an attempt at analysing the problems of the export sector within a consistent framework. The advantage of using a structural model is that the relationships of all endogenous variables in the model are made explicit, thus making it easier to trace linkages among variables.

This chapter will be concerned with two of the most prominent hypotheses. The first hypothesis views instability as exerting a negative influence on economic development mainly because of the public and private problems of planning under uncertainty, risk aversion and asymmetrical responses (D. Mac Bean, A. J., 1966; Coppock, J.D., 1962). The second hypothesis, however, contends that instability has little effect on economic activity.

The contention of the first group of hypotheses is based on the reasoning that a reduction in export earnings will result in a smaller import capacity, directly through reducing foreign exchange, and indirectly, through higher costs of foreign borrowing as interest rates charged by foreign banks adjust upwards reacting to greater uncertainty. In addition for those countries which are faced with a severe balance of payment constraint, the loss of export earning may have to be compensated for by the imposition of import restrictions. The restrictions on imports may very well include basic capital equipment and essential intermediate goods. Consequently, gross domestic investment would be adversely effected by a reduction in machinery imports. Moreover, the presence of uncertainty increases the risk and at the same time reduces the rate of return on investment as well as shortening the planning horizon. Such a change in the investment climate may result in a rise in inventory investment instead of an expansion in the productive capacity of the economy. The reduction in investment would certainly reduce the long run growth of the economy. Another channel through which export instability can influence economic activity is the public sector. Since for most developing economies, the public sector relies heavily on tariffs and commodity taxes as its major sources of revenue, fluctuations in export earnings and also in imports are invariably reflected in the fluctuation of government revenue. Due to these fluctuations and because of the limitations of foreign borrowings, the public sector may be forced to adopt procyclical instead of countercyclical expenditure policies, thereby exacerbating rather than smoothing out the cyclical movements.

The reduction in export earnings would also depress the income level of the export industry. Both consumption and investment expenditure of the export industry would fall. This would then work through the multiplier process to bring down the level of GDP. An export boom on the other hand is expected to raise the overall price level significantly and thus the real effects on economic activity due to export booms are greatly reduced. Price inflation arises mainly from the occurrence of excess liquidity which is created by the transfer of export earnings into domestic demand for goods and services. Moreover, if the economy was already operating at close to capacity output before the export booms, the injection of higher levels of purchasing power as the result of an export boom could cause prices to soar even higher.

While this hypothesis claims to explain the growth issues, all the episoders used by its proponents seem to focus on the short-run consequences of export fluctuations. It is doubtful that the long-run affects of export instability have actually been convincingly demonstrated by the proponents of this hypothesis.

The second hypothesis is based on Friedman's theory of consumption. Knudsen and Parnes (1975), demonstrate that in the absence of any correlation between the transitory and permanent components of either income or consumption, the exporters of commodities are able to save the increased earnings from the good years. Thus the fluctuations are mainly absorbed by the exporters who offset the bad years with savings accumulated during the good ones.

8.2 The characteristics of the export prices

Before we continue in our investigation into a determination of the characteristics of the export prices, though, it is useful to give a brief review of the literature of the measurement of instability, which is still a matter of debate among economists. The first attempt to examine the correlation between instability indices was made by Coppock who found that the correlation coefficients for the log-variance index, and the index using the average of percentage of deviations around the log-linear trend for export over 1959-1971 was 0.897. Later comparison of instability indices made by Knudsen and Parnes confirm Coppock's results of a high correlation. In particular, they found that the correlation coefficient between the log-variance index and the five-years moving average was 0.94, that between the log-variance index and the deviations from an exponential trend index was 0.94 too, and between the deviations from an exponential trend index and the five-year moving average there was 0.86. These findings of the early studies led Mac Bean, 1966, p.34. To conclude that *"... as long ... as each index is calculated for the same period of time, the results are invariably, highly correlated"* (p.34).

Other studies, however, found that this conclusion was not entirely warranted. Glezakos, for instance, found that the correlation between the five-year moving average index used by MacBean and the log-variance index of Coppock was only 0.44. Leith (1970) also pointed out that, depending on the period chosen and on whether the sample includes only DCS or only LDCS, the correlation coefficient between the log-variance index and the deviations from a linear trend index varies from a high of 0.75 to a low of 0.50. Furthermore, Offut and Blandford's (1981) study confirms Glezakos and Leith's findings of low correlation coefficient between instability indices. This is the most recent study in this field and compares the rank correlation between the coefficient of variation, the three and five years moving average, yield, output, price and revenue for ten United States field crops over the 1950-1970 period. They found very little concurrence between rankings and made the conclusion that *"the results of this application should eliminate any remaining scepticism as to the dependence of the characterisation of instability on the choice of empirical technique"*.

From this brief review it is obvious that no clear picture emerges from the empirical evidence; indeed, much of the evidence is conflicting. A number of reasons to explain the inconclusiveness of the studies is in Dmitris Diakosavas, no. 8302 (see also Glfzakos (1983), Gerald Tan (1983) and C. Morgan (1983)).

Generally, most indices measure the sensitivity of instability, some of them detrended and some non-detrended. The indices are classified into two groups:

1. Those which measure deviations from the mean of the series, i.e. non-detrended indices;
2. Those with measure deviation from a trend, i.e., detrended indices.

The latter contains all those indices that are based on OLS and MA methods to estimate the trend.

In this chapter we will attempt to show the sensitivity of instability from the indices made by Coppock who found the correlation coefficients for the log-variance index (see Table 8.2a). Meanwhile, we will attempt to use the other measurements the sensitivity of instability detrended indices, which are based on the OLS method (see Table 8.2b in appendix to Chapter 8).

The export prices of the principal commodities, such as crude oil, date, leather, grains and the manufacturing industry are chosen as the subject of investigation in this chapter. As shown in Table 8.1, these prices appear to be highly positively correlated in the sample period, indicating that they move together most of the time. Although the correlation between the prices of manufactured and other prices appear to be relatively low, their correlation is nevertheless statistically significant at the 95 per cent level of confidence.

In Table 8.2a Coppock's instability indices (Coppock, J.D. (1962)) measure the extent of fluctuation in the export earnings, and it is shown that with the exception of grains, export prices for the other commodities all fluctuate more widely than export volumes. Moreover, the movement in export prices and volumes are additive that is they move in the same direction, thus leading to a large fluctuation in export earnings.

Table 8.1   Bivalent correlation matrix of the main goods

	Export for the Period 1970-1980					
Products	1	2	3	4	5	6
Vegt. Oil (1)	0.1					
Dates (2)	0.88	0.10				
Crude oil (3)	0.90	0.90	0.10			
Leathers (4)	0.93	0.94	0.92	0.10		
Grains (5)	0.88	0.84	0.91	0.84	0.10	
Manf. Ind. (6)	0.58	0.65	0.59	0.71	0.64	0.10

Note: R > 0.4393 are significant at 95% level.

Table 8.2a   The Instability Indices for the major goods during the period 1970-1980**

Commodities	Exports value	Exports volume	Exports prices
Dates	1.020	1.361	1.680
Leather	1.108	1.275	1.369
Veget. Oil	1.109	1.217	1.605
Crude oil	1.101	1.143	1.160
Manuf.	1.038	1.020	1.092
Grains	1.277	1.095	1.142

** This table calculated from the Coppock measure of export instability is given by;

$$I = \text{anti}\log\left[\frac{1}{n-1}\sum_{t-1}^{n-1}\left(\log\frac{X_{t+1}}{X_t} - m\right)^2\right]^{1/2} \qquad [8.1]$$

$$m = \frac{1}{n-1}\sum_{t=1}^{n-1}\log\frac{X_{t+1}}{X_t}$$

Where; I = represents the trend in export, X_t = is export at time t, n = is the number of observation.

8.3 An economic model simulation of the effects of export instability

This section explores the effects of instability on goal attainment as well as on the other important variables in the model. As export earnings are made up of both price and volume, the fluctuations in export earning could be attributed to either fluctuations in export prices or export volume.[2] We have chosen to study export instability principally through the export price route for two important reasons. Firstly, as indicated in Table 8.2 historically, export prices were shown to fluctuate more than export volumes. Secondly, the structure of the model is such that the causal relationships run from export prices to export volumes. A decline in the export price of a commodity, grain for instance, would lead ultimately to a reduction in the volume of a grain export. In this sense, the fluctuations in export volumes, are to some extent induced by fluctuations in export price. Furthermore, the current interest in the commodity price stabilisation scheme makes the choice on price instead of volume particularly relevant.[3]

As we have mentioned, the methodology used in this chapter to compare two hypothetical simulation results, consists of one generated under the assumption of smooth export price and, the other simulated under varying export prices. The smooth export prices series are presented by underlying growth paths, while the actual export price series are used to represent the varying export price series.[4]

There are several approaches for estimating the alternative growth path of a time series. Some of the most commonly used methods are:

1. A Linear time trend approximation
2. A Log-linear time trend approximation
3. A moving average approximation.

In this chapter, for each commodity price in the model, two alternative smoothed export price series were generated; one by means of a linearly fitted time trend and other by a log-linear time trend.[5] Table 8.3 and 8.3a (in appendix to Chapter 8) show the two alternative versions of the smooth export price used in the simulation tests. The period of simulation is from 1970 to 1980, and for the purpose of making comparisons, the simulation result based on the actual historical export price is used as the control solution. The comparisons of simulation results between the smoothed and the varying export price are shown in Tables 8.4 and 8.5. In Table 8.4, the linear time trends of export prices were used to represent the smooth export price series, while in Table 8.5 the smooth export price series were obtained by log-linear time trends. To make a comparison of the overall differences between the three alternative simulation paths: linearly smoothed export price, log linearly smooth export prices and varying export prices, both the arithmetic means and the standard deviation of principal variables are computed according to the first assumption of estimate the linear smooth export price, and the results as shown in Table 8.6a. By comparing the mean value of the principal variables in the model simulated under the varying export prices with that simulated under the smooth export prices, it is possible to get an indication as to the impact of export instability on the goal attainment of the economy. The sample standard deviations of these variables, on the other hand, indicates the extent to which fluctuations in export prices would be transmitted to the fluctuations of the other principal variables.

Meanwhile, though it is useful to compute the coefficient of the variation of principal variables and compare the C.V of principal variables in the model simulated under the varying export prices with that simulated under the smooth export prices, it is also possible to get an indication as to the impact of export instability on the goal attainment of the economy. The results of C.V of these variables, also, indicate the extent to which fluctuations in export price would be transmitted to the fluctuations of the other principal variables, the result as shown in Table 8.6b.

The percentage deviations of the simulation results, under the two alternative assumptions about the smooth export price series from their control solution, are shown respectively in Tables 8.4a and 8.5b. However, due to the presence of a complicated dynamic large structure and also because the deviations between the actual and smoothed export price series are not uniform but vary from year to year, it is extremely difficult to separate out this multitude of causes and attribute the change, say in a particular variable, to any specific cause. However, the mechanism through which variations in commodity prices are being transmitted to other sectors of the economy pears many similarities to some of the earlier simulations where the model was shocked with either a sustained increase or a sustained decrease in commodity prices. What is different though, is that in is this case, the year-to-year variation in export price is allowed to swing from a large positive to a large negative in accordance with their deviation from trend. Moreover, because not all commodities exhibit the same pattern of fluctuation around their time trend a further complication in the sense that change in commodity prices may offset each other is introduced. Generally, the initial impact of price fluctuation is still in the production and export of the commodities. These effects are however, transmitted through government revenue, and private sector income to other components of aggregate demand, such as, the demand for import, private consumption, government consumption and investment and private investment. The interaction of these variables then determines the level of foreign reserve, money supply, prices the wage rate, employment and loan rate.

As shown in Table 8.4 in 1974, for instance, since the trend which determined export prices for most commodities was substantially lower than the actual export prices of the control solution, the output level of most commodities as determined by the smoothed export prices were relatively lower compared with the variable

Table 8.4a* Linearly smoothed export prices versus variable export prices

Economic sectors	1970	1971	1972	1973	1974	1975	1976	1977	1978	1979	1980
GDP	227.0	667.0	888.5	--78.00	--51.9	227.9	88.71	88.35	44.94	--12.2	--8.3
Non-oil GDP	112.7	557.1	559.30	--47.3	--53.6	116.2	66.70	66.8	33.7	--17.8	--12.2
V. add. agriculture	77.49	224.5	660.31	113.7	--3.57	113.5	--6.96	445.8	334.5	--4.39	11.0
Consumer prices	66.96	33.8	11.11	77.30	--21.9	77.2	33.52	223.23	118.44	--4.51	--6.14
Wages and salaries	99.87	225.6	339.63	222.92	--42.7	118.2	88.49	660.4	442.6	--5.8	0-0.31
Aggregate demand	88.4	554.1	111.36	330.80	--46.40	221.1	99.30	--69.2	--46.94	--6.6	--0.18
GDP deflator	114.6	332.1	66.58	33.91	--23.3	77.23	44.89	226.5	222.7	--0.6	--3.73
Balance of payment	110.6	226.0	991.82	--52.8	--47.2	223.4	77.48	669.7	442.95	--12.4	--6.8

Note:* Derived from Table 8.4 in the appendix (% deviation from control solution).

Table 8.5a* Log linearly smoothed export prices versus variable export prices

Economic sectors	1970	1971	1972	1973	1974	1975	1976	1977	1978	1979	1980
GDP	88.33	998.73	116.42	--5.57	--3.47	--15.41	--10.81	--15.23	--10.63	66.75	--8.26
Non-oil GDP	117.00	772.20	223.36	--14.91	33.59	--5.45	--2.42	--5.38	--2.27	112.57	11.39
V. add. agriculture	--4.37	115.97	66.20	33.59	--3.07	77.27	66.71	77.34	66.64	--3.72	--4.89
Consumer prices	11.59	55.93	22.34	1.30	--1.81	--3.87	--3.79	--3.97	--3.77	--2.79	--1.14
Wages and salaries	114.01	224.27	115.86	13.19	--26.49	--10.27	--17.95	--60.39	--25.1	5-2.79	--0.32
Aggregate demand	88.89	440.23	113.19	77.23	337.14	--11.31	117.32	--43.91	--9.34	--5.79	--0.06
GDP deflator	44.13	99.65	55.19	33.75	336.38	--3.61	--4.50	--3.76	--4.53	00.51	--3.73
Balance of payment	115.24	664.03	221.49	--12.79	--5.79	--12.32	110.69	112.42	110.54	--3.70	--1.60

Note:* Derived from Table 8.5 in the appendix (% deviation from control solution).

export price simulation. The net effect of variation in agriculture sector commodity prices is that the value-added in the agriculture sector declined by 3.57 per cent in 1974 compared to the control solution. The fall in agriculture output then led to a decline in employment in the agriculture sector. As a result of a lower level of agriculture output, real exports (agriculture export) of goods fell by 59.97 per cent as well. This large percentage fall in total export was due to the decline in the value-added in the oil sector in the same year. The decline in total export in 1973, for instance, was not mainly due to a decline in the output of the oil sector or in the value-added in crude oil or because of a decline in export prices generally, but was chiefly a result of the nationalisation of foreign oil companies in Iraq. This operation had an effect on the level of production in the oil sector because of the lack of experience of production and export at that time.

Although exports had fallen, imports continued to remain at a relatively high level, sustained mainly by a large increase in the aggregate demand of the previous years. As a result, there was substantial reduction in the balance of payment account. The worsening in the balance of payments led then to a reduction in the money reserve which in turn brought about a reduction in the level of the money supply and a relatively lower level of aggregate demand resulted in a decline in both the GDP deflator and consumer prices index.

Meanwhile, the income variables in the model were adversely affected by the decline in export prices. Among them, wages and salaries and corporate income appeared to have suffered decline.

Due to the complexity and the multitude of factors involved in bringing about the response pattern as shown in Tables 8.4 and 8.5, no further attempt is made here to provide a detailed analysis for the deviation of the simulated path from its control solution. In general, it is observed that except during the export boom years of 1974, 1978, 1979 and 1980, the simulated values under smooth export prices appear to be higher than those under varying export prices for most of the variables in the model.

Table 8.6a presents a summary table of the mean and the standard deviations of the principal variables, simulated under the first alternative assumptions about the export prices series. While Table 8.7 shows the mean and the standard deviation of principal variables computed under the second alternative assumptions value of the same set of variables. We shall make use of these two tables to discuss the effects of export fluctuations on goal attainment of the economy. It is moreover, noted in Table 8.6 and 8.7 that the simulation results in terms of the mean value and those in terms of the standard deviation value are quite different. In Table 8.6a, in particular, a variable which has a higher mean say under the smooth export prices as such, when making a comparison between the two alternative export price regime: the fluctuating export price and; the smoothed export prices, a selection criterion has to be determined. The simulation results could only be compared either in terms of their means and coefficient variation. We shall first use the mean value as the yardstick for comparison.[6] This will be followed by an analysis of the differences in the coefficient variation under the two alternative assumptions as well.

In terms of output growth, on average, both non-oil and total GDP are higher and less variable under the variable export prices. This is because the level of output of all sectors of the economy is, on the average, larger under smoothed than under varying export prices.

Thus in terms of the objective of steady growth, smooth export prices appear to out-perform varying export prices. These simulation results appear to support the Government's measures to stabilise commodity prices through its participation in various international commodity agreements. The level of non-oil GDP under the linear price trend is, on the average, 3.1 per cent higher than the level of non-oil GDP according to the log-linear price trend and the varying price simulations at 0.45 per cent is, however, lower. In either case non-oil GDP appears to be higher under smooth export prices. The level of smooth export prices generated by the linear time trend appears to be higher than that generated by the log-linear time trend. As shown in Table 8.6 under either the first or the second assumption about the smooth export price series, values-added in the agriculture sector, the mining sector, construction, the manufacturing, transport and the services sector are, on the average, higher than their base solution. Moreover, in either case the standard deviations for non-oil GDP and total GDP are also shown to be lower than base solution which is simulated under the varying export price assumption.

As a result of a higher level of output brought about by the hypothetical change in export prices, employment in both the non-agriculture sectors and the agriculture sector were raised. We can thus conclude that the smooth export prices have the tendency to produce higher average values of both output and employment.

In the area of price stability, the level of both the consumer prices index and the GDP deflator are, on the average, higher under smooth export prices than under varying export prices. In terms of this variability as measured by the standard deviation, both variables seem to have a smaller standard deviation under the smooth prices simulation. This is due to the fact that with more stable export prices, both production and export of commodities would improve. Export price fluctuation would affect production directly through lagged export prices, while they also influence the behaviour of private sector income, private investment and government investment, and Government consumption indirectly through either export earnings or real output. The improvement in production would result in a large export volume and would therefore, bring about an increase in export earnings.

Moreover, with the existence of stable export prices, greater stability in export earnings is assured. This would be likely to bring about a greater stability in the climate for investment. At the same time, there would be an increase in aggregate demand generated through higher export earnings as well as through higher investment expenditure. Moreover, with an improvement in the balance of payment account, the monetary base would probably expand, leading to an increase in the level of the money supply. Although the price levels are expected to be higher,

213

their growth rate would be more uniform in the absence of export price fluctuations.

On average, the total export of goods is higher and less variable under the smooth export prices than under the variable export prices. Likewis, imports of goods were also higher. The stable export prices stimulate the expansion of productivity capacity and the export volumes, leading ultimately to higher export earnings. Higher output also generates higher income and thus higher demand for imports. The increase in imports, however, appears to be less than the growth in export earnings. Consequently, there is an improvement in the current account. The capital account of the balance of payment is also improved mainly due to an increase in the foreign revenues in response more stable export prices. As a result, the level of the money reserve is higher under the smooth export price simulation. So is the level of money supply. The simulation results thus indicate that the balance payment position would improve with greater stability in export prices.

In the simulation under the smoothed export prices, the income indices are higher and more stable, indicating that they have higher means and a lower standard deviation. The total wages and salaries (wage earners) derive substantial benefit from both the increases in total employment and the wage rate. Since the change in wage income has kept pace with the change in national income, its relative share has not been affected.

In the public sector, both revenue and expenditure are higher in the simulation with smooth export prices than with varying export prices. Higher government revenue is the direct result of the higher level of oil revenues from oil export as well as from export and import duties. As the level of public sector consumption expenditure depends mainly on the availability of government revenues, public Consumption expenditure is also raised to a higher level.

Table 8.6b in appendix to Chapter 8, shows the percentage of coefficients of variation of all principal variables under the first alternative assumption. Moreover, it is noted in Table 8.6b that the simulation results in terms of coefficients of variation are quite different. In particular, variables which have a lower C.V as say under the smooth export prices simulation. Moreover, from Table 8.6b it appears that the results under actual export prices have the largest C.V than the other two under simulation cases, such as, the linear smoothed and log-linear smoothed export prices.

In Table 8.7 the mean values and standard deviation values under the second alternative assumptions about the export prices are compared. Moreover, in this case we examine the residual's variability from the trend regression. It is shown that generally the simulation results under either linearly or log-linearly smoothed export price have lower standard deviation values than the simulation results under the assumption of varying export prices. Meanwhile, the mean values of our principal variables in our model under either linearly or log-linearly smoothed and varying export.

Table 8.6d in appendix to Chapter 8, shows the percentage of coefficients of variation under the second assumption in the estimated linear smooth export prices.

214

That the C.V result of the actual export prices has the largest of the C.V than the other two under simulation cases which the linear smoothed and log-linear smoothed export prices. This might be attributed to the fact that this index does not account for trend; deviation are measured from the mean of the observations.

This points out the weakness of the simulation results, in particulars they are unable to indicate conclusively whether or not fluctuating in export is uniformly better or worse for the economy, the export smoothed export prices appear to produce higher prices under the first assumption, see Table 8.6a. In terms of mean values the fluctuating export prices appear equal to the other two alternatives (see Table 8.6c). Therefore, the conclusion, depends on the choice of the comparison. Moreover, in order to take both attributes: means actual value into account, some weighting schemes which reflect the results of attaining each of them to the policy makers have to be devised. This is too involved to be dealt with here.

The existence of a significantly higher level of export prices then stimulated greater production and more exports as well as resulting in a general level of real output, income, employment and a larger external balance.

8.4   An alternative export instability

The above simulation results appeared to indicate that export fluctuation would be detrimental to the Iraqi economy only in terms of achieving S. D and C.V. Export fluctuations may even be beneficial if the policy objectives were to hit a certain target by the mean values. This led to the conclusion that in order to judge whether or not export instability produced an overall adverse effect on the economy it is necessary to assign weight to reflect the relative importance of both the attainment of a high average growth rate S. D and C.V, in terms of their contribution to the social welfare function. However, the derivation of such a weighted scheme is too complicated and involved to be adequately dealt with here. Hence our inquiry will be limited more narrowly to the effects on a number of major variables in the model.

However, the concept of instability as applied to the above simulation tests appears to be rather weak, particularly because it is observed that in quite a number of export prices series, the smoothed paths appear to be systematically lower S.D and C.V than the varying price paths during the earlier part of the simulation period. while the situation reverses itself towards the mean values appear equal under the second alternative assumption of linear time trend. To overcome this weakness of systematic deviation of the varying price series from the smoothed price series, instead of using the historical price series to represent the varying export prices, a set of artificially generated fluctuating export prices was used. The generated prices series have the desirable characteristics of fluctuating randomly around the smooth trend. Moreover, the extent of fluctuation of the artificial series is also made to reflect the fluctuation of the actual price series around their linear trends.

Table 8.6a The mean values and standard deviations of the principal variables in the model, when simulation under alternative one assumptions about the export prices*

Variables	1	2	3	Difference	
				2/1	3/1
Total GDP	5245.91	5280.45	5255.45	0.66	0.18
	(2112)	(2028)	(2033)		
Non-oil GDP	4986.91	5140.64	5003.27	3.08	0.45
	(1633.00)	(1521.00)	(1949.00)		
Aggregate final demand	3981.00	4037.90	3981.99	1.43	0.03
	(1671.00)	(870.00)	(875.80)		
Consumer price index	174.02	174.89	174.09	0.49	0.04
	(24.08)	(13.57)	(12.56)		
GDP deflator	179.00	181.00	180.00	1.12	0.56
	(42.73)	(20.32)	(20.32)		
Wages and salaries	10202.09	10252.09	10220.18	0.49	0.18
	(3543.00)	(1077.00)	(1077.00)		
Balance of payments	1416.91	1417.90	1441.80	3.83	1.76
	(892.30)	(885.30)	(887.30)		

Note: This table derives from Table 8.6 in appendix. P = a +T* Trend *Log (P) = a +T * Trend 1= Actual export price 2= Linearly smooth export prices 3= Log-linearly smooth export 4= Percentage difference.

Table 8.7 The mean values and standard deviations of the principal variables in the model, when simulation under alternative two assumptions about the export prices*

Variables	Actual	Linearly	Log-lin
GDP	245.5 (4142)	5245.5 (108)	5245.5 (565)
Non-oil GDP	5130 (3706)	5140.00 (152.)	5190.3 (662)
Aggregate final demand	3981.0 (2506)	3181.00 (150)	3981.0 (494)
Consumer prices	104.60 (21)	6114.10 (3)	174.00 (9)
GDP deflator	181.00 (44)	181.00 (9)	181.00 (15)
Wages and salaries	833.00 (226)	835.60 (32)	833.60 (37)
Balance of payments	1441.90 (987)	1441.90 (436)	1441.9 (564)

Note: * This table is derived from Table 8.7 in the appendix. P = a+T+T².

In this section, the issue of export price instability will be studied by comparing the model solution generated under fluctuating prices with the control solution obtained with a smooth linear trend of export prices. The fluctuating export prices are generated so as to have their means on the smooth trend. This is done by imposing a normally distributed disturbance term with zero mean and unit variance on the smooth trend. The standard deviation of the disturbance term is also constrained by the trend adjusted standard deviation of historical price series. The trend-adjusted standard deviation is derived from the regression result of the actual export prices against a linear time trend. In this case we limit the standard deviation to 1.0 standard error of estimate of the line trend.

A fluctuating export price series y is obtained by the following identity:

$$y = x + c \cdot z \cdot d \qquad\qquad [8.2]$$

Where;
x = linearly smoothed export prices
z = random number
c = scalar variable equal one in our case
d = standard error of estimate of the linear trend of export price.

Let z be a series of normally distribution random numbers each with mean zero and standard deviation.

Finally, the fluctuating export prices generated from the simulation test is shown in Table 8.8. The percentage deviation of the simulation results under the assumption of fluctuating export prices from their control solution is shown in Table 8.9. While the comparison of means and S.D of the principal variables under assumption of fluctuating export prices with the linearly smoothed export prices is shown in Table 8.10. As can be seen from Table 8.9, with the introduction of the randomly fluctuating export prices, most variables show as many as there are downs over the simulation period, compared with their control solution which was simulation smooth export prices.

217

Table 8.8 **Artificially generated fluctuating export prices for the period 1970-1980**

Years	L	C	D	G	M	V
1970	114.15	314.16	105.10	119.18	120.30	78.55
1971	138.94	374.15	114.32	147.50	168.50	88.55
1972	152.40	399.89	122.90	163.14	183.50	133.30
1973	179.61	447.33	131.87	190.90	219.50	128.70
1974	190.57	569.21	140.37	208.44	230.70	155.10
1975	227.62	532.40	149.65	237.67	282.00	163.72
1976	237.24	551.99	158.11	254.52	290.90	201.00
1977	255.38	585.20	166.83	275.29	313.20	212.28
1978	273.86	650.65	176.14	305.17	366.80	220.28
1979	202.05	668.03	184.56	321.42	373.60	248.64
1980	238.56	730.34	193.83	350.39	424.10	257.62
SEE*	32.41	22.10	4.75	23.73	11.73	28.16

Note: SEE* = Standard error estimate L= Leathers C= Crude oil D= Dates G= Grains M= Manufacturing Industries V= Vegetables.

The rises and falls of the export prices from their actual value are also on the whole well distributed. There were however, exceptions in 1974 and 1975 when it happened that a large number of fluctuating export prices were simultaneously lower than their control solutions.

As shown in Table 8.10, the average values of more than four-fifths of the variables being examined are equal under smooth export prices than under fluctuating export prices. There are, however, a number of variables whose average values are higher under smooth export prices.

Table 8.9a*   Comparison of the simulation results of the artificially generated export prices with linearly smoothed export prices

Economic sectors	1970	1971	1972	1973	1974	1975	1976	1977	1978	1979	1980
Total GDP	44.68	19.66	1.67	-2.99	-4.08	-3.03	11.69	-2.55	-1.73	-1.38	-1.41
Non-oil GDP	26.69	11.65	1.09	-2.82	-0.44	-0.76	-1.35	-1.22	2.26	0.56	0.34
Aggregate final demand	20.70	24.88	1.07	0.04	0.03	-2.79	1.53	2.32	-1.63	-1.32	-1.33
Consumer prices	1.09	-1.60	1.51	-0.66	1.05	-1.03	0.64	1.07	-0.78	0.72	-0.70
GDP deflator	1.14	-2.29	0.05	-0.89	1.23	-1.23	0.78	1.29	-0.81	0.91	-0.67
Wages and salaries	4.57	8.35	-20.32	-7.02	-13.05	8.94	2.36	-27.36	-27.93	31.60	31.30
Government's revenues	7.24	27.01	4.91	-3.89	-4.97	-3.64	1.83	2.64	-20.06	1.35	-1.70
Balance of payment	2.27	23.72	-1.81	-3.54	2.71	-2.64	1.73	1.70	-0.90	2.05	-0.41

Note: This table derived from Table 8.9 in the appendix (per cent deviation from control solution).

In particular, the total GDP appear to be marginally equal under the linearly smoothed export prices with the mean value under the fluctuating prices. Among the components of the aggregate demand, only Government investment, as well as private consumption and private investment appears equal under the linearly smooth export prices with the under fluctuating prices, while real export, imports and the non-oil GDP are higher.

In the price block, both the consumer price index and the GDP deflator are, on average, higher than the smooth export prices simulation.

In the employment block, agriculture employment is equal but non-agriculture employment is lower under smoothed export prices regime. Moreover on aggregate, the smooth export price regime tends to produce a higher level of total employment average.

In the value-added block, the smooth export prices regime tends to produce, on average, a higher level of service sector and manufacturing sector, but a equal level of mean under the smoothed prices and under the fluctuating of the other sector.

Meanwhile, wages and salaries are also higher under the smooth export price regime. The overall government revenue also appears to have a higher mean under the smooth export price regime.

Table 8.10a **A comparison of the mean and the standard deviation of the principal variables under the assumption of fluctuating export prices with the linearly smoothed export prices***

	Mean values	
Principal variables	Fluctuating export prices	Linearly smoothed
Total GDP	5245.45(2008)	5280.54(2028)
Non-oil GDP	5130.36(1524)	5140.64(1521)
Aggregate final demand	3980.82(858)	4037.90(876)
Consumer prices	174.09(13.50)	174.82(12.57)
GDP deflator	180.90(20.85)	181.31(20.32)
Wages and salaries	764.21(559.)	10252.10(1077)
Government's revenues	3105.82(1937)	3434.46(1961)
Balance of payment	1442.00(906.1)	1471.89(887.3)

Note: *This table is derived from Table 8.10 in the appendix.

The results of this table are dependent on the first alternative assumption; P = a + T* Trend. The simulation results thus indicate that the smooth export price regime has the tendency of producing a higher average value for most variables As such, the results should be interpreted carefully. For some variables the smoothed export price regime may give rise to both high average values and lower S. D values when compared with fluctuating export prices. For many variables the answer for the comparison of mean value and S. D value is conflicting. Therefore, the results are rather mixed. Moreover, a great deal of subjective judgement may be needed to determine the relative importance in the attainment of either policy objective: a higher average value or a lower S.D value. In any case, it is most likely that some variable would be adversely affected by fluctuating prices while other variables may benefit from it.

8.5   A statistical test for the difference in the mean GDP

As indicated by Table 8.10, the mean for real GDP under fluctuating export prices was only marginally lower than the mean value of real GDP under the linearly smoothed export prices. In order to determine whether or not these two series are statistically different, a test is derived. This involves testing the null hypothesis that the differences between the two series are Zero against the alternative hypothesis that they are not. The test producer used is the approximate t ratio test. The numerator of the ration is the mean of the difference between the two series while the denominator is the standard deviation of these differences.

The test result indicates that the two series are not statistically different from one another. Moreover, the test of smoothed and non-smoothed export prices under two alternative assumptions were (-0.36) and (-0.004) respectively. Consequently, the result of the alternative simulation test contradicts the result of the earlier simulation test on export instability. Given that the concept of export instability is more accurately defined in the alternative test, we can conclude that from the simulation test of the model, export price fluctuation does not appear to adversely influence the level of GDP.

Table 8.10b   A statistical test for the difference in real GDP under fluctuating and smooth export prices*

Year	Fluctuations export price	Smooth export price	Differences
1970	762	722	40
1971	566	423	143
1972	1554	1571	-17
1973	2786	2717	69
1974	3377	3862	-140
1975	5055	5010	45
1976	6056	6156	-100
1977	7123	7301	-178
1978	8469	8449	20
1979	9454	9595	-136
1980	10882	10741	142
Mean	5098.63	5140.64	-42
Standard deviation	(1524)	(1521)	(113.784)

T ratio = $\dfrac{-24}{113.784}$ = -0.37. Note: * The smoothed export prices calculated from the first alternative assumption; P = a + T *Trend.

Table 8.10c   A statistical test for the difference in real GDP under fluctuating and smooth export price*

Year	Fluctuations export price	Smooth export price	Differences
1970	762	4798	-4036
1971	565	4905	-4340
1972	1554	4874	-3320
1973	2786	4950	-2164
1974	3377	5625	-2248
1975	5055	5806	249
1976	6056	5829	227
1977	7123	5226	1897
1978	8469	5166	3303
1979	9454	5075	4379
1980	10882	4855	6027
Mean	5098.63	5100.9	-2.27
S.D	(1524)	(251)	(1273)

S.D= Standard deviation. T ratio = $\dfrac{-2.27}{1273}$ = -0.01. Note: * The smoothed export prices are calculated from second alternative assumption P= a + T + T^2.

8.5.1 Simulation with alternative growth trends of export prices

The purpose of this simulation is to explore the possible effects of the economy when a shift in the underlying growth trend of export prices occurs. The major export prices of Iraq are determined in the world markets. Although Iraq influences are limited, yet a change in the price trend of her commodity would most certainly produce widespread influence on the entire economy. This is due largely to the important role assumed by the export sector. As noted earlier, the economy depends heavily on the export sector to generate government revenues, investment, employment, income, and foreign revenue.

While the future course of export prices is clouded in uncertainties, it would be useful nevertheless for the economic planners to project the growth paths of the major economic variables under alternative plausible assumption about the future course of export prices, in order to get a better understanding as to the influence of export price on the future course of the economy, to have an indication of the sustainable growth path of the economy and finally to use the projections as a base for formulating contingency plans to deal with these problems should they arise. The simulation results would also enable the policy makers to assess the resources required to achieve certain economic objectives under alternative export price scenarios. For instance, if the growth path of export prices were such that the rate of sustainable growth were much lower than desirable, the public sector could step up its spending programme to take up the slack in economic activity. But before doing that the policy makers may want to know the level of additional spending needed, how it could be financed and what impact it may have on the economy. New resources could be mobilised through raising taxes, through channelling private sector saving to the public sector by raising the rate of provident fund contribution, through foreign borrowing, or through direct financing by the central bank. Alternatively the government may deliberately reallocate resources from a slow growth sector, say the agriculture sector, to a high growth sector, say the manufacturing sector. Such a policy measure would also affect the other sectors of the economy.

The simulations for studying the effects of alternative growth paths on the economy are carried out in the forecasting period 1981-1995. It is therefore necessary first to construct a base line forecast solution, with which the impact of the alternative export price scenarios may be compared.

8.6 Assumption of the base line forecast solution

The base line forecast solution is constructed by making an assumption about the exogenous variables in the model for the period 1981-1995. Since the data for 1981 and 1982 are now partially available, the actual values of the exogenous variables are used wherever possible. The assumptions about some of the most important exogenous variables in the forecast period are examined below.

In making an assumption about the future course of the exogenous variables, care is taken to ensure that they bear a close resemblance reality, and to their historical patterns as well as to reflect any insights gained from other work on Iraq. Moreover, it has also been found necessary to realise some of the endogenous variables at the beginning of the forecast period by making constant adjustments. This is done to reduce the divergence between the actual value and the forecast value of the endogenous variables at the beginning of the forecast period of import prices. It is assumed that the prices of the import of consumption goods and investment goods will grow at 6 per cent per annum, while the prices of imports of the intermediate goods will grow at 6.5 per cent. Historically the prices for intermediate goods were always higher than those of final goods. The assumption about the growth of the real output of the industrial countries is obtained from the most recent forecast solution of the Wharton world model and is expected to grow at an annual rate of about 3.2 per cent. Import duties are assumed to grow gradually from an average of 6.7 per cent in 1981 to 8.9 per cent by 1995. This assumption is made to reflect the current Government Policy of raising import duties to encourage the domestic production of consumer durable. The current trend is expected to continue into the future to promotion the national industries and the current structure of export duty is expected to remain unchanged. The agriculture sector, in particular, is expected to continue to receive favourable treatment from government. Since the imposition of a higher export tax rate would affect the income of the farmers, it is unlikely that the government would risk raising export taxes for the purposes of boosting public sector revenue when one of its central concerns is with regard to reducing the income disparity. Although the control solution constructed in this context is not intended to produce the best possible prediction of the future, it should nevertheless represent a feasible path of the economy.

For the purpose of this simulation study, all exports prices are treated as exogenously determined. Furthermore, in the control solution, the export prices of the commodities in our study are assumed to follow the log-linear growth trend established earlier in the study on the instability issue.

The level of public sector investment is also exogenised and it is assumed that public investment will expand at an annual rate of 15 per cent for the entire forecast period. Judging from the previous growth experience of the public investment expenditure, this assumption seems plausible.

The other major exogenous variables in the model are the import price indices, the tax rate, the tax exceptions on corporate income, the exchange rate, the foreign interest rate and on wages and salaries and the contribution to employees provident funds made by the wage earners. The price indices of exports of developed countries to developing countries are assumed in the determination of import prices.

In the mining sector, the Government is assumed to pursue a national depletion policy with respect to both crude oil and other mining materials, such as phosphate. Thus the output of these materials is expected to grow at a steady 1.2 per cent per annum (excluding crude oil). In the case of the crude oil it is difficult to expect growth of output, due largely to the war between Iraq and Iran.[7]

The tax expenditure on wage income as being currently practised are likely to remain unchanged for the entire forecast period. The non-tax revenue, which consists of profits from the public sector is expected to grow at an annual rate of 1 per cent, its average growth in the 1970s.

In view of the need for financing 1 per cent of real public sector investment it is assumed that net government borrowing from abroad would increase from 10 million I.D in 1981 to about 31 million in 1982 largely offset by an increase in the current account deficit due to a fall in the oil export or in total export earnings and an increase in import payments because of the effects of the war between Iraq and Iran and the Iraqi balance of trade. Meanwhile, in spite of the continuing war as mentioned, after 1983 with a number of large public projects coming on stream, the need for external financing is expected to be increased. Thus, in any case we will note that after 1982, the foreign debt is expected to increase by the government at the level of 2.5 per cent per annum for the rest of the forecast period.

Using the projection of the exogenous variables and the adjustments made for some of the endogenous variables, a base line forecast was obtained. The base line forecast shows an average growth rate of real GDP of 6.62 per cent per annum for the period 1981-1995, while the consumer prices index should grow at an annual rate of 1.48 per cent. The growth rate of real GDP is however expected to be significantly lower than that achieved in the 1970s.

8.6.1 Effects of a change in secular growth trend of export prices

To examine the effects of change in the growth rate of export prices, besides the log-linear trend projection used in the construction of the control solution, two alternative growth paths of export prices are assumed.

Alternative one The export prices of the commodities are assumed to be sustained at the level reached in their most recent peaks for the entire duration of the forecast period. For most commodities, 1980 was the year in which the recent peak was hit. The assumption is denoted as the low growth path in export prices.

Alternative two In this alternative, the export prices are assumed at an average rate of 2.5 per cent per annum from their most recent peak levels. This assumption is denoted as the medium growth path in export prices.

By substituting each of these two assumptions in turn into the model and assuming that all the exogenous assumptions remain valid, two additional sets of the forecast results are obtained for the most significant variables in the model, and it is possible to get an indication as to the effect of change in the secular growth rate of export prices.

225

Since the export prices used in the construction of base line forecast alternative are based on the projection of the log-linear time trend estimated for the 1970s, and because the events of the 1970s were shown to be especially favourable to the primary commodities, the average annual growth of export prices for most of the commodities were relatively high. The smaller growth was in manufacturing production prices which average 2.4 per cent per annum while the highest growth was in crude oil. Comparing all the three export price scenarios, the baseline solution appears to represent a high export price scenario.

The smallest growth was in Date prices which averaged 5.7 per cent per annum while the highest rate of growth was in vegetable oil. Comparing all the three export price scenarios, the baseline solution appears to be represented by a high export price scenario.

Table 8.11 shows the percentage deviation of the forecasting solution under low export price assumption from a control solution, while Table 8.12 shows the percentage deviation of the forecast solution under medium export prices assumption from the control solution and Table 8.13 presents a summary of the mean values and growth rates of the principal variables in the model under the three alternative export price assumptions.

In Table 8.11, the results of low export prices simulation are compared with the baseline forecast period. It is shown that if export prices were to be sustained at the previous peak level for the entire duration of the forecast period, it would result in a significant all round reduction in the level of output, employment, price and balance of payment current account and overall account balance. In the first two years, however, the simulated results generated under the assumption of low export price are significantly higher than their control solution values. This is because at their peaks in 1980, the export prices are very much higher than their trend projected values in the same years, as such it is expected to take about two to three years for the trend projected export prices to reach the same level as that of their previous peak. Thus during the period the trend projected export prices surpassed the previous peak level and began to rise increasingly higher. Thus by 1995, real GDP under the low prices assumptions is 35.4 per cent lower than the base solution. The output of all sectors of the economy is also adversely affected. The most severe reduction in output appears to occur in the agriculture sector. The output of the construction, manufacturing, transport and the service sector as also considerably lower than their base solutions values.

The deviation in the output of the mining sector (excluding oil) appears to be relatively small. This is largely due to the assumption concerning the implementation of the National Depletion Policy to regulate the supply of mining materials to a steady level. As a result, the influence of a fall in export prices on output trends to be reduced.

The combined effect of a lower agriculture output level and lower export prices is that the level of agriculture income falls. Meanwhile, a lower level of employment which was brought about by a lower level of economic activity

226

coupled with a decline in the wage rate imply that the level of wage income is lower than its control solution.

Reflecting a general reduction in overall income, the level of wages and salaries is also lower than the control solution. The reduction in income then led to a private consumption expenditure. Real private investment expenditure has fallen by as much as 32.6 per cent below its control solution value in 1995. Government consumption was also lower than the base solution value. The reduction in government consumption is largely the result of a result of a decline in the level of total government revenues. As a result of a reduction in incomes which was accompanied by a reduction in export and imports, the level of government revenue was significantly lower than its base solution. By the end of the forecast period 1995, for instance, the level of government revenue has fallen about 34.5 per cent from its control solution.

The level of private sector investment expenditure in the lower export prices simulation is also significant lower than its control solution. This is caused largely by a decline in the profitability condition as well as a fall in the level of real output.

Compared to the forecast, both the consumer price index and the GDP deflator are lower in the low export prices simulation. The reduction in the consumer price index is directly the result of a decline in excess liquidity and a fall in aggregate demand while the fall in GDP deflator could be attributed to a decline in both the export prices as well as the consumer prices index.

In the balance of payment account, in the "low export prices" simulation runs are lower than their control solution values. A reduction in the balance of payments of the external account then leads to a decline in the money reserve. Consequently, the money supply is adversely affected by the shift in export prices to a lower growth path. Thus by 1995, the money supply would be 31.3 per cent lower than its control solution.

Table 8.12 compares the forecast result generated under the assumption of a medium growth trend for export prices over the forecast period 1981-1995, with that of the baseline forecast.

The picture presented in Table 8.12 is very similar to that given by Table 8.11, there is therefore no need to repeat the reasons for the simulation results under medium export prices which deviate from the control solution in detail. However, a few significant differences between the two tables do exist. It is noted that in Table 8.12, the positive percentage deviation of the simulation values from this control solution linger on for a longer period in the initial years. This again may be due to the fact that for most export prices, at the time when the peak export price was attained, the peak value was substantially higher than the trend projected export prices. Furthermore, with the previous peak price raised by 2.5 per cent per annum from 1981 to 1995, it naturally needs a longer time for the trend growth path to catch up with the medium growth path.

As expected, the percentage deviation of the simulated result from the control solution under the assumption of a medium growth path for the export prices are

227

uniformly lower than that under the assumption of no growth in export prices, especially towards the later part of the forecast period.

The effect of variation in the growth trend of export prices on the growth rate and the average level of the principal variables in the model over the entire forecast period 1981-1995 are shown in Table 8.13.

As the three forecasts are based, each on an alternative assumption about the future growth paths of export price while all the other exogenous assumptions are identical, it is legitimate to attribute the differences in the simulation results solely to the difference in the growth trend of export prices.

As the results of Table 8.13 are self-evident, we shall limit our comments only to the effects of alternative the growth paths of export prices on the attainment of major economic goals. These goals are: growth and job creation, price stability, income distribution, and equilibrium in the balance of payment position.

In terms of growth, low export price would produce an average growth rate of GDP at 2.55 per cent per annum, while medium prices world produce 4.55 per cent per annum; and high export prices 9.75 per cent per annum. Moreover, output of all productive sectors is also affected by changing export price trend. Output of the agriculture sector appears to be especially sensitive.

Job creation in both non-agriculture and agriculture sectors are affected. The annual rates of the growth of employment in non-agriculture sectors are 1.6 per cent, 1.97 per cent and 2.78 per cent per annum respectively under the assumption of low, medium and high growth paths of export prices.

In the area of price stability, the consumer price index and the GDP deflator are both higher under the assumption of a 'high' growth path in export prices than under a 'low' growth path: the average growth rate for the consumer price index changes from 0.95 per cent per annum under a 'low' growth path to 1.48 per cent per annum under 'high' export prices.

Likewise, the average growth rate of the GDP deflator was raised from 1.01 per cent to 1.52 per cent when the export prices shifted from a low growth path on to a higher growth path.

The wages and salaries in the model show a higher growth rate under the "high" commodity prices assumption compared to the low prices alternative. For instance, the rate of growth in wages was raised from 0.83 per cent to 2.83 per cent. The model appears to have under predicted the rate of growth in corporate income which was significantly raised from 1.73 per cent in the low price scenario to 4.43 per cent in the high price scenario.

The balance of payments' sector, shows that significant gains would be made by a shift of export price from the low growth path on to a higher growth path.

Table 8.11 Comparing a sustained export price at 1980 levels with the trend projected export price

Variables	1981	1982	1983	1984	1985	1986	1987	1988	1989	1990	1991	1992	1993	1994	1995
GDP	3.9	2.97	2.09	-5.96	-9.95	-11.93	-15.9	-17.8	-25.79	-22.94	-25.7	-29.64	-31.6	-33.51	-35
Real GDP	3.29	2.59	0.59	-6.43	-10.24	-12.28	-16.2	-18.2	-25.90	-23.89	-25.8	-29.68	-31.6	-35.49	-35
Private consumption	1.96	1.40	-3.64	-6.99	-10.38	-12.06	-15.4	-17.2	-32.84	-22.10	-23.8	-27.11	-28.8	-30.41	-32
Private investment	4.01	3.36	1.50	-5.18	-8.87	-10.71	-16.2	-16.2	-23.57	-1.67	-23.5	-27.14	-28.9	-30.75	-32
Govt. consumption	1.97	1.76	-3.62	-7.27	-11.09	-12.95	-16.7	-18.5	-25.99	-24.07	-25.9	-29.60	-31.5	-33.27	-33
Govt. investment	2.49	1.58	-3.63	-7.71	-11.82	-13.85	-17.92	-20.0	-28.15	-26.03	-28.1	-32.11	-34.1	-36.11	-38
Export	4.74	2.87	-8.59	-12.41	-14.31	-18.15	-20.02	-27.7	-25.61	-27.57	-27.6	-31.35	-33.3	-35.10	-36
Import	0.72	-2.96	-4.80	-8.48	-12.19	-14.03	-17.70	-19.5	-26.93	-26.79	-26.9	-30.51	-32.3	-34.13	-35
Final demand	2.03	1.66	-3.51	-7.19	-10.90	-12.74	-16.42	-18.3	-25.65	-23.75	-25.6	-29.16	-31.1	-32.86	-34.
GDP deflator	1.35	-3.50	-4.33	-6.56	-6.56	-8.84	-12.24	-13.4	-17.91	-16.74	-17.9	-20.12	-21.3	-22.35	-23
Consumer prices	1.38	1.16	-1.72	-3.82	-5.87	-6.90	-8.96	-10.0	-14.15	-13.08	-14.1	-16.16	-17.2	-18.20	-19
Employment in agri.	2.82	0.37	-0.41	-0.49	-0.58	-0.61	-0.70	-0.9	-0.93	-0.91	-1.0	-1.96	-1.0	-1.99	-2
Non- agri employment	4.44	0.49	-5.67	-8.12	-10.59	-14.30	-14.26	-15.5	-20.71	-19.15	-20.4	-22.81	-24.0	-25.23	-26
V. added agriculture	1.59	1.45	-2.96	-5.98	-9.04	-10.55	-13.59	-15.1	-21.16	-21.13	-19.5	-21.11	-24.1	-37.09	-38
V. added mining	0.15	0.33	0.41	0.14	-0.08	-0.26	-0.42	-0.6	-0.68	-0.78	-0.8	-0.86	-0.9	-0.95	-1
V. added construction	1.69	1.32	-4.32	-8.33	-12.37	-14.37	-18.37	-20.4	-28.41	-26.43	-28.3	-32.31	-34.3	-36.19	-38
V. added manufacturing	2.66	1.66	-3.37	-6.72	-10.10	-11.75	-15.12	-13.8	-32.53	-21.80	-23.5	-26.79	-28.5	-30.09	-31
V. added transport	2.78	1.80	-2.69	-6.34	-11.87	-11.84	-15.48	-17.3	-34.60	-22.71	-24.5	-29.99	-31.8	-33.57	-34
V. added service	3.21	0.22	-1.94	-5.38	-8.86	-10.58	-14.02	-15.8	-22.66	-20.82	-22.6	-26.09	-27.7	-29.41	-31
Corporation income	20.16	11.33	3.40	-0.33	-5.41	-10.53	-15.48	-19.9	-26.01	-31.55	-36.1	-39.98	-71.1	-45.10	-46
Wage and salaries	4.32	2.51	1.51	-6.88	-8.21	-10.87	-13.54	-14.9	-17.52	-18.80	-24.2	-22.82	-24.2	-26.79	-28
Wage rate index	1.00	-2.61	-5.84	-9.09	-10.71	-13.93	-15.54	-22.0	-32.04	-20.37	-22.0	-25.19	-26.8	-28.37	-29
Govt. revenues	2.03	1.64	-3.49	-7.15	-10.86	-12.69	-16.35	-18.2	-25.56	-23.66	-25.5	-29.12	-30.9	-32.70	-34
Money supply	6.12	3.57	-2.33	-5.74	-9.19	-10.90	-14.31	-16.0	-22.89	-21.11	-22.8	-26.22	-27.9	-29.58	-31
Balance of payments	2.71	1.26	-4.66	-8.56	-12.49	-14.45	-18.33	-20.3	-28.16	-26.09	-28.0	-31.09	-33.3	-35.7	-37

Note: (% deviation from control solution).

Table 8.12 Comparing a 2.5 per cent annual growth in the export prices with the trend projected export prices

Variables	1981	1982	1983	1984	1985	1986	1987	1988	1989	1990	1991	1992	1993	1994	1995
Total GDP	6.49	4.97	2.02	0.19	-1.91	-3.89	-5.83	-7.88	-9.73	-11.71	-11.67	-13.61	-15.57	-17.49	-19.00
Real GDP	5.27	3.35	1.41	-2.47	-4.42	-6.36	-8.26	-10.21	-12.10	-12.06	-14.00	-13.92	-15.86	-17.70	-19.00
Private consumption	3.11	1.46	-2.24	-1.88	-1.85	-3.53	-6.88	-8.55	-10.21	-11.91	-11.84	-13.49	-15.17	-16.80	-16.00
Private investment	5.88	4.07	2.23	0.44	-1.41	-3.24	-5.09	-6.88	-8.68	-10.50	-10.46	-12.26	-14.09	-15.88	-17.00
Government's consumption	3.85	2.02	0.16	-1.67	-3.53	-5.39	-7.23	-9.07	-10.90	-12.75	-12.71	-14.53	-16.39	-18.20	-18.00
Govt. investment	4.57	2.56	0.52	-1.49	-3.53	-5.57	-7.57	-9.60	-11.60	-14.18	-13.59	-15.58	-17.61	-19.60	-19.00
Exports	8.95	3.07	-0.84	-2.72	-4.62	-6.53	-8.40	-10.31	-12.17	-14.07	-14.84	-15.90	-17.80	-19.66	-19.00
Imports	2.59	0.32	-1.06	-2.77	-4.71	-6.55	-8.36	-10.20	-11.19	-13.80	-13.79	-15.65	-17.43	-18.22	-21.00
Aggregate final demand	3.90	2.69	2.42	-1.57	-3.41	-5.26	-7.06	-8.89	-10.71	-12.54	-12.51	-14.31	-16.14	-17.94	-17.00
Consumer prices	2.43	1.50	0.38	-0.64	-1.67	-2.70	-3.72	-4.75	-5.76	-6.80	-6.78	-7.78	-8.81	-9.82	-10.00
Employment in agriculture	5.24	2.24	0.32	-0.36	-0.41	-0.45	-0.48	-9.49	-0.53	-0.57	-0.62	-0.66	-0.70	-0.70	-0.00
Non-agri. Employment	5.40	1.95	-3.18	-4.38	-5.61	-6.84	-8.04	-9.27	-10.47	-11.69	-11.67	-12.88	-14.09	-15.30	-16.00
V. added agriculture	3.10	1.63	0.12	-1.37	-2.93	-2.86	-4.30	-4.32	-5.81	-7.32	-10.35	-11.84	-13.34	-14.83	-14.00
V. added mining	0.23	0.46	0.49	-0.29	-0.13	-0.02	-0.14	-0.26	-0.15	-0.35	-0.44	-0.49	-0.53	-0.59	-0.00
V. added construction	3.74	1.76	-2.49	-2.22	02.19	-6.23	-8.19	-10.19	-12.16	-14.15	-14.11	-16.07	-18.06	-20.02	-21.00
V. added manufacturing	5.06	3.37	0.01	-1.70	-1.16	-3.26	-4.86	-6.66	-8.22	-8.89	-11.57	-11.61	-13.20	-14.87	-16.00
V. added transport	4.64	2.84	1.01	-0.88	-2.60	-4.43	-6.22	-8.04	-8.82	-11.64	-11.61	-13.39	-15.21	-16.99	-17.00
V. added service	3.18	1.54	0.19	-1.88	-3.60	-5.33	-5.67	-6.19	-8.68	-10.36	-10.36	-10.30	-13.76	-15.44	-15.00
Corporation income	25.91	13.93	7.67	-5.47	-8.99	-1.64	-5.09	-8.44	-12.70	-16.72	-19.11	-22.81	-26.71	30.11	32.00
Wages and salaries	8.97	5.18	4.51	-6.83	-8.15	-9.48	10.79	-10.79	-12.11	-13.42	-14.74	-14.72	-16.03	-18.65	-18.00
Wage rate index	3.89	2.30	0.68	-0.91	-2.52	-4.14	-5.73	-7.37	-8.92	-10.53	-10.51	-12.09	-13.69	-15.27	-16.00
Govt. revenues	3.91	2.10	0.27	-1.54	-3.37	-5.20	-8.41	-8.83	-10.62	-12.45	-12.41	-14.20	-16.02	-17.80	-17.00
Money supply	8.56	4.87	1.16	0.53	-2.24	-3.95	-5.63	-7.33	-9.01	-10.63	-10.68	-12.35	-14.05	-9.13	-15.00
Balance of payment	6.46	3.18	1.26	-0.69	-2.62	-4.57	-6.51	-8.43	-10.38	-12.29	-14.23	-14.19	-16.09	-18.04	-19.00

Note: (% deviation from control solution).

Table 8.13 The effects of change in the secular growth rate of export prices in the model for the period 1981-1995

Variables	Mean			Rate of growth		
	L	M	H	L	M	H
Current GDP	12495.5	13299	16728.00	2.55	4.80	9.75
Real GDP	11422.2	12287	14691.59	1.44	3.76	6.62
Private consumption	28641.6	3311.9	3587.16	0.39	1.51	2.26
Private investment	489.68	519.64	567.65	0.42	1.68	2.56
Govt. consumption	2424.30	2628.8	2869.93	0.44	1.83	2.75
Govt. investment	2344.52	2389.3	2800.76	0.51	1.67	2.50
Exports	5193.18	5687.2	6215.84	1.40	1.69	2.75
Imports	2036.54	2231.3	2431.61	1.48	1.63	2.63
Agg. final demand	8317.97	9006.1	2825.36	1.63	1.69	2.46
Consumer prices	246.82	257.6	271.30	0.33	0.95	1.48
GDP deflator	257.65	276.4	291.88	0.55	1.01	1.52
Agri. employment	661.60	666.6	968.73	0.97	1.09	1.39
Non-agri employment	2049.83	2280.2	2417.28	1.55	1.97	2.78
V. add. agriculture	659.95	705.3	758.73	0.32	1.36	2.06
V. add. construction	767.35	898.8	922.50	0.64	1.71	3.64
V. add. transport	498.93	535.9	584.58	0.13	1.78	2.45
V. add. manufact. ind.	670.43	722.3	782.43	0.74	1.51	3.78
V. add. mining	37.99	39.9	43.39	0.54	1.51	2.13
V. add. service	1405	1495.9	1625.49	0.44	1.75	2.35
Corporation income	11673	11967	12350.00	1.73	3.51	4.43
Wages and salaries	1269.17	1452.2	1958.07	0.83	1.45	2.82
Wage rate index	701.27	748.87	809.47	0.38	1.15	2.20
Total Govt. Revenue	8340.25	9006.0	9825.35	1.52	2.32	2.66
Money supply	1006.84	1007.6	1025.20	1.42	4.55	7.32
Balance of payment	3150.49	3455.8	3784.12	2.39	5.86	8.84

Note: L= Low, M= Medium, H= High.

8.7 Conclusion

Numerous simulation exercises on the export sector have been carried out in this chapter. The simulation results demonstrated the powerful-influence of the export sector particularly through changes in export prices on the other sectors of the economy.

Two alternative simulation tests on the effects of export price fluctuations on real GDP have produced inconclusive results. The first test seems to support the contention that a smooth export price would produce higher real GDP on the average, compared with the fluctuating one. In the second simulation test, while real GDP is, on average, marginally higher in the case of smooth export prices compared with the fluctuating export prices, neither of them are statistically different. Thus if we take export price instability to mean random fluctuations around some underlying trend, then it does not appear that instability is inherently bad in terms of affecting the level of real GDP.

Perhaps the main problems of export fluctuations are found at more micro level and not the level of real GDP. One contention is that export fluctuations are per se burdensome. This is mainly due to the difficulties caused to the businessman who has to adjust to changing economic conditions. For instance, a firm may find it necessary to lay off experienced workers in severe economic recession brought about by a sharp decline in export prices. As the economy recovers, there is no guarantee that it would be able to re-hire its old workers, because they may have found new employment in the mean time. This is an obvious loss to the company. Furthermore, by temporarily shutting down their business operations to minimise losses in severe recession, the businessman may also find he has lost their customers and markets share when they open for business later.

The most serious problem of export fluctuation is the uncertainty associated with the magnitude and duration of export fluctuations. Thus in either an export boom or an export slump, the businessman has to be watchful for the signs of changing export conditions. An incorrect reading or poor assessment of the export sector can be very costly. For instance, if he expects the export sector to recover soon and undertakes to restock his inventory by importing, and if the recovery does not materialise, he may end up having to bear a large cost for holding an additional inventory.

Some costs of adjustment are also incurred by the public sector and households. In the household sector, a decline in export prices may mean unemployment for some members of the family who now need the support of the family for food and shelter. In the public sector, poor economic performance often means the need for government aid and subsidies for the needy.

However, since our model does not capture these micro aspects, it is difficult to use the model to show the effects of export instability on the risk bearing behaviour of the private or the social adjustments required to deal with export fluctuation. In order to do that the model has to be further disaggregated to incorporate various aspects of social behaviour.

Furthermore, it appeared that the social and political repercussions of export instability are much more severe. Unfortunately, these effects could not possibly be captured with the use of an econometric model. However, it was concluded that a shift in the growth path of the export prices would have important effects on the economy.

Notes

1. Adams and Behrman review these earlier studies and find them defective both on a priori and methodological grounds. They conclude that only simulation studies which are carried out through the use of an integrated econometric model of a particular country that incorporates the primary commodity sector, the complete structure of the economy, and perhaps the specific international commodity markets of interest would be useful in providing a reasonable test of the commodity problems. Following their suggestions, an econometric analysis with the use of an integrated macroeconometric model is being used here to examine the export fluctuation of the Iraqi economy.

2. The relative contribution of price and quantity variations to export instability has been examined by Murray (1978), who looked only at aggregate indices, and the distinction between price and quantity components is neglected. See also Chung M. Wong (1986).

3. The distinction between oil and non-oil exports was made in this study, in order to bring out the importance of the oil sector in terms of its huge contribution to its foreign exchange earnings in the country. Therefore, the function of the demand for Iraq oil exports was determined in this study by the exogenous variables. One of the most important was the oil prices variable. Therefore, the study provided that the long-run elasticities of Iraqi crude oil exports with respect to the oil prices was (-1.71). The elasticities seem quite high and they indicate how sensitive Iraqi oil exports were to the price variable. The size of these elasticities seem consistent with Iraqi experience. Moreover, the events of the Middle East in the late 1970s were another indication. When the oil prices increased, the Iraqi oil exports (in volume) increased from 0.544 billion barrels in 1972 to 0.754 billion barrels in 1973, and the overall balance of trade surplus increased from I.D 221.5 million in 1968 to I.D 4659 million in 1979. Meanwhile, revenues derived from oil exports provided foreign exchange for essential imports and strengthened Iraq's external account. The strengthening of external position was indicated by the rise in gold and foreign exchange reserves held by the Central Bank from $781 million at the end of 1972 to $6990 million at the end of 1977 (Europe Publications, op. cit., p. 391).

4. Voivodas (1974), Mac Bean and Nguyen (1981) used the terms of linear time trend in analysis of total earnings instability.

5. In this chapter we are dependent on the two sorts of equation to estimate the linear smooth export prices, which are:
   (1) $p = a + b\,T$. (2) $p = a + b_1\,T + b_2\,T^2$

6. These circumstances did not appear under assumption of the linear smoothed export prices estimated by the linear regression equation which is:
   Price = $a + b_1\,T + b_2 T^2$ (see Table 8.6c in appendix to chapter 8).

7. Until 1960 oil producing countries had acted largely individually with the international major companies, whose collective interest dictated a co-ordinated policy over the company-host country distribution of revenue. *OPEC*, after its establishment in 1960 (this organisation, the founding members of which were in Iraq, Saudi Arabia, Iran, Kuwait, Venezuela and Nigeria etc.) succeeded in stopping the decline in oil prices and in establishing posted prices until early 1970. The establishment of *OPEC* shifted the subject of conflict from the division of revenues to pricing and production policies and altered the balance of power of antagonists with the inception of a collective front of oil producers. The picture of *OPEC* as setting the price of oil without regard to usual market forces fares little better than that of a unified *OPEC* determining the quantity to be supplied. True, *OPEC*'s members do meet periodically to agree on prices, but the

233

important question is what determines the prices on which they agree. Although the existence of *OPEC* has almost cancelled out the differences in the oil prices of exporting countries, the existence of non-*OPEC* members among the oil producing countries coupled with the fact that there are differences in the oil quality. We speculated that the Iraqi oil prices can differ from the world's average of the same commodity. It, therefore, implies that if the export price of Iraqi oil falls relative to the world price, more Iraqi oil will be in demand and vice-versa. *OPEC* has always attempted to put agreements between *OPEC* countries and the international oil companies. These agreements reflected the buoyant world oil demand and the determination of these countries to protect their oil revenues from fluctuations in the value of the USA dollar, the currency in which most prices are quoted, in order to save the prices from decline.

It is possible to outline the role of *OPEC* in preserving its members' interests throughout the period of study in the following points:

a. In 1960-1970 *OPEC* succeeded in stopping the decline in the oil price and in stabilising posted prices until 1970. In 1971 the Teheran agreement fixed the income tax rate at 55 per cent and raised posted price by 40.5 cents per barrel and adopted a schedule for oil price increase.
b. In Teheran in 1973 a compromise price was adopted between the auction price and the October 1973 level of $11.65.
c. In 1974 *OPEC* countries turned their attention to increasing their take on company's equity oil (40 per cent share). The net effect was to raise royalties from 12.5 per cent to 20 per cent of posted prices, and income tax from 55 per cent to 85 per cent.
d. In December 1975, oil prices were raised by 10 per cent to offset part of the world price inflation and in 1976 and 1977, the price of oil increased 10 per cent and 5 per cent respectively. This small summary for the role of *OPEC* countries in the world oil market.

Iraq, despite its reputation for being one of the *OPEC* 'hawks', does not favour such high petroleum prices as some other producers, though it wishes to get a good return for its natural resource, it nevertheless cannot afford to price itself out of the market. If Iraq can retain its customers, its income from petroleum exports will give a vital boost to the economy.

Just as Iraq has taken a more moderate line on oil price, so it has opposed concerted production cuts. After the Arab-Israeli war of October 1973, Iraq opposed the restrictive sales policy of the organisation of Arab Petroleum Exporting Countries. Iraq even increased sales to favoured countries. It did, however, follow *OPEC*'s policy embargoing supplies to the USA and the Netherlands (Europe Publication, op. cit.).

9 Summary and Conclusion

At the beginning of this study two goals were defined, the construction of a workable econometric model for Iraq and the application of the model to analyse some of the macro-economic policies currently pursued by the Government. In particular, the model was to be used to study both the effects of export fluctuation on the Iraqi economy as well as the manner in which discretionary policy measures may be taken to mitigate the effects of export fluctuations.

Interest in econometric analysis in Iraq has grown rapidly in recent years partially due to a more active use of discretionary policy measures since the early 1970s, as the Government took entirely new approach to economic development. In particular, the public sector began to play an increasingly large role in economic activity in the pursuit of its new economic policy. This change development strategy was followed by more frequent use discretionary fiscal and monetary measures, both for the purpose of short-term stabilisation and also for the promotion of long-term economic growth and development.

In order to accomplish this task, the study began in Chapter two by giving a brief survey of the economy with a view to presenting descriptive picture of it. In that chapter were considered the structure of the economy with the emphasis on sectoral contribution to GDP and foreign exchange earnings. Most importantly, the chapter reveals how the agricultural sector's share of the GDP and its export earnings has fallen during the period 1968-1980. It also reveals how, in contrast to this, oil began to emerge as the leading sector in terms of its contribution to the GDP and foreign exchange earnings. In fact, as from the mid-70s, the oil sector has been contributing more than 90 percent of foreign exchange earnings. Because of the growing importance of and high dependence on the oil sector, it is observed that fluctuations in this sector (oil) have largely dictated the shape of the economy. By this we mean that a downward trend in the performance of this sector in recent times, has meant a recession for the economy while an upward trend has often proved to accompany a period of boom.

Also because of the high dependence on the export sector, we have paid particular attention to the oil export sector both in the strategy of development, economic growth, and the estimation of the model in the macro-economic model in Chapter 5.

The indirect impact of the export sector on the Iraqi economy, which is represented in chapter three, i.e. the benefit of foreign exchange receipts which Iraq derived from her export sector, has been examined and analysed. It was difficult to show the utilisation of all foreign exchange receipts which Iraq earned from her export sector during the period of study, as it was difficult to obtain the relevant statistical data. Nevertheless, such data as were available concerning the utilisation of revenues derived from oil sector, i.e., oil revenues. Statistical and economic analysis of the utilisation of oil export revenues and the influence of such utilisation on Iraq's economy, show significantly the indirect benefits which Iraq derived from her trade. This necessitated an examination and evaluation of the utilisation of the oil export sector in the economic development plans and the ordinary budgets. During the period 1968-1980, at current prices, oil revenues accounted on average for more than 90 percent and 58.7 percent of the economic development plans and ordinary budget's revenues respectively.

This chapter revealed the fact that during the period under investigation the increase in export revenues, particularly revenues for oil exports, has been the fundamental factor behind the development of the indigenous economy, and the increased economic growth which characterised Iraq's economy during the period of 1968-1980.

As regards the direct impact of export sector, the study indicates that although the direct benefit of the oil sector for the economy was limited, on the whole, such benefits were not felt on a large scale. In other words, the forward linkages have become stronger, through the supply of low cost raw material to the domestic economy, for instance, petrochemical industries, while the contribution of the backward linkages was some what insignificant. This could be attributed, in part, to the highly capital-intensive nature of the oil industry and to the failure of the domestic economy to meet the oil sector's requirement in capital equipment. So the result of this study corroborates Hirschman's theory of unbalanced growth and, refutes Rollin's pessimistic arguments, and what is more, it is the forward linkages, rather than the backward linkages as Hirschman tends to believe, which have been the prime factor in the development of the Iraqi economy.

In addition, it was found that the direct benefits of Iraq's merchandise non-oil sector could be substantial, as compared with those of the oil export sector as a result of:

1. certain economic characteristics of the non-oil sectors in the Iraqi economy,
2. the relatively strong integration between the non-oil sectors with Iraqi indigenous sectors and,
3. the suitability of the Iraqi economy.

In order to create an interlocking between sectors and linkages (forward and backward) and a high rate of growth and indeed for Iraq to develop its full economic potential it is strongly contended that more attention should be given to solving the problems of the agricultural sector, and that the Government should continue to expand and improve the manufacturing sector. The period of study shows that Iraq's foreign trade, to a limited extent directly, and to a very large extent indirectly benefited Iraq's economic development.

Before formulating our model, we undertook a brief survey of some of the relevant existing work in this field. Chapter five of our thesis took up this exercise. In view of the fact that analysis of macro-economic model equations has been one of the leading areas to gain the attention of researchers, we considered the previous work on macro-model functions for Iraq. In that section we observed that these earlier investigations have suffered from miss-specification error.

The chapter showed that existing macro-economic models of the economy by UNCTAD staff (1968) and A. Kader's model have largely concentrated on the demand side and ignored the supply function. None of them paid attention to prices, wages, financial sector, Government activities, employment or the income distribution. Even deflator equations were excluded by these earlier models.

In the light of facts obtained from previous existing works and our prior knowledge of the economy, we built up in chapter five a plausible model of the economy.

The macro model that provides the framework for our investigations, is a disaggregated multi-sector model. The major building block of the model includes the production block, the aggregate demand block, the employment wages and factor income block, the foreign trade and balance of payments block; the prices block, the Government block, and financial block. In specifying the macro-model, the characteristics of the economy as well as data limitation were taken into account, the length of the estimation period for the equations to another, with the maximum number of observations being 21 (1960-1980)and the minimum being 15(1966-1980). We used the OLS methods for all the equations and estimated by 2TSL numbers of equations, in view of the simultaneity of the system. The principles were that the model should incorporate sufficient policy instruments and that it should reflect the real world situation reasonably well. In many of the specified equation, we included the nationalisation of oil industry and the oil price hike dummies on the speculation that the general level of economic activity may have been affected by these events.

On the whole, the macro model performed satisfactorily, the historical dynamic simulation result showed that the model was able to track most variables reasonably well. Although a number of endogenous variables suffered from a systematic downwards bias after 1975, the extent of this downwards bias was relatively small over time. consequently, this problem was resolved through the use of a small adjustment factor. Two main lessons were learnt from the construction of the macro-model. Firstly, in designing the structure of the model, it pays for the model builder to acquire a good understanding of the forces that operate in the economy. While the basic economic principles may hold true in different economies, there also exist certain unique characteristics and institutional differences between one economy and another and as such, modification to the general principles is often necessary. Failure to take these special factors into account would result in a weak representation of the economy. Consequently, familiarity with the economic history of the nation being modelled as well as the occurrence of major econometric events in the sample period would greatly enhance the quality of the model.

Secondly, the estimated relationship reveals some important characteristics in the model. Some of the major findings are as follows: in the agriculture sector the production of grains is shown to be insensitive to price changes. The production of vegetable oil is responsive to price variations, while Dates production is only moderately responsive to price changes. In the mining sector, oil sector is shown to be sensitive to lagged value added in the oil sector; the production of other mining such as sulphur and phosphates are both responsive to the value added in the oil sector and value added in the other mining sectors. The output of the manufacturing sector is strongly influenced by domestic demand and exports.

In the estimation of private consumption equation, it is shown that aggregate national savings is sensitive to real interest rate. This relationship implies that in order to raise the level of national savings, a desired policy measure would be to liberalise the interest rate policy. The model confirms the importance of both the availability and cost of bank credit in influencing the level of private sector investment.

Due mainly to the existence of a severe under employment situation in the rural sector, as well as, the measures taken towards mechanisation in a large number of farm operations, the demand for labour in the agriculture sector has a relatively low elasticity with respect to changes in agriculture output.

The Philips curve phenomenon has been shown to be operative in Iraq, which in turn suggests a legitimate role for the use of stabilisation policies. The demand for wage increases is influenced largely by gains in productivity as well as current and past movements in consumer prices. The existence of excess aggregate demand presumes and higher production costs are major factors in influencing the level of consumer prices. The export volume of primary commodities is governed by its level of output. Neither stockpiling nor domestic usage of the primary commodities has had any significant influence on the volume of export. The volume of manufactured exports is largely determined by the world's general economic conditions; the prices of Iraqi manufactured goods relative to those of the rest of the world does not seem to be statistically significant.

The demand for imports of consumption goods is sensitive to price variations, as is the demand for intermediate and investment goods.

In the multiplier and sensitivity tests, the model appeared to perform reasonably well. All the policy simulations appeared plausible and conformed well to both a priori expectation as well as to empirical observation. From these exercises, the following points are observed:

1. Of particular significance was the role played by import of goods. Due largely to the fact that the import of goods constituted a major component of the gross domestic expenditure, and at the same time they were highly sensitive to variation in aggregate demand, as such there were substantial import leakage's whenever stimulate economic policies were used.

2. In general, the total export volume was relatively sluggish to stimulate economic policies. This was due mainly to the fact that in Iraq primary exports were from the bulk of total export of goods. While the manufactured exports

were relatively responsive to stimulate economic policies, primary exports were not.

3. Fiscal policy simulations involving the use of both tax measures and Government expenditure were examined. The tax measures examined include a sustained five percentage points increase in export duties, and a sustained five percentage points increase in the tax rate of all categories of income. In addition, a stimulates fiscal policy measure in the form of a 10 percent increase in real Government consumption was also studied.

4. A sustained increase in export duties affected other economic variables through two principal channel, the commodity prices channel and the Government revenue channel. Consequently, both the production and exports of the primary commodities declined. Since output of all productive sectors of the economy was adversely affected by the policy change, both real and total GDP declined. Reacting to a fall in output, employment fell too. In the Government sector, the increase in the export tariff rate significantly boosted the tax revenue from export duties while revenue from other sources declined marginally. However, on balance the increases in export duties were more than enough to offset the declines in income tax, excise duties and import duties. Consequently, Government revenue rose which in turn brought about an increase in public consumption expenditure. In response to this policy change, the external position worsened, but the inflation situation improved. In an environment without public sector intervention, an increase in the export tariff rate resulted in a slower economic growth, a decline in employment, an increase in the balance of payment deficits a lower price level and a smaller Government deficit.

5. In the case of a sustained five percentage points increase in the tax rate of all categories of income, which was simultaneously accompanied by a measure to channel the additional revenue collected to raise the level of Government investment, the simulation results indicated that such a policy measure would lead to a marginally higher of output and employment; a marginally lower consumer price index, a higher interest rate, a lower level of money supply as well as a lower level of bank credit available to the private sector. It was also shown that after lapse of a few years, the initial positive output effect on a number of sector quickly diminished due to the onset of tighter credit conditions.

6. The results indicated that a sustained 15 per cent increase in the oil export, in particular, has little effect on domestic non-oil economic activities and the major part of the gain from these exports comes through their effect on domestic demand.

239

7. Simulative policies such as the increase in money supply and Government expenditure also produced desirable results.

In Chapter 6, we examined the tracking ability of the model using standard statistical criteria. For this exercise, the model is shown to be reasonably successful, particularly for the sample period. This fact is demonstrated further by the use of the graphical techniques which shows that the model is able to capture turning-points.

The export sector simulation chapter explored the effects of both short-term fluctuations of export prices as well as variations in the underlying growth trend of export prices on the economy. As expected, changes in export prices as well as variations in the underlying growth trend of export prices are shown to have a significant impact on most variables in the model. Two alternative simulation tests for export instability were carried out. One test used actual export prices, while the other used artificially generated export prices to represent fluctuating prices. Moreover, this alternative assumption examined under two alternative of measure of trend of export price as well. The comparison of fluctuating various smoothed export price was inconclusive. In the first case where the historical export prices were used to represent fluctuating export prices, the simulation results led one to the conclusion that smooth export prices were able to give, on the average, higher levels of output and employment growth as well as a better external balance position. But due to the presence of long cyclical swings in export prices during the simulation period, there exists a systematic deviation between the time paths of smoothed export prices and fluctuating prices for most commodities studied. In particular, at the beginning of the simulation period, the smoothed export prices were higher than fluctuating export prices. This systematic deviation makes the choice of historical export prices as representative of fluctuating prices series rather weak because it is too presumptuous to assume that fluctuating export prices would follow a set pattern. Consequently, a more acceptable way of generating fluctuating export prices was used. In the second case, the export price series were artificially generated. From each export price, an artificial price series was generated by taking into account both its underlying growth trend and the extent of its variation from the trend. In the simulations where the artificially generated export prices were used, the levels of real GDP under the smoothed and fluctuating prices were not statistically different from one to another which implied that export price fluctuations did not have any effect on real output growth. However, it should be recognised that the constructed model did not adequately capture the micro aspect of decision making under uncertainties nor did it capture the possibility of welfare loss incurred by farmers due to export fluctuations.

Consequently, the present conclusion should be treated as being tentative. Further investigations suggested several directions, in which further research on the commodity problems may proceed. In particular, it may be necessary to evaluate the effect of export fluctuations in an optimal control framework. In such a framework, the social cost incurred due to export price fluctuations can be explicitly introduced as a target variable in the objective function. Moreover, by making use of the optimum control framework it is possible to evaluate the existence of trade-off in the attainment of different economic goals such as price stability; economic growth, private sector investment, external balance and employment growth when the economy is subjected to varying degrees of export fluctuations.

The export sector simulation demonstrated the pervasive influence of the export sector on the rest of the economy. It was shown that a sustained decline in export prices exerted a greater negative effect than a sustained increase in export prices exerted a positive effect, even when the magnitude of change in either direction was identical. Meanwhile, a shift in export price to a higher growth path would be beneficial to most variables in the model.

9.1 The problems and limitations of this study

During the course of this study we have encountered a number of problems. The first section of this part addresses itself to discussion of some of these problems and the last section considers the limitation of our study and suggests a number of areas where further development is needed.

9.1.1 The problems of the study

By far the most intractable problem which an econometric model builder in a developing country faces arises from his poor data base. The set of data which exists prescribes the level of detail, disaggregation and sophistication of the model, determines the estimation horizon and affects the reliability of the model.

Whereas data problems are a matter of degree, they are so serious for model building in developing countries that some of these problems should be detailed. The discussion is organised according to four major characteristics of available data in developing economies, namely:

1. incompleteness
2. short sample period
3. low reliability of the data; and
4. constant revisions of data.

Data do not exist for some vital variable. As already mentioned in the study this problem has further created an econometric problem of errors-in-variables. This problem of incomplete data has effected, to a very great extent, the level of detail, disaggregation and sophistication of the model. Another dimension of this problem is that in most cases, data on certain aggregates are not sufficiently broken down to allow for further disaggregates. For example, data on consumer expenditures are not broken down into durable and non-durable forms to allow for treating these

241

expenditure categories differently. Also, the available data do not distinguish between domestic private investment expenditure, stock building and foreign private investment. This kind of problem makes explicit specification of certain relationships unfeasible a case in point being those of private investment expenditure and stock building equations.

Apart from the earlier problem of the incomplete data, some of the existing data is not available for a long period. This definitely reduces the scope of the study. It further creates an econometric problem of there being an insufficient degree of freedom. This has effected the choice of estimation methods adopted.

There is also the problem of the quality of data. In so many cases data are not from the same source and the method of reporting and units used may be different, thereby necessitating conversion from one unit to another with its attendant problem of rounding up. In some cases, data are not available in the form desired. For example, it would have been more useful if data on wages had been given as unit labour costs or at least if the available data had made it possible to generate the required series. This would have made the interpretation of the coefficient of this variable in the price equation a lot easier. The quality of most data is so poor that it will have a spill-over effect on the quality and hence the reliability of our results.

The constant revisions of data (which are very common in this type of economy) make such a model tentative; the estimates of the coefficients for the structural equations may change or the revised data are used in re-estimation. This problem implies that models need to be revised as and when new data become available.

9.2 Limitations of the macro model and further research work

In general, the objectives of this study have been met. But the model presented above is a highly simplified one and it is difficult to envisage that such a simple model will adequately represent an economy of the diversity and size of the Iraqi type. Thus, our attempt is primarily exploratory and we hope that subsequent attempts will expand the model. A few of the directions in which development is needed are noted below:

1. To use the constructed model in formulating optimal policy packages through the use of an optimal control framework.
2. To incorporate a demographic sector which takes into account rural-urban migration. The issue of urban congestion is becoming increasingly important. So are the problems of high unemployment among the unskilled workers in the cities and urban poverty. Unfortunately information on rural- urban migration is rather scanty at the moment, as such work in this area has to be preceded by data compilation.

3. To further disaggregate the public expenditure and take into account the effect of development expenditure allocation on the economy.
4. We do note an explicit stock building and foreign private investment function. In our study, we have assumed that these components be regarded as the balancing items. With the availability of data on these components there is the need to explore this area further.
5. We have constructed an annual model because there are no quarterly data. A quarterly model would be more suitable for dynamic analysis and hence further work in this area is desirable when quarterly data are available.
6. We do not divide the private consumption into urban and rural. In our model, we have only the total private consumption. With the availability of the data on these components there is a need to explore this area further.

Finally, we have not considered the details of fiscal and monetary policy which should be included in a detailed model. This is another area that could be fruitfully explored with the availability of data.

Appendix to Chapter 4

The fiscal (direct) effects of the exports sectors on the economic sectors in the Iraqi Economy

Table 4.5   (Inverse of 1968 $(1-A)^{-1}$ (input inverse))

Economic sectors	1	2	3	4	5	6	7	8	9	10	11
1. Agriculture	1.122897	0.019140	0.002014	0.233075	0.111633	0.028540	0.027218	0.057788	0.003528	0.000000	0.0269
2. Mining and Quarrying	0.000455	1.008932	0.000080	0.006237	0.064600	0.000765	0.001516	0.002261	0.000822	0.000000	0.0053
3. Crude Oil	0.000891	0.001319	1.000169	0.019635	0.009376	0.002404	0.002235	0.003907	0.000295	0.000000	0.0021
4. Mfg. Indus.	0.066274	0.098051	0.012327	1.459932	0.697161	0.178767	0.166218	0.290505	0.021933	0.000000	0.1614
5. Construction	0.003012	0.006008	0.000434	0.004398	1.010283	0.000552	0.013681	0.017563	0.011989	0.000000	0.0769
6. Electric and Water	0.004285	0.003892	0.000161	0.013083	0.008693	1.023266	0.025696	0.008008	0.003068	0.000000	0.0110
7. Wholesale and Retail Trade	0.149548	0.066997	0.002016	0.233274	0.114547	0.028564	1.029982	0.049094	0.003601	0.000000	0.0261
8. Transport and Communication	0.072276	0.313977	0.002523	0.094161	0.064351	0.011532	0.070662	1.025660	0.003267	0.000000	0.0175
9. Banking and Insurance	0.008951	0.005059	0.000358	0.013904	0.007075	0.002836	0.060053	0.006671	1.013027	0.000000	0.0033
10. Public Administration	0.000003	0.000004	0.002937	0.000058	0.000028	0.000007	0.000007	0.000011	0.000001	1.629434	0.0000
11. Services	0.017056	0.073013	0.001286	0.022304	0.125211	0.002738	0.018309	0.238197	0.006548	0.000000	1.0778

Table 4.6 (Inverse of 1968 $(1-A)^{-1}$ (output inverse))

Economic sectors	1	2	3	4	5	6	7	8	9	10	11
1. Agriculture	1.122879	0.000438	0.002415	0.230960	0.037864	0.001707	0.012108	0.021701	0.000225	0.00000	0.0129
2. Mining and Quarrying	0.019800	1.008932	0.004168	0.268969	0.954484	0.001990	0.029361	0.037106	0.002286	0.000000	0.1166
3. Crude Oil	0.000743	0.000025	1.000169	0.016221	0.000120	0.000830	0.001228	0.00016	0.000295	0.000000	0.0009
4. Mfg. Indus.	0.066870	0.002274	0.014921	1.45928	0.23883	0.010791	0.074666	0.110548	0.001414	0.000000	0.0814
5. Construction	0.008871	0.000407	0.001535	0.012836	1.010283	0.000097	0.017936	0.019508	0.002255	0.000000	0.1133
6. Electric and Water	0.071613	0.001495	0.003215	0.216717	0.049343	1.023266	0.191954	0.050481	0.003277	0.000000	0.0926
7. Wholesale and Retail Trade	0.335919	0.003458	0.005433	0.519284	0.087362	0.003838	1.029979	0.041563	0.000517	0.000000	0.0292
8. Transport and Communication	0.191613	0.019131	0.008026	0.247395	0.057927	0.001829	0.083397	1.025642	0.000553	0.000000	0.0232
9. Banking and Insurance	0.140169	0.001821	0.006718	0.215785	0.037621	0.002657	0.418676	0.039390	1.013027	0.000000	0.0260
10. Public Administration	0.000004	0.000000	0.006022	0.000098	0.000016	0.000001	0.000005	0.000007	0.000000	1.629434	0.0000
11. Services	0.017056	0.073013	0.003085	0.044198	0.085019	0.00328	0.016298	0.179651	0.000837	0.000000	1.0778

Table 4.7 (Inverse of 1976 $(1-A)^{-1}$ (output inverse))

Economic sectors	1	2	3	4	5	6	7	8	9	10
1. Agriculture	1.201802	0.003797	0.000677	0.376470	0.376470	0.001694	0.011670	0.078751	0.002400	0.0129
2. Crude Oil	0.000396	1.000045	0.000010	0.000158	0.006203	0.000028	0.001850	0.000726	0.000038	0.0002
3. Sulphur	0.000010	0.024811	1.000000	0.000004	0.000154	0.000001	0.000046	0.000018	0.000001	0.000000
4. Mining	0.015792	0.002934	0.000742	1.007694	0.227130	0.001075	1.052087	0.030453	0.011285	0.0077
5. Mfg. Indus.	0.110801	0.012548	0.002753	0.044108	1.734147	0.007789	0.517061	0.202915	0.010689	0.0571
6. Electric and Water	0.053055	0.016248	0.006182	0.024853	0.457012	1.028772	0.157222	0.161994	0.010895	0.0494
7. Construction	0.001058	0.001400	0.000066	0.002143	0.006031	0.000086	1.057977	0.004217	0.010642	0.0004
8. Wholesale and Retail Trade	0.232176	0.034779	0.03272	0.124498	0.543223	0.002520	0.296916	1.116638	0.000559	0.0191
9. Banking and Insurance	0.052206	0.030819	0.001132	0.043313	0.247010	0.001785	0.133527	0.217110	1.118364	0.0377
10. Services	0.110981	0.072467	0.002616	0.067646	0.580334	0.003220	0.234167	0.428798	0.015856	1.0769

Table 4.8 (Inverse of 1976 (1-A) $^{-1}$ (input inverse))

Economic sectors	1	2	3	4	5	6	7	8	9	10
1. Agriculture	1.201802	0.00849	0.071264	0.074580	0.208029	0.036466	0.077619	0.070673	0.009622	0.0999
2. Crude oil	0.001772	1.000045	0.004632	0.003977	0.015328	0.002683	0.005501	0.002913	0.000685	0.0070
3. Sulphur	0.000000	0.000053	1.000000	0.000000	0.000001	0.000000	0.000000	0.000000	0.000000	0.000000
4. Mining	0.02802	0.000116	0.013845	1.007695	0.022264	0.004105	1.124127	0.04848	0.08025	0.0105
5. Mfg. Indus.	0.200519	0.005077	0.524063	0.449982	1.734148	0.303485	0.622349	0.329553	0.077551	0.7970
6. Electric and Water	0.002464	0.000169	0.030210	0.006507	0.011729	1.028772	0.004856	0.006752	0.02029	0.0177
7.Construction	0.001591	0.000471	0.010349	0.018163	0.005011	0.002775	1.057977	0.005691	0.064150	0.0055
8.Wholesale and Retail Trade	0.258711	0.00866	0.383509	0.782037	0.334476	0.060364	0.220046	1.116637	0.024984	0.1639
9. Banking and Insurance	0.013022	0.001719	0.029690	0.060901	0.034045	0.009580	0.022152	0.048599	1.118364	0.07248
10. Services	0.014410	0.002104	0.035732	0.049512	0.041636	0.008997	0.020221	0.049963	0.008253	1.0769

Table 4.9 (Inverse of 1980 $(1-A)^{-1}$ (output inverse))

Economic sectors	1	2	3	4	5	6	7	8	9	10	11
1. Agriculture	1.157718	0.001242	0.054606	0.075280	0.178341	0.025092	0.078337	0.121481	0.063771	0.009083	0.0902
2. Crude Oil	0.001445	1.000056	0.003288	0.004152	0.012088	0.001689	0.005175	0.001782	0.003004	0.000601	0.0058
3. Sulphur	0.000034	0.000001	1.000077	0.000097	0.000283	0.000040	0.000121	0.000042	0.000070	0.000014	0.0001
4. Mining	0.002859	0.000202	0.011696	1.017052	0.023361	0.003629	0.126282	0.003655	0.006159	0.009494	0.0116
5. Mfg. Indus.	0.200174	0.007795	0.455417	0.575206	1.674462	0.233976	0.716858	0.246781	0.416107	0.083225	0.8111
6. Electric and Water	0.003924	0.000272	0.023044	0.012953	0.009674	1.018218	0.00600	0.006883	0.004422	0.004153	0.0168
7. Construction	0.001261	0.000883	0.004060	0.084771	0.005451	0.004115	1.070194	0.002754	0.004607	0.076800	0.0059
8. Wholesale and Retail Trade	0.142039	0.003852	0.058533	0.077886	0.194181	0.027253	0.084691	1.039714	0.062385	0.010003	0.0945
9. Transport and Communication	0.150499	0.008451	0.363922	0.806763	0.208214	0.037569	0.193547	0.084927	1.081114	0.019975	0.1081
10. Banking and Insurance	0.010030	0.001039	0.041841	1.184000	0.047962	0.017639	0.160008	0.010114	0.045764	1.089524	0.0693
11. Services	0.014047	0.002198	0.073621	0.065907	0.037265	0.009103	0.023353	0.022352	0.075102	0.007087	1.0649

Table 4.10 (Inverse of 1980 $(1-A)^{-1}$ (input inverse))

Economic sectors	1	2	3	4	5	6	7	8	9	10	11
1. Agriculture	1.182096	0.011357	0.001167	0.035088	0.410724	0.001866	0.158866	0.095092	0.158646	0.003638	0.0101
2. Crude Oil	0.000339	1.000058	0.000008	0.000169	0.005400	0.000023	0.001736	0.000291	0.000492	0.000041	0.0001
3. Sulphur	0.003359	0.000574	1.000079	0.001674	0.053490	0.000231	0.017194	0.002880	0.004873	0.000407	0.0012
4. Mining	0.017136	0.005240	0.000715	1.017375	0.266534	0.001280	0.074242	0.015228	0.025696	0.016471	0.0064
5. Mfg. Indus.	0.105531	0.018034	0.002472	0.052585	1.680294	0.007263	0.540130	0.090459	0.153060	0.012775	0.0395
6. Electric and Water	0.066943	0.020096	0.003991	0.038129	0.316716	1.018238	0.147767	0.081413	0.055641	0.020546	0.0266
7. Construction	0.000889	0.002649	0.000030	0.009989	0.007339	0.000170	1.070230	0.001345	0.002199	0.015659	0.0003
8. Wholesale and Retail Trade	0.206258	0.024686	0.000961	0.022756	0.546251	0.002383	0.182368	1.041402	0.079212	0.004368	0.0129
9. Transport and Communication	0.231398	0.056520	0.005751	0.211322	0.620028	0.003457	0.431003	0.091816	1.103880	0.009069	0.0156
10. Banking and Insurance	0.034682	0.05479	0.001475	0.683754	0.316510	0.003586	0.786150	0.024369	0.106335	1.089553	0.0221
11. Services	0.152463	0.102401	0.008121	0.122223	0.775596	0.005839	0.365376	0.168311	0.545148	0.022368	1.0651

Appendix to Chapter 5

1. Estimating model by two stages least squares (TSLS)

Table 5.1   The equations of the model which estimated by (TSLS) two stages least squares method

Eq. No.	Dependent variables	Estimated coefficient and t ratios (parenthesis)
17 DL	VMAU	34.07+0.135 (CP+XMAU-MCG) + 0.975TIN+0.813 (1.82) (3.89) (3.29) (2.01) SEE=24.87, R^2 =0.9887, D.W =1.80, Period=1963-1980
22	V. Const.	-18.38+0.327TINV+ 104DL7576+0.04Tim (-2.07) (48.42) (5.54) (2.02) SEE=24.74, R^2 =0.994, D.W =22.10, Period=1966-1980
26	V. Service.	100.4 + 0.157AER (92.54) (17.20) SEE=89.66, R^2 =0.96, D.W=0.96, Period=1963-1980
39	PINV.	53.74 - .155RINTR + 1.113RINVR + 0.257EXG (6.98) (-1.40) (4.54) (3.21) SEE=22.24, R^2 =0.981, D.W =1.52, period=1963-1980
59	LN PDP Con	1.04+0.830LN CP (1.63) (16.31) SEE= 0.051, R^2 =0.96, D.W =1.02, Period=1963-1980
60	LN PDGC	24.79 + 0.107 LN CP + 1.018 LN W (2.201) (4.07) (4.975) SEE=6.213; R^2 =0.985; D.W=1.18, period=1963-1980
82	DET	1.25GRGDP + 0.349PlanTARG (2.67) (-2.17) (5.96) SEE=2.99, R^2 =0.80, D.W= 1.88, Period=1963-1980

Eq. No.	Dependent Variables	Estimated coefficient and t ratios (parenthesis)
89	CISDU	3.547 + 0.51MANU+0.114RGDP (1.225) (8.735) (2.301) SEE=4.94, R^2=0.976, D.W= 2.179, Period=1963-1980
	TMG	1.6859 + 0.482PM (6.74) (14.32) SEE=0.17, R^2=0.88, D.W= 1.23, Period=1963-1980
	GC	126.97 + 0.743Gr-TRF + 0.60TIN (2.64) (3.28) (3.57) SEE=0.05, R^2=0.98, D.W= 2.00, Period=1963-1980
	DFGC	0.87 + 0.174W + 0.70CP (1.95) (1.75) (3.20) SEE=0.36, R^2=0.99, D.W= 1.02, Period=1963-1980

2. Identities and definitional equations

1. GDP = V. AGR. + V. MANU + V.OIL + V. oth MIN + V. CONST + V.TR + V. SER.
2. PDGDP = (N GDPT/GDPT) 100
3. KMANU = KMANU(t_{-1}) (1-0.62)+ INVMANU
4. TRINV = PINV + GINV
5. GNP = GDP + NETF1
6. CHGDP = GDP- GDP$_{-1}$
7. ADJGDP = GDP + TTAD
8. TTAD = (XGC/MP) - XG
9. AER = TCON + TIF + EXG
10. TCON = PCON + GC
11. EXG = XOIL+ X non - OIL + XSER
12. TRINVN non-Agri = TINV (excluding Agri.)
13. ADJGREV = GR - TFR
14. Δk = V. Xt - (Vot-1/kt-Cxt+Mt)
15. WR/PCON = MPI/PGDP
16. GDP(non - Agri) = VMANU + VOIL + VOTHMIN + VCONST + VTRC + VSER
17. DDMANU = CP + XMANU - MCG
18. GR = OIL-REV + TAX- REV + OTHE
19. NADD = GC + GINV + PCON + PINV + PDTINV

20. BP = XG + S (oil + non-oil commodity) - MG + S) + NGT + NPT +NGB + NFI + EMTF + SDRS + IMF
21. NFSSTB = NFABNT$_{-1}$ + OBM

3. Summary of the behaviour equations of the model

1. V. Agr = DE Agr (-1) + V. Agr (-l) (Value added in agriculture sector)
2. LN Y grain = LN TIME + LN (X Price/xp TOB) (Grain output)
3. LN Y Vegt. oil = LN DL + LN XP vegt. oil (-1) + LN XP Vegt. oil/PDGDP (-1) + LN XPvegt/PDGDP-2 +LN XP vegt oil/PDGD p(-3) (vegt. oil output)
4. LN Y Date = X P Dat/PDGDP+LN XPDate/PDGDP-5 + Y Palm Date (-1)+DL (Date output)
5. POMANU = KMANU (-1)+CRAMAU/MP+LMANU (Potential of manufacture output)
6. VMANU = (CP+XMANUMCG)+TINV+DL (Value added in manufacture sector)
7. V. Oil = V. oil(-1) + DL (Value added in oil sector)
8. V. Min. = opthmin + oth min. (Value added in other mining sector)
9. V. Const. = TRINV(-1) + DL (Value added in construction sector)
10. V.Tran. = ADJGDP(-l) (Value added in transport sector)
11. V. Ser. = AER (Value added in service sector)
12. PCon = IMGC (-1) + GNP (-1) + DL (Private consumption)
13. GC = GC(-1) + (GR-TFR) + TIM (Government consumption)
14. PINV = EXG -TRINTR + RNVCR/MP (Private investment)
15. GINV = CHGDP + MINTKG + GINV (-1) + RDPE(-l) (Public investment)
16. EMoth = GDP non- agri (-1)+TRINV non-agri (-1)-WR/RCML (-2)-WR/RCML(-3) (Employment in other sector non-agriculture)
17. LN EM Agr = LN Agr.(-1) - DL1972 - LN WR/Prcom (-1) -LN WR.Prcom(-2) (Employment in agriculture sector)
18. LN W = LN UN + LN LPROD + LN PC(-1) + TIM (The rate of wage)
19. LNCP = LN CAUT + LN MP + LN MS + LN W(-1) + W(-2) (The consumer price)
20. LN PD P Con = LNCP (The deflator of private consumption)
21. LN PDGC = LN CP + LN W (The deflator of government consumption)
22. LN PINV = LN PMKI + LN UNCOL (The deflator of private investment)
23. LN PDGINV = LN PMKI + LN UNCOL (The deflator of government investment)
24. LN XP Oil = LN XP oil ECH (The export prices of oil)
25. LN XPMANU = LN MPINTG + LN UN CoL (The export price of manufacture)
26. XP PRIM = XP Date + XP Leather + XP Vegt. Oil + XP grain (The export price of primary goods)

27. LN PMCON = LN (PWMC TM EH) (The import prices of consumer goods)

28. LN PMINV = LN (PWINV TM LH) (The import prices of investment goods)

29. LN PMINMT = LN (PWINMT TM XH) (The import prices of intermediate goods)

30. MMANU = MANU (-1)+DL-TRM-MPINMT-1/PDINMT(-1) (The imports of manufactured goods)

31. MINVG = TRINV+TRINV(-1)+DL-MPINV(-1)/PDINV(-1)(The imports of investments goods)

32. MCON = P Con-PMCON/PGDP-PMCON/PGDP (-1) + DL-TRM (The imports of consumer goods)

33. LNX oil = LN PX oil/PW+LN INP+LN X oil (-1)+DL73+DL72 (The export of oil)

34. LN XP rim = LN P income + LN PX non/P (-1)- LN WY + LN XPRIM (-1) (The exports of primary goods)

35. LN XMANU = LN WY-LN (PXMANU/PW(-l) (The export of manufactured goods)

36. DET = GRGDP + Plan TAR (The development expenditure)

37. CISDU = MANU + CHGDP (The excise duties)

38. RM = NFSSTB + NCG + OTF (The reserve money)

4. List of variables

A) Endogenous variables

1. V. Agri. = Value added in agriculture sector.

2. Y. grain = Grain output.

3. Y. vegt oil = Vegetable oil output.

4. Y. date = Date output.

5. V. Oil = Value added in oil sector.

6. V. MIN = Value added in other mining sector.

7. V. CONST = Value added in construction sector.

8. V. TRC = Value added in transport sector.

9. NADD = The national total demand.

10. V. MANU = Value added in manufacturing sector.

11. V. SER = Value added in service sector.

12. AER = Real aggregate expenditure (including the consumption and investment expenditure of both the private and government as well as the level of real exports).

13. POMANU = The potential of manufacturing output.

14. P Con = Private consumption.

15. TINV = The total investment.

16. MINMT = The imports of intermediate goods.

17. MCG = The imports of consumer goods.

18. MINV = The imports of investment goods.

19. PINV = The private investments.

20. GC = The government consumption.

21. GINV = The government investment.

22. GDP = Gross domestic products.

23. ADJGDP = GDP adjusted.

24. Tcon = The total consumption.

25. CP = The consumer prices, 1970 as the base year.

26. CHGDP = Real change in GDP.

27. GNP = The gross national production.

28. PDGDP = The gross domestic production implicit price deflator.

29. PDPINV = The private investment deflator.

30. PDGINV = The government investment deflator.

31. PDPCON = The private consumption deflator.

32. PDGC = The government investment deflator.

33. PXMANU = The export price of manufacturing goods.

34. PXPRIM = The export price of primary goods.

35. PXOIL = The export price of oil.

36. WR/Prcom = The relative prices.

37. PMGC = The import price of consumer goods.

38. PMINMT = The import price of intermediate goods.

39. PMINV = The import price of investment goods.

40. X Oil = Volume of the oil export.

41. Xprim = The export of primary goods.

42. XMANU = The export of manufacturing goods.

43. EXG = The total exports of goods.

44. DDMANU = Real consumption of domestic production of the manufacturing sector.

45. KMANU = Capital stock in manufacturing sector.

46. W = The average wage index.

47. GR = Government total revenues.

48. TTAD = Term of trade adjusted.

49. BP = Balance of payments in current account.

50. DET = The total development expenditure.

51. NFAMNI = The foreign assets of the Central Bank.

52. CISDU = The excise duties.

53. RM = Reserve money.

54. GDP non-agri = The gross domestic production for all sectors (excluding agriculture sector).

55. TINV non-agri = The real investment of all the sectors excluding the agriculture sector.

56. EM. Agri. = The employment in agriculture sector.

57. EMOTH = The employment in other sectors (excluding agriculture).

58. ADJGREV = The Government revenues adjusted.

59. Δ Kt = Change in venture.

B) Exogenous variables

1. DE Agri. = Development expenditure in agriculture sector.

2. LMANU = Labour productivity of manufacturing sector.

3. MS = Money supply.

4. UNCOL = Unit labour cost.

5. DL = Dummy variable.

6. CMBLR = Bank credit interest rate.

7. MP = Domestic price of imports:1970=100.

8. CRAMAU/MP = The capital working in manufacturing sector, which is deflated from import price.

9. PXMANU/PW = The relative price of manufacturing export adjusted of the world price.

10. WR/RCML = Relative factor price which the Commercial Bank's lending rate.

11. W. Agr. = The rate of wage of the agriculture sector.

12. TRM = The tariff rate import.

13. PW = The world price.

14. YW = OECD income index: 1970=100.

15. CAUT = Index of capacity of utilisation.

16. DDET = Total government expenditure.

17. TIM = Trend time index.

18. Oil Rev. = Oil revenues.

19. Plan TARG. = The development plan target.

20. WPMCON TM EH = World prices of consumption goods in domestic currency and adjusted from import tariff.

21. WPMINTG = World prices of intermediate goods in domestic currency and adjusted from imports tariff.

22. WPMINVG = World prices of investment goods in domestic currency and adjusted from import tariff.

23. WY = The level of the world's economic activity.

24. WP = The world prices of oil.

25. NCG, OTHF = Government bonds held by the commercial banks and other assets of commercial banks apart from credit.

26. Un = Unemployment.

Appendix to Chapter 6

Total Import Prices

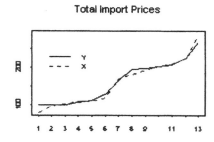

Value Added in Agricultural Sector

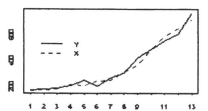

Value Added in Manufacture Sector

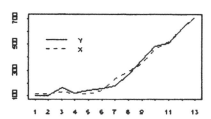

Value Added in Oil Sector

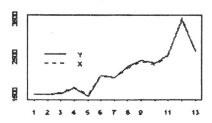

Y: Actual Values
X: Predicted Values

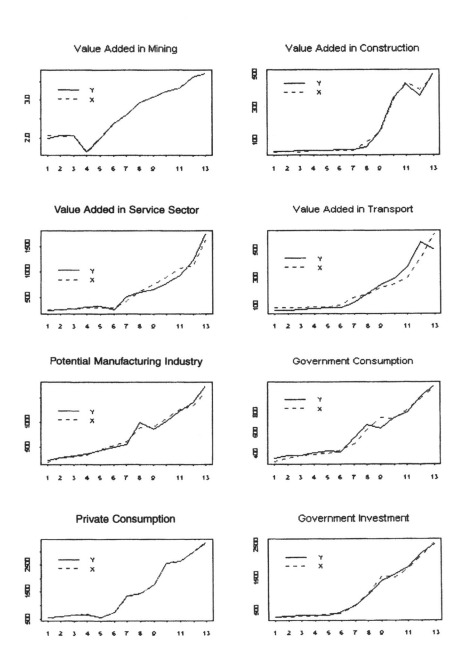

260

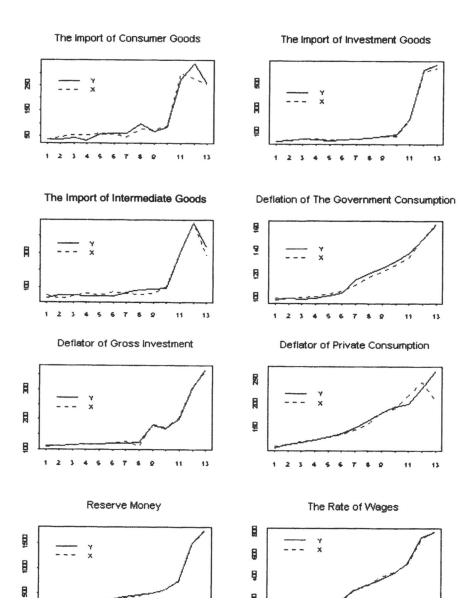

261

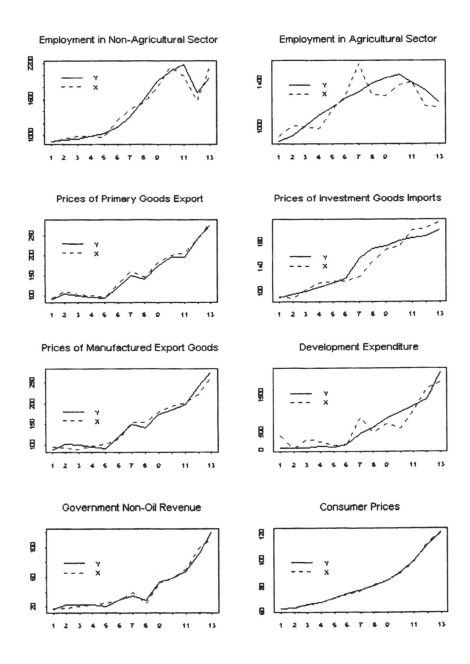

262

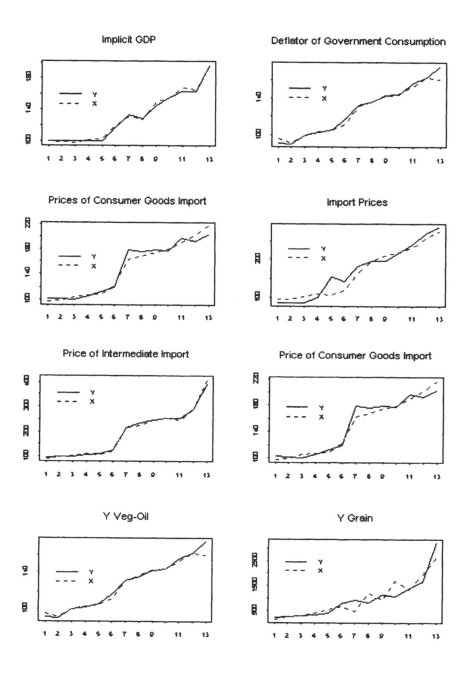

Private Investment

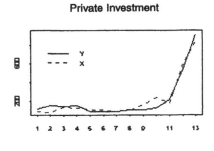

The Export of Oil

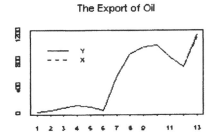

The Export of Primary Goods

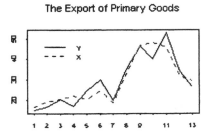

The Export of Manufacturing Goods

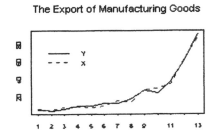

Y: Actual Values
X: Predicted Values

264

Appendix to Chapter 8

Table 8.2b **Instability indices for the major export goods of Iraq for the period 1970-1980**

Major export	D	E	F	G	H
1. Vegetable oil	123.082	2.5668	27.837	15.729	10.7126
2. Crude oil	32.490	0.7534	1.235	0.02954	3.7713
3. Leathers	120.342	2.225	29.008	13.915	8.6076
4. Grains	74.294	1.70235	15.498	9.52945	9.2115
5. Manf. Ind.	81.3695	1.65435	19.3765	13.2102	5.0760
6. Dates	25.0564	1.24467	1.3848	3.01855	4.0589

$$D = 100 \frac{\sum \left| C_t - \hat{C}_t \right|}{\bar{C}_t} \;;$$

$$E = 100 \frac{\sqrt{\sum \left| C_t - \hat{C}_t \right|}}{\frac{N}{\bar{C}_t}}$$

$$F = 100 \sum \left[\frac{C_t - \hat{C}_t}{\hat{C}_t} \right]^2 \;;$$

$$G = 100 \frac{\sqrt{\frac{\sum \left(C_t - \hat{C}_t \right)^2}{N-1}}}{\bar{C}_t}$$

$$H = 100 \frac{\sum^t \frac{\left| C_t - \hat{C}_t \right|}{\hat{C}_t}}{N} \;;$$

(H) Represents the exponential index. The average of percentage absolute deviation around the log-linear trend.

Table 8.3 Two alternative versions of smooth export prices

Alternative one: Smooth export price derived from linear time trend, price = a+b *Trend

Years	Leather	Crude oil	Dates	Vegt. Oil	Grains	Mfg. Ind.
1970	131.00	339.15	107.41	90.59	137.69	135.24
1971	144.17	367.14	114.29	1010.25	151.67	152.20
1972	158.34	397.44	121.62	113.16	166.84	171.24
1973	173.86	430.24	129.41	126.47	183.65	192.71
1974	190.94	465.73	137.70	141.35	202.21	216.87
1975	209.65	504.17	146.53	157.98	222.59	244.01
1976	230.25	545.78	155.92	176.56	245.02	274.60
1977	252.81	590.20	165.91	197.33	269.71	308.96
1978	277.65	639.57	176.54	220.55	296.89	347.70
1979	304.86	692.36	187.85	246.49	326.81	391.20
1980	334.81	749.50	199.89	275.49	359.75	440.25
Average growth rate	9.7%	8.25%	6.41%	11.76%	10.07%	12.54%

Note: *Trend = Time.   (Continued)

Alternative two: Smooth export prices derived from log linear time trend, Log price = a+b *Trend

Years	Leather	Crude oil	Dates	Vegt. Oil	Grains	Mfg. Ind.
1970	112.85	321.79	105.24	74.33	120.61	118.59
1971	134.47	361.50	114.08	93.43	143.28	147.11
1972	156.08	401.20	122.92	112.53	165.95	175.63
1973	177.78	440.90	131.75	131.63	188.62	204.15
1974	199.32	480.60	140.59	150.73	211.30	232.67
1975	220.94	520.30	149.42	169.83	233.97	261.19
1976	242.56	560.01	158.26	198.93	256.64	289.71
1977	264.18	599.71	167.10	208.03	279.31	318.23
1978	285.80	639.41	175.93	227.13	301.98	346.75
1979	307.42	679.11	184.77	246.23	324.65	375.27
1980	329.04	718.81	193.60	265.33	347.32	403.79
Average growth rate	10.27%	7.8%	5.7%	12.45%	10.17%	11.95%

(Continued)

Alternative one: Smooth export price derived from linear time trend,
     price = a+b$_1$ T + b$_2$ T^2

Years	Leather	Crude oil	Dates	Vegt. oil	Grains	Mfg. Ind.
1970	156.68	322.28	99.32	102.02	149.87	110.60
1971	152.00	361.69	111.71	104.50	154.99	149.40
1972	153.16	401.17	123.31	110.68	164.00	185.90
1973	160.17	440.71	134.12	120.55	176.92	220.10
1974	173.02	480.31	144.14	134.11	193.74	252.00
1975	191.72	519.98	153.37	151.37	214.46	281.70
1976	216.26	559.71	161.82	176.31	239.08	309.00
1977	246.65	599.51	169.47	196.95	267.60	334.20
1978	282.88	639.38	176.54	225.28	300.03	357.00
1979	324.95	679.31	182.40	257.30	336.36	377.50
1980	372.88	719.30	1987.68	293.02	376.59	395.80
Average growth rate	8.39%	7.66%	6.01%	10.18%	7.89%	12.68%

Note: T= Time.   (Continued)

Alternative two: Smooth export prices derived from log linear time trend,
     Log price = a+b1T+b2T^2

Years	Leather	Crude oil	Dates	Vegt. oil	Grains	Mfg. ind.
1970	152.05	321.68	99.70	98.13	147.84	118.95
1971	152.90	359.45	110.94	103.04	155.96	147.57
1972	156.78	398.84	122.22	112.56	166.07	177.91
1973	163.95	439.43	133.32	122.49	178.52	210.33
1974	174.82	480.76	143.99	134.71	193.73	243.84
1975	190.11	522.28	153.99	149.76	212.23	277.08
1976	210.81	563.38	163.05	168.31	234.75	308.75
1977	238.40	603.35	170.93	191.12	262.12	337.29
1978	274.92	637.24	177.42	219.38	295.46	361.24
1979	323.30	677.86	182.33	254.51	336.28	379.31
1980	387.70	710.89	185.54	300.88	386.37	390.57
AG	9.03%	7.52%	6.28%	10.83%	9.20%	11.55%

Note: AG= average growth rate.

Table 8.4　Linearly smoothed export prices versus variable export prices

Variables	1970	1971	1972	1973	1974	1975	1976	1977	1978	1979	1980
Total GDP	12.66	57.09	59.30	-47.34	-53.60	16.21	6.70	6.45	3.69	-17.80	-12.17
Real GDP	27.00	67.00	88.53	-78.00	-51.90	27.90	8.71	8.35	4.94	-12.24	-8.30
Real private consumption	13.55	24.43	87.63	16.28	41.01	16.53	8.71	57.12	42.08	-3.56	-10.64
Real private investment	1.63	47.40	76.61	44.10	-47.79	22.99	8.63	23.58	46.29	-10.60	-3.61
Real Govt. investment	7.78	11.24	63.36	68.36	-53.37	28.17	10.01	70.21	47.32	-6.96	-0.54
Real Govt. consumption	-10.69	26.02	91.82	52.79	-47.19	23.35	7.48	69.67	42.95	12.36	-6.75
Total export	-34.46	94.56	17.20	-41.39	-59.87	3.09	7.96	67.43	43.47	-10.19	-4.37
Total import	8.42	43.09	97.63	0.17	58.58	4.55	9.58	-64.29	-44.09	-6.81	-0.69
Aggregate final demand	8.14	54.12	11.36	30.80	-46.39	21.07	9.30	-69.18	-46.94	-6.60	-0.18
Consumer prices	6.86	31.83	1.11	7.30	-21.86	7.15	3.52	23.23	18.44	-4.51	-6.14
GDP deflator	14.57	32.13	6.58	3.91	-23.29	7.23	4.89	26.48	22.66	-0.75	-3.73
Export price of leather	-15.57	3.76	2.17	0.45	33.17	7.86	1.64	8.48	-3.56	-11.78	-6.58
Export price of crude oil	4.35	6.45	0.66	7.16	-1.39	7.17	2.65	-0.06	2.77	7.77	-1.09
Export price of dates	12.97	13.23	-3.17	2.82	-6.25	-4.73	3.00	-0.65	1.98	3.48	-0.64
Export price of veget. oil	-3.69	0.31	3.74	-9.56	-11.64	40.35	23.76	9.98	2.60	-8.10	-4.16
Export price of grains	1.48	2.72	9.26	1.84	26.36	-4.38	3.97	0.41	1.15	-6.09	-2.16
Export price of mfg. industries	5.13	14.22	-10.21	4.07	-4.16	-10.71	4.97	1.09	-1.91	-1.26	-2.97

Note: (% deviation from control solution).

(Continued)

Table 8.4 Linearly smoothed export prices versus variable export prices (continued)

Variables	1970	1971	1972	1973	1974	1975	1976	1977	1978	1979	1980
Agri. employment	0.36	2.20	0.34	0.35	-0.41	0.14	0.05	0.26	-0.05	-0.59	-0.61
Non-agri. employment	8.06	14.99	28.84	0.62	-12.18	5.50	4.72	22.10	20.32	-2.34	-6.61
V. added agriculture	7.39	24.48	60.31	13.66	-3.57	13.52	-6.96	45.78	34.47	-4.39	1.00
V. added mining	2.50	5.67	8.54	10.75	8.95	4.48	1.55	0.87	-0.40	-1.10	-1.33
V. added crude oil	80.39	136.66	39.36	-137.18	-55.69	32.81	9.16	95.94	53.35	-14.46	-8.21
V. added mfg.	9.74	35.23	82.37	19.08	40.72	16.69	8.15	56.03	40.47	-5.07	-0.89
V. added transport	4.82	44.05	88.88	35.69	-46.15	21.36	8.58	67.98	45.03	-8.38	-2.29
V. added construction	15.49	20.35	97.09	48.71	51.55	-25.72	-10.5	-83.51	53.51	-7.62	-0.78
Corporation income	44.46	71.07	80.91	22.41	-16.28	23.74	-0.05	-1.39	-0.51	-22.72	-30.96
Wages and salaries	9.77	25.60	39.63	22.92	-42.73	18.18	8.49	60.38	42.57	-5.79	0.31
Wages rate index	0.10	17.97	61.81	23.23	-38.33	15.88	6.40	44.83	34.68	-8.44	-3.32
Government revenue	26.44	51.57	11.93	34.20	-58.05	36.69	9.19	10.48	10.48	55.29	-16.18
Money supply	35.56	89.56	6.79	-25.36	-42.70	18.42	8.13	59.99	41.64	-6.84	-0.95
Balance of payment	10.64	26.02	91.82	-52.79	-47.19	23.35	7.48	69.66	42.95	-12.36	-6.75

Note: (% deviation from control solution).

Table 8.5 Log-linearly smoothed export price versus variable export price

Variables	1970	1971	1972	1973	1974	1975	1976	1977	1978	1979	1980
Total GDP	8.33	98.73	16.42	-5.57	-3.47	-15.41	-10.81	-15.41	10.63	6.75	-8.26
Real GDP	17.00	72.20	23.36	-74.91	3.59	-5.59	-2.42	-5.38	-2.27	12.57	1.39
Real private consumption	6.86	24.76	9.58	5.83	-3.89	-8.70	-8.07	8.88	8.02	3.70	-2.64
Real private investment	4.09	38.94	8.56	2.49	-2.94	12.78	9.31	12.66	9.16	-6.58	-8.02
Real Government investment	9.05	42.25	13.68	7.38	-4.14	-11.62	-44.74	9.45	4.76	-0.11	-0.53
Government consumption	16.54	68.18	26.50	13.21	-4.61	-15.12	-11.58	-15.17	11.47	-5.36	-2.88
Total export	13.48	52.13	18.71	11.45	-4.85	-11.46	-10.23	-11.57	10.11	10.18	-4.35
Total import	11.40	40.06	15.31	9.66	-4.93	-10.26	9.56	-10.39	-9.39	-3.39	-0.79
Aggregate final demand	8.89	40.23	13.19	7.23	37.14	-11.31	17.32	-43.91	-9.34	-4.65	-0.06
Consumer prices	1.59	5.93	2.34	1.30	-1.81	-3.87	-3.79	-3.97	-3.77	-2.79	-1.14
GDP deflator	4.13	9.65	5.19	3.75	36.38	-3.61	-4.50	-3.76	-4.53	0.51	-3.73
Export price of leather	-27.27	-10.16	2.78	1.90	39.02	13.67	7.08	13.36	-0.73	-11.04	-8.19
Export price of crude oil	1.00	2.75	2.52	-4.75	1.57	-4.20	-0.12	1.44	2.75	5.70	-5.09
Export price of date	9.66	8.69	-7.69	-10.30	-4.28	-2.85	-1.55	-0.35	1.63	1.78	1.04
Export price of veget. Oil	-20.98	3.76	1.78	-5.87	-5.77	51.05	39.44	-5.10	0.38	-8.20	-7.53
Export price of grains	0.51	7.05	-3.24	17.87	-5.49	4.65	0.67	3.99	-2.89	-7.19	-5.34
Export price of manufacture	7.54	10.41	-7.91	9.45	2.81	-4.43	0.24	-1.31	-2.18	-5.52	-11.00
Agriculture employment	0.20	2.28	1.89	0.19	0.99	-0.70	-0.14	0.60	0.14	-0.17	-0.16
Non-agriculture employment	18.57	26.09	19.87	17.95	-2.58	4.48	-0.13	4.04	-0.25	-0.26	-2.37
V. added in agri. sector	-4.37	15.97	6.20	3.59	-3.07	7.27	6.71	7.34	6.64	-3.72	-4.89
V. added in mining	1.82	5.03	3.20	6.73	5.53	2.60	0.64	0.19	-0.89	-1.38	-1.45

Note: (% deviation from control solution).

Table 8.5 Log-linearly smoothed export price versus variable export price (continued)

V. added in crude oil	15.09	29.66	-32.27	9.93	-3.81	-18.09	-12.09	-17.75	11.75	-7.03	-81.39
V. added in manufacture	6.34	24.13	9.07	5.28	-3.73	-8.94	7.99	-8.99	-7.92	-4.99	-5.24
V. added in transport	8.08	38.11	11.41	8.36	19.12	18.31	16.02	-24.10	-22.53	-18.99	-7.38
V. added in construction	15.82	86.01	23.65	33.42	-0.95	-13.72	-11.13	-13.73	-10.98	-4.58	-6.03
V. added in services	1.17	9.48	5.37	3.29	0.10	1.51	-1.28	1.94	1.54	-2.58	-3.41
Corporation income	20.09	31.40	37.18	4.32	-4.15	10.94	-1.59	-10.89	-7.34	-9.88	-14.23
Wage and salaries	14.01	24.27	15.86	13.19	-26.42	-10.27	-17.95	-60.39	-25.07	5.79	-0.32
Wages rate index	4.76	20.00	7.16	3.87	3.22	8.56	7.45	8.60	7.41	-4.42	-5.66
Government revenue	10.43	15.39	43.94	-2.76	-3.12	-20.55	-12.43	-20.02	-12.15	16.17	4.91
Money supply	4.87	25.13	7.83	-3.76	-3.21	-10.05	-8.23	-10.06	-8.09	5.14	0.91
Balance of payments	15.24	64.03	21.49	-12.79	-5.79	-12.32	10.69	12.42	10.54	-3.70	-1.60

Note: (% deviation from control solution).

Table 8.6 The mean values and standard deviations of the principal variables in the model, when simulation under alternative assumption about the export prices

Variables	Actual export prices (1)	Linearly smooth export prices* (2)	Log-linearly smooth export prices* (3)	Per cent difference	
				2/1	3/1
Total GDP	5245.91 (2112.00)	5280.45 (2028.00)	5255.45 (2033.00)	0.66	0.18
Non-oil GDP	2205.09 (1633.00)	5009.30 (1521.00)	5009.27 (1949.00)	-	-
Real private consumption	1623.09 (678.50)	1673.00 (330.60)	1672.89 (330.60)	3.07	3.06
Real private investment	225.18 (105.20)	228.16 (86.79)	226.83 (86.87)	1.32	0.73
Real govt. consumption	1089.64 (553.50)	1248.63 (376.40)	1109.36 (375.50)	14.59	1.81
Real govt. investment	982.90 (433.20)	1049.35 (246.10)	986.18 (431.40)	5.84	0.33
Total exports	3444.27 (1016.00)	2454.45 (879.70)	2444.73 (886.70)	0.40	0.19
Total imports	1002.73 (390.90)	1004.60 (194.90)	1002.82 (364.20)	0.19	0.009
Aggregate final demand	381.00 (1671.00)	4037.90 (870.00)	3981.99 (875.80)	1.43	0.03
Consumer prices index	174.02 (24.08)	174.89 (13.57)	174.09 (12.56)	0.49	0.04
GDP deflator	179.00 (42.73)	181.00 (20.32)	180.00 (20.32)	1.12	0.56
Value added agriculture	377.79 (383.80)	388.77 (315.60)	378.88 (325.60)	2.91	0.29
Value added mining	18.72 (7.43)	18.72 (4.00)	16.73 (4.09)	-	-10.63
Value added crude oil	2804.18 (1189.00)	3193.37 (1173.00)	3003.46 (1174.00)	13.88	7.11
Value added manufacturing industries	303.77 (128.00)	353.69 (57.46)	353.00 (67.43)	16.43	16.20
Value added construction	336.26 (165.10)	383.23 (94.84)	352.23 (94.83)	13.97	4.75
Value added transportation	237.40 (93.80)	238.43 (63.17)	237.43 (27.17)	0.43	0.01
Value added service	8403.90 (2153.00)	8776.40 (1821.00)	8492.80 (1945.00)	4.43	1.06
Non-agri. employment	1529.64 (383.80)	1549.70 (315.60)	1529.70 (325.60)	1.27	0.004
Wages and salaries	10202.09 (3543.00)	10252.09 (1077.00)	10220.18 (1077.00)	0.49	0.18
Wages rate index	376.26 (96.40)	379.26 (67.89)	377.16 (69.79)	0.80	0.27
Money supply	478.21 (182.90)	479.88 (114.60)	478.21 (122.50)	0.35	-
Corporate income	10311.40 (5613.00)	10347.00 (3225.00)	10323.40 (4548.00)	0.35	0.12
Balance of payment	1416.91 (892.30)	1417.19 (885.30)	1441.80 (887.30)	3.83	1.76

Note: * Smooth price was estimated by the regression; Log price = a + b 1 T.

* The smooth prices were estimated by the linear regression; Price = a + b 1 T.

The standard deviation is shown in parentheses: * a = constant, b1 = regression coefficient, T = time.

Table 8.6b   The coefficient of variation of the principal variables in the model, when simulation under alternative assumptions about the export prices

Variables	Actual export prices	Linearly smooth export prices	Log linearly smooth export prices
Total GDP	40.26	30.84	38.68
Non-oil GDP	32.64	29.56	38.91
Real private consumption	41.80	19.75	19.76
Real private investment	46.72	38.04	38.29
Real govt. consumption	50.80	30.15	33.85
Total exports	44.07	35.72	43.74
Total imports	41.57	19.40	36.27
Aggregate final demand	42.65	21.55	21.99
Consumer prices index	13.84	7.59	7.21
GDP deflator	23.87	11.23	11.29
V. add. agriculture	101.59	81.18	85.94
V. add. mining	39.70	21.37	24.45
V. add. crude oil	42.40	36.73	39.09
V. add. mfg. ind.	42.14	16.25	19.10
V. add. construction	49.10	13.01	26.92
V. add. transport	39.51	26.49	30.40
V. add. service	25.62	20.75	22.90
Non-agri. employment	25.09	20.37	21.29
Total gov. revenues	87.12	57.11	57.51
Wages rate index	25.62	17.90	18.04
Money supply	38.25	23.88	25.62
Balance of payment	62.98	60.18	61.57

Note: This table calculated from Table 8.6.

Table 8.7b The coefficient of variation of the principal variables in the model, when simulation under alternative assumptions about the export prices

Variables	Actual export prices	Linearly smooth export prices	Log-linearly smooth export prices
Total GDP	40.26	2.17	11.00
Non-oil GDP	32.75	4.90	12.90
Real private consumption	41.80	1.40	10.20
Real private investment	46.72	4.00	6.70
Real govt. consumption	50.80	4.40	16.30
Real govt. investment	44.07	20.30	27.10
Total exports	41.57	6.00	9.60
Total imports	41.57	3.70	12.40
Aggregate final demand	42.65	1.70	5.20
Consumer prices index	13.84	1.70	5.20
GDP deflator	23.87	5.50	8.30
V. add. agriculture	101.59	2.10	9.30
V. add. mining	39.69	63.10	6.80
V. add. crude oil	42.40	6.30	15.40
V. add. mgf. ind.	42.14	4.80	13.90
V. add. construction	49.10	1.50	6.00
V. add transport	39.51	5.50	14.80
Non-agri. employment	25.09	1.40	1.00
Total govt. revenues	87.12	7.70	7.70
Wages and salaries	34.73	1.10	8.10
Wage rate index	25.62	28.50	38.30
Money supply	42.13	6.90	13.40
Corporate income	54.43	4.60	10.90
Balance of payment	62.98	30.20	39.11

Note: This table calculated from Table 8.7.

Table 8.7 The mean values and standard deviations of the principal variables in the model, when simulation under alternative assumption about the export prices

Variables	Actual export prices (1)	Linearly smooth export prices* (2)	Log-linearly smooth export prices* (3)	Per cent difference 2/1	Per cent difference 3/1
Total GDP	5245.45 (4142.00)	5245.45 (108.00)	5245.45 (565.00)	-	-
Non-oil GDP	5100.30 (4066.00)	5100.90 (251.00)	5100.90 (662.00)	0.12	-
Real private consumption	1622.99 (678.50)	1622.99 (23.00)	1622.99 (165.00)	-	-
Real private Investment	225.18 (105.20)	225.18 (51.30)	225.18 (15.00)	-	-
Real government Consumption	1149.70 (553.50)	1149.70 (73.80)	1149.70 (153.60)	-	-
Real government Investment	983.00 (433.20)	983.00 (63.00)	983.00 (16.00)	-	-
Total exports	2444.73 (1016.00)	2444.73 (496.00)	2444.73 (662.00)	-	-
Total imports	1003.00 (390.90)	1003.00 (60.00)	1003.00 (96.00)	-	-
Aggregate final Demand	3981.00 (1671.00)	3982.00 (149.00)	3981.00 (493.00)	0.03	-
Consumer prices Index	174.02 (24.08)	174.09 (3.00)	174.09 (9.00)	0.49	0.49
GDP deflator	179.00 (42.73)	180.00 (10.47)	179.00 (15.00)	0.60	-
Value added agriculture	377.00 (383.80)	378.00 (32.43)	377.77 (47.41)	0.26	0.26
Value added mining	18.72 (7.43)	18.72 (0.12)	18.72 (1.30)	-	-
Value added crude oil	2804.00 (1189.00)	2804.00 (743.00)	2804.00 (1044.00)	-	-
Value added mfg. ind.	303.77 (128.00)	305.00 (17.00)	303.77 (49.00)	0.57	-
Value added construction	336.000 (165.10)	336.00 (5.00)	336.00 (21.00)	-	-
Value added transportation	237.40 (93.80)	328.41 (13.00)	237.43 (35.00)	0.42	-
Value added service	701.00 (2153.00)	701.00 (15.00)	701.00 (62.00)	-	-
Non-agri. employment	1529.00 (383.80)	1529.00 (13.00)	1529.00 (10.00)		
Total Govt. revenue	1439.00 (379.00)	1439.00 (111.00)	1439.00 (111.00)	-	-
Wages and salaries	3152.00 (2746.00)	3152.00 (35.00)	3152.00 (251.00)	-	
Wage rate index	10202.09 (3543.00)	10203.00 (238.00)	10203.00 (320.00)	0.12	0.12
Money supply	376.26 (96.40)	377.16 (26.00)	377.16 (52.00)	0.239	0236
Corporate income	478.21 (182.90)	478.21 (22.00)	478.42 (52.00)	-	-
Balance of payment	1416.91 (892.30)	1416.91 (436.00)	1461.91 (564.00)	-	-

Note: * Smooth price was estimated by the regression; Log price = a+ b_1 T+ b_2 T^2.

* The smooth price was estimated by the linear regression; Price = a+ b_1 T + b_2 T^2.

* The standard deviation is shown in parentheses; *a = constant, b1, b2 = regression coefficient, T = time.

Table 8.9 Comparing the simulation results of the artificially generated export prices with the linearly smoothed export prices

Variables	1970	1971	1972	1973	1974	1975	1976	1977	1978	1979	1980
Total GDP	44.68	19.66	1.67	-2.99	-4.08	-3.03	1.69	-2.55	-1.73	-1.38	-1.4
Real GDP	26.69	11.65	1.09	-2.82	-0.40	-0.76	-1.33	-1.27	-2.26	0.56	0.3
Real private consumption	8.94	33.21	0.73	-1.98	-2.91	-2.37	1.38	2.13	-1.47	1.25	-1.2
Real private investment	20.69	25.50	1.54	-2.44	-3.46	-2.84	1.50	2.26	-1.75	.121	-1.4
Government consumption	21.76	2.11	1.26	-2.61	-3.45	-2.78	1.50	2.30	-1.68	1.25	-1.4
Government investment	7.00	86.95	1.62	-3.80	-4.28	-3.38	-1.82	2.67	-1.77	1.53	-1.3
Aggregate final demand	20.70	24.88	1.07	0.04	0.03	-2.79	1.53	2.32	-1.63	-1.32	-1.3
Consumer prices	1.09	-1.60	1.51	-0.66	1.05	-1.03	0.64	1.07	-0.78	0.72	-0.7
GDP deflator	1.14	-2.29	0.05	-0.89	1.23	-1.23	0.78	1.29	-0.81	0.91	-0.6
Export prices of leather	-13.00	-3.60	-3.75	3.30	-0.20	8.57	3.03	1.01	-1.36	-9.20	1.1
Export prices of crude oil	-7.36	1.87	0.62	3.97	0.75	5.60	1.14	-0.95	1.73	-3.51	-2.5
Export prices of date	-2.14	2.62	6.57	1.86	1.90	0.02	1.40	0.55	-0.22	-1.75	-3.0
Export prices of veg. oil	-13.29	-12.54	1.24	1.76	9.73	3.75	13.84	7.57	-1.12	0.87	-6.4
Export prices of grains	-13.44	-2.68	-2.23	3.95	3.08	6.77	3.88	2.07	-2.78	-1.65	-2.6
Export prices	-11.12	10.72	7.16	13.90	6.53	15.53	5.93	-1.81	-5.21	-4.90	-3.6
Of manufacture											
Agriculture employment	0.05	-4.94	-0.03	-2.30	-0.06	0.01	0.01	0.03	-0.01	-0.05	0.0
Non-agriculture Employment	13.64	21.01	12.59	9.07	-8.95	-4.76	5.23	-41.41	-1.13	1.94	-0.5

Note: (% deviation from control solution).

Table 8.9 Comparing the simulation results of the artificially generated export prices with the linearly smoothed export prices (continued)

Added in agri. sector	-5.13	-5.22	2.93	-1.54	-2.20	-1.95	1.16	-1.16	-1.22	1.17	-1.0
Added in mining	-10.41	57.14	1.67	-2.27	-2.92	-2.50	1.43	2.22	-1.45	1.35	-1.6
Added in crude oil	6.63	13.78	1.75	-4.03	-4.81	-3.42	1.83	2.70	-1.79	1.54	-1.3
Added in construction	8.40	81.30	2.22	-3.18	-4.35	-3.17	-1.72	2.60	-1.80	1.40	-1.4
V. added in manufacturing	8.75	16.30	0.31	-2.09	-2.73	-2.29	1.38	2.16	-1.32	0.64	-1.0
Added in transport	15.90	24.13	0.34	-2.67	-3.25	-2.62	1.55	2.43	-1.45	1.49	-1.1
V. added in services	-18.88	-8.13	0.94	-1.79	-2.79	-2.35	1.29	1.99	-1.54	-1.12	-1.3
Corporation income	12.94	4.21	-5.77	7.03	-2.56	-16.60	-8.79	4.00	7.68	-2.75	10.4
Wage and salaries	4.57	8.35	-20.32	-7.02	-13.05	8.94	2.36	-27.36	-27.36	31.60	31.3
Wages rate index	5.60	6.15	0.30	-1.67	2.27	-2.09	1.24	12.38	-1.22	1.23	-0.9
Government revenue	7.24	27.01	4.91	-3.89	-4.97	-3.64	1.83	2.64	-20.06	1.35	-1.7
Money supply	10.88	30.58	0.63	-2.16	-2.87	-2.47	1.39	12.15	-1.47	1.30	-1.1
Total exports	-33.33	-19.33	-6.34	-3.04	-2.88	-2.62	1.60	2.50	-1.19	1.73	-0.7
Total imports	10.76	16.94	0.96	-2.26	-3.14	-0.64	1.44	-2.20	-1.59	1.56	-1.3
Balance of payments	2.27	23.72	-1.81	-3.45	2.71	-2.64	1.73	1.70	-0.90	2.03	-0.4

Note: (% deviation from control solution).

Table 8.10a A comparison of the mean values and standard deviation of the principal variables under second assumption of linear smoothed export price and fluctuating export price

	Mean Values	
Variables	Fluctuating	Smoothed export price
Total GDP	5245.45 (2008.00)	5245.45 (108.00)
Real GDP	5130.36 (1622.87)	5121.00 (1673.00)
Real private consumption	1622.90 (325.00)	1622.90 (230.60)
Real private investment	225.18 (85.40)	228.16 (86.79)
Real government consumption	1149.82 (369.90)	1149.63 (375.50)
Real government investment	982.95 (244.70)	1049.35 (246.1)
Total exports	2474.82 (905.50)	2445.00 (876.70)
Total imports	1009.68 (212.10)	1004.63 (194.90)
Aggregate final demand	3980.82 (858.00)	4037.90 (876.00)
Consumer price index	180.90 (20.85)	181.91 (20.32)
V. add. agriculture	377.79 (60.60)	388.77 (60.53)
V. add. mining	20.01 (4.12)	18.07 (4.09)
V. add. crude oil	2804.10 (1171.00)	3193.37 (1174)
V. add. mfg. ind.	354.00 (58.78)	353.00 (57.46)
V. add. construction	336.27 (92.14)	383.23 (94.84)
V. add. transport	237.44 (64.12)	238.43 (63.17)
V. add. service	701 (191.10)	701 (182)
Non-agri. employment	1553.01 (427)	1549 (314)
Total Govt. revenues	3105.82 (1937)	3434.46 (1961)
Wages and salaries	764.21 (559.04)	10252.10 (1077)
Wage rate index	377 (69.22)	379.26 (67.89)
Money supply	478.22 (144.2)	479.88 (114.6)
Balance of payment	1442 (906.10)	1441.89 (887.30)

Note: The smooth estimated by linear regression, $P = a + T + T^2$.

Table 8.10b A comparison of the mean values and standard deviation of the principal variables under second assumption of linearly smoothed export price with fluctuating export price

Principal variables	Mean values and standard deviation	
	Fluctuating export price	Smoothed export price
Total GDP	5245.45 (2008.00)	5245.45 (108)
Real GDP	5098.6 (1524.00)	5100.9 (250)
Aggregate final demand	3980.83 (858.00)	3981 (150)
Consumer prices	174.09 (13.50)	174.1 (3.1)
GDP deflator	180.90 (20.9)	181.9 (9.8)
Wages and salaries	764.21 (559)	833.6 (237.9)
Government revenues	3105.8 (1937)	3105.95 (35)
Balance of payment	1442.00 (906)	1472 (436)

Note: This table derived from Table 8.10 in appendix. The smoothed export prices are calculated from second alternative assumption; $P = a + T + T^2$.

Bibliography

Abdul, Kader, A. (1976), *The Role of the Oil Sector in the Economic Development of Iraq*, PhD Thesis, unpublished, West Virginia University.

Adam, F.G. and Jonos, P. E. (1966), 'On the Statistical Discrepancy in the Revised US National Accounts', *Journal of the American Statistical Association*, No. 61, pp. 1219-1229.

Adam, F.G., Behrman, J.R. and Roldam, R.A. (1979), 'Measuring the Impact of Primary Commodity Fluctuating on Economic Development: Chile and Brazil', *American Economic Review*, vol.69, May.

Adam, F.G. and Behrman, R. (1982), *Commodity Export and Economic Development*, Wharton Economic Studies, Lexington Books, D.C. Heath and Company, pp. 144-145.

Adler, J.H. (1969), *Fiscal Policy in Developing Country, and Accelerating Investment in Development Economic*, edited by Agarwala and Singh, New Delhi, Oxford University Press, p. 415.

Ahmed, N.Z. (1976), *A Description of the Impact of Crude Oil Export on the Economic Growth of Iraq, 1953-1970*, PhD Thesis, unpublished, University of Graduate, School of Business Administration, London.

Ahn Singh, C.Y.I. and Squire, L. (1981), 'A Model of an Agriculture Household in a Multi-crop Economy: The case of Korea', *Review of Economics and Statistics*, November.

Akhan, N. (1979), 'Pattern of Agriculture Development in Arab Countries', *The Arab Planning Institute*, Kuwait, pp. 167-71.

Al-eyd, A. K. (1979), *Oil Revenues and Accelerated Growth*, Praeger Publisher, USA.

Allen, R.G.D. (1967), *Macro Economic Theory: A Mathematical Treatment*, New York, Macmillan.

Al-Sayhig, Y. (1980), The *Arab Economy, Past Performance and Future Prospects*, Oxford University Press, pp. 77-79.

Al-Sefou, M. I. (1980), *Structural Analysis of Iraqi Exports and their effects on the Development of the Domestic Economy, 1945-1975*, PhD Thesis, unpublished, Swansea.

Arthur, W.L. (1969), *Development Planning: The Essentials of Economic Policy*, New York, Harper and Row, p. 15.

Artis, M.J. (1982), 'Why do forecasts differ?', paper presented to the panel of Academic Consultants, No. 17, Bank of England.

Artis, M.J., Bladen-Hovell, R. and Zang, W. (1992), 'Leading indicators in forecasting', mimeo, *University of Manchester*.

Artis, M.J., Leslie, D.G. and Smith, G. M. (1982), 'Wage Inflation: a Survey' in H.J. Artis et. al. (ed), *Demand Management, Supply Contraction And Inflation*, Manchester, Manchester University Press.

Askin, A.B. (1977), *Macroeconomics Policy In Developing Country; An Econometric Investigation Of The Post War Chilean Experience*, Amsterdam, North Holland Publishing Company.

Askin, B.A and John, A. (1974), *Econometric Wage and Price Models*, Assessing the Impact of Economic Stabilisation Program, Lexington Books, Lexington, Massachusetts.

Askin, A.B. and Kraft, J. (1974), *Econometric Wage And Price Models, Assessing The Impact Economic Stabilisation Program*, Lexington Books, Lexington, Massachusetts.

Ball, R.J. (1973), *The International Linkages of National Economic Models*, North Holland, America Elsevier, p. 109.

Bank of England (1981), 'Factors underlying the recent recession', papers presented to the panel of Academic Consultants, No.15, *Bank of England*, London.

Barrell R.J. and Whitley, J.D. (eds) (1992), 'Macroeconomic Policy Coordination in Europe', *The ERM and Monetary Union*, Sage, London.

Barro, R. and Grossman, H. (1976), *Money, Employment and Inflation*, Cambridge.

Behrman, J.R. (1968), *Supply Response in Underdeveloped Agriculture; A Case Study of Four Major Annual Crops in Thailand; 1973-1963*, Amsterdam, North Holland Publishing Company.

Behrman, J.R. and Klein, L. (1970), 'Economic Growth Model For The Developing Economy, Growth and Trade', *Essays in Honor of Sir Roy Harrod* (eds), V.A. Eltis, M.F.G. Scott and Wolfe, Oxford Press.

Behrman, J.R. (1974), 'Modelling Stabilisation Policy For The LDCS In An International Aspects Of Stabilisation Policy', Proceedings of ISPE, Boston et.al. (eds), *Federal Reserve Bank Conference*.

Behrman, J.R. and Hanson, J.A. (1979), 'The Use Of Econometric Models In Developing Countries', in Behrman, J.R., *National Bureau Of Economic Research*.

Behrman, J.R. and Verges, R. (1979), *A Quarterly Economic Model of Panama in Short-term Macro Economic Policy in Latin America*, edited by Behrman, Jere and James A. Hanson, NBER.

Berndt, E. R., Darrought, M.N. and Diewert, W.E. (1977), 'Flexible Functional Forms and Expenditure Distributions: An Application to Canadian Consumer Demand Functions', *International Economic Review*, October.

Blackburn, K. (1987), 'Economics policy evaluation and optimal control theory: a critical review of some recent development', *Journal of Economic Theory*, 7, pp. 53-65.

Bodkin, R.G., Klein, L.R. and Marwah, K. (eds) (1991), *A History of Macroeconometric Model-Building*, Aldershot, Edward Elgar.

Britton, A.J. and Pain, N. (1992), 'Economic Forecasting in Britain', *National Institute of Economic and Social Research*, Report Series, No.4.

Brown, A. (1979), 'On Measuring the Instability of Tim Series Data: A Comment', *Oxford Bulletin of Economics and Statistics*, vol. 41, pp. 249-50.

Brown, M. (1952), 'Habit Persistence and Lags in Consumer Behaviour', *Econometric*, 20 July.

Bruce, L.D. and Wottsiungchen, D. (1984), 'Endogenous Versus Exogenouse Price Targets for Commodity Market Stabilisation', in A. J. Hughes (ed), *Applied Decision Analysis And Economics Behaviour*, Martinus Nijhoff Publishers, Netherlands.

Brundell, P.H. and Savedberg, P. (1983), 'More on the Causes of Instability in Export Earnings', Reply, *Oxford Bulletin of Economics and Statistics*, 45, pp.385-388.

Burhead, J. (1956), *Government Budgeting*, New York, John Wiley and Sons, Inc., p. 466.

Byung Nak, S. (1981), 'Empirical Research on Consumption Behaviour: Evidence From Rich and Poor LDCs', *Economic Development And Cultural Changes*, No. 3.

Canavese, A.J. (1982), 'The Structure Explanations in the Theory of Inflation', *Working Paper*, Vol. 10, No. 70, pp. 523-529.

Carlin, W. and Soskice, D. (1991), 'Macroeconomics and the Wage Bargain', Oxford, Oxford University Press.

Caves, D.U. and Christensen, L.R. (1980), 'Econometric Analysis of Residential Tim-of-use Electricity Pricing Experiments', *Journal of Econometrics*, December.

Central Bank of Iraq (1978), 'Economic Development in Iraq', *Bulletin Statistical Department*, January to December.

Chenery, H.B. and Watanable, T. (1958), 'International Comparison of the Structure of Production', *Econometrica*, 26, pp. 487-521.

Chichester, L.R. (1984), 'The Myth OPEC Cartel', *OPEC*, pp. 60-65.

Christensen, L.R. and Manser, M.E. (1977), 'Estimating U.S. consumer Performance for Meat with Flexible Utility Function', *Journal of Econometrics*, January.

Christensen, L.R., Jorgenson, D.U. and Lau, L.J. (1975), 'Transcendental Logarithmic Utility Functions', *American Economic Review*, June.

Clower, R.U. (1965), *Monetary Theory Selected Readings*, edited by Clower, R.W., Penguin.

Coppock, J.D. (1962), *International and Economic Instability*, New York, McGraw-Hill.

Corden, V.M. and Oppenheimer, Peter (1976), 'Economic Issues for the Oil-Importing Countries', in Rybczynski, T.M. (ed), *The Economics of Crisis* London, Macmillan.

Corden, V. M. (1982), 'Booming Sector and Dutch Disease Economics: *A Survey*', *Working Paper*, No. 79, November.

Corden, V.M. (1981), 'The Exchange Rate, Monetary Policy and North Sea Oil: The Economic Theory of the Squeeze on Tradable', *Oxford Economic Paper*, No. 33 July, pp. 23-46.

Cuthbertson, K., Hall, S. and Taylor, M.P. (1992), *Applied Econometric Techniques*, London, Harvester Wheatsheaf.

Davis, E.P. (1984), 'The Consumption Function in Macro-Economic Model, a Comparative Study', *Applied Economics*, 16, p. 800.

Dehaghi, G. (1980), *A Macro-econometric Study Of The Iran Economy*, PhD Thesis, unpublished, University of Birmingham.

Dhrymes, J. (1970), *Econometrics: Statistical Foundation and Application*, Harper and Row Publisher, pp. 174-176.

Diakossavas, D. (1986), 'The Measurement of Commodity Market Instability with Particular Reference to Food Consumption Instability', *Manchester Discussion*.

Diakossavas, D. (1984), *Food Insecurity in Low Income Countries: Measurement, Sources and Some Policy Implications*, PhD Thesis, unpublished, University of Manchester.

Easton, W.W. (1985), 'The Importance of Interest Rates in Five Macroeconomic Models', *Bank of England Discussion Paper*, No. 24.

Eckstein, Z. (1984), 'Rational Expectations Model of Agricultural Supply', *Journal of Political Economy*, Vol. 92, No. 1, February.

Edith and Penrose, E.F. (1978), *Iraq: International Relation and National Development*, London, Ernest Benn, Boulder, Westview Press.

Europe Publication Limited (1983/1984), *IRAQ*, London Staples Printers Limited.

Europe Publication Limited (1957), *The Middle East*, London Staples Printers Limited, p. 186.

Fair, R.C. (1983), Specification, Estimation and Analysis of Macroeconometric Models, Harvard University Press.

F.A.O. (1977), *Census Bulletin*, No. 17, May.

Feder, G. (1983), 'On Export and Economic Growth', *Journal Development Economics*, 12, No.1-2. pp. 59-37.

Fel, J.L. and Ranis, G. (1961), 'A Theory of Economic Development', *American Economic Review*, 51.

Fisher, P.G. (1992), *Rational Expectations in Macroeconomics Models*, London, Kluwer Academic Publishers.

Fisher, P.G., Turner, D.S., Wallis, K.F. and Whitley, J.D. (1989), 'Comparative properties of models of the UK economy', *National Institute Economic Review*, 133, pp. 91-104.

Fisher, W.B. (1978), *In the Middle East and North Africa 1978-1979*, 25th edition, London Europe Publications.

Fisher, W.B. (1981), *Change and Development in the Middle East*, edited by John Clarke and Howard Bowen Jones, pp. 101-102.

Forsyth, P.L and Kay, J.A. (1980), 'The Economic Implications of North Sea oil Revenues', *Fiscal Studies*, 1 July, pp. 1-28.

Frederick, A. and Axelgard, U. (1986), *Iraq in Transition A Political, Economic and Strategic Perspective*, published in Britain by Mansell Publishing Limited, London, INC.

Friedman, M. (1957), 'A Theory of the Consumption of Function', *National Bureau of Economic Research*, Princeton, NJ.

George, F. (1977), 'An Illustrative Model', in *National Institute Model II.*

Gerald, T. (1983), 'Export Instability, Export Growth and GDP Growth', *Journal of Development Economics*, 12, pp. 219-227.

Glezakos, C. (1983), 'Instability and the Growth of Export', *Journal of Development Economics*, 2, pp. 229-236.

Glezakos, C. (1983), 'More on the Causes of Instability in Export Earning', *Oxford Bulletin of Economics and Statistics*, 42 , pp. 379-383.

Goldberger, A.S. (1964), *The Impact Multiplies and Dynamic Properties of Klein, Goldberger Model*, Amsterdam, North Holland Publishing Co.

Granger, C.W.J. and Newbold, P. (1986), *Forecasting Economic Time Series*, 2nd edition, New York, Academic Press.

Green, C. and Diakosavvas, D. (1986), 'Assessing the Impact on Food Security of Alternative Compensatory Financing Schemes: A Simulation Approach, with an Application to India', unpublished paper, October.

Green, C. and Kirkpatrick, C. (1982), 'A cross section Analysis of Food Insecurity in Developing Countries: Its Magnitude and Sources', *Work paper*, Vol. 18, No. 2, January.

Gregory, R.G. (1976), 'Some Implications of The Growth of The Mineral Sector', *Australian Journal of Agricultural Economics*, 20, August, 71-91.

Gupta, K. L. (1984), *Finance and Economic Growth in Developing Countries*, Croom Helm, London.

Hagen, E.E. (1975), *The Economic of Development*, Irwin Hamewood.

Hall, P. (1983), *The Economics of Growth and Development*, St. Martin's Press, New York.

Hall, S.G. (1985), 'On the solution of large economic models with consistent expectations', *Bulletin of Economic Research*, 37, pp. 157-61.

Hall, S.G. (ed) (1994), *Applied Economic Forecasting Techniques*, Hemel Hempstead, Harvester Wheatsheaf.

Hansen, L. P. and Sargent, T.J. (1980), 'Formulating and Estimating Dynamic Linear Rational Expectations Models', *Journal Economic Dynamic and Control*, 2, February.

Harvey, A.C. (1983), *The Econometric Analysis of Time Series*, Philip Allen.

Harvey, A.C. (1981), *Time Series Models*, Halsted, New York.

Harvey, A.C. (1980), 'On Comparing Regression Models in Levels and First Differences', *International Economic Review*, 21, pp. 707-720.

Hasan, M.S. (1982), 'The Role of Foreign Trade in Economic Development of Iraq, 1964-1980: A study in the Growth of Independent Economy', in M.A. Cook (ed), *Studies in the Economic History of Middle East*, published by School of Oriental and African Studies, pp. 348-358.

Hati, J.A. (1987), 'Key Sectors and the Structure of Production in Kuwait an Input-Output Approach', *Applied Economic*, 19, pp. 1187-1200.

Hendry, D.F. and Von Ungern-Sternberg, T. (1981), *Essays in The Theory and Measurement of Consumer Behaviour*, Cambridge University Press.

Hendry, D. H. (1993), *Lectures in Econometric Methodology*, Oxford University Press.

Hendry, D.H. and Clements, M. (1992), 'Towards a theory of economic forecasting', mimeo, *Institute of Economics and Statistics*, Oxford.

Hendry, D. H. and Richard, J.F. (1983), 'The econometric analysis of economic time series', *Statistics Review*, 51, pp. 111-63.

Hendry, S.G.B., Karakitsos, E. and Savage, D. (1982), 'On the derivation of the "efficient" Phillips Curve', *The Manchester School*, 50, pp. 51-77.

Hill, J.W and Low, S.A. (1982), 'Imperfect Capital Markets and Life-Cycle Consumption', *Journal Development Economics*, 10, pp. 257-269.

Hirschman, A. O. (1966), *The Strategy of Economic Development*, New Haven and London, Yale University Press, p.109.

Holtham, G. and Hughes-Hallett, A.J. (1992), 'Policy cooperation under uncertainty: the case for some disagreement', *American Economic Review*, 82,1043-51.

Ibrahim, A. (1983), *Arab Resources, the Transformation of a Society*, Washington, D. C., Croom Helm, London.

International Bank for Reconstruction and Development (1958), *The Economic Development of Iraq*, Baltimore, The Hopkins Press.

International Monetary Fund, Washington, D.C., various issues.

Johnston, J. (1963), *Econometric Methods*, New York, McGraw-Hill.

Jorgenson, D.W. (1961), 'The Development of a Dual Economy', *Economic Journal*, p. 71.

Jorgenson, D.W. (1965), 'Anticipation and Investment Behaviour', in J. Duesenberry, L.R. Klein, and G. Kuh (eds), *The Quarterly Econometric Model of the Unit State*, Amsterdam, North Holland Publishing Company.

Kalder, N. (1955), 'Alternative Theories of Distribution', *Review of Economic Studies*, No. 2, p. 23.

Keating, G. (1985), 'Fooling all the people: LBS forecast release', London: *London Business School*, Vol. 9, p.11.

Kelley, A.C., Williamson, J.G. and Cheetham, R.J. (1972), *Dualistic Economic Development: the Theory and History*, University of Chicago Press.

Kelley, A.C. and Williamson, T.G. (1969), 'Household Saving Behaviour in the Developing Economies; The Indonesian Case', *Economic Development And Development Cultural Change*, Vol. 1, p. 16.

Kenneth, P.J. (1981), *Economic Development Competing Paradigms*, Washington, D.C., University Press of America.

Kiker, B.F. (1971), *Human Capital*, Columbia University Press, New York.

Kindleberger, C.P. (1965), *Economic Development*, Wiley, New York, p. 84.

Klein, L.R. (1950), *Economic Fluctuations in the United States 1921-1941*, Wiley, New York.

Klein, L.R. (1965), 'What Kind of Macroeconomic Model for developing Economies', *The Indian Economic Journal*, Vol. 10, pp.163-175.

Klein Lau L. (1975), *A Bibliography of Macroeconomic Models of Developing Economic Development*, D.C. Heath Company.

Knudsen, O. and Parnes, A. (1975), *Trade Instability and Economic Development*, Lexington, Lexington Books.

Korliras, P.G and Thorn, R.S. (1979), *Modern Macro-economic, Major Contributions to Contemporary Thought*, Harper and Row Publisher, New York.

Koyck, L.M. (1954), *Distribution Lags and Investment Analysis*, Amsterdam, North-Holland Publishing Company, p. 30.

Krishnaswany, K.S. (1965), 'The Evaluation of Tax Structure in a Development Policy', in T.A. Peacock and G. Hanser (eds), *Development Finance and Economic Development*, Paris, OECD, p. 81.

Laidler, D. and Bentley, B. (1983), 'A Small Macro-Model of the Pasture United State', *The Manchester School*, Vol. 51, pp. 317-340.

Laidler, D. and Shea, P. O. (1983), 'A Small Model of an Open Economy Under Fixed Exchange Rates, The United Kingdom, 1954-1970', *Economica*, Vol. XLXVII, pp. 141-158.

Larsen, F. and Llewellyn, J. (1983), 'Estimated Macroeconomic Effects of a Large Fall in Oil Prices', *OECD Department of Economics and Statistics*, Working Paper, No. 8.

Lasaga, M. (1979), *An Econometric Analysis of the Impact of Copper on the Chilean Economy*, PhD Dissertation, unpublished, University of Pennsylvania.

Layard, P.R.G., Nickel, S.J. and Jackson, R.A. (1991), *Unemployment: Macroeconomic Performance and the Labour Market*, Oxford, Oxford University Press.

Leith, J.C. (1970), 'The Decline in World Export Prices Instability, A Comment', *Bulletin Oxford University*.

Leontief, U.U. (1983), *Input-Output Economics*, Oxford University Press, New York.

Lewis, W.A. (1954), *The Theory of Economic Growth*, London, pp. 274-283.

Litterman, R. B. (1986), 'Forecasting with Bayesian vector autoregressions: five years of experience', *Journal of Business and Economic Statistics*, No. 4, pp.25-38.

Lloyd, G.R. (1985), *Economic Growth in the Third World 1950-1980*, Yale University, p. 339.

Lloyds Bank Group, *Iraq*, London, various issues.

Lluch, C. and William, R. (1975), 'Dualism in Demand and Saving Patterns, the Case of Korea', *Economic Record*, p. 51.

London Business School (1981), *Consumption Function*, LBS.

Lord Saltier (1955), *The Development of Iraq*, London, Caxton Press Ltd, p. 97.

Love, J. (1983), 'Concentration and Diversification and Earning Instability: Some Evidence on Developing Countries, Export Manufactures and Primary Products', *World Development*, Vol. 11, No. 9, pp. 787-93.

Love, J. (1985), 'Export Instability: An Alternative Analysis of Causes', *The Journal of Development Studies*, Vol. 21, p. 2.

Lucas, R. (1976), 'Econometric Policy Evaluation A Critique, in the Philips Curve and Labour Market', *Journal of Monetary Economics*, Supplements, pp. 19-43.

Lynne, S. (1981), *Employment Policy in Developing Countries; A Survey of Issues and Evidence*, New York, Oxford University Press.

MacBean, A.I. (1966), *Export Instability and Economic Development*, London, Allen and Uwin.

Mackie, D., Miles, D. and Taylor, C. (1989), 'The impact of monetary policy on inflation: modelling the UK experience 1978-86', in Britton, A. (ed), *Policy-Making with Macroeconomic Models*, Aldershot, Gower.

Maddala, G. S. (1977), *Econometrics*, New York: McGraw-Hill.

Maddock, R. and Mclean, I. (1982), Rushes and Booms: The Adjustment of the Australian Economy to Export Shocks, *mimeo, Australian National University*.

Maizels, A. (1968), 'Review of Export Instability on Economic Development', *American Economic Review*, 58, June.

Malgrange, P. and Muet, P.A. (eds) (1984), *Contemporary Macroeconomics Modelling*, Oxford, Basil Blackwell. .

Mariano, R. S. and Brown, B.W. (1984), 'Residual based procedures for prediction and estimation in nonlinear simultaneous system', *Econometrica*, Vol. 52, 321-43.

Marzouk, M. S. (1986), 'A Econometric Model of Sudan', *Journal of Development Economics*', pp. 37-358.

Massel, B.F. (1970), 'Export Instability and Economic Structure', *American Economic Review*, Vol. 1, p. 56.

Mckibben, W. and Sachs, J.D. (1991), *Global Linkages: Macroeconomic interdependence and cooperation in the world economy*, Washington, D.C., Brookings Institution.

Mckinnon, R.I. (1976), 'International Transfer and Non-Traded Commodities: The Adjustment Problem', in D.M. Leipziger (ed), *The International Monetary System and the developing Nations*, Washington, D.C., Agency for International Development.

Mclachlan, K. (1981), 'The Oil Industry in the Middle East', in J. Clark and H. B. Jones (eds), *Change and Development in The Middle East*, p.9.

McNees, S. K. (1982), 'The role of macroeconometric models in forecasting and policy analysis in the United States', *Journal of Forecasting*, Vol. 1, pp. 37-48.

McNees, S. K. (1986), 'Forecasting accuracy of alternative techniques: a comparison of US macroeconomic forecasts', *Journal of Business and Economic Statistics*, Vol. 4, pp.5-23.

McNees, S. K. (1991), 'Comparing macroeconomic model forecasts under common assumptions', in L.R. Klein (ed), *Comparative performance of US Econometric Models*, Oxford, Oxford University Press.

Meier, M. G. (1976), *Leading Issues in Economic Development*, Third Edition, Oxford University Press, New York.

Ministry of Planning, C. O. S. (1976-1983), *Annual Abstract of Statistics*, Iraq.

Ministry of Planning, C.O.S. (1984), *The Manpower Planning Commission: The Realities of Population, Manpower Wages*, Iraq.

Modigliani, F. (1975), 'The consumption function in a Developing Economy and the Italian Experience', *An American Economic Review*, Vol. 2, pp. 33-43.

Mohsin, S. (1982), *Transportation and Communication sector in Iraq and its development during the period 1970-1980*, PhD Thesis, University of Lodz, Poland.

Molho, L.E. (1986), 'International Monetary Fund', *Staff Papers*, March, Vol. 33, No.1.

Moran, D. R. (1979), 'Fiscal Policy in Oil Exporting Countries 1972-1978', *International Monetary Fund, Staff Papers*, Vol. 26, No. 1.

Morgan, C. (1983), 'Export Fluctuations and Economic Growth', *Journal of Development Economics*, No. 12, pp. 195-218.

Nerlove, M. (1958), *The dynamic of supply Estimation of former Response Prices*, Baltimore, Johns Hopkins Press.

Newlyn, W.T (1961), 'The Role of Fiscal and Monetary Policy', in U.R. Hicks (ed), *Federalism and Economic Growth in Under-Developed Countries*, London.

Ngugen, D. T. (1980), 'Commodity Concentration and Export Earnings Instability: A Mathematical Analysis', *Economic Journal*, Vol. 90, pp. 345-62.

Nicholes, C. B. (1974), *An Econometric Investigation of Inter-relationship Between Capital and Economic Growth of Greece*, PhD Thesis, unpublished, University of Birmingham, p. 58.

Nurkse, R. (1958), 'Trade Fluctuation and Buffer Policies of Low Income Countries', *Kyklos*, 11, pp. 141-154.

O.E.C.D., 'Main Economic Indicators', various issues.

O.E.C.D., 'Economic Outlook', various issues.

Olivera, J.H.G (1979), 'On Structural Stagflation', *Journal of Development of Economics*, Vol. 6, No. 4.

Olofin, S. and Iyariwura, J.O. (1983), 'From Oil Shortage to Oil Cult: Simulation of Growth Prospects in the Nigerian Economy', *Journal of Policy Model*, Vol. 5, pp. 363-378.

Olofin, S., Iyaniwura, J., Adeniyi, J. and Olayide, S. O. (1985), 'An Operational Econometric Model of the Nigerian Economy', *Empirical Economics*, Vol. 10, pp. 231-262.

O.P.E.C. (1978), 'Annual Report 1977', Vienna, *Publishing Department of OPEC*, Vienna.

Ormerod, P. (1979), 'The National Institute Model of the U.K. Economy; some Current Problems', in O. Paval (ed), *Economic Modelling, Current Issues and Problems in Macro-economic Modelling in the UK and the US*, London, Graduate School of Business Studies.

Osborn, D. and Teal, F. (1979), 'An assessment and comparison of two NIESR econometric model forecasts', *National Institute Economics Review*, 127, pp. 64-75.

Patterson, K.D. (1986), 'The Stability Of Some Annual Consumption Functions', *Oxford Economic Paper*, 38, pp. 1-30.

Patterson, K.D. and Ryding, J. (1984), 'Dynamic Time Series Models with Growth Effects Constrained to Zero', *Economic Journal*, 94, pp. 137-143.

Pesaran, M.H. (1986), 'The New Classical Macroeconomics: A critical exposition', University of Cambridge, Dept. of Applied Economics, *Economics Reprint*.

Phillips, A.W. (1958), 'The Relationship between Unemployment and the Rate of change of Money Wage Rate in UK 1961-1957', *Economica*, No. 5, p. 27.

Pindyck, R.S. and Rubinfeld, D.I. (1981), '*Econometric Model and Economic Forecasts*', McGraw-Hill International Book Company, 2nd edition.

Prakash, Y.R. (1975), *A Econometric Model for the Foreign Trade Sector of India, 1961/1962-1971/1972*, PhD Thesis unpublished, Graduate School of Comel University.

Priovolos, T.G. (1979), 'An Econometric Model of the Ivory Coast', *A Report Prepared for the Wharten EFA - Agent of the International Development Project*.

Priovolls, T.G. (1980), *Coffee and the Ivory Coast*, Lexington Books, Lexington, Massachusetts.

Puttrus, A. B. (1978), *The Performance of the Iraq, National Development Plan 1970-1974; An Econometrics Analysis*, MSC Thesis, unpublished, University of Birmingham.

Quarterly Economic Review of Iraq, 'Annual Supplement', *The Intelligence United Limited*, London, various issues.

Raja, T.C. (1969), 'Fiscal Policy, Development Planning and Budgeting', *International Monetary Fund Staff Paper*, No. 1, March, p. 65.

Rangarajan, C. and Sundararajan, V. (1976), 'Impact of export fluctuations on income, a cross country analysis', *The Review of Economics and Statistics*, Vol. 58.

Rascheed, O.K. (1969), 'Fiscal Policy, Development planning and annual budgeting', *International Monetary Fund Staff Paper*, Vol. 16, No. 1, March, p. 81.

Ray, R. (1980), 'Analysis of a time series of household expenditure surveys for India', *Review Of Economics And Statistics*, November.

Resnick, B. (1973), 'A Model of trade and Government Sectors in Colonial Economies', *American Economic Review*, 63, September, p. 3.

Robert, B. B. (1968), *Financing Economic Development*, University of Chicago Press, p. 20.

Rodon, R. and Paval, N. (1961), 'Notes on the theory of the Big Push', in H. Ellis (ed), *Economic Development for Latin America*, St. Martin's Press, New York.

Rollin, C. E. (1956), 'Mineral Development and Economic Growth', *Social Research*, Autumn.

Salman, D.J. (1985), *Dualism in the Iraqi Economy: Its Relevance to Economic Planning*, PhD Thesis, unpublished, University of Wales Institute of Science and Technology, Cardiff.

Samara, I.A. (1981), '*The Economic Growth of Iraq: The Role of Oil Revenues, Government Policies and Strategies Since 1950*', PhD Thesis, unpublished, University of Wales, Swansea.

Sanders, B.G. (1982), *International Commodity Agreement: A Simulation Analysis of Performance Criteria*, PhD Thesis, unpublished, University of Oklahoma.

Sandford, C. (1984), *Economics of Public Finance*, Pergamon Oxford Press.

Schiderinck, J.H.F. (1978), 'Regression Factor Analysis in Economics', *Tilbury School of Economics Social Science and Law*, Vol. P. 1.

Schultze, C. L. (1985), 'Micro Economic Efficiency and National Wage Stickiness', *American Economic Reviews*, March.

Schultze, C. L. and Tryon, J.L. (1965), *Prices and Wages in the Brooking Quarterly Econometric Model of the United States*, Duesenberry, J. S. and From, G., Klein, L.R., Kuh, E., North Holland Publishing Company.

Schyrris, R. and Homan, P. (1970), *Middle East Oil and Western World, Prospects and Problems*, N.Y. Publishing Co., p.105.

Sebastain, M.A. (1988), 'A New Approach to the Relationship Between Export Instability and Economic Development', *Economic Development and Cultural Change*, January, No.2, Vol. 36.

Sherbbiny, N.A. (1981), 'Labour and Capital Flows in the Arab World', in Sherbing, N.A. (ed), *Manpower planning in the Oil Countries*, Greenwich, T.A. Press INC. and Conn., Research in Human Capital and Development.

Simmons, P. and Weiserbs D. (1979), 'Translog Flexible Functional Forms and Associated Demand Systems', *American Economic Review*, December.

Singh, S. K. (1975), *Development Economic*, London.

Smith, R.P. (1990), 'The Warwick ESRC Macroeconomic Modelling Bureau: an assessment', International Journal of Forecasting, 6, 301-9.

Smith, R. P. (1994), 'The macro-modelling industry: structure, conduct and performance', in S.G. Hall (ed), London: Harvester Wheatsheaf.

Stanffer, T.H. (1981), 'Growth Versus Expansion in a Renter Economy', *Middle East Economic Survey*, Vol. XXIV, No.5, p.16, November.

Streeten, P. (1970), 'Balanced versus Unbalanced Growth', in Meier, G. M. (ed), *Leading Issues in Economic Development*, Oxford University Press, 2nd edition, pp. 366-371.

Struass, J. (1982), 'Determinants of Food consumption in rural Sierra-Leone: Application of the quadratic expenditure system to the Consumption-Leisure component of a Household-firm Model', *Journal of Development Economics*, December.

Summer, M. (1984), 'The Philips Curve', *The Economic Review*, Vol. 1, No. 5.

Sushil, B. W. (1987), 'The Effects of Inflation and Real Wages on Employment', *Economica*, 54, pp. 21-40.

Symons, J.S.V. (1982), 'The Real Interest Rate and Demand for Labour', *London School Of Economics, Working Paper*, No. 410.

Taylor, L. (1983), 'A Stagnationist Model of Economic Growth', *Cambridge Journal Of Economics*, 9, pp. 383-403.

Taylor, L. (1983), *Structuralist Macro-Econometrics*, Basic Books, New York.

Tazer, M. (1969), *The Political Economy of International Oil and the Underdevelopment Countries*, Temp Smith Ltd., London.

Theil, H. (1971), *Principles of Econometrics*, New York, N.Y, John Wiley and Sons Inc.

Thelbald, R. and Jamad, S. (1983), *Problems of Rural Development in Oil Rich Economy, Iraq,1958-1975: The Contemporary State*, edited by Niblock, T., University of Exeter.

Thompkinson, P. (1978), 'The Prices Equation and Excess Demand', *Bulletin of Economics and Statistics.*

Turner, D. S. (1990), 'The role of judgement in macroeconomic forecasting', *Journal of Forecasting*, 9, pp. 315-45.

UNCTAD (1968), 'Trade Prospects and Capital Needs of Developing Countries', United Nations publication, R.J. Ball (ed), *Reprinted in the International Linkages of National Economic Models*, sales no. 68.11.D.13.

United Nation (1961), 'Department of Economics and Social Affairs, use of Model in Programming Industrialisation and Productivity', *Bulletin*, 4, April.

United Nation, Statistical Year Book for Asia and the Pacific', various issues.

Valuline, V.G. (1978), *A Bibliography of Econometric Models of Developing Countries*, UNCTAD, Geneva.

Voicodas, C. S. (1974), 'The Effects of Foreign Exchange Instability Growth', *Review of Economics and Statistics*, pp. 410-412.

Von Ungern-Sternberg, T. (1981), 'Inflation and savings: International Evidence Inflation Induced Income Losses', *Economic Journal*, pp. 961-976.

Wadhwani, B. S. (1987), 'The Effects of Inflation and Real Wages on Employment', The London School of Economics', *Economica*, 54, pp. 21-40.

Wallis, K.F. (1979), *Topics in applied econometrics*, Basil Blackwell, Oxford.

Wallis, K.F. (1989), 'Macroeconomic forecasting: a survey', *Economic Journal*, 99, pp. 28-61.

Wallis, K.F. and Whitley, J.D. (1987), 'Long-run properties of large-scale macroeconometric models', *Annals d'Economie et de Statistique*, 6/7, pp. 207-24.

Wallis, K.F. and Whitley, J.D. (1991), 'Sources of error in forecasts and expectations: UK economic models, 1984-88', *Journal of Forecasting*, 10, pp. 231-53.

Wallis, K.F., Andrews, M. J., Bell, D.N.F., Fisher, P.G., and Whitley, J. D. (1985), *Models of the UK Economy: A second review by the ESRC Macroeconomics Modelling Bureau*, Oxford, Oxford University Press.

Walter, H. (1975), 'Fiscal Polices for Underdevelopment Countries' *in Readings on Taxation in Development Countries*, edited by R.M. Bird and Oldman-Baltimore, Johns Hopkins University Press, p. 9.

Watcher, S.M. (1979), *Latin American Inflation. The Structuralist Monetarist Debate*, Lexington Books, D.C. Heath and Company.

Weber, W.G. (1971), 'Interest rate and the Short-run Consumption Function', *American Economic Review*, 61, June.

Weber, W.E. (1970), 'The effect of interest rate on aggregate consumption', *American Economic Review*, 60, September.

Whitley, J.D. (1992), 'Comparative simulation analysis of the European multicountry models', *Journal of Forecasting*, 11, pp. 423-58.

Whitley, J. D. (1992), 'Aspects of monetary union: model-based simulation result', in R.J. Barrell and J.D. Whitley (eds), *Macroeconomic policy coordination in Europe: The ERM and monetary union*, Sage, London.

Whitley, J. D. (1992), 'Comparative properties of the Nordic models', in L. Bergmann and O. Olsen (eds), *Economic modelling in the Nordic Countries*, Amsterdam, North-Holland.

Wijnbergen, V. (1982), 'Stagflationary Effects of Monetary Stabilisation Policy', *Journal of Development Economic*, pp.133-169.

Wijndergen, V. (1983), 'Interest rate Management in LDCs', *Monetary Economics*, 12, September, pp. 433-452.

Wijndergen, V. (1982), 'Inflation, Employment and the Dutch Disease in Oil Exporting Countries: A Short-run Disequilibrium Analysis', *Quarterly Journal of Economics*, March.

Willson, P.D. (1977), 'Export Instability and Economic Development: A survey Parts I and II', Warwick University, *Economic Discussion paper*.

World Bank (1979), World Department Report Social Indicator Data Sheet', *World Bank*, August.

Index

296

M

MacBean, 206
macroeconomic, 1
manufacturing, 15, 16, 23, 24, 42, 44, 73, 99, 100, 101, 102, 218, 256, 257, 258
marginal, 48, 121, 123, 124, 126, 128, 172, 179, 181, 182, 191
efficiency, 119, 163, 173, 181, 182, 185, 190, 191, 192, 220, 221, 231, 240
market, 11, 30
mean, 6, 49, 158, 159, 160, 164, 204, 207, 209, 212, 214, 215, 216, 217, 220, 221, 222, 225, 231, 232, 236, 273, 275, 279
money, 82, 169, 171, 174, 177, 180, 184, 198, 199, 229, 230, 231, 257, 270, 272, 273, 274, 275, 276, 278
money supply, 39, 123, 137, 138, 139, 140, 172, 174, 175, 179, 181, 185, 189, 210, 212, 213, 214, 227, 240
moving averages, 205
multiplier, 92, 168, 176, 206, 239

N

nationalisation, 68, 96

O

OECD, 5, 8, 138, 147, 148, 258
oil, 36, 37, 46, 53, 57, 59, 64, 69, 73, 77, 94, 95, 100, 102, 151, 155, 169, 245, 246, 258, 279
OLS, 6, 106, 107, 108, 109, 110, 207, 238
OPEC, 2, 45, 61, 85, 147, 156, 233, 234
output, 40, 105, 115, 118, 181, 227

P

Parnes, 206
permanent, 76, 109, 120, 122, 123, 206
permanent income, 109, 120, 122, 123
plan, 8, 31, 34, 40, 50, 51, 52, 53, 54, 55, 57, 58, 60, 61, 62, 63, 64, 65,
66, 67, 68, 69, 70, 71, 72, 73, 74, 75, 76, 77, 78, 79, 111, 124, 202
potential, 114, 139, 161, 253
price, 138, 171, 174, 177, 184, 206, 233, 253, 266, 267, 269, 273, 276
price equation, 140, 186, 189, 242
private, 1, 10, 17, 18, 19, 21, 22, 34, 37, 39, 40, 50, 51, 60, 61, 63, 69, 75, 77, 111, 115, 118, 119, 120, 121, 122, 123, 124, 125, 126, 128, 129, 130, 137, 140, 141, 144, 145, 151, 153, 155, 161, 162, 164, 166, 172, 175, 178, 179, 180, 181, 183, 185, 188, 190, 191, 205, 210, 213, 220, 223, 226, 232, 238, 240, 241, 242, 243, 253, 255, 256, 269, 271, 273, 274, 275, 276, 277, 279
consumption,investment,product, 279
production, 2, 3, 12, 13, 14, 20, 26, 28, 29, 31, 32, 34, 39, 46, 47, 48, 49, 50, 52, 53, 62, 73, 74, 75, 88, 91, 92, 93, 94, 98, 104, 105, 108, 111, 112, 113, 114, 115, 116, 117, 118, 119, 121, 124, 127, 131, 132, 136, 139, 142, 146, 147, 148, 150, 160, 162, 172, 173, 175, 179, 181, 182, 183, 187, 188, 189, 191, 201, 210, 212, 213, 215, 224, 225, 234, 238, 239, 256, 257
production function. *See* Cobb-Douglas
productivity, 8, 9, 28, 40, 41, 44, 49, 52, 74, 75, 95, 96, 112, 133, 135, 136, 139, 176, 191, 214, 239, 257
public, 24, 48, 65, 99, 101, 105, 131, 141, 245, 246, 253

R

Rascheed, 49, 85
real, 8, 115, 117, 130, 146, 171, 172, 174, 176, 177, 180, 184, 191, 198, 199, 226, 229, 230, 231, 255, 256, 269, 271, 273, 274, 275, 276, 277, 279
real wage rate, 132
restriction, 132, 133, 175

For Product Safety Concerns and Information please contact our EU
representative GPSR@taylorandfrancis.com Taylor & Francis Verlag GmbH,
Kaufingerstraße 24, 80331 München, Germany

Printed and bound by CPI Group (UK) Ltd, Croydon, CR0 4YY
01/05/2025
01858342-0009